INSIDERS' GUIDE® TO

ST. LOUIS

FOURTH EDITION

DAWNE MASSEY

INSIDERS' GUIDE®

GUILFORD, CONNECTICUT
AN IMPRINT OF THE GLOBE PEQUOT PRESS

HELP US KEEP THIS GUIDE UP TO DATE

We would love to hear from you concerning your experiences with this guide and how you feel it could be improved and be kept up to date. Please send your comments and suggestions to: editorial@ GlobePequot.com

Thanks for your input, and happy travels!

INSIDERS' GUIDE®

Copyright © 2009 Morris Book Publishing, LLC

Text design by Sheryl Kober
Maps by XNR Productions, Inc. © Morris Book Publishing, LLC

ISSN 1547-321X
ISBN 978-0-7627-5037-5

Printed in the United States of America
10 9 8 7 6 5 4 3 2 1

The prices and rates in this guidebook were confirmed at press time. We recommend, however, that you call establishments before traveling to obtain current information.

CONTENTS

Directory of Maps

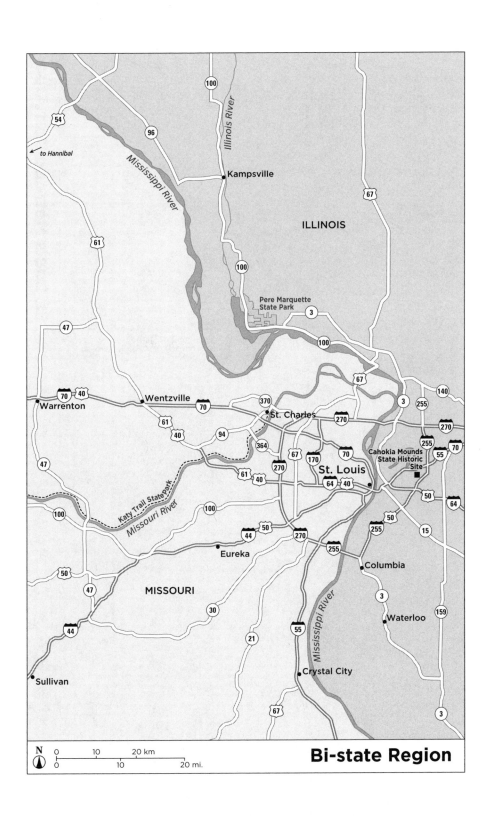

Bi-state Region

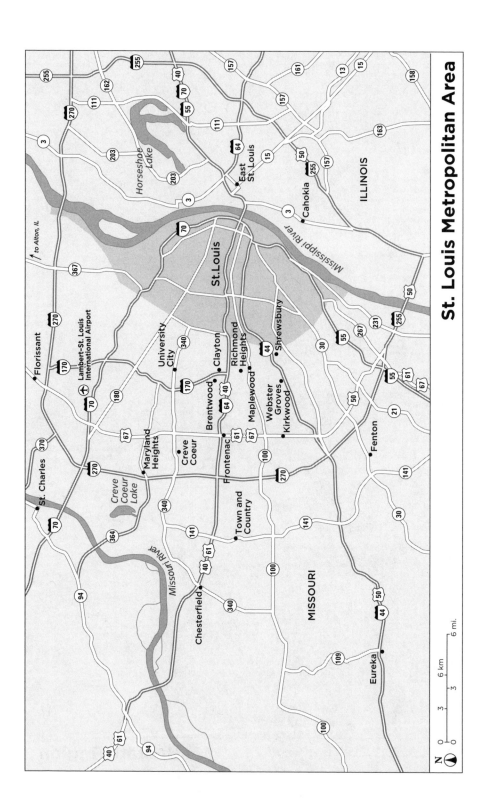

St. Louis Metropolitan Area

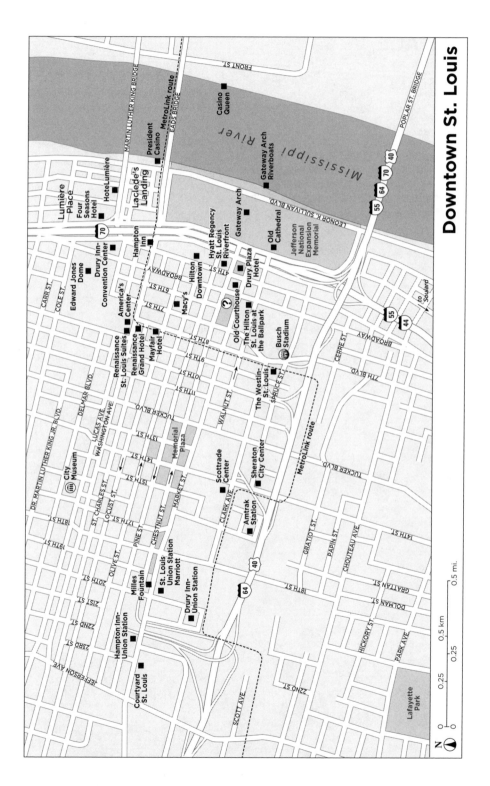

Downtown St. Louis

PREFACE

Welcome to St. Louis! St. Louis is a city that represents the crossroads of America—everybody who's anybody had to pass through these parts. Known as the Gateway to the West, St. Louis seems to have a bit more in common with cities of the Northeast than the wild westerners on our left. Our diverse population features a variety of cultures, and most of the citizenry shares a dedication to family, friends, sports, music, and an honest day's work—although not necessarily in that order.

While St. Louis is known for the sleek and contemporary monument that pays tribute to the awakening of America's pioneer spirit, if you ask ten people what St. Louis is all about, you'll likely get nine different answers. Some will say the Gateway Arch, while others won't be able to focus on anything other than the St. Louis Cardinals' rich baseball history. Football fans will probably flash back to Super Bowl XXXIV and the triumphant St. Louis Rams, while old-school types will harken back to the days when names like Dan Dierdorf, Jackie Smith, Jim Hart, and Conrad Dobler roamed the Cardinals football turf. Many will point to St. Louis's hometown brewer, Anheuser-Busch, while others might identify more closely with the red and white checkerboard of the old Ralston Purina camp. But, whatever you think about St. Louis, it's probably a good idea to withhold judgment until you've had a taste of St. Louis in the 21st century. A lot of things have changed in the area during the last few decades, but, true to form, a lot of things have stayed exactly the same. And that's the way St. Louisans seem to like it: sprinkle in a little new, but serve up a lot of tradition. That's St. Louis.

HOW TO USE THIS BOOK

This book is divided into self-contained, stand alone chapters that detail specific aspects of life in St. Louis. From the nightlife and restaurant options to the best things to do when you're traveling with kids, there's something for every taste in this guidebook. After starting out with an overview of the city, the book launches into the myriad things that make St. Louis such a unique place to live and to visit.

Area maps have been provided so you can get your bearings in the St. Louis area, and vital statistics have been included in the Area Overview chapter. Throughout the book you'll find Insiders' Tips (indicated by [i]) with brief nuggets of information that will help you feel like someone "in the know," as well as Close-ups that focus on some of the more interesting and unique aspects of St. Louis.

Find out how to get around in the appropriately named Getting Here, Getting Around chapter, then check out the Accommodations chapter for some suggestions of places to rest your travel-weary head. When you get hungry, turn to the Restaurants chapter for a few suggestions on places to get a quick bite or where to enjoy a leisurely meal, and check out the Nightlife chapter for a listing of St. Louis–area hot spots. St. Louis has plenty of casinos to keep you occupied when Lady Luck is on the horizon, which are detailed in their own chapter, and the Kidstuff chapter helps explain why St. Louis is such a family-friendly place to live and to visit.

Most of the chapters are divided into geographic areas or neighborhoods that are popular with locals and visitors alike. Listings located in the downtown area are featured first, which are followed by the offerings available in other neighborhoods and municipalities. There are also a few items of note on the eastern side of the Mississippi River, in Illinois, and these are included at the end of the Missouri listings. Other chapters, such as Attractions, Kidstuff, and Spectator Sports, are organized by subject so you can find what you want to see quickly and easily, and the Annual Events chapter is listed chronologically.

The Accommodations, Restaurants, and Attractions chapters include pricing guides to help give you an idea of how much each choice will end up costing you. Luckily, many of St. Louis's attractions are free, and when this is the case it's been noted.

Please remember that in a growing city such as St. Louis, things are bound to change. Restaurants and attractions come and go, so by the time you read this book there may be new and different options for you to explore. If your heart is set on something, please call ahead of your visit so you're not disappointed.

AREA OVERVIEW

The visitors who trek to St. Louis each year are all but certain to find something they like in the Gateway to the West. But where to find it? Since St. Louis is relatively spread out, the following overview of the area will give you an idea what to expect in the different neighborhoods. The chapter has been arranged by the geographical sections that have been used throughout the book.

DOWNTOWN

Geographically speaking, downtown St. Louis is largely bordered by Cole Street on the north, Jefferson Avenue to the west, Chouteau on the south, and the Gateway Arch/Memorial Drive on the east. The central business district is largely contained between Washington Avenue (north), Interstate 64/U.S. Highway 40 (south), Memorial Drive (east), and the Wachovia Securities complex just west of Jefferson Avenue. Washington Avenue is the current hot spot for residential and commercial development, as dozens of new condos, apartments, restaurants, galleries, and boutiques are breathing new life into the area. The city's three sports arenas are located downtown as well, with Busch Stadium (MLB Cardinals), Scottrade Center (NHL Blues), and the Edward Jones Dome (NFL Rams) within ten blocks of each other. Anything located north of Cole Street and the Edward Jones Dome is referenced as the "near-north" side by locals. There are two additional entertainment areas in downtown, including Laclede's Landing and the historic Soulard neighborhood.

Laclede's Landing

At the far eastern edge of the city is Laclede's Landing, an entertainment district with restaurants and clubs. The collection of renovated 19th-century warehouses are listed on the National Register of Historic Places. Named for St. Louis's founding father, Pierre Laclede, "The Landing" features cobblestone streets and unique architecture along the Mississippi riverfront. Leonor K. Sullivan Boulevard is the district's eastern border, with Washington Avenue to the south, Third Street to the west, and Carr Street serving as the northern border.

Soulard

Just south of downtown is the Soulard neighborhood, a conclave of 19th-century red brick homes, historic churches, cozy bars, restaurants, and music clubs. The lively neighborhood was named for Antoine Soulard, a Frenchman who surveyed colonial St. Louis for the King of Spain. Today, this tract of land is one of St. Louis's favorite places to play, with live music filtering out of the various bars on an almost nightly basis. The Soulard Farmers' Market, which has been operating continuously since 1779, serves as the district's centerpiece, and is a popular destination for locals and visitors alike. Soulard's borders are Seventh Street to the east, the Anheuser-Busch brewery complex to the south, Interstate 55 to the west, and Park Avenue to the north.

Lafayette Square

West of Soulard is Lafayette Square, a revitalized area that includes some of the most beautiful Victorian architecture in the Midwest. The stately 1870s and 1880s "painted ladies" that frame the square have been called the finest and largest collection of Victorian-era architecture in the country. The picturesque neighborhood square surrounds Lafayette Park, a lush oasis of greenery within the urban landscape. Upscale eateries and bars have set up shop in the area, and new loft spaces are being carved from old warehouses and manufacturing sites. It has become one of the city's most popular neighborhoods. Lafayette Square is bordered by Chouteau Avenue to the north, Jefferson Avenue to the west, Interstate 44 to the south, and 18th Street to the east.

MIDTOWN

Midtown, located about a mile west of downtown, is most recognizable as the location of Saint Louis University's (SLU) sprawling campus and the booming Grand Center arts and entertainment district. SLU students live in various on-campus residence halls, and they eat and drink at the numerous bars, restaurants, and fast-food places located nearby. In addition to the fabulous Fox Theatre, Powell Symphony Hall, and the Sheldon Concert Hall, Grand Center is bustling with new development, including stylish new residential units, restaurants, and the premiere jazz club, Jazz at the Bistro (see listing in Nightlife). Midtown is bordered by Forest Park Parkway to the south, Compton Avenue to the east, Vandeventer on the west, and Washington Boulevard to the north.

WEST OF DOWNTOWN

Central West End

The Central West End—often called the CWE—is filled with charming sidewalk cafes, restaurants, art galleries, bookstores, shops, and cozy pubs. The neighborhood's commercial district, largely centered at Maryland and Euclid Avenues, is surrounded by block after block of tree-lined streets and large, stately homes. One of the most popular events held here is the annual house tour that allows visitors to get a look inside these beautiful homes. The area boundaries are I–64/US 40 to the south, Delmar Boulevard to the north, Boyle Avenue on the east, and Forest Park on the western edge.

The Hill

The Hill, St. Louis's own version of Little Italy, is home to a variety of restaurants, delis, bakeries, and shops, as well as at least two places to play a game of bocce—Italian lawn bowling. Even the fire hydrants, which set a colorful boundary for the neighborhood, are painted green, white, and red in tribute to Italy. Elegant gourmet restaurants, mom-and-pop trattorias, and tiny Italian grocery stores stand alongside small brick homes and businesses in this charming and close-knit neighborhood. Located south of I–44, Kingshighway is The Hill's eastern boundary, with Hampton Avenue to the west and Arsenal Street to the south.

i The Hill neighborhood has an active civic organization known as Hill 2000. The group formed in 1970 as a neighborhood improvement association and continues to draw positive attention to the area through various events. Proceeds from these festivals and activities are used for neighborhood improvements and to promote housing for new residents.

Maplewood

Just northwest of The Hill is a charming enclave called Maplewood. The formerly neglected municipality is enjoying a renaissance, as rehab-happy residents are moving into the economically accessible and quaint houses and storefronts. Along Manchester Road, Maplewood's charming main street, a variety of new restaurants, clubs, cafes, and specialty shops are popping up alongside the city's longtime antiques shops, jewelers, office supply stores, and other retailers. The quaint neighborhood is located between McCausland Avenue (east), Hanley Road (west), I–44 (south), and Manchester Road (north).

The Loop

To the north of I–64, next door to Washington University, is University City, or as it's more commonly called, The Loop. Named after an old streetcar turnaround, The neighborhood offers a diversity of ethnic and traditional American restaurants, shopping in one-of-a-kind stores, a variety of entertainment options, and the St. Louis Walk of Fame. University City is located between North and South Road, Forest Park Parkway, Roseland Avenue, and the residential areas just north of Delmar Boulevard. Delmar is the "main drag" of U City, and it connects The Loop with the Central West End neighborhood and Clayton.

Clayton

Clayton is the seat of the St. Louis County government, but it is probably best known for its thriving corporate business culture, beautiful homes, and its multitude of dining options. This near-west suburb of St. Louis features dozens of fine restaurants and casual eateries, along with elegant hotels, art galleries, and upscale shops. The annual St. Louis Art Fair is held in downtown Clayton each September, and it is one of the most popular festivals in the region. Clayton is perched between I–64 (south), Delmar Boulevard (north), Skinker Boulevard (east), and Interstate 170 (west).

NEAR-NORTH SIDE/NORTH COUNTY

The "near-north" side of the city features the historic African-American neighborhood known as The Ville and a series of older neighborhoods undergoing rejuvenation. Some local developers are slowly making progress on this front, with new low-income family housing units taking over vacant lots and deteriorating buildings. Annie Malone, one of the country's first African-American millionaires, was the most famous resident of The Ville, and the neighborhood's Sumner High School is the alma mater to St. Louisans Tina Turner, Arthur Ashe, and Chuck Berry. Cole Street is the area's southern border, with Interstate 70 to the north, Goodfellow Boulevard to the west, and

the Mississippi River to the east. North County is a largely suburban area that includes a number of small municipalities, as well as Lambert–St. Louis International Airport.

SOUTH/SOUTHWEST

Located just past The Hill and the St. Louis Hills neighborhood (home of Ted Drewes Frozen Custard) in the southwestern part of the city is another of St. Louis's nebulous regions called "South County." South County includes a number of bedroom communities and municipalities, including Affton, Oakville, Mehlville, Lemay, and Arnold. The main commuter artery for this region is I–55, with the Mississippi River serving as the southern border, Highway 141 as its western edge, and I–44 to the north. There are also several other charming small towns and suburbs in the southwest portion of St. Louis County (north of I–44, west of Interstate 270, south of I–64, and east of the St. Louis city limits), including Webster Groves, Kirkwood, and Glendale. These areas have preserved a certain small-town charm, and both Webster Groves and Kirkwood have unique "main-street" shopping and entertainment in addition to beautiful homes and tree-lined streets.

WEST COUNTY

"West County" is a vague and often deceptive term used to describe just about any of the seemingly endless municipalities located north of I–44, south of I–70, and west of Lindbergh Boulevard. Town and Country, Chesterfield, and Wildwood are suburban outposts that fall under this heading, along with Creve Coeur, Ballwin, and Manchester. There are a few attractions and notable restaurants sprinkled throughout West County, but the area(s) are more well known for large-scale shopping malls and suburban, family-friendly neighborhoods.

St. Louis Vital Statistics

Mayor/Governor: Francis G. Slay (D)/Jay Nixon (D)

Population (in 2008): City: 353,837; metro area: 2,600,000; Missouri: 5,586,114

Area: City: 61 square miles; business district: 2 square miles; Missouri: 69,706 square miles

Nicknames: Gateway to the West, Mound City, The Lou

Average temperatures: July: 79; January: 29

Average rainfall: 39 inches per year

Average snowfall: 19.8 inches per year

Founded: City: 1764; Missouri: 1821

Major cities: Jefferson City (state capital), Columbia, Kansas City, Rolla, St. Louis, Springfield

Major colleges/universities: Lindenwood University, Maryville University, Saint Louis University, St. Louis College of Pharmacy, University of Missouri–St. Louis, Washington University, Webster University, Fontbonne University

Major area employers: Anheuser-Busch, Inc., AT&T, Boeing, Emerson, Enterprise Rent-A-Car, BJC Health Care Systems, Washington University, Saint Louis University, Tenet Health Systems, Daimler-Chrysler Corporation, Wachovia Securities

GETTING HERE, GETTING AROUND

St. Louis is located at the epicenter of an amazing network of interstate highways, so it is virtually accessible from almost every direction. Downtown St. Louis streets are laid out on a grid pattern with alternating one-way north- and southbound streets. Abundant parking is available in high-rise garages and surface lots throughout downtown. Parking meters on the street generally have two-hour time limits, which are strictly enforced. Right turns are allowed on red lights unless otherwise posted.

BY CAR

From the east, Interstate 70, Interstate 64, and Interstate 55 go west, young man (or woman), and all three will take you across the Poplar Street Bridge and into downtown St. Louis. From there, I-70 goes through downtown, past the airport, and westward across Missouri, while I-55 turns south past the Anheuser-Busch brewery and continues along the Mississippi River through southwest Missouri and into Arkansas. Take I-64 west through the center of St. Louis County, and don't be surprised if locals refer to it as Highway 40 instead of 64. The Interstate 44 route begins in St. Louis and runs southwest along parts of historic Route 66 to Springfield and points west, ending up—eventually—in Santa Monica, California, and the foot of the Pacific Ocean.

In 2009, one of the region's most traveled roadways began to undergo extensive construc-

i Car trouble? Visit one of the 38 Dobbs Tire & Auto centers (636) 677–2101 located throughout the bi-state region. There's even one in downtown St. Louis. They offer fast service, honest pricing, and a free one-way shuttle within a 5-mile radius of each location. To find out where road construction is located on the Missouri side of the Mississippi River, call the Missouri Department of Transportation (MODOT) at (888) ASK–MODOT or log on to www.modot.org.

tion. Interstate 64/Highway 40 will be completely closed between I-170 and Kingshighway throughout 2009. Allegedly, all construction will be completed by December 31, 2009. For the most recent traffic snarls and construction updates, call the Missouri Department of Transportation—or MODOT—at (888) ASK–MODOT or log on to www.modot.org.

BY PLANE

Just minutes from downtown St. Louis, Lambert–St. Louis International Airport offers hundreds of convenient domestic and international flights into and out of St. Louis. The airport includes 12 major airlines in two terminals, which are connected by walkways and a shuttle bus. Plan to arrive at the airport at least an hour before takeoff Tuesday through Thursday, two hours prior Friday through Monday. For more information, call the airport at (314) 426–8000 or visit www.flystl.com.

Airport services include on- and off-site parking shuttles, ATMs, bookstores, coffee and snack shops, fax machines, full-service restaurants and lounges, foreign currency exchange and a full-service bank, game room, interfaith chapel, long-term parking, newsstands and gift shops, shoe-shine stands, TT/TDD phones, a visitor information booth, and a U.S. Post Office. There are two visitor information centers in the baggage claim areas of the Main and East Terminals on the lower levels, where friendly and informed volunteers are on hand to answer questions and

Airline	Phone Number	Concourse(s)
Air Canada	(888) 247–2262	A
American West Airlines	(800) 235–9292	A
American Airlines	(800) 443–7300	B,C
Big Sky Airlines	(800) 237–7788	E
Comair	(800) 354–9822	A
Continental Airlines	(800) 525–0280	A
Delta Airlines	(800) 221–1212	A
Frontier Airlines	(800) 432–1359	D
Midwest Connect	(800) 452–2022	E
Northwest/KLM Airlines	(800) 225–2525	A
Skyway	(800) 452–2022	E
Southwest Airlines	(800) 435–9792	E
United Airlines	(800) 241–6522	A
US Airways	(800) 428–4322	A

offer suggestions about things to see and do in St. Louis. There's also a healthy stock of free brochures, maps, and the latest event information for area attractions and restaurants.

A list of airlines that service Lambert–St. Louis International Airport and the concourses where they're located is on this page. Concourses A, B, C, and D are located in the Main Terminal, and Concourse E is in the East Terminal. There is a connecting hallway between the Main and East Terminals, but it is a bit of a walk—especially if you're running late for a flight.

For more information call (314) 426-8000 or log on to www.flystl.com or check www .flightarrivals.com for real-time flight arrival and departure information.

TAXIS, LIMOUSINES, AND CAR RENTALS

Taxis and Limos

Taxi fares are about $2.50 for the first $\frac{1}{10}$ mile and 17 cents for each additional $\frac{1}{10}$ mile. There's a $1 charge for each additional passenger and a $20 per hour waiting charge. A cab ride from Lambert Airport to downtown St. Louis should average

$33, and a cab ride from the airport to the Clayton business district averages about $22.

County Cab Company: (314) 991-5300; www .stlouiscountycab.com

Harris & Eagle Cab Company: (314) 535-5087

JED Limousine Services, Inc.: (314) 429-2200 or (800) 800-JED1; www.jedlimousine.com

Laclede Cab Company: (314) 652-3456

Style Limousines: (314) 521-6506 or (800) 789-5311; www.stylelimousines.com

TransExpress Transportation: (314) 428-7799 or (800) 844-1985; www.transexpress-stl.com

Car Rentals

Most of the major car rental agencies have offices in St. Louis, both at the airport and throughout the greater metropolitan area.

> **i** When local residents give driving directions, they will refer to Interstate 64 as Highway 40.

Enterprise Rent-A-Car, a St. Louis–based car rental company, has numerous locations throughout the bi-state area and will send someone to pick you up at your hotel and bring you to their closest rental office. When you return the car, they will take you back to your hotel or point of origin as well, so if you're looking for the most convenience, Enterprise "picks you up."

Avis Rent-A-Car: (314) 426-0279; www.avis.com

Budget Rent-A-Car: (314) 948-9565; www.bud get.com

Enterprise Rent-A-Car: (314) 863-0110 or (800) 227-9449; www.enterprise.com

Thrifty Car Rental: (314) 423-3737; www.thrifty .com

i The good news: Parking meters throughout downtown are free after 7:00 p.m., Monday through Saturday and all day on Sunday. The bad news: If you do get a parking ticket, you must pay it within 15 days or the fine will double and continue to increase until it's paid in full. You can pay tickets by phone, 24 hours a day, seven days a week via your Visa, MasterCard, or American Express card at (314) 450–2830 or (800) 611–3009.

BY TRAIN OR BUS

Amtrak

St. Louis's new Gateway Transportation Center (GTC) is home to Amtrak, MetroLink, and Greyhound Bus Line. The center, located on South 15th Street adjacent to the MetroLink light rail system's Civic Center stop, provides passengers with a clean, safe, and friendly transportation center featuring 24-hour operations staff and security. For Amtrak information call (314) 331-3300 or (800) 872-7245, or visit the Amtrak Web site, www.amtrak.com. Greyhound Bus Line info is available at (314) 231-4485 or (800) 231-2222, or www.greyhound.com. MetroLink fares and schedules are available at www.metrostlouis.org.

PUBLIC TRANSPORTATION

MetroLink

St. Louis's light-rail system, MetroLink, has been called one of the best mass-transit systems in the country. The clean, efficient trains are a big hit with visitors and locals alike who want to see many of St. Louis's attractions without a car. The system, which starts at Lambert–St. Louis International Airport, covers more than 46 miles and stops at more than 30 locations throughout Missouri and Illinois. The popular system recently expanded, with westward routes extending to the Clayton business district and eastward into Illinois.

A one-way ride on MetroLink costs about $2, and tickets may be purchased and validated at any station. Visitors can take MetroLink from the airport to downtown St. Louis for around $3.50, and the ride usually takes about half an hour. Daily passes for MetroLink and buses are $4.50. Trains usually run every 7 minutes during peak hours and every 10 minutes throughout the rest of the day. On weeknights, trains run every 15 minutes or so. From 11:30 a.m. to 1:30 p.m. on weekdays there's a Free Ride Zone that allows passengers to board MetroLink at any of the stations from Laclede's Landing to Union Station at no charge. For schedule information call (314) 231-2345 or (314) 982-1555 (TTY).

i MetroLink, the bi-state region's light-rail system, is an affordable and fast way to get from Lambert–St. Louis International Airport to downtown St. Louis.

MetroLink shuttle bus

Zip2, a summertime shuttle service that operates Memorial Day weekend through Labor Day, lets visitors leave the driving to Metro. The brightly colored shuttle buses connect the popular Forest Park cultural attractions with must-see sites in downtown and along the St. Louis riverfront. Zip2 operates from 10:00 a.m. to 6:30 p.m. daily, and one-day passes are about $4.50.

MetroBus

The bi-state bus system, MetroBus, serves most areas of the city of St. Louis and many of the municipalities in St. Louis County. For schedule information call (314) 231-2345, or visit the Transit Information Center, Monday through Saturday, at Seventh and Washington Streets in downtown St. Louis. Buses generally run from 4:00 a.m. to 2:00 a.m., and the fare is around $1.75. For more information log on to the Metro Web site www .metrostl.org.

During the week, MetroLink travels the St. Louis area around 4:00 a.m. to midnight. On weekends, the trains run between 5:00 a.m. and 12:30 a.m., so make sure that you don't get caught waiting for a train after the clock strikes 12!

HISTORY

St. Louis is known around the world for its fascinating attractions, great restaurants, and exciting blues music and nightlife. But what was here on the banks of the Mississippi River before the modern, lively city you see today? Clues abound in the city's interesting and varied history, which dates back more than four centuries.

EARLY SETTLERS

Early settlers of the St. Louis region allegedly were Indian mound builders, a group that scientists later called the Mississippians, who occupied the area from 850 to 1300 AD (this is why you'll occasionally hear St. Louis referred to as "Mound City"). The Native Americans built a complex culture on terraced land where Cahokia Mounds Historic Site is now. As many as 40,000 people lived in what was then the largest city north of Mexico; however, the civilization died out mysteriously by 1300 AD. During the 15th century, scientists believe that the Algonquin Indian civilization extended from Missouri to Maine along the Mississippi and St. Lawrence Rivers. That group, which included the Illinois nation, occupied the state of Illinois and the land to the north and east.

In 1673 Pere Marquette, a Jesuit missionary, and French-Canadian explorer Louis Joliet traveled the upper Mississippi and discovered the Missouri River. They explored the confluence of the two rivers and stopped near present-day Grafton, Illinois, before continuing south. Because of this exploration, the French claimed the Mississippi Valley north of the Ohio as part of Canada.

THE BIRTH OF ST. LOUIS

Almost a century later, in 1754, the French and Indian War resulted in the defeat of France. France ceded its holdings east of the Mississippi to Great Britain in 1763. That same year, Pierre Laclede, a partner in a fur trade company in New Orleans, began scouting for an ideal Indian fur trading location. He took along his 13-year-old stepson, Auguste Chouteau, on a journey up the Mississippi. After looking at two sites that proved unsuitable for their needs, they journeyed approximately 18 miles south of the confluence of the Missouri and Mississippi Rivers and discovered what would become St. Louis. Laclede and Chouteau liked the area's river access and the bluff that would prevent flooding. They marked the site and returned to it one year later to found the settlement of St. Louis, named for King Louis IX of France. Laclede predicted in a journal entry in 1763 that "I have found a situation where I am going to form a settlement which might become hereafter one of the finest cities in America." St. Louis developed into a thriving river town and eventually into a cultured city of the time.

The French soon began settling in St. Louis and established a fur trading community. The town developed into a center for north–south commerce along the Mississippi River and was closely modeled on a French colonial city of the times. Since the early settlement had no retail centers, cargoes of flour, sugar, whiskey, blankets, fabrics, tools, and household goods were brought to St. Louis by keelboat.

While the French founded St. Louis, others also flocked to and had an interest in the new city. French Canadians brought African slaves, and the community traded with the local Indian tribes. Even though France had rights to the land, the Spanish administered the city, which became part of the United States in 1804.

GROWTH AND PROSPERITY

By the time of the Louisiana Purchase in 1804, St. Louis had grown in population and established a bustling river landing. With city growth came new warehouses, supply stores, and a need for boat makers and repair shops. Keelboats transported furs to the north in exchange for manufactured goods. After the Lewis & Clark expedition returned from exploring the Louisiana Purchase, St. Louis became a hub for trappers in a new trade oriented to the far west and served as the final outpost where travelers could outfit themselves before their journeys began.

In 1817 the steamboat Zebulon M. Pike marked a new era in transportation along the river as it docked in St. Louis for the first time. The sandy beach levee in St. Louis was no longer adequate for these new steam vessels, so levees were transformed into stone wharves, and warehouses were built to receive goods. Steamboats became the preferred mode of river transportation and gradually replaced the keelboat.

By 1849 St. Louis was a major trading city, with travelers passing through to the gold rush in California and moving on to follow the Oregon Trail mapped by Lewis and Clark. In that same year a steamboat blew up on the crowded levee, and fire quickly spread to the city, destroying 15 blocks of the city's center and causing more than $6 million in damage. Only the Old Courthouse and the Old Cathedral, made of stone, survived. St. Louis set about the task of rebuilding, and this time brick and iron were used rather than easily kindled wood.

St. Louis entered the Victorian Age with style and a massive growth of industry and commerce. Resources of iron, the era of the steamboat and railroad, and the age of invention molded the city into a thriving metropolis. St. Louis was also home to diverse customs and a tapestry of cultures. The iron resource some 60 miles south of St. Louis led to a booming factory and foundry industry, as iron pipes, plows, stoves, and tools were produced from pig iron, and decorations on some of the city's grand homes and elaborate fences were made of wrought iron. The demand for iron increased substantially after the fire of 1849. During this time an influx of German and Irish immigrants, often leaving their homelands to escape political unrest and famine, arrived, and they left their mark on the city. The Germans, for example, brought their brewing expertise, and their ability to make bricks from the region's red clay significantly contributed to the area's unique architectural style.

THE CIVIL WAR

Several years before the beginning of the Civil War, a famous, historic case took place at the Old Courthouse in downtown St. Louis. Dred Scott and his wife, Harriet, slaves belonging to a St. Louis slave owner, sued for their freedom in 1847 after living for a time in states that prohibited slavery. After a protracted court battle, a final ruling by the U.S. Supreme Court in 1857 declared that slaves were not citizens and thus had no rights under the law. This only added to the already mounting pre–Civil War tensions in the nation.

At the time of the Civil War, St. Louis was one of the most important cities in the West and was the nation's third busiest port. Although the war brought a lot of hardship and suffering to the city, St. Louis was not directly involved as a theater for battle. While Missouri was nominally a slave state, it had remained loyal to the Union; however, the war still divided the city as it had the rest of the country.

MANUFACTURING AND TECHNOLOGY

The steamboat, which had ruled the rivers for 30 years and faithfully transported overlanders up the Missouri River for the journey along the Oregon Trail, was in decline by the 1880s. The 1874 completion of Eads Bridge across the Mississippi River simultaneously signaled the death knell for the steamboat and the beginning of east–west railroad commerce in St. Louis. St. Louis's Union

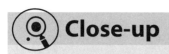

Close-up

Beer City, USA

It almost seems that St. Louis was destined to become a major beer brewing locale. In the 1800s, a lot of things just seemed to fall into place that helped make St. Louis the epicenter of American beer.

As large numbers of immigrants from Germany and Bohemia found their way to St. Louis beginning around 1830, a substantial portion of these newly-minted Americans settled in Soulard, the city's oldest neighborhood. This area was home to a number of breweries over the years, and it eventually became the home of the world's largest brewer, Anheuser-Busch. The immigrants' principal skills lay in making bricks and beer, so a number of breweries began to open in the city. And it helps explain the number of red brick buildings throughout the area. In addition to Eberhard Anheuser's Bavarian Brewery and Adam Lemp's Western Brewery, others like the Arsenal Brewery, Anthony and Kuhn's, Excelsior, Green Tree and English breweries established themselves in St. Louis.

Location and resources also spurred the growth of brewing in St. Louis. A large German population, plenty of water, rail connections, limestone caves, and entrepreneurial spirit provided the foundation for the city's beer business. By 1850, 43 percent of all St. Louisans were born in either Ireland or Germany—what a great foundation of customers for local beer-makers—and brewers began using caves in the Benton Park neighborhood for beer storage. The caves' cool, constant subterranean temperatures provided the best circumstances for brewing and storing.

AMERICA'S FIRST LAGER BEER BREWERS

John Adam Lemp arrived in St. Louis from Eschwege, Germany in 1838, and sought his fortune as a grocer. What set him apart from other grocers was his ability to supply an item that wasn't sold by any of his competitors—lager beer. Lemp learned the art of lagering beer under the tutelage of his father in Germany and the natural cave system under the city provided the perfect temperature for aging beer. Lemp soon realized that the future of lager beer in America was a force to be reckoned with, so in 1840 he gave up the grocery business and built a modest brewery on South Second Street. A St. Louis industry was born, as the brewery enjoyed tremendous success and John Adam Lemp died a millionaire.

William J. Lemp succeeded his father as the head of the brewery and soon built it into an industrial giant. When the Civil War started in 1861, Lemp had about 40 local competitors, but only 19 remained by the end of the century. He erected a new plant in 1864, as the size of the brewery grew with the demand for its product. By 1870, it was the largest brewery in St. Louis and controlled the lion's share of the St. Louis market, a position it held until Prohibition. In 1892 the brewery was incorporated as the William J. Lemp Brewing Co. In 1897 two of the brewing industry's were brought together by the marriage of William Lemp's daughter, Hilda, to Gustav Pabst of the noted Milwaukee brewing family.

The first Falstaff brand beer appeared in mid-1899, and Lemp Brewing registered the Falstaff trademark and logo four years later. Named for the Shakespearean character of Sir John Falstaff, the beer name was a tribute to the character's philosophy to "eat, drink, and be merry." However, all was not well within the Lemp beer dynasty. The first fracture occurred when Frederick Lemp, William's favorite son and the heir apparent to the brewery presidency, died under mysterious circumstances in 1901. Three years later, William J. Lemp shot himself in the head in a bedroom at the family mansion, apparently still grieving the loss of his son. William J. Lemp Jr. then took over as company president.

The brewery's fortunes continued to decline until 1919 when Prohibition forced the plant to close permanently. Continuing what seemed to be a family tradition, Elsa Lemp, considered the wealthiest heiress in St. Louis, committed suicide in 1920. In June of 1922, the Lemp brewery, once valued at $7 million, was sold at auction to International Shoe Company for less than

$600,000. Although most of the company's assets were liquidated, the Lemps were able to keep the family home. After presiding over the sale of the brewery, William Lemp Jr. shot himself in the same building where his father had died 18 years earlier. William's brother, Charles continued to reside at the house after his brother's suicide but led a reclusive existence. He also died of a self-inflicted gunshot wound, and his body was discovered by his brother, Edwin. In 1970, Edwin Lemp died of natural causes at the age of ninety. Today, the family's home has been turned into a restaurant and bed-and-breakfast called Lemp Mansion Restaurant & Inn (3322 DeMenil Place; 314-664-8024, www.lempmansion.com) and is available for tours.

In 1917, the Griesedieck family purchased Forest Park Brewing's property and formed the Griesedieck Beverage Company. In 1918, the Lemp Brewery ceased production and closed, and Griesedieck went into receivership two years later. Joe Griesedieck eventually obtained the Falstaff trademark from the Lemp family and bought the Griesedieck Company back, renaming it the Falstaff Corporation. The company made it through Prohibition with a variety of side businesses as well as brewing "near beer" brands, or nonalcoholic brews. When Prohibition ended in 1933, the company became Falstaff Brewing Corporation and was granted the very first federal permit to resume brewing beer. The Griesedieck and Falstaff breweries merged in 1957, and in 1985, Falstaff acquired Pabst Brewing. However, the brand's sales continued to drop throughout the 1990s, so in 2005, Pabst announced that it would no longer produce the Falstaff brand.

Still going strong is St. Louis's own, Anheuser-Busch. In 1860, Eberhard Anheuser acquired the Bavarian Brewery from the original owner, George Schneider, and renamed it E. Anheuser & Company. The next year, Adolphus Busch married Anheuser's daughter Lily, and began working at his father-in-law's brewery in 1864. The company, which grew quickly and began dominating the local beer market, changed its name to Anheuser-Busch Brewing Association in 1879. After Anheuser's death in 1880, Busch became president of the company. In 1913, Adolphus Busch died and the company was turned over to his son, August A. Busch, Sr. Busch lead the brewery through Prohibition, as the company began producing everything from ice cream and ginger ale syrup to non-alcohol Budweiser and refrigerated cabinets. Busch pioneered refrigerated railroad cars that extended the shelf-life of un-pasteurized lager so it could be shipped farther. Anheuser-Busch capitalized on this newfound technology to nurture a national market for its products. It was the first step in making Budweiser, introduced in 1876, the most popular beer in America.

August A. Busch Jr. took over the reins of the company when his father died in 1946, and "Gussie," as he was known, diversified the company by adding regional breweries, opening Busch Gardens, and creating the Metal Container Corporation as a subsidiary. Gussie's son, August A. Busch III, took over the company as president in 1973. Busch III, who is often referred to as "The Third," was at the helm when Bud Light was introduced in 1982 and when Anheuser-Busch broke the billion dollar mark of beer brewed since the company's founding. During this period, Anheuser-Busch expanded its brewing practices around the globe, including purchasing a majority interest of Grupo Modelo in Mexico (in 1993) and the Chinese company, Wuhan Brewing Company (in 1995). Busch III retired in 2002, naming Patrick Stokes as president of the brewery, the first non-family member to oversee the company since its inception. In 2006, August A. Busch IV ("The Fourth") assumed the role of president and the company continued to introduce new beer brands and expand into the distilled spirits category. In 2008, Anheuser-Busch agreed to a takeover by Belgium's InBev, the world's largest brewer. InBev's brand portfolio includes such popular beers as Beck's, Stella Artois, and Labatt Blue. The St. Louis brewery will serve as the North American headquarters for the company, re-named Anheuser-Busch InBev.

Visitors can still take a free tour of the Anheuser-Busch Brewery (I-55 & Arsenal Street, 314-577-2626, www.budweisertours.com), which includes stops at the Brew House, Budweiser Clydesdales' stables, lager cellar, packaging plant, and gift shop. At the end of the tour, guests ages 21 and over can sample a variety of Anheuser-Busch brands.

Station, designed by architect Theodore Link, opened in 1894, and it was the largest railroad station in the United States at the time.

In addition to the advent of the railroad, other technological advances introduced in the latter part of the 19th century made a difference in the lives of St. Louisans, including the foot-powered sewing machine and gas or oil lamps. In 1876 Alexander Graham Bell invented the telephone, and within a year it was introduced to St. Louis. During the next decade, wealthy home owners began using electricity to light up their houses, and no home was complete without a piano. In 1898 the first player piano was introduced to the market, and Ralston Purina produced the world's first hot cereal, called "Ralston" after the doctor who endorsed it. The "good old days" of letter writing, hand-darning socks by candlelight, and lack of efficient transportation seemed to be vanishing.

> **i** The oldest known building in St.
> Louis, the Old Rock House, was built
> on the land where the Jefferson National
> Expansion Memorial is currently located.
> Built by Manuel Lisa in 1818, it was used to
> house furs of buffalo, deer, badger, skunk,
> and beaver. Symbolic of St. Louis's first
> industry, the building was disassembled
> and partially reconstructed in the St. Louis
> Revisited Gallery at the Old Courthouse.

THE WORLD'S FAIR

The Louisiana Purchase Exposition of 1904, also known as the St. Louis World's Fair, commemorated the centennial of the Louisiana Purchase. The exposition, which was visited by nearly 20 million people, featured exhibits from more than 40 nations, 12 palaces that displayed technological advances, beautifully designed exposition halls, lakes and gardens, and amusement rides and food. The Louisiana Purchase Exposition Company installed 75 miles of roads and walkways and 15 miles of railroad for the World's Fair, and built the more than 1,000 buildings that occupied the fairgrounds in what is now Forest Park. Many modern-day items that are considered "all-American" actually debuted at the fair, including Buster Brown shoes, ice-cream cones, hot dogs served in a bun, and iced tea.

The fair's electric Intramural Railroad had 17 stops throughout the fairgrounds, and visitors could see demonstrations of new inventions like the heavier-than-air flying machine, coin changers, electric clocks, and automatic telephone answering machines. One exhibit that drew a lot of attention was the baby incubator, which dramatically increased the chances of survival for premature infants Performers included a 24-year-old cowboy-storyteller named Will Rogers; musician Scott Joplin, who introduced the world to ragtime; and an exotic entertainer called "Little Egypt," who lured fairgoers to "The Pike," the fair's. amusement area. The phrase "coming down the Pike," which is still used today, referred to all the wonders of the world a visitor could see displayed on the fairgrounds.

A CITY ON THE MOVE

A significant transition to the 20th century came after the Worlds' Fair. People were becoming less community-oriented and kept to themselves more thanks to the invention of the radio, the phonograph, and electric fans. The days of gathering at the Old Courthouse to listen to orators vanished, and walking by the river to feel the cool breeze went by the wayside. Electric trolley cars enabled anyone to commute easily and inexpensively.

Another form of transportation, the automobile, was taking folks out to the surrounding areas of the city and dispersing its population. The world's first gas station opened in St. Louis in 1905 at 412 South Theresa Avenue, and the same year, George Dorris, one of the founders of the St. Louis Motor Carriage Company, organized the Dorris Motor Car Company. Other car makers followed, and by 1909 St. Louis had 20 automobile manufacturers and another eight firms that custom-built cars to order. From 1900 to 1929 St. Louis was home to more than 219 car manufacturing companies.

Transportation also took to the skies around St. Louis, and in 1905 the dirigible California Arrow gave local residents their first look at controlled flight. Watching gas-filled balloons was a popular spectator event, and the First International Balloon Race was held in St. Louis in 1908. Two years later Thomas Scott Baldwin made St. Louis's first extensive airplane flight, during which he flew over and under the Mississippi River bridges. Other air-flight firsts followed, including Arch Hoxsey's nonstop cross-country record, when he flew 87 miles from Springfield, Illinois, to St. Louis; Theodore Roosevelt's 1911 flight that originated in St. Louis, which was the first time a president had ridden in an airplane; and, of course, Charles Lindbergh's historic nonstop transatlantic flight in 1927. Lindbergh was sponsored by 12 St. Louis businessmen who dubbed his plane The Spirit of St. Louis. After the successful flight and a ticker tape parade in New York, a triumphant Lindbergh returned to St. Louis, where 500,000 people cheered him along a parade route through the city.

i The ice-cream cone was first concocted by Ernest Hamwi, who served Persian waffles, called zalabia, filled with ice cream at the St. Louis World's Fair. He later founded the Missouri Cone Company, which became the country's largest producer of ice-cream cones.

PROHIBITION

A movement to prohibit alcohol had increased support in the new century, the theory behind which was that abstention from alcohol would reduce crime and alcoholism—two increasing problems in St. Louis and throughout the nation. Instead of solving these problems, however, the Prohibition Act that was passed as a constitutional amendment in 1920 had the opposite effect. Outlawing the sale, manufacture, or transportation of alcohol merely encouraged the vice prohibitionists wanted eliminated. People secretly brewed alcohol and sold it at speakeasies, secret gathering places that resembled bars,

and this was a tremendous period of growth for organized crime. Prohibition greatly affected St. Louis's breweries. Since Anheuser-Busch could no longer make beer, it began producing yeast and a soft drink called Bevo. IBC (Independent Breweries Company) root beer also made its way to store shelves as an alternative to alcoholic beverages in 1920, and the Seven-Up Company introduced its new soft drink in 1929. Like Anheuser-Busch's line of alcoholic and nonalcoholic beverages, IBC and Seven-Up's soft-drink syrups are still produced in St. Louis.

When Prohibition—the "failed social experiment"—came to an end in 1933, August A. "Gussie" Busch Jr. presented the Budweiser Clydesdale eight-horse hitch to his father at the brewery in St. Louis. The team traveled to New York and then Washington, D.C., to deliver the first case of post-Prohibition Budweiser to the White House. The Clydesdales became synonymous with Anheuser-Busch and eventually appeared in commercials and at parades across the country.

THE GATEWAY ARCH AND THE PUSH TOWARD THE 21ST CENTURY

In 1948 Eero Saarinen won $225,000 in an architectural competition to design the Gateway Arch for the Jefferson National Expansion Memorial, which encompassed the city's original historic district. Before any demolition at the memorial site, the National Park Service researched, surveyed, and photographed existing structures of historical significance in an effort to make certain that the monument and its surroundings contributed to the revitalization of the riverfront area. In accordance with this urban renewal concept, the area surrounding the memorial grounds was designed to include a stadium, motels, offices, and commercial buildings.

Steamboats represented the majority of river traffic between 1850 and 1870, and in St. Louis the steamboats were reported to be anchored three deep and a mile wide along the levee.

The stainless-steel-faced Gateway Arch, completed in 1965, is 630 feet wide (between the

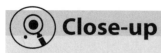 **Close-up**

St. Louis's Musical Heritage

The honor roll of musicians with ties to St. Louis reads like a who's who of modern American music: Cornell Haynes, aka Nelly; trumpeter Jeremy Davenport; Grammy award-winning musician Sheryl Crow; jazz saxophonist David Sanborn; former Doobie Brother Michael McDonald; Bobby "Don't Worry, Be Happy" McFerrin; Rock and Roll Hall of Fame inductee Johnnie "B. Goode" Johnson; Fontella "Rescue Me" Bass; sax man Oliver Sain; and the Father of Rock 'n' Roll himself, Chuck Berry. It wasn't just a coincidence that St. Louis produced so many successful musicians; the city's varied and fascinating musical heritage played a part.

Situated in the nation's heartland, St. Louis's location has lent itself to absorbing myriad cultures and eccentricities, serving as a crossroads between north and south, east and west. Many credit the Mississippi River, which runs along the edge of the city, for bringing the blues up to St. Louis from its birthplace in Mississippi. Many black Mississippians who followed the river en route to Chicago, Detroit, and other destinations stopped over in St. Louis, and some remained. Blues music had been born in the cotton fields of the Mississippi Delta by the late 1800s, and this "new" folk music spread quickly north to Memphis and St. Louis, where the blues became the dominant secular music in the African-American community.

Inspired by early Mississippi blues, Memphis bandleader William Christopher "W. C." Handy penned "Memphis Blues," the first blues song ever published. At one point Handy journeyed upriver, settling for a brief period in St. Louis. During the 1890s he spent time on the riverfront, listening to the workers on the levee sing their way through the long, laborious days. Their melodies sounded a lot like the "field hollers" he was used to hearing from field workers who picked cotton in the Mississippi Delta. He remained in St. Louis for a time, performing in taverns and pool halls on what was then known as Targee Street, which today is the site of the Scottrade Center, home to the St. Louis Blues NHL ice hockey team. Several years later, in 1916, Handy would pen "St. Louis Blues," which went on to become the most published blues song in history.

Around the turn of the 20th century, a new kind of music would find its way out of St. Louis. Ragtime, a heavily syncopated piano-based music that was "ragged" to give it more feeling, was popularized during the 1904 World's Fair in St. Louis by Scott Joplin. Joplin, considered by many to be the Father of Ragtime, published his "Maple Leaf Rag" in 1899, turning ragtime into

outer faces of its triangular legs) and soars 630 feet into the St. Louis skyline. Each leg is an equilateral triangle with sides that are 54 feet long at ground level and taper to 17 feet at the top. The double-walled, triangular sections were placed one on top of another, then welded inside and out to build the legs of the Arch. Reinforced concrete foundations were sunk 60 feet into the ground, extending 30 feet into bedrock. Sections range in height from 12 feet (at the base) to 8 feet for the two keystone sections at the top. The complex engineering design and construction is completely hidden from view—all that can be seen is the stainless-steel "skin" and the inner

skin of carbon steel. These combine to carry the gravity and wind loads to the ground. At the top, the observation platform is 65 feet long and 7 feet wide, with plate-glass windows that provide miles of views to the east and west. Structural engineers report that in a 150-mph wind, the top of the Arch will deflect, or sway, only 18 inches in the east–west direction.

The construction of the Gateway Arch and the nearby Busch Memorial Stadium (in 1966) helped promote the revitalization of St. Louis's central business district. For the next 30 years, downtown underwent a building boom that included projects like the Cervantes Convena pop-music craze. Joplin taught piano and performed in bordellos and barrooms in St. Louis from 1900 to 1904, influencing a generation of ragtime and jazz musicians.

While ragtime's popularity was short-lived, it resurfaced under a pseudonym farther downriver. During the early 1900s, brass bands were extremely popular, and New Orleanians put their own spin on the ragged rhythm, "jazzing" it up a notch. Piano players like Jelly Roll Morton perfected the new approach, and his style translated to other keyboard jockeys throughout Storyville, New Orleans's famous red-light district. These jazz influences steamed back into St. Louis aboard northbound riverboats from New Orleans, and they blended with established ragtime and blues music to enhance the St. Louis blues.

Jazz music continued to evolve and grow in popularity over the years, and by the end of World War I, Louis Armstrong hit the spotlight and moved jazz to the next level. Armstrong and other music legends such as King Oliver, Duke Ellington, Ma Rainey, and Bessie Smith were the pioneers who laid the foundation for jazz as well as a new music genre, rhythm and blues, that would explode in the next decades.

During the late 1940s and early 1950s, rhythm and blues got its start in the nightclubs of East St. Louis, Illinois; St. Louis, Missouri; and Memphis, Tennessee. The popularity of Big Band orchestras was waning, and musicians such as Ike Turner, Louis Jordan, and others recorded by musical mad scientist Sam Phillips at Sun Studio in Memphis filled the niche. In early 1954 a youngster named Elvis Presley ventured into Sun to make a recording. A Mississippi native, he had been greatly influenced by the style and mannerisms of blues and jazz musicians. After he recorded with Sam Phillips, the rest was rock 'n' roll history—the boy who would be King had arrived.

While Elvis was getting his break in Memphis, the man considered to be the Father of Rock 'n' Roll was kicking things around upriver in St. Louis. Chuck Berry was busy whipping up a few essential elements—namely blues, rhythm and blues, gospel, and country—into a rock 'n' roll frenzy. His hard-driving guitar sounds and rockabilly-style vocals took him to the top of the charts, but he didn't reap nearly as many benefits as his light-skinned counterparts. Meanwhile, Ike Turner was taking himself to the big time with another Memphis/St. Louis hybrid, Anna Mae Bullock—better known as Tina Turner.

Today, blues music is alive in St. Louis's neighborhood clubs, taverns, and entertainment districts such as the Soulard neighborhood. Just south of the city's famous Gateway Arch, blues clubs are tucked into the various red brick buildings of the historic district of Soulard.

tion Center (1978), the rehab of St. Louis Union Station (1985), and downtown's only shopping mall, the St. Louis Centre (1986). At the same time, growing interest in preservation of historic neighborhoods, which was fueled mostly by federal tax credits, led to the revitalization of the Central West End, Soulard, and Lafayette Square neighborhoods during the 1970s and early 1980s. Although the recession of the late 1980s and early 1990s slowed growth to a degree, several major projects were completed in downtown during this time period. The popular MetroLink light-rail line opened in 1993, and the renamed America's Center convention complex expanded

tremendously. In 1994 the expanded and refurbished Kiel Civic Center reopened, and the facility, now called Scottrade Center, is home ice for the NHL's St. Louis Blues and home to Saint Louis University's Billikens basketball. Scottrade Center also hosts numerous concerts and family entertainment events throughout the year.

Another big event that took place in 1993 was the "great Mississippi River flood," which detracted from urban revitalization efforts somewhat. The rising river waters didn't hamper construction of the new 67,000-seat domed stadium in downtown St. Louis, however. St. Louis was rewarded for its forethought in January 1995,

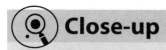

Route 66

St. Louis is the largest city along Route 66 between Chicago and Los Angeles, and there are a number of sites related to the "Mother Road" within the region. Some of the streets have new names, but these locations are all part of the Route 66 journey through the area. Just north of St. Louis is the Old Chain of Rocks Bridge, situated across the mighty Mississippi River south of Interstate 270. The bridge is open to pedestrian traffic only, and it offers a good spot for "eagle-watching." On the outskirts of downtown is the tiny Eat Rite Diner, whose motto is "Eat Rite or Don't Eat at All."

Grab a burger here then head out for Ted Drewes Frozen Custard, perched at its historic location since the 1940s. Farther west, the street name changes to Watson Road, and you'll see the location of the old Coral Court Motel. The motel was torn down in 1995, and the land is now filled with a subdivision of newer homes, but you can see one of the old motel's units that was saved and reconstructed at the National Museum of Transportation in West County. Across the street and down Watson Road a bit is the Wayside Motel, built in 1930. While it's not nearly as glamorous as the deco-style Coral Court, it is one of many vintage motels and buildings representative of the era still standing.

Out in Eureka, Route 66 State Park features a visitor center housed in the former Bridgehead Inn, a 1935 roadhouse. The center features Route 66 memorabilia and tells the story of "The Main Street of America." As you pass through Pacific, you'll see the old Pacific 66 Liquor sign that has been restored as a Route 66 sign, and the Red Cedar Inn, built in 1943. Villa Ridge is home to the Sunset Motel, and nearby Stanton features the Jesse James Museum. The Circle Inn Malt Shop is still around in Sullivan, and Cuba remains heavy with Mother Road icons such as the Wagon Wheel Motel and the Old Phillips 66 Service Station, both of which were built in the 1930s.

So "if you ever plan to motor west," visit www.missouri66.org for more tips and history from the Route 66 Association of Missouri. For information about Route 66-related stops in Illinois, log on to the Route 66 Association of Illinois's Web site at www.IL66assoc.org.

---

i In the mid-1930s, the "juniors" division of women's clothing was born in St. Louis. Irving Sorger, a merchandising manager at St. Louis's Kline's Department Store, realized a need for a younger look in women's clothing. He contacted the Washington University Department of Dress Design in the School of Fine Arts and convinced them to create dresses that would appeal to young women in their late teens and early twenties.

when the NFL's Los Angeles Rams announced that they were pulling up stakes and moving the team to St. Louis. In November of the same year, the Dome at America's Center hosted its first St. Louis Rams game. The venue was later renamed the TWA or Trans World Dome and is now known as the Edward Jones Dome. The St. Louis Rams won Super Bowl XXXIV in January 2000.

Today, downtown and neighborhood revitalization efforts continue in St. Louis, as evidenced by the resurgence of such areas as Washington Avenue, Lafayette Square, Maplewood, and the Central West End. There are currently five Fortune 500 corporations headquartered within the city limits and eight within St. Louis County. Many of the older industrial buildings in St. Louis serve as incubators for growing small businesses and explorations in technology and the bio-tech industry.

Important Dates in St. Louis History

1764   St. Louis is founded by French fur traders Pierre Laclede and Auguste Chouteau

1804   President Thomas Jefferson purchases the Louisiana Territory from France.

1804   Meriwether Lewis and William Clark head west from St. Louis under orders from President Jefferson to explore the Louisiana Territory

1809   St. Louis is incorporated as a town

1821   Missouri becomes the 24th state

1847   Dred Scott, a slave, and his wife, Harriett, sue for their freedom in what became one of the most celebrated court cases in U.S. history and a contributing cause of the Civil War

1860   Eberhard Anheuser acquires a small brewery in south St. Louis that he and son-in-law Adolphus Busch build into one of the top-producing breweries in the world

1904   Forest Park hosts the Louisiana Purchase Exposition, more commonly referred to as the St. Louis World's Fair

1926   In the first of their ten World Series titles, the St. Louis Cardinals defeat the New York Yankees in seven games

1927   Charles Lindbergh, flying The Spirit of St. Louis, becomes the first person to fly the Atlantic solo

1933   Prohibition ends and August A. "Gussie" Busch Jr. celebrates by sending the Budweiser Clydesdale eight-horse hitch to deliver the first case of post-Prohibition Budweiser to the White House

1965   Construction of the Gateway Arch is completed

1993   The Mississippi River overflows its banks in what is called a "500-Year Flood," causing billions of dollars worth of damage to the St. Louis region

2000   The St. Louis Rams win Super Bowl XXXIV by defeating the Tennessee Titans 23–16

2003   The historic Eads Bridge, the first structural steel span to cross the Mississippi River, reopened to vehicular and pedestrian traffic on July 4, exactly 129 years after the bridge's original grand opening date

2004   Groundbreaking ceremonies are held for a new Busch Stadium being built adjacent to the existing Busch Stadium

2005   The Edward Jones Dome hosts the NCAA Men's Final Four Basketball Tournament and the University of North Carolina is crowned champion of college hoops

2006   A new Busch Stadium opens in downtown and the St. Louis Cardinals christen the venue by winning their tenth World Series championship in franchise history

2008   The Loop, St. Louis's Delmar Boulevard, was named one of "10 Great Streets in America" by the American Planning Association (APA)

2009   St. Louis hosts the 2009 NCAA Women's Final Four and the Major League Baseball All-Star Game

ACCOMMODATIONS

St. Louis has more than 38,000 places for you to spend the night while you're in the metropolitan region. Accommodations range from the utmost in upscale hotels to charming bed-and-breakfast facilities to Lewis & Clark–style "roughing it" at area campgrounds. Whether you're in the market for luxury and pampering or just need a place to rest your head at night, there's something in every price range available. Most of the major hotel chains are represented in the area, and downtown St. Louis is in the middle of a tremendous hotel building boom. New hotels have opened around the America's Center convention complex, and they range from economic convenience to four-star luxury.

The listings begin with downtown St. Louis properties, then proceed westward, northward, and southward from there. Hotels or chains located on the Illinois side of the river aren't included here because they aren't particularly convenient to St. Louis–area attractions—you'll come out better by staying on the Missouri side of the Mississippi River. There are some Illinois bed-and-breakfasts as well as campgrounds and RV parks listed here, however. The Illinois area immediately across the river from St. Louis lends itself to these types of properties more easily than hotel chains, due to the fact that these kinds of accommodations are more likely to be found in less densely populated areas. (For more information on properties located outside of St. Louis County, see the Day Trips and Weekend Getaways chapter.)

Almost all of the properties listed in this chapter offer wheelchair-accessible and nonsmoking rooms for their guests. Some of the hotels list their facilities as "limited wheelchair accessible," so it's a good idea to call ahead and make sure the property that you choose can accommodate your individual needs. Unless otherwise noted, all of these hotels, motels, and bed-and-breakfasts accept most major credit cards, and I've noted a few properties that allow pets.

Price Code

The following price code is based on a regular room with double occupancy and reflects basic room rates (known in the industry as "rack rates"). These prices do not include the local sales and hotel taxes on rooms, tips, service charges, or additional fees.

$	Less than $100
$$	$100-125
$$$	$125-175
$$$$	More than $175

DOWNTOWN

COURTYARD ST. LOUIS DOWNTOWN $–$$
2340 Market Street
(314) 241-9111, (800) 321-2211
www.marriott.com/stlch
Located just a few blocks west of the immediate downtown area, this Courtyard feels more like a suburban hotel than a downtown property. Services offered include complimentary self-park parking, an indoor pool, on-site limited-service market, and free in-room, high-speed Internet access. There are laundry valet and self-service laundry facilities, as well as fax, copying, and printer service available. The hotel frequently offers special package deals that include a dis-

counted price on rooms and assorted extras, such as coupon booklets, free passes to area attractions, and other incentives.

i Headquartered in St. Louis, the Drury hotel chain is one of the best bargains in the region. Ideal for traveling families or business travelers, Drury hotels offer reasonable room rates and free parking, as well as free continental breakfasts. Plus, many of the chain's hotel rooms are outfitted with a mini refrigerator and microwave oven. There are a total of sixteen Drury inns and hotels across the metropolitan St. Louis area, including three downtown. The hotels frequently offer special deals that include coupon books, free admission to attractions, and special room rates, so it's worth calling (800) 378-7946 or logging on to www .druryhotels.com for more information.

DRURY INN & SUITES–ST. LOUIS CONVENTION CENTER $$
711 North Broadway
(314) 231-8100, (800) 378-7946
www.druryhotels.com
There are three Drury hotel properties in downtown St. Louis, and all offer free continental breakfast each morning as well as free parking. They all have indoor pools and Jacuzzis, fitness rooms, and on-site guest laundry services. This Drury property is located on the northern edge of downtown, directly across the street from the Edward Jones Dome and the America's Center convention complex. The hotel is within easy walking distance of the Arch, Laclede's Landing, Washington Avenue, Busch Stadium, and several MetroLink stations. The hotel has a full-service restaurant on-site, J. F. Sanfilippo's, which serves up traditional Italian favorites, fresh-baked bread, and house-made desserts.

DRURY INN–ST. LOUIS UNION STATION $$
201 South 20th Street
(314) 231-3900, (800) 378-7946
www.druryhotels.com

Conveniently located downtown adjacent to historic Union Station, this hotel is housed in what once was the Railroad YMCA. In addition to the restaurants and shops at Union Station, the Drury is close to the Scottrade Center, which hosts basketball and hockey games, as well as concerts and family entertainment shows. There's also easy access to a MetroLink stop nearby, which can take visitors to Busch Stadium, the convention center, Lambert-St. Louis International Airport, or to the Illinois side of the river and the Casino Queen gambling boat. Lombardo's Trattoria Restaurant, a spin-off of The Hill neighborhood's popular Lombardo's restaurant, is located in the hotel.

DRURY PLAZA HOTEL–ST. LOUIS $$–$$$
Fourth and Market Streets
(314) 231-3003, (800) 378-7946
www.druryhotels.com
The Plaza location is the flagship hotel in St. Louis and the newest addition to the collection of Drury hotels downtown. The lobby is part of the former Fur Exchange Building, which is one of the oldest buildings in St. Louis. The term "affordable elegance" may seem cliché, but things at this hotel definitely look a lot more expensive than they are. From the marble and granite lobby area, complete with its Lewis & Clark diorama, to the 365-plus guest rooms, the Plaza is a very nice, reasonably-priced option. Many of the rooms offer spectacular views of downtown and the Gateway Arch, and the hotel provides easy access to Busch Stadium and the historic riverfront. There are two full-service restaurants on-site: Max & Erma's is a casual and family-friendly St. Louis sports-themed restaurant—part of the national chain—and Carmine's Steakhouse features hand-cut, custom-aged steaks and Italian cuisine.

FOUR SEASONS HOTEL $$$$
999 North Second Street
(314) 881-5800
www.fourseasons.com
Missouri's only Four Seasons hotel is part of the $500 million Lumière Place casino complex. The luxury hotel, which offers unparalleled views

of the Gateway Arch, has 200 guest rooms, a 10,000-square-foot luxury spa, outdoor pool, and 20,000 square feet of meeting space. Cielo restaurant features upscale Italian cuisine, while the elegant Cielo Bar serves up cocktails and a tapas-style menu.

HAMPTON INN–GATEWAY ARCH $$
333 Washington Avenue
(314) 621-7900, (800) HAMPTON
www.hamptoninn.com

Located in the heart of downtown St. Louis and right across the street from the famous Gateway Arch, Edward Jones Dome and the America's Center convention complex. The hotel is convenient to the dining and nightlife at Lumière Place, Washington Avenue and the burgeoning Loft District. The property features Tigin's Irish Pub, an indoor pool and whirlpool, a game room, and three levels of parking. Limited wheelchair accessibility.

HAMPTON INN–UNION STATION $$
2211 Market Street
(314) 241-3200

While the "Union Station" part of this hotel's name is slightly misleading (it's a couple of blocks away), it is in the general vicinity and convenient to many downtown attractions. This Hampton is owned and run by the Drury family as well, so you get the same good deal on a room rate, along with free "deluxe continental" breakfast, free parking, and free local calls. There's also an indoor pool and whirlpool, exercise facilities, and an on-site bar and restaurant, Syberg's on Market. You can catch Syberg's shuttle to baseball, hockey, and football games here, too.

HILTON ST. LOUIS AT THE BALLPARK $$$–$$$$
One South Broadway, Broadway and Market Streets
(314) 421-1776, (800) 228-9290
www.hilton.com

Conveniently located directly across the street from Busch Stadium and Kiener Plaza, the Hilton is located near the Busch Stadium MetroLink stop

and the heart of the downtown business district. It has 675 deluxe guest rooms, an Executive Floor, laundry valet, self-service laundry facilities, shoe-shine stand, and a full business center, as well as personal computer and printer availability. There's valet and self-parking available, along with an on-site Hertz Car Rental desk, gift shop, newsstand, and an ATM. The property, rated three stars by Mobil Travel Guide and three diamonds by AAA, features an on-site Starbucks, the Pavilion full-service restaurant, and the Market Street Cafe.

HILTON ST. LOUIS DOWNTOWN $$–$$$
400 Olive Street
(314) 436-0002
www.hilton.com

Located within the beautifully renovated Merchants Laclede Building, the historic building retains the beauty of its late 18th-century architecture. In addition to covered parking, a complimentary business center, state-of-the-art fitness center, and same-day valet dry cleaning, the hotel features an award-winning restaurant, 400 Olive. The full-service restaurant is open for breakfast, lunch, and dinner and features traditional and contemporary cuisine. Each of the 195 sleeping rooms has free high-speed wireless Internet access; a refrigerator with complimentary bottled water; two telephones with voice mail, data-port, and free local phone calls; a coffeemaker with complimentary coffee and tea; and a large work desk with desk-level outlets and ergonomic chairs.

HOTELUMIÈRE $$–$$$
901 North First Street
(314) 881-7800, (877) 450-7711
www.lumiereplace.com

The former Embassy Suites has undergone a $16 million renovation and been re-branded as HoteLumière. The all-suite hotel has nearly 300 guest rooms, an indoor pool, and the House of Savoy, a Tuscan-themed restaurant. HoteLumière connects to the new Lumière Place casino complex located on the historic riverfront.

HYATT REGENCY ST. LOUIS
RIVERFRONT $$–$$$
315 Chestnut Street
(314) 655-1234, (800) 223-1234
www.stlouisriverfront.hyatt.com

The recently renovated and re-branded Hyatt Regency St. Louis Riverfront (formerly the Adam's Mark Hotel) features 910 guest rooms and 96 deluxe suites outfitted with cable TV, in-room movies, same-day laundry/dry-cleaning service, and phones with voice mail and free high-speed Internet access. There's a fully equipped health club on-site, plus heated outdoor and indoor pools, saunas, and racquetball courts. Business travelers will appreciate the hotel's full-service business center, which offers typing, faxing, mailing, FedEx/UPS, notary services, and audiovisual equipment and technical service. The hotel is home to a number of dining and entertainment options, including the Tiffany Rose Lobby Lounge, which offers premium cocktails in a cigar-friendly atmosphere, and Chestnut's, a casually elegant restaurant with a great Sunday brunch.

MILLENNIUM HOTEL ST. LOUIS $$$$
200 South Fourth Street
(314) 241-9500, (800) 325-7353
www.millenniumhotels.com

The 780-room Millennium Hotel's circular tower is one of downtown's most recognizable landmarks, and the hotel's location makes it a convenient place for business, leisure, and convention travelers. There are three on-site restaurants, two lounges, seasonal indoor and outdoor swimming pools, an exercise room/fitness center, game room, attached parking garage, and an ATM in the hotel lobby. Twenty-eight stories above street level, the revolving Top of the Riverfront restaurant offers diners a panoramic view of St. Louis, along with a menu of innovative American cuisine and an all-American wine list.

NAPOLEON'S RETREAT $$–$$$
1815 Lafayette Avenue
(314) 772-6979, (800) 700-9980
www.napoleonsretreat.com

This beautiful 1880 Victorian offers elegant yet relaxed accommodations in the historic Lafayette Square neighborhood. There are five large guest rooms in this restored town house, and all include private baths, TVs, phones, and wireless Internet service. The house is furnished with antiques, and it was named one of Better Homes & Gardens magazine's "Prettiest Painted Places" in America. The nearby 30-acre Lafayette Park is a Victorian jewel that offers a glimpse into St. Louis's architectural past, with its original wrought-iron fence, gazebos, park house, and duck pond. It's a perfect place for an evening stroll or a quick walk after breakfast.

THE OMNI MAJESTIC HOTEL $$$$
1019 Pine Street
(314) 436-2355, (800) THE-OMNI
www.omnihotels.com

Listed on the National Register of Historic Places, this elegant, concierge-style, European boutique hotel was built in 1913. Tucked away in the midst of the downtown business district, the 91-room Majestic offers access to laundry services, a full-service business center, the hotel chain's Omni Kids Program, and a complimentary shuttle service within the downtown area. The hotel allows pets less than 25 pounds for a $50 nonrefundable fee. Valet parking is available for an additional charge. The hotel has a full-service fitness center with state-of-the-art cardiovascular equipment and offers complimentary high-speed Internet access. The Mahogany Grille serves traditional American cuisine in a relaxed pub-style environment. There's also a big-screen TV for sports fans or news hounds.

RENAISSANCE ST. LOUIS GRAND
HOTEL $$$$
800 Washington Avenue
(314) 621-9600
www.marriott.com

Located adjacent to the America's Center convention complex, the Renaissance Grand Hotel certainly lives up to its name. The beautifully restored, historic building features more than 900 guest rooms and public areas that elicit the grandeur of the 1920s era. The architectural beauty won awards when the hotel opened in 1917, and much care has been taken to restore the property to its original magnificence. This AAA four-diamond hotel features a lobby lounge that offers light snacks and Capri, the hotel's casual, full-service restaurant where guests can enjoy contemporary Mediterranean cuisine from the coast of Italy, south France, Greece, and Spain, and An American Place, and upscale yet casual restaurant open for dinner only. High-speed Internet access is available in all guest rooms.

RENAISSANCE ST. LOUIS SUITES
HOTEL $$$$
827 Washington Avenue
(314) 241-9100

The sister hotel to the Renaissance Grand Hotel (located right across the street) is just as spectacular in its decor and guest amenities. The all-suites hotel combines luxury with historic elegance and has the look and feel of a boutique hotel. This property was built in 1929, and it remains an ideal place for business travelers or families who need a little room to spread out. Each suite has a bedroom that is separated by French doors to the living area, work area, and a wet bar with a refrigerator and coffeemaker. High-speed Internet access is available in every sleeping room. The in-house eatery is the Washington Avenue Bistro and Lounge, which serves breakfast, lunch, and dinner. Pets are allowed with payment of a nonrefundable sanitation fee.

THE ROBERTS MAYFAIR, A WYNDHAM
HISTORIC HOTEL $$$
806 St. Charles Street
(314) 421-2500, (800) 996-3426
www.wyndham.com

Located in the heart of downtown, this beautifully restored hotel, built in 1925, is one of the most charming in the city. Throughout its history, the Mayfair was the place for visiting luminaries such as Irving Berlin, Cary Grant, and Harry Truman. In fact, legend has it that Grant "invented" the idea of putting a chocolate on hotel guests'

pillows. It seems that Grant was trying to woo a female occupant of the hotel during a visit, so he left a trail of chocolates from her pillow to his hotel room. The Mayfair, which is listed on the National Register of Historic Places, is elegant without being stuffy and has retained its regal 1920s ambience while incorporating modern amenities. Each guest room features high-speed Internet access and incredibly comfortable pillow-top mattresses. Located within walking distance to the Arch, Busch Stadium, the Edward Jones Dome, America's Center convention complex, and MetroLink stations, the hotel is truly a unique jewel. The cozy cocktail bar is a great place to enjoy a drink after work or to grab breakfast or lunch during the day.

SHERATON ST. LOUIS CITY CENTER
HOTEL & SUITES $$-$$$
400 South 14th Street
(314) 231-5007, (888) 627-8096
www.starwoodhotels.com

A beautifully renovated downtown historic hotel, the Sheraton St. Louis City Center Hotel & Suites offers great amenities in a convenient location. The oversize guest rooms and suites feature queen-size sofa sleepers, refrigerators, wet bars, Sony Playstations, two-line speakerphones, coffeemakers, and Internet access through the 27-inch television. Dining options include upscale ambience and American cuisine at bistro 14, lighter fare at the Columns Lounge and Piano Bar. For more strenuous recreation check out the indoor, heated, Olympic-size pool, or work out while overlooking the St. Louis skyline in the fitness center. There's also a rooftop sundeck and an oversize Jacuzzi tub. The hotel is across the street from the MetroLink light-rail system and across from the Scottrade Center sports and entertainment facility.

ST. LOUIS UNION STATION MARRIOTT $$$
1820 Market Street
(314) 231-1234
www.marriott.com

The newly re-branded Marriott (formerly the Hyatt Regency) is located inside Union Station, the National Historic Landmark retail, restaurant, and entertainment complex. The hotel, which features more than 525 luxurious guest rooms and suites, offers guests a choice between the traditional elegance of the restored train station in the Headhouse and the contemporary design of the Garden Hotel. In-room Internet access is available for a fee. There's an outdoor heated pool and a fitness room that features free weights, Life Cycles, treadmills, stair-climbers, and rowers, as well as saunas in the men's and women's locker rooms. There are a number of dining options within the hotel, including The Shed Bar and Grill, Station Grill, and the Grand Hall, which features a full bar and hors d'oeuvres menu.

THE WESTIN ST. LOUIS $$–$$$
811 Spruce Street
(314) 621-2000, (800) WESTIN1
www.starwoodhotels.com

Located directly across the street from Busch Stadium, the Westin's Clark Street Bar is a favorite gathering place before and after baseball games. The sleek, modern smoke-free hotel offers more than 250 luxurious guest rooms and suites with contemporary flair and high-tech touches. In addition to high-speed Internet access in every room, the property has a well-equipped 24-hour fitness center and full-service day spa, a business center, and limousine service. The Clark Street Grill allows diners to enjoy international cuisine and the interactive display kitchen in a unique urban loft setting. It's actually good "hotel food" and is a popular dining destination for locals.

> **i** The Chase, built by and named for Chase Ullman in 1922, was the destination for upscale business and leisure travelers. It became the "home away from home" for renowned actors and singers performing in St. Louis and hosted every U.S. president from the 1920s to the 1980s. The "Chase Club" (now the hotel's five-screen movie theater) featured top-name entertainers such as Frank Sinatra, Dean Martin, Jerry Lewis, and Bob Hope.

WEST OF DOWNTOWN

Central West End

CHASE PARK PLAZA HOTEL $$$$
212–232 North Kingshighway
(314) 633-3000, (877) 587-2427
www.chaseparkplaza.com

"The Chase," the more common moniker of the legendary Chase Park Plaza Hotel, is a contemporary blend of distinctive charm and upscale sophistication in the Central West End neighborhood. The Chase Park Plaza, comprised of two buildings, the Chase and the Park Plaza, encompass more than 1 million square feet of luxurious guest suites with high-speed Internet access, restaurants, meeting facilities, shops, and a five-screen movie theater. The hotel features more than 100 luxury suites for overnight and extended-stay guests, and amenities include a beautiful heated outdoor pool, an 18,000-square-foot fitness and exercise facility, and a full-service business center with computers, high-speed Internet access, e-mail, and fax machines. There's a car rental desk where guests can access vehicles on-site. Five unique restaurants within the complex offer an array of culinary options. Eau Bistro specializes in new American cuisine, with fresh seafood and meats from around the country, complemented by its 300-bottle wine list. The Sunday Champagne Brunch is spectacular and features a lavish spread that includes seafood, omelets cooked-to-order, desserts, and much more. Cafe Eau, which is one of St. Louis's most popular nightspots, features an ice bar to keep liquid refreshments perfectly chilled and a diverse menu for breakfast, lunch, and dinner. The Tenderloin Room is known for its masterfully seasoned steaks, such as the famous Pepperloin a la Tenderloin. The menu includes fresh seafood and classic soups and salads. The Marquee Cafe offers seasonal American cuisine in a casual atmosphere for breakfast, lunch, and dinner, but the dessert menu is pretty incredible as well. Outdoor seating is available, weather permitting, and the menu offers room service and carry-out options.

And, finally, Chaser's Lounge is a full-service bar conveniently located next to the five-screen multiplex movie theater.

HOTEL INDIGO $$-$$$
4630 Lindell Boulevard
(314) 361-4900
www.ichotelsgroup.com

Located in the heart of the Central West End neighborhood, this new full-service, 130 guest room property is a sophisticated, smoke-free boutique hotel designed to be an oasis for travelers who want something more than a typical hotel environment. Indigo features complimentary high-speed Internet access, a 24-hour business and fitness center, Phi Bar, Restaurant and the quick serve Bistro—Golden Bean for cutting edge cuisine and Starbucks coffee.

Clayton

HILTON ST. LOUIS FRONTENAC $$$-$$$$
1335 South Lindbergh Boulevard, Clayton
(314) 993-1100, (800) 325-7800
www.stlouisfrontenac.hilton.com

The Frontenac Hilton offers more than 260 spacious guest rooms and 37 suites and is convenient to both the Clayton and downtown St. Louis business districts. Guest rooms feature dual-line telephones with voice mail and dataports, and recreational facilities include an outdoor swimming pool and a health club that features Nautilus equipment and a sauna. The hotel's casual dining room, Provinces Grille, offers American cuisine. Provinces Restaurant serves breakfast, lunch, and dinner in a "business casual" atmosphere. Guests can take advantage of free transportation to and from Lambert–St. Louis International Airport.

MOONRISE HOTEL $$$-$$$$
6177 Delmar Boulevard
(314) 721-1111
www.moonrisehotel.com

Located in the heart of The Loop, the new Moonrise Hotel features sophisticated, contemporary design with first class amenities mixed with some quirky signature features. Guest rooms are outfitted with the Enrapture Eurotop beds, plush feather pillows, down duvets, flat screen TVs, Technology Docking Station, Wi-Fi, and cordless telephones. Moonrise offers ten "Walk of Fame Suites," each designed to showcase a different honoree from the nearby St. Louis Walk of Fame. The boutique hotel's on-site eatery Eclipse features a menu of classic favorites reinterpreted with unique ingredients for breakfast, lunch, and dinner. The rooftop terrace bar offers cocktails and small plate specialties, as well as incredible views of the Gateway Arch.

> **i** Even when big events are in town, you can usually find a room at the 62-room Water Tower Inn (3545 Lafayette Avenue, 314–977–7500; www.slu.edu/ events/wti.html), owned and operated by Saint Louis University. The hotel isn't on most travelers' radar, so you can find a clean, low-cost, no frills hotel room with easy access to I-44.

RITZ-CARLTON–ST. LOUIS $$$$
100 Carondelet Plaza, Clayton
(314) 863-6300, (800) 241-3333
www.ritzcarlton.com/hotels/st_louis

The Ritz is—well, it's the Ritz. It's everything you'd expect a luxury hotel to be. Located in the heart of Clayton, the hotel is about 15 minutes from Lambert–St. Louis International Airport and only a short walk from a plethora of Clayton's finest restaurants and art galleries. There are more than 300 large, luxurious guest rooms and suites, each with French doors that open onto private balconies. The standard room is more than 500 square feet, while the Executive Suites are more than twice that size. All guest rooms at the hotel feature three telephones and two phone lines, voice mail, an honor bar with refrigerator, Nintendo, cable TV, twice-daily housekeeping service, plush terry cloth bathrobes, complimentary morning newspaper, and in-room safes. The hotel fitness center is outfitted with climate-controlled indoor

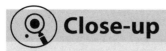

Close-up

Spas

Two of the city's most popular hotels—The Westin St. Louis in downtown and the Chase Park Plaza Hotel in the Central West End—have ways to reduce the overall stress level of travelers with a slate of "hands-on" personal services. Both have on-site, full-service day spas to serve guests in search of some much needed TLC. The facilities offer everything from massages and facials to body wraps and pedicures, so if your stressful existence could use some exfoliation, schedule some "quality time" with your body, mind, and spirit.

The Solera Spa and Health Club (The Westin St. Louis, 811 Spruce Street; 314–621–2000) offers a variety of body treatments, including the seaweed body wrap and Sedona Mud body wrap, which are intended to detoxify and revitalize the skin, while the Peppermint Rosemary Herbal Body Scrub and the Dead Sea Salt Glow treatments exfoliate the skin. Solera also offers European facials and signature treatments like sunless bronzing, feet and hands rejuvenation treatments, and the centuries-old technique of ear candling. Guests can choose one of ten different massages, including the traditional Swedish massage, a deep-tissue massage, or the Acu-Roma, which combines Swedish massage techniques with aromatherapy oils for additional relaxation. Both the Executive and the Signature massages are designed to soothe and relax stressed-out patrons, and the Solera Thermo-Stone Massage works on easing aching muscles, improving circulation, and removing impurities by using warm basalt volcanic stones and soothing oils. There's a prenatal massage to help de-stress moms-to-be, and the rejuvenating Shiatsu/Thai Massage that uses techniques from the Far East. Services are available Monday through Saturday; Sunday by appointment only.

The Salon & Spa at the Chase (Chase Park Plaza Hotel, 232 North Kingshighway, Suite 104; 314–633–3081, www.chaseparkplaza.com/amenities/salon/) is open daily and features a variety of personal services including massages, facials, waxing, peels, pedicures, and manicures, as well as a full menu of hair salon services. Or, if you want to make a day of it, take advantage of one of the facility's packages like "A Day at the Chase" (Swedish massage, facial, manicure, pedicure, haircut and finish, and makeup application) or the "Day of Indulgence" (aromatherapy massage, deep-cleansing European facial, manicure, pedicure, and exfoliating polish). The "Make It a Date" package is built for two and features one-hour Swedish massages, European facials, and his-and-hers manicures and pedicures. If you don't have time to pamper yourself completely, try the "Short & Sweet" option, which includes a 30-minute aromatherapy massage, an express facial, manicure, and pedicure.

Other highly recommended spa treatment centers located throughout the area include The Face and The Body (2515 South Brentwood Boulevard, Brentwood; 314–725–8975; www.face andbody.com), for men and women; Stonewater Spa, Salon & Boutique (3 Plaza Frontenac, Frontenac; 314–569–2111; www.stonewater.com); and the Solace Spa at the Wellbridge Athletic Club (7620 Forsyth Boulevard, Clayton; 314–746–1500; www.wellbridgeac.com).

lap and hydrotherapy pools, a private sundeck, steam, sauna, and massage services. On-site dining options include the Grill, which combines classic American beef and seafood dishes with customized sauces and side dishes, and the Restaurant, specializing in continental or "fitness" cuisine for breakfast and lunch. In the Lobby Lounge, guests can choose from a menu of lighter fare, as well as an extensive sushi bar and a large variety of martinis. (Check out the Close-up feature in the Nightlife chapter for more information.) The private Cigar Club, furnished with rich leather and mahogany furnishings, serves a light-fare menu along with more than 250 cigars and premium cognacs, grappas, ports, sherries, scotch, and American whiskies. The Wine Room has more than 7,000 rare vintages and select labels, and is the city's largest "dine-in" wine cellar.

> **i** For a complete list of St. Louis–area hotels, call the St. Louis Convention & Visitors Commission at (800) 916–0040, or log on to its Web site at www.explorestlouis.com.

SEVEN GABLES INN $$$
26 North Meramec, Clayton
(314) 863-8400, (800) 433-6590
www.sevengablesinn.com
The Seven Gables, built in 1926, is a Tudor–style inn with steep, pitched roofs; a massive chimney; tall, narrow windows in multiple groups; and decorative half-timbering. This European-style luxury hotel blends old-world charm and modern conveniences. Stucco walls, parquet floors, Oriental rugs, and country French antiques grace the common areas, creating an elegant and inviting atmosphere. The 32-room inn has two restaurants on-site. Molly Darcy's is an Irish pub with a casual, "clubby" feel, and offers a menu of reasonably priced pub grub. Not wheelchair accessible.

SHERATON CLAYTON PLAZA HOTEL–ST. LOUIS $$-$$$
7730 Bonhomme Avenue, Clayton
(314) 863-0400, (888) 337-1395
www.starwoodhotels.com
Location, location, location. This Sheraton is situated in the heart of Clayton's business district and allows guests to literally step out to dozens of neighborhood bars, restaurants, galleries, and shops. Located in the heart of St. Louis County's financial and judicial center, the hotel features more than 250 guest rooms and 31 suites, an indoor pool, health club, complimentary airport shuttle, shuttle service within the Clayton area, and Alexander's Restaurant.

NORTH COUNTY

COMFORT INN & CONFERENCE CENTER $-$$$
9600 Natural Bridge Road, Bridgeton
(314) 427-7600, (888) 444-CLUB
www.choicehotels.com
This Comfort Inn features dual-line telephones with voice mail, dataports, coffeemakers, and 25-inch TVs with CNN, ESPN, HBO, and pay-per-view movies. There's also a fitness facility, video arcade, billiards, and an indoor pool under a retractable roof. Business travelers can utilize the business center's printers, fax machine, copier, express mail services, two small conference rooms, business work tables, and den-style seating. The hotel offers free high-speed Internet access, as well as a free airport shuttle. On-site dining is limited to the Comfort Inn Restaurant, which serves breakfast, lunch, and dinner.

CROWNE PLAZA ST. LOUIS AIRPORT $$-$$$
11228 Lone Eagle Drive, Bridgeton
(314) 291-6700
www.ichotelsgroup.com
The Crowne Plaza St. Louis Airport Hotel, located just 1 mile from Lambert–St. Louis International Airport, features more than 350 guest rooms and suites with large business-class desks, ergonomic chairs, two phone lines, dataports, and high-speed Internet access. The hotel's restaurants include Cloud's Restaurant for breakfast and a T.G.I. Friday's that serves lunch and dinner. The fully equipped exercise facility is located within the hotel's spectacular eight-story, glass-enclosed atrium that features a two-story waterfall, heated indoor pool, whirlpool, and fitness center that includes a treadmill, free weights, stair-stepper, exercise bike, and universal weight machine.

> **i** You can often find better rates by checking out an individual hotel's Web site, which may offer Internet-only rates or hotel package deals.

DRURY INN–AIRPORT $$

10490 Natural Bridge Road, Bridgeton
(314) 423-7700, (800) 378-7946
www.druryhotels.com

This Drury hotel property, located 1/4 mile from the airport and the MetroLink light-rail system, features 172 guest rooms and two-room suites, free parking, and a free 24-hour airport shuttle. Guests can enjoy a free continental breakfast daily, a manager's reception with free beverages on Monday through Thursday evenings, and access to an on-site exercise room, indoor pool, and whirlpool.

HOLIDAY INN AIRPORT–OAKLAND PARK $$

4505 Woodson Road, Bridgeton
(314) 427-4700, (800) 426-4700
www.holiday-inn.com/stl-woodsonrd

This standard-issue Holiday Inn offers all of the usual trappings of the chain, but what makes it stand apart is its European decor and a collection of more than 200 original oil paintings on display throughout the hotel. The hotel is located about 1/2 mile from the airport MetroLink station that provides transportation to downtown St. Louis and area attractions. It offers complimentary airport transportation, free parking, an outdoor pool, and an on-site fitness facility with a sauna, treadmill, Life Cycle, and stair-stepper. Business travelers have access to a full business center featuring personal computers, e-mail, Internet, printer, fax, and copy services. Free high-speed Internet access is available in all guest rooms. The Oakland Park Restaurant is open daily and serves breakfast, lunch, and dinner.

ST. LOUIS AIRPORT MARRIOTT $$–$$$

10700 Pear Tree Lane, Bridgeton
(314) 423-9700, (800) 228-9290
www.marriott.com/stlap

Located at Lambert–St. Louis International Airport, the newly renovated Marriott is a full-service hotel that caters to business travelers. In addition to more than 600 guest rooms, all of which offer free high-speed Internet access, the property offers a complimentary airport shuttle, concierge services, news and shoe-shine stand, and a full business center complete with secretarial services. Restaurants in the hotel include the Rock River Tavern and the Rock River Grill for casual American-style dining. There's also an on-site Starbuck's, an indoor and outdoor pool, health club, whirlpool, and sauna, as well as a full-service spa located nearby.

SOUTH/SOUTHWEST

BEST WESTERN KIRKWOOD INN $$

1200 South Kirkwood Road, Kirkwood
(314) 821-3950, (800) 435-4656
www.bestwestern.com/kirkwoodinn

This Best Western is a small, comfortable hotel located in the southwest corner of St. Louis County, right off Interstate 44. It is convenient to the Magic House children's museum, Laumeier Sculpture Park, Grant's Farm, and the Museum of Transportation, and it's only a 15-minute drive from Six Flags amusement park. The 114-room hotel offers free parking and free continental breakfast and has discount admission tickets available for Six Flags. There's a Chili's Bar & Grill on-site. Pets are allowed in certain room types, and there is a daily charge of $10 per pet.

DRURY INN & SUITES–FENTON $$

1088 South Highway Drive, Fenton
(636) 343-7822, (800) 378-7946
www.druryinn.com

Located minutes from Six Flags via I–44, this Drury property has 141 standard guest rooms and two-room suites, which feature separate bedroom and living areas. The hotel offers the usual list of Drury amenities, including free continental breakfast, high-speed Internet access in every room, manager's reception with free beverages Monday through Thursday evenings, an exercise room, guest laundry, indoor/outdoor pool, and whirlpool. There's a Cracker Barrel, Denny's Restaurant, Sonic, and Bandana's BBQ restaurant adjacent to the hotel.

HOLIDAY INN FOREST PARK $-$$
5915 Wilson Avenue
(314) 645-0700, (800) 465-4329
www.ichotelsgroup.com

This Holiday Inn offers budget-level accommodations in an ideal Mid-County location on I–44, 2 miles from Forest Park and less than 10 minutes from downtown. There's an outdoor pool, an on-site restaurant and lounge, and free parking. The hotel is located about 1 mile from The Hill Italian neighborhood, so good food is only a short drive away. On-site, there's the Forest Park Cafe, serving American cuisine for breakfast, lunch and dinner, and the Forest Park Lounge for cocktails.

HOLIDAY INN, ST. LOUIS SOUTH
INTERSTATE 55 $$
4234 Butler Hill Road, Arnold
(314) 894-0700, (800) 785-2328
www.ichotelsgroup.com

Located in the South County area, this Holiday Inn is about 15 miles from downtown St. Louis and convenient to I–55. The property has 163 guest rooms and suites, as well as a Holidome, which features indoor and outdoor pools, a whirlpool, an exercise room, a variety of games, and a sunning area. Remington's is the hotel's on-site restaurant, serving breakfast, lunch, and dinner, along with Sunday brunch. There's a cash machine on-site, as well as a business center featuring copy service, e-mail and Internet access, fax, and personal computer and printer service. High-speed Internet access is available in guest rooms. The hotel staff speaks a variety of languages, including Tagalog, Finnish, French, German, Croatian, and Spanish.

HOLIDAY INN AT SIX FLAGS $$$
4901 Six Flags Road, Eureka
(636) 938-6661, (800) 782-8108
www.stlouissixflags.holiday-inn.com

Located directly across from the Six Flags amusement park, the heart of the Holiday Inn is a spacious old stone barn offering an unusual combination of rich, colorful history and modern facilities. Guests can take advantage of the hotel's game area, which features video games, shuffleboard, and an indoor putting green. There's also an on-site exercise room, whirlpool, sauna, and indoor swimming pool. The full-service Haymarket Restaurant serves up breakfast, lunch, and dinner. Complimentary shuttle to Six Flags St. Louis.

THE LODGE AT GRANT'S TRAIL BY
ORLANDO'S $$-$$$
4398 Hoffmeister Avenue
(314) 638-3340, (866) 314-7829
www.lodgeatgrantstrail.com

The Lodge at Grant's Trail is located in the southwest portion of St. Louis. It has the amenities of a fine hotel and a casual rustic charm that offers guests a unique place for entertaining or just unwinding. There are two presidential suites—Washington and Lincoln—and six specialty rooms, each with a different theme, private bath, satellite TV, and fireplace. Breakfast is served each morning, wine and cheese are served at check-in, and special-event catering is available, but there is no on-site restaurant.

TOWNEPLACE SUITES BY MARRIOTT $
1662 Fenton Business Park Court, Fenton
(636) 305-7000
www.marriott.com/stltf

This Marriott-brand property, located in west St. Louis County, is designed for extended-stay travelers. The town house community offers economical studios and one- and two-bedroom suites with fully equipped kitchens. High-speed Internet access is available in every guest room. Guests can use the laundry valet or self-service laundry facilities, and have access to simple business services such as faxing, copying, and printing. There's also an exercise room and an outdoor pool.

WEST COUNTY

DOUBLETREE HOTEL & CONFERENCE
CENTER ST. LOUIS $$$
16625 Swingley Ridge Road, Chesterfield
(636) 532-5000, (800) 222-8733
www.doubletree.com

This deluxe hotel and conference center features more than 220 rooms, 15 tennis courts, racquetball facilities, indoor/outdoor pool, and a Cybex-equipped health club. Each guest room includes two telephones—one with dual ports—and a large work table. High-speed Internet access is also available in each room. For a little more luxury, there's the Executive Registry Level, where the guest rooms feature wet bars, plush seating arrangements, and more spacious bathrooms. American cuisine is served at Chaucer's, Racquets Bar & Grill, and Gulliver's Lounge.

DRURY INN & SUITES–CREVE COEUR $$
11980 Olive Boulevard, Creve Coeur
(314) 989-1100, (800) 378-7946
www.druryhotels.com
Part of the Drury chain, this hotel offers more than 180 guest rooms located within easy access of Interstate 270 in West County. Amenities include a free continental breakfast, indoor pool and whirlpool, exercise room, meeting rooms, guest laundry, free local calls, and covered parking. This property also offers two-room suites with microwaves and refrigerators. The hotel is located right next to an Applebee's restaurant.

DRURY INN & SUITES–WESTPORT $$
12220 Dorsett Road, Maryland Heights
(314) 576-9966, (800) 378-7946
www.druryhotels.com
This Drury property features 130 guest rooms and is located minutes away from the shops and restaurants of Westport Plaza. The hotel is also close to the outdoor Verizon Wireless Amphitheater, which hosts top-name bands and entertainers throughout the warmer months. Guests can enjoy a free continental breakfast, local phone calls, parking, and access to the outdoor pool.

HARRAH'S ST. LOUIS CASINO & HOTEL $$$
777 Casino Center Drive, Maryland Heights
(314) 770-8100, (800) HARRAHS
www.harrahs.com
Harrah's Hotel features 455 deluxe rooms, 47 luxury suites, a complimentary 24-hour fitness center, free airport shuttle service, and free parking. Dining options are as varied as the casino games, with a total of seven (lucky seven) on-site

restaurants and lounges. Club Aroma, Jester's Deli, and Town Square Buffet serve up lighter fare in a casual atmosphere, while Charlie Gitto's From the Hill and The Range Steakhouse offer more extensive menus. Moby's Fish Tales offers fresh seafood at reasonable prices, and the VooDoo Lounge is a haven for sports fans, complete with a giant video wall full of live sports action.

LA QUINTA INN & SUITES ST. LOUIS–WESTPORT $–$$
11805 Lackland Road, Maryland Heights
(314) 991-3262, (800) 687-6667
www.laquinta.com
This hotel offers 131 guest rooms and two-room suites with coffeemakers, dataport phones, 25-inch TV sets/entertainment packages, free airport shuttle, local phone calls, and daily continental breakfast. There's also a pool, spa, and fitness center, and business center services are available. Free high-speed Internet access is available in guest rooms.

RESIDENCE INN BY MARRIOTT–WESTPORT $$
1881 Craigshire Road, Maryland Heights
(314) 469-0060, (800) 331-3131
www.residenceinn.com/stlrw
Located about ½ mile from the Westport Plaza entertainment district, this Residence Inn features 127 one- and two-bedroom suites with separate living and sleeping areas, as well as a fully equipped kitchen complete with refrigerator, microwave, and coffeemaker. Pets are allowed, with payment of a nonreturnable sanitation fee. Guests can enjoy a complimentary hot breakfast buffet each morning and a complimentary hospitality hour Monday through Thursday. There's an on-site pool, heated spa, fitness center, and a Sport Court for basketball, volleyball, and tennis. Free high-speed Internet access is available in each guest room.

SHERATON WESTPORT PLAZA HOTEL $$$$
900 Westport Plaza, Maryland Heights
(314) 878-1500, (800) 822-3535
www.sheraton.com/westportplaza

The Sheraton Westport Hotel is a first-class high-rise hotel centrally located in the Westport Plaza business and entertainment complex. It offers a variety of services, including a car rental desk and business center, along with an indoor pool, health club and fitness center, and Jacuzzi and sauna. Complimentary parking and airport shuttle, in-room coffee, and weekday editions of *USA Today* are also featured. Pets are allowed. High-speed Internet access is available for an additional charge.

SHERATON WESTPORT LAKESIDE
CHALET $$$$
191 Westport Plaza, Maryland Heights
(314) 878-1500, (800) 822-3535
www.sheraton.com/westportchalet
The Sheraton Westport Lakeside Chalet is a European-style hotel with 300 guest rooms that include dataports, coffeemakers, and cable television with HBO. The Lucerne Restaurant is open daily and overlooks Westport Lake. Like its sister Sheraton property next door, the hotel offers complimentary parking, airport shuttle, and in-room coffee service. High-speed Internet access is available in all guest rooms for an additional charge. Pets are allowed.

SPRINGHILL SUITES BY MARRIOTT–
ST. LOUIS/CHESTERFIELD $-$$
1065 Chesterfield Parkway, Chesterfield
(636) 519-7500, (800) 287-9400
www.springhillsuites.com
Rooms in this moderately priced all-suite hotel have about 25 percent more space than a traditional hotel room. The studio suites feature separate areas for sleeping, eating, working, and relaxing; complimentary breakfast buffet; two-line telephone with dataport and voice mail; free high-speed Internet access; in-room coffee service; minifridge; and microwave—perfect for business travelers or families with small children.

ST. LOUIS MARRIOTT WEST $$-$$$
660 Maryville Centre Drive, Chesterfield
(314) 878-2747, (800) 352-1175
www.stlmarriottwest.com

Located about 16 miles west of downtown St. Louis, this full-service Marriott features rooms with high-speed Internet access and 27-inch televisions with premium cable, pay-per-view movies, Nintendo, and WebTV. The hotel is nestled among a beautiful tree-lined setting and includes an on-site health club with indoor and outdoor pools, as well as a full-service restaurant.

YOGI BEAR'S JELLYSTONE RESORT AT
SIX FLAGS $
5300 Fox Creek Road, Eureka
(636) 938-5925, (800) 861-3020
www.eurekajellystone.com
Jellystone Resort has premium camping facilities less than ½ mile from the Six Flags St. Louis amusement park. The 35-acre facility offers paved roads; full or water/electric hookups; shaded, level sites; 50-amp electric; pull-throughs; clean restrooms and hot showers; propane; a dump station; Laundromat; and fire rings and picnic tables at each site. There are computer modem hookups at the nearby Ranger Station and a fully stocked camp store complete with groceries, camping and RV supplies, firewood, ice, and souvenirs. Jellystone also offers tent/pop-up sites with the aforementioned amenities or deluxe (water/electric) or primitive sites. Oh yeah, and you can meet Yogi Bear "in person," swim in the pool, play mini-golf or arcade games, watch movies, or take a train ride. Camping cabins are available, and there's free high-speed Internet access, too.

OUT OF TOWN

THE BEALL MANSION . . .
AN ELEGANT BED & BREAKFAST $$-$$$
407 East 12th Street, Alton, IL
(618) 474-9100, (866) 843-2325
www.beallmansion.com
The Beall Mansion offers luxurious, nonsmoking guest rooms in a beautifully restored early 20th-century house featuring hardwood floors, crystal chandeliers, leaded glass, and the original woodwork. Guest rooms feature private baths

with whirlpools and showers or claw-foot tubs; fireplaces; Wi-Fi; full-, queen-, or king-size feather beds; and expanded cable TV. Special package deals include everything from a complimentary glass of champagne on arrival and a package of gourmet chocolates to plush monogrammed robes and breakfast in bed.

BOONE'S LICK TRAIL INN $$-$$$
1000 South Main Street, St. Charles
(636) 947-7000, (888) 940-0002
www.booneslick.com
This 1840s Federal-style building houses a charming bed-and-breakfast in St. Charles's historic district. Located just 8 miles from Lambert-St. Louis International Airport, the inn is tucked in among the shops and restaurants along a brick street, the inn includes two gathering rooms and six guest rooms, all with private baths and air-conditioning controls. The house is furnished with regional antiques, and guests are treated to full breakfasts each morning. It's conveniently located within minutes of Katy Trail State Park, as well as many of St. Charles's popular dining, entertainment, and gambling options.

CAHOKIA RV PARQUE $
4060 Mississippi Avenue, Cahokia, IL
(618) 332-7700
www.cahokiarv.com
The Cahokia RV Parque offers a variety of amenities for those who are looking to "rough it" while visiting the St. Louis area. There's a swimming pool, lounge, restrooms and showers with wheelchair facilities, laundry room, playground area, and tent-camping availability. The park has two party pavilions; pay phones; a propane station; a dump station; long, level gravel sites—pull-throughs and back-ins; 30/50-amp full-service sites; and telephone lines available at most of the sites. They also have wireless, high-speed Internet access for campers with laptops. Cahokia RV Parque is located "just across the river" at the corner of Illinois Highway 157 (Camp Jackson Road) and Illinois Highway 3.

CASINO QUEEN HOTEL $-$$
200 South Front Street, East St. Louis, IL
(800) 777-0777
www.casinoqueen.com
Guest room amenities include high-speed Internet access, cable TV, in-room movies, Nintendo with multiple gaming options, an oversize desk, two phones, a coffeemaker, and laundry valet services. There's also an indoor swimming pool, a fitness/workout room, and meeting and banquet facilities. The hotel is fully ADA compliant. A $100 deposit per room is required, payable via credit card or cash. One side of the hotel has tremendous views of the Gateway Arch.

CASINO QUEEN RV PARK $
200 South Front Street, East St. Louis, IL
(800) 777-0777
www.casinoqueen.com
The casino's RV park is right across the river from downtown St. Louis and extremely convenient to area attractions and the MetroLink light-rail system. Equipped with more than 130 full-service spaces, pull-through sites, full hookups with cable TV and Internet access, a bathhouse, laundry facilities, a convenience store, and 24-hour security, the park also offers shuttle service to the casino and nearby MetroLink station. If you visit the casino Web site, you'll find various packages that include everything from breakfast for two in the Queen's Courtyard Buffet and free slot club points to gift shop discounts and "plus-size" sites and landscaped areas. Not wheelchair accessible, and deposit/guarantee by credit card required.

CORNER GEORGE INN BED & BREAKFAST $$-$$$
1101 Main Street, Maeystown, IL
(618) 458-6660, (800) 458-6020
www.cornergeorgeinn.com
Located 35 miles south of St. Louis, the Corner George Inn was originally built as a hotel and saloon in 1884. Today, the restored bed-and-breakfast consists of four buildings, including the original inn, summer kitchen, and two rock houses. There are sitting rooms on both floors

of the inn, as well as a wine cellar and an elegant ballroom that serves as a common area for guests and the breakfast dining area. There are seven guest rooms, each with a private bath, and the inn is furnished with antiques. Bicycle rental and horse-drawn carriage rides in the country are available upon request.

JEROME PLACE BED & BREAKFAST $
827 Ester, Cahokia, IL
(618) 337-1537
www.bbonline.com/il/jerome

This bed-and-breakfast is located about 10 minutes from downtown St. Louis and offers visitors a quiet, peaceful place to get away from it all without leaving the finer things behind. The inn features a fireplace, Jacuzzi, swimming pool, lawn sports, and relaxing music and rocking chairs on the expansive decks. Guests are treated to a full breakfast that features breakfast casseroles and exotic flavored coffees. Families are welcome.

KOA GRANITE CITY CAMPGROUND $
3157 West Chain of Rocks Road
Granite City, IL
(618) 931-5160, (800) 562-5861
www.koa.com

This full-service campground is located on historic Route 66 and features 70-foot-long sites, a swimming pool, full hookups with 30/50-amp service, LP gas, modem dataport, a state park–type playground, and laundry facilities. The Granite City Campground is about 11 miles from downtown St. Louis and 8 miles from Gateway International Raceway. Not wheelchair accessible.

SUNDERMEIER RV PARK & CONFERENCE CENTER $
111 Transit Street, St. Charles
(636) 940-0111, (800) 929-0832
www.sundermeierrvpark.com

The park has paved streets, 106 level concrete pads, 39 pull-throughs, 30/50-amp electric service, hookups for water and sewer, two instant phone and Internet hookups at each site, free Wi-Fi, expanded cable TV, and sleeping cottages available to rent. Sundermeier can accommodate any size unit; offers daily, weekly, or extended-stay rates; and is open year-round. Reservations can now be made online. There's also a full-service restaurant on-site, the Beef Eaters Pub & Grill.

RESTAURANTS

You can always find something good to eat in St. Louis. In a region with such a diverse collection of neighborhoods and cultures, it's not too surprising to find an ever-increasing list of great places to eat, drink, and be merry. What else would you expect from a city whose intense relationship with food became even clearer during the beloved 1904 St. Louis World's Fair, where merchants presented iced tea, ice-cream cones, and hot dogs to the world? Plus, St. Louis has strong ties to the German and French cultures, so it's safe to say that this town definitely knows how to cook—and eat.

Today, visitors will find excellent chefs behind the scenes at restaurants that offer every kind of cuisine. From its elegant steak houses and fashionable Euro-style bistros to the courtyard cafes and neighborhood barbecue joints, St. Louis will have something to offer, whatever your style. The tradition of infusing different cultures with so-called American cuisine has continued to evolve, as new Americans from Asia, India, Bosnia, Africa, and Eastern Europe continue to bring their dining delights to St. Louis. These tasty additions to an already eclectic culinary culture succeed in spicing up St. Louis's Midwestern gumbo of cultures and styles.

The eateries in this chapter are listed geographically, then categorized by cuisine. Most of these restaurants offer a nonsmoking section and wheelchair access for their patrons, unless otherwise noted, and almost all accept major credit cards. Some venues extend their hours during the summer months if they are located in an area known for being popular with tourists.

Price Code

The price code for this chapter is based on a lunch or dinner entree with a nonalcoholic beverage.

$. . . . . $17 or less per person
$$ . . . . $18–$32 per person
$$$ . . . . $33–$45 per person
$$$$ . . . More than $45 per person

DOWNTOWN

After-Dinner Delights

BAILEY'S CHOCOLATE BAR $
1915 Park Avenue
(314) 241-8100
www.baileyschocolatebar.com
Chocoholics will want to set up camp inside this delectable Lafayette Square dessert and dessert-drinks haven. In addition to a mouth-watering array of chocolate and non-chocolate sweets

(such as bread pudding, rustic apple cake, brownies, and more), the bar-side house specialty is the Chocolate Bar Signature, which servers describe as "pure chocolate, alcohol, and milk." There's also a better-than-average wine list, an assortment of unique (and not-so-unique) beers, and nonalcoholic drinks including coffees, shakes, and hot chocolate. Open daily.

33 WINE SHOP & TASTING BAR $–$$
1913 Park Avenue
(314) 231-9463
www.33wine.com
When wine lovers die, they hope they end up at the pearly gates of the 33 Wine Shop & Tasting Bar in Lafayette Square. This intimate neighborhood wine and beer bar offers more than 300 wines from around the world and does so with a casual flair. The bar also offers an assortment of more than 30 bottled beers from around the world, including Bell's Kalamazoo Stout, Anchor

Liberty Ale, Harviestoun Old Engine Oil, and Lindeman's Framboise. There's a wine- and beer-friendly snack menu available that features a diverse list of sausages and cheeses, including Thuringer, Fontini Fontal, dill Havarti, Jarlsberg, and Drunken Goat, and an assortment of crackers and hearty breads. Closed Sunday and Monday.

American

AN AMERICAN PLACE $$$$
800 Washington Avenue
(314) 418-5800
www.aapstl.com
Located in the Renaissance Grand Hotel is An American Place, an upscale yet somewhat casual restaurant that features the food of noted chef Larry Forgione. This is St. Louis fine dining at its finest, with a gourmet menu and a host of imported and domestic wines available. Open for dinner only, the menu of entrees features such specialties as pan-roasted mignon of elk, lobster ravioli, cedar plank wild Columbia River salmon, Missouri buffalo loin, and fresh Fontina cheese and forest mushroom agnolotti pasta. The menu changes seasonally, and everything is made to order from scratch. Reservations are strongly recommended. Closed Sunday and Monday.

CLARK STREET GRILL $–$$
811 Spruce Street
(314) 552-5850
www.clarkstreetgrill.com
Open for breakfast, lunch, and dinner daily, the Clark Street Grill serves contemporary French- and Asian-influenced American cuisine. Located in the lobby of the Westin hotel, Clark Street is a great place for a meal or drinks, and it has become a popular gathering place before and after Cardinals baseball games. It has an upscale look and feel about it, but it's still a casual place to meet friends or have a business lunch. The lunch menu includes a variety of soups, salads, and sandwiches such as the arugula chicken wrap and grilled vegetable calzone, with dinner entrees ranging from the Portobello scaloppini to the Pan-Pacific pesto-crusted beef tenderloin

and Berkshire center cut pork chop. Clark Street has an extensive dessert menu that also includes an assortment of after-dinner drinks.

i City Grocers (920 Olive Street; 314–621–0010) provides downtown residents, workers, and visitors with a cornucopia of fresh fruits and vegetables, prepared foods, and tasty options along with the basic necessities. There's a full-service deli that offers ready-made lunch and dinner options as well as some truly decadent desserts. You can eat in at one of the tables, both inside and outside, or get it to go.

ELEVEN ELEVEN MISSISSIPPI $$–$$$
1111 Mississippi Avenue
(314) 241-9999
www.1111-m.com
This Lafayette Square eatery features Tuscan- and Northern California–influenced cuisine in a casual, rustic, and charming environment that is also slightly upscale. The wine country bistro is housed in a historic brick warehouse that showcases plenty of hardwoods, brick, and copper along with two fireplaces in the main dining room and loft lounge. Open for lunch and dinner, Eleven Eleven's daytime menu includes oven-baked flatbreads, soups, salads, pastas, and assorted bistro fare. The dinner options expand to include such specialties as the house-made wild boar ravioli, potato-wrapped grouper, black pepper fettuccine, and the honey-roasted duck. The wine list and the dessert menu are as intricate as the entrees. Reservations suggested. Closed Sunday.

FRAZER'S RESTAURANT $$
1811 Pestalozzi Street
(314) 773-8646
www.frazergoodeats.com
Frazer's is one of those rare restaurants that offers upscale eats in a casual atmosphere. The tiny storefront restaurant has had to expand several times since it opened in 1992, with a new outdoor dining area being the most recent improvement.

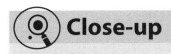 **Close-up**

St. Louis's Brewpubs

A crop of new St. Louis breweries came to light near the end of the 20th century, as the increasing demand for craft beers and microbrews took flight. Just as it was in the 1800s, a number of enterprising beer-lovers began brewing and selling a variety of beers, and a new age of brewing was born.

In 1991, the St. Louis Brewery & Tap Room (2100 Locust Street, 314–241–2337, www.schlafly. com) began operations in a building at the corner of 21st and Locust streets on the western edge of downtown. The first new brewery in more than 50 years started making and selling a line of Schlafly beers named after its founder, Tom Schlafly. What began as a simple brewpub with limited distribution to a few local restaurants has continued to grow and evolve into a popular local beer-maker that now features a second brewery, Schlafly Bottleworks (7260 Southwest Avenue, 314–241–2337, www.schlafly.com) in nearby Maplewood, and a distribution network that includes more than 1,200 restaurants, bars, grocery and convenience stores across the region.

The award-winning specialty beers at Morgan Street Brewery (721 North Second Street, 314–231–9970, www.morganstreetbrewery.com) are handcrafted on-site to produce their own distinctive colors and flavors. The brewing equipment (specially designed for the building) produces many styles, such as the Honey Wheat and Steam Lager that are available year around. Some beers will be on tap from time to time to compliment the changing St. Louis seasons. MSB features a number of specialty brews, including Honey Wheat, Morgan Street Vienna, a Golden Pilsner, Dark Wheat, Red Lager, Oatmeal Stout, Irish Stout, Cobblestone Steam Lager, and seasonal beers including Maibock, Altbier, Doppelbock, Oktoberfest, Winter Lager, and Krystäl. New Morgan Street Signature Beers pop up throughout the year, and there's a "Brewski Sampler" available that features four different styles.

The O'Fallon Brewery (26 West Industrial Drive, O'Fallon, MO, 636–474–BEER, www.ofallon brewery.com) is a small manufacturing brewery located in St. Charles County, just northwest of St. Louis. Founded in January 2000, the facility brews approximately 1,850 barrels of beer annually, or about 25,000 cases. The newest kid on the beer block has already established itself as a player in the national beer market, as O'Fallon Unfiltered Wheat took the Bronze Medal in 2005, and O'Fallon Smoked Porter won a Gold Medal in 2004 at the Great American Beer Festival. In addition to brewing three "everyday" beers—O'Fallon Gold, O'Fallon Wheat, and O'Fallon Smoked Porter—the brewer offers O'Fallon 5-Day IPA, available on draught only, and a seasonal beer for each of the four major seasons: O'Fallon Cherry Chocolate for winter, O'Fallon Blackberry Scottish for Spring, O'Fallon Wheach (peach-wheat) for summer, and O'Fallon Pumpkin Beer for the fall. O'Fallon's brews are sold locally through 20 retailers in Missouri and to distributors in Colorado, Illinois, Indiana, Iowa, Kansas, Kentucky, Michigan and Wisconsin.

Additional brewpubs in the area include Square One Brewery (1727 Park Avenue, 314–231– ALES, www.squareonebrewery.com), which serves up Light Squared, Pilsner, Bavarian Weizen, Grand Cru, Front Range, Saison, Park Avenue Pale Ale, I.P.A., Anniversary Ale, Single Malt Scotch Ale, Imperial Stout, Barley Wine, Cask Park Avenue Pale Ale, and Belgian Wit on tap. Trailhead Brewing Company (921 South Riverside Drive, St. Charles, MO; 636–946–2739, www .trailheadbrewing.com) offers a variety of pilsners, stouts, and ales, all of which are made on-site.

The menu changes often (but only slightly) to accommodate the availability of seasonal items; however, the food is always good. Appetizers like the mushroom strudel, carpaccio, and hummus are solid mainstays, along with the tasty pasta dishes and the fish, chicken, and beef entrees. There's a good selection of vegetarian items—including a delicious vegetarian Reuben—along with comfort-food desserts like carrot cake, bread pudding, and blackberry cobbler. Open for lunch and dinner; closed Sunday.

HARRY'S RESTAURANT & BAR $$
2144 Market Street
(314) 421-6969
www.harrysrestaurantandbar.com
Harry's is an elegant, comfortable restaurant that features innovative American cuisine and a lovely view of the St. Louis skyline. In addition to an impressive wine list, Harry's dinner menu features a variety of salads and appetizers as well as entrees such as grilled chops, steaks, and seafood. The lunch menu is inviting as well, and it includes a variety of sandwiches, salads, and even vegetable lasagna. Reservations are highly recommended. Open daily.

KITCHEN K $$
1000 Washington Avenue
(314) 241-9900
www.kitchen-k.com
Kitchen K features a comfortable mix of high-end cuisine made from familiar items along with more casual favorites including sandwiches, paninis and burgers. The restaurant offers an impressive selection of wines that pair nicely with such newfound favorites as the handmade veggie spring rolls, Ahi Togarashi, and the Baja Chicken Enchilada. There are also a number of daily specials including meat loaf, pasta dishes, and fresh seafood. Try the sweet potato fries as a starter. Open Monday through Saturday for lunch and dinner.

LUCAS PARK GRILLE $$
800 Washington Avenue
(314) 418-5800
www.lucasparkgrille.com
In addition to being part of Washington Avenue's popular bar scene, Lucas Park Grille is known for its five-star filets, locally raised lamb, sea bass, and the wine list of more than 250 varieties. Lunch or dinner patrons can choose from an array of salads, appetizers, and entrees such as Macadamia Encrusted Hawaiian Sea Bass, Pepper Grilled Flat Iron, and Roasted Vegetable Galette. There's also an extensive wine list. Open daily for lunch and dinner.

SOULARD'S RESTAURANT $-$$
1731 South Seventh Street
(314) 241-7956
www.soulards.com
Soulard's is one of the few restaurants in town that serves a full breakfast on weekdays. Now, we're not talking about a sticky bagel and a cup of coffee to go—the restaurant offers everything from poached eggs and a Spanish omelet to whole wheat buttermilk waffles and hearty breakfast sandwiches. For lunch Soulard's features baked Brie with almonds, house-made salad dressings, grilled chicken salad, sandwiches, and entrees including peppered pork tenderloin with garlic mayonnaise and crab cakes over capellini pasta with beurre blanc sauce. The dinner menu ranges from grilled Portobello mushrooms and chicken Spedini to New York strip steak, marinated grilled French cut pork chops, barbecued shrimp, and house-made desserts. Closed Sunday.

SQWIRES RESTAURANT & MARKET $-$$
1415 South 18th Street
(314) 865-3522
www.sqwires.com
SqWires serves fresh seafood and innovative menu items using the freshest seasonal ingredients. The dinner menu offers a host of seafood entrees, such as raspberry balsamic barbecue glazed salmon and Golden Trout, along with vegetable lasagna, wild mushroom fettuccine,

and herb Provençal Canadian pork loin. Desserts include chocolate ravioli, Brandy Alexander and bread pudding. The bar features a variety of martinis, draft and bottled beers, and an impressive wine list. Breakfast, lunch, and dinner are served daily, and there's also an impressive brunch available on Saturday and Sunday.

SWEETIE PIE'S $

4270 Manchester Avenue

(314) 371-0304

If you have a hankerin' for some down-home, southern-style comfort food, then Sweetie Pie's at the Mangrove is where you want to be. This location, situated in the up-and-coming Grove neighborhood, was opened due to the popularity of the authentic soul food menu at the original Sweetie Pie's in North County (9841 West Florissant Avenue; 314-521-9915). Daily "meat and two" or "meat and three" plates (meat plus two or three side orders) offer stick-to-your-ribs, homemade goodness like smothered pork steak, baked chicken, barbecued rib tips, catfish, and meat loaf alongside delicacies like black-eyed peas, yams, okra, mashed potatoes, and dressing. But whatever you do, do not leave without trying the macaroni and cheese—it is truly some of the best in town. The food is served cafeteria style, and the menu changes regularly—but there's never a shortage of tasty options. Sweetie Pie's owner Robbie Montgomery is a former "Ikette," a back-up singer for St. Louis R&B legends Ike & Tina Turner. Open Tuesday through Sunday.

i Most St. Louis restaurants are truly family-friendly operations that have special menus for the smaller fry. Call ahead if your plans include something fancier.

VIN DE SET $$–$$$

2017 Chouteau Avenue

(314) 241-8989

www.1111-m.com/vindeset

Perched atop the restored Centennial Mill Building is one of St. Louis's newest food and drink destinations, Vin de Set. It gained instant notoriety for its spacious rooftop deck area, a definite rarity in these parts. The menu, which features the seasonal cuisine of southern France with a contemporary American twist, includes a variety of salads, soups, and gourmet sandwiches prepared croque-monsieur style and served with a knife and fork. Appetizers range from toasted lobster ravioli and frog legs to escargot and seared tenderloin tartare. Entrees include burgundy braised short ribs, whole yellowtail snapper, and duck confit and julienne zucchini crepes. The extensive wine list features numerous options to complement your feast. The bar is open Tuesday through Sunday, while the restaurant serves lunch and dinner Tuesday through Friday; dinner only Saturday through Sunday.

Asian

SEN THAI ASIAN BISTRO $

1221 Locust Street

(314) 436-3456

www.senthaibistro.com

Sen Thai—as it's often called—is tremendously popular among downtown workers and residents looking for an infusion of Thai, Chinese, and Japanese cuisine. Open for lunch and dinner, Sen's food is always fresh and always good. The spring rolls and the coconut shrimp are excellent appetizers, and the voluminous choices of soups, salads, rice, and noodle and curry dishes make ordering just one dish almost impossible. Start with one of the appetizer platters to get a taste of several items, then go back to the menu for an entree. Beer and wine are available, along with nonalcoholic beverages including Thai iced coffee and tea. Open for lunch and dinner Monday through Friday; dinner only Saturday and Sunday.

WASABI SUSHI BAR $

1228 Washington Avenue

(314) 421-3500

www.wasabistl.com

Wasabi has scored big with St. Louis sushi fans. The menu, which features both sushi and non-sushi items, offers traditional Japanese cuisine as well as some items that put a new twist on old favorites. Some of the restaurant's specialties include sukiyaki (sliced beef and vegetables in a hot, sweet broth), tonkatsu (deep-fried breaded pork loin with a fruit and vegetable sauce), unagi don (smoked eel on a bed of rice), and the niku don (a beef and veggie omelet on a bed of rice). The sushi bar itself features more than 60 items. There's a second location at 16 South Central Avenue (314) 721-9970 in Clayton. Both locations are open for lunch and dinner Monday through Saturday.

Brazilian

YEMANJA BRASIL RESTAURANTE $–$$
2900 Missouri Avenue
(314) 771-7457
www.brazildining.com
Cozy, warm, and tropical, Yemanja offers authentic Brazilian food in an inviting, casual atmosphere. In addition to a variety of vegetarian, seafood, and steak specialty dishes, the Benton Park eatery features various salads, homemade sobremesas (desserts), a selection of appetizers (such as acarajé, deep-fried black-eyed pea croquettes served with a side of spicy vatapá sauce), and a menu of Brazilian drinks. Try a caipirinha, the country's national drink, made from crushed lime, sugar, and Brazilian rum and topped with ice, or a cup of cafézinho, Brazilian espresso. Dinner only, Tuesday through Sunday. Reservations recommended.

Continental

AL'S RESTAURANT $$$$
1200 North First Street
(314) 421-6399
Al's Restaurant has an elegant decor and an array of international specialties. This out-of-the-way restaurant follows the old-school tradition of a verbal menu, with no prices mentioned unless you ask. There's a dress code (men must wear a jacket), which usually isn't a problem for the business clientele that frequent the place. The menu includes voluminous lists of appetizers and first courses, and the wait staff is truly helpful

and professional in their duties. Steaks, seafood, salads, and Italian specialties are the favored fare at Al's, along with a selection of desserts. Closed Sunday and holidays.

SIDNEY STREET CAFE $$–$$$
2000 Sidney Street
(314) 771-5777
www.sidneystreetcafe.com
Sidney Street Cafe is the place for contemporary American and continental cuisine in a cozy, romantic atmosphere complete with flickering candlelight, linen tablecloths, and exposed brick. A well-rounded wine list complements the menu of seafood, steaks, and pastas in this romantic restaurant that's tucked inside a century-old building in the Soulard/Benton Park neighborhood. Sidney Street's menu is anything but ordinary and features unique delicacies like blue cheese tarts, veal dumplings, Szechwan tuna, and kumquat and BBQ glazed quail. The selection of desserts changes nightly, but it's safe to assume that the sweets are as good as the entrees. Reservations required. Closed Sunday.

Italian

ANTHONY'S BAR $
10 South Broadway
(314) 231-7007
A popular lunchtime and happy-hour mainstay for downtown workers, Anthony's now also serves dinner. The cozy bar area offers limited dining tables and bar seating—both fill up quickly during the noontime rush—but the food is worth the wait. Anthony's shares the same owners/managers as the legendary Tony's Italian restaurant on the other side of the building, as well as the same kitchen—but that's where the similarities end. Anthony's Bar is a casual cocktail bar, circa 1962, while Tony's is as upscale and classy as you can get. The good news is that the food is excellent in both places, though the menu—and the prices—are smaller at Anthony's. Lunch is served Monday through Friday only. Closed Sunday.

CHARLIE GITTO'S PASTA HOUSE $

207 North Sixth Street
(314) 436-2828
www.charliegittosdowntown.com

Gitto's is a favorite lunch spot and dinner destination for downtown workers and residents, as well as visiting sports celebrities. Since 1974 the restaurant has been serving up authentic Italian fare, incredible salads, and decadent desserts in this family-style neighborhood eatery. One entire wall is filled with photos of international celebrities who have enjoyed their meal with Charlie, and the rest of the restaurant's decor looks like something out of a movie starring the Rat Pack. Closed Sunday except on Rams football or Cardinals game days.

CIELO $$$–$$$$

999 North Second Street
(314) 881-5800
www.fourseasons.com/stlouis/dining.html

Located inside the Four Seasons Hotel, Cielo features a contemporary Italian menu, and exceptional array of Italian wines and magnificent views of the Mississippi River and Gateway Arch. The upscale-casual restaurant offers indoor and outdoor dining for breakfast, lunch and dinner. There's a children's menu available, as well as a decadent variety of dessert options.

HOUSE OF SAVOY $$–$$$

901 North First Street
(877) 450-7711
www.lumiereplace.com

Authentic regional Italian cuisine with savory sauces, fresh salads, hearty pastas, and an array of grilled entrées. The upscale eatery features an extensive wine list and house made desserts in an atmosphere of Old World splendor. Specialties include Grilled Wild Salmon, Pork Chop Milanese, Seafood Risotto, and grilled calamari. Open daily for dinner only.

JOSEPH'S ITALIAN CAFÉ $–$$

107 North Sixth Street
(314) 421-6636

Legendary for its handmade stromboli, Joseph's features a number of homemade traditional and contemporary Italian dishes. Pastas, salads, and appetizers are available for lunch or dinner, along with some unique St. Louis–style pizzas. The Botticelli is a Joseph's original that is made with roasted garlic–infused olive oil and mozzarella cheese topped with a cold, crisp Caesar salad. The Buffalo Chicken pizza features grilled chicken tossed in a hot sauce with caramelized onions and Gorgonzola cheese on a basil pesto crust. Joseph's Gnocchi Diablo is a popular pasta dish made with fresh handmade gnocchi in a chipotle cream sauce with Italian sausage and roasted peppers. Main course options include pork saltimbocca (seared pork rib chop wrapped in prosciutto and stuffed with herbs), chicken and wild mushroom risotto, and veal marsala, among others. Closed Sunday.

KEMOLL'S RESTAURANT $$–$$$

One Metropolitan Square
(314) 421-0555
www.kemolls.com

Located on the 40th floor of the "Met Square" building, Kemoll's is a landmark restaurant offering superb Italian dishes, steaks, and seafood in an elegant atmosphere. In addition to a long list of authentic Italian dishes, Kemoll's serves up some of the freshest seafood in town. Try the Manicotte Alla Toscana, Broiled Oysters Alla Gaetana, or Linguini Monte Mare, and save room for dessert. House made specials include tiramisu, Bananas Foster, and creme brûleé. The restaurant is open for dinner only Monday through Saturday. Kemoll's also offers a specially priced, early-evening dinner nightly from 5:00 to 6:30 p.m. Reservations are recommended—and so are a jacket and tie for men.

10TH STREET ITALIAN $

504 North 10th Street
(314) 241-9988
www.10thstreetitalian.com

Even though it looks like it, this is not your standard fast-food Italian eatery. 10th Street Italian specializes in high-quality—and delicious—Italian food that is made to order and served up quickly. A popular spot for lunch, the restaurant fills up quickly, but the turnover is a lot faster than your average sit-down restaurant. The menu features tasty soups, salads, appetizers, hot and cold sandwiches, and pasta dishes that are as good as any you would find at the restaurants on The Hill. Specialties include the lasagna, cannelloni, and chicken or eggplant Parmesan. They also do a big take-out dinner business after 5:00 p.m. during the warm weather months, so it's a great option for travelers who would prefer in-room dining without the room service prices. Open Monday through Friday.

TONY'S RESTAURANT $$$$
410 Market Street
(314) 231-7007
www.tonysstlouis.com

Tony's is considered by many to be St. Louis's finest restaurant. From appetizers like fresh Beluga caviar and stuffed calamari to entrees such as grilled scampi and lobster tails, Tony's has mastered the art of combining gourmet Italian dining with first-class service. Tony's is a AAA four-diamond award winner and a Mobil four-star award winner, and the atmosphere has been voted "Most Romantic" in various readers' polls. *Condé Nast Traveler* selected Tony's as the No. 1 Italian restaurant in the country. Reservations are required, along with a coat and tie for male patrons. Closed Sunday.

Mexican

ARCELIA'S $-$$
2001 Park Avenue
(314) 231-9200

Arcelia's is a legendary, authentic Mexican restaurant in Lafayette Square. The simple neighborhood eatery is casual and kitschy, with the usual Mexican-style decor, but the food is what makes this place stand out. Excellent margaritas are a good way to start, followed by the chile-spiked salsa and a first course of nopales salad (slices of prickly pear cactus paddles tossed with diced tomatoes, onions, and a drizzle of lemon juice), or one of the traditional Mexican soups, tamales,

empanadas, or chalupas. Arcelia's also serves traditional breakfast foods, including chilaquiles, a hash of fried tortilla strips, as well as eggs and chorizo sausage. Open daily.

CHAVA'S MEXICAN RESTAURANT $-$$
925 Geyer Avenue
(314) 241-5503

Outstanding Mexican food in a casual, comfortable environment with a friendly staff. Chava's salsa is some of the best in town and you will be tempted to fill up on chips while you wait for your meal. The Soulard eatery serves plentiful portions of fresh and tasty entrees, including a number of vegetarian options. The margaritas are so smooth and refreshing that they're dangerous. Open daily for lunch and dinner.

Pizza

B & T PIZZA $
1131 Washington Avenue
(314) 621-2400
www.bntpizza.com

Good, fresh hand-tossed pizza by the slice or by the pie. B&T's New York-style pizzas are made with tomatoes from California, mozzarella cheese from Wisconsin, and a variety of vegetable and local meat toppings, including Volpi's pepperoni and DiGregorio's Italian sausage from The Hill, St. Louis's Italian neighborhood. They also serve gourmet salads, beer, and wine in a casual, fast-food atmosphere. Dine-in, take-out, and delivery. Open until 3:00 a.m. on Friday and Saturday. Closed Sunday.

JOANIE'S PIZZERIA $
2101 Menard at Russell
(314) 865-1994
www.joanies.com

Joanie's is one of the few St. Louis pizza places that doesn't assume that everyone wants their pizza in the St. Louis style (topped with Provel—a processed cheese—instead of mozzarella). Instead, Joanie's staff serves up three types of pizza crusts, including a homemade hand-tossed crust; a baked, double-crust pie; and a thinner-crust version for those St. Louis pizza diehards. The toppings are virtually unlimited, and the specialty pizzas are as creative as they are tasty. The menu also includes various appetizers, salads, sandwiches, and pastas, and an ever-changing choice of daily specials. Great outdoor patio. Open daily.

ℹ️ In St. Louis, pizza is an entirely different animal than in most parts of the country. Most St. Louisans grew up eating a style of pizza that features a thin, cracker like crust topped with sweet tomato sauce and Provel, a processed cheese. Be sure to ask your server what kind of cheese is used—and if he isn't sure, you should probably request mozzarella on your pie. You may get some funny looks, but it could be better than the alternative.

MAURIZIO'S PIZZA & SPORTS CAFE $
1107 Olive Street
(314) 621-1997
www.maurizios.com

Maurizio's is always open—or it always seems to be open—at least until 3:00 a.m. This is another place in St. Louis where you can get "real" pizza (topped with mozzarella instead of Provel), along with pasta, salads, sandwiches, and chicken wings. There's a daily all-you-can-eat buffet that features various kinds of pizza, chicken wings, and soda for one low price, plus you can get a full line of packaged liquors to go. Open daily.

Pub Food

ATOMIC COWBOY $
4140 Manchester Road
(314) 775-0775
www.atomic-cowboy.com

This self-described "Baja Grille/Tequilaria/Art Lounge/Espresso Bar" is one of the anchors of the revitalized Grove neighborhood. Featuring a kitchen staff from Mexico City, the restaurant specializes in foods indicative of the Baja-style of cooking. The eatery offers sandwiches, salads,

tacos, burritos and entrees with a unique flair, including specialties like the Mexican tuna melt, Aztec chicken banquette, banana leaf–wrapped tilapia, citrus lime shrimp skewers, fish tacos, and wild mushroom tamales. Do yourself a favor and order the delicious Gaucho Fries with serrano ketchup as a starter. The ambience is casual and funky, with a definite artistic vibe, and it is a great place to enjoy lunch or dinner or a late-night snack. Atomic Cowboy, which features one of the best patios in the neighborhood, has a great selection of desserts and specialty coffee drinks. Open for lunch Tuesday through Friday, and dinner Tuesday through Sunday. Closed Monday.

THE DUBLINER $–$$
1025 Washington Avenue
(314) 421-4300
www.dublinerstl.com

This European-style "gastropub" has taken steps to set itself well apart from other Emerald Isle–themed taverns in St. Louis. The bar serves lunch and dinner daily, along with a Pub Fare menu that includes bangers and mash, beef and Guinness stew, fish and chips, and The Full Irish, a fried egg with sausages, rashers, beans, and tomato. "Gastropub" is a British term for a public house ("pub") that focuses on a particular cuisine and prepares it at a higher quality—more like meals in prestigious restaurants. The food must also complement the beers and wines served. There's a vegan sandwich and a Farmer's Salad for the veggie fans, but the majority of the menu is geared toward carnivores. Here the food is as important as the drinks—there are no pizzas, no pastas, and no quesadillas on the menu. It's all traditional Irish food, which is based on French cooking.

MAGGIE O'BRIEN'S RESTAURANT $
2000 Market Street
(314) 421-1388
www.maggieobriens.com

Maggie O'Brien's is a favorite gathering spot for sports fans to get together and watch a game. There are seven satellites, 27 televisions, and three 10-foot big screens, as well as a shuttle service to major sporting events. Open for lunch and dinner, Maggie's Irish beef stew and corned beef and cabbage with Irish potatoes are just two of the preferred specialty dishes. The bar is open until 2:00 a.m. nightly, and there's a covered outdoor patio for dining and drinking during the warmer months.

MORGAN STREET BREWERY $

721 North Second Street
(314) 231-9970
www.morganstreetbrewery.com

Morgan Street's creative menu and great daily specials always seem to coincide with what goes best with beer. The Brewski is a four-beer sampler that lets you try a few brews before deciding which one goes best with your food. The eatery's comfortable mountain-lodge ambience offers a variety of indoor and outdoor dining options. Appetizers range from hot baked pretzels to blue crab cakes, and the selection of salads includes a grilled Portobello salad and an apricot-chicken creation. Some of the brewery favorites on the menu include Coniques (breaded mashed potato balls), bacon-wrapped buffalo meat loaf, lobster ravioli, and grilled chicken and andouille pasta in cream sauce. For dessert there's a white chocolate bread pudding and the Death by Chocolate cake with fudge filling. The brewpub serves its own handcrafted microbrews, as well as popular bottled domestics and imports. Closed Monday.

SCHLAFLY TAP ROOM $

2100 Locust Street
(314) 241-2337
www.schlafly.com

The Schlafly brewpub features more than 30 handcrafted beers throughout the year and serves them up alongside traditional American and European "pub grub," burgers, salads and sandwiches. Tap Room specialties include the steak and mushroom pie, schnitzel, Moules Frites, and the incredibly tasty fish and fries. The chef's special tartar sauce is legendary, and it tastes just as good on the fries as it does on the fish. For dessert try the sticky toffee pudding. It's open

daily for lunch and dinner, and the bar stays open until 1:00 a.m.

SKY BOX SPORTS BAR & GRILL $-$$

800 North Third Street
(314) 241-5100
www.skyboxstl.com

Owned by St. Louis hip-hop star Nelly, former St. Louis Rams running back Marshall Faulk, and NBA stars Darius Miles and Larry Hughes, this upscale sports bar and lounge serves up a variety of snacks and entrees. Specialties include St. Louis Ribs (glazed with Nelly's spiced BBQ sauce), crawfish étouffée, and grilled salmon, and the "Minor League" menu offers kids' favorites such as burgers, chicken fingers, and mac and cheese. More than 70 HD TVs line the walls, making it an ideal perch for sports fans, and the lounge atmosphere is comfortably casual. Open for lunch Monday through Friday, and dinner nightly.

Sandwiches

BLUES CITY DELI $

2438 McNair
(314) 773-8225
www.bluescitydeli.com

Tucked into a turn-of-the-century storefront in the Soulard/Benton Park neighborhood, Blues City Deli serves up a side order of live blues with their menu of po' boys, muffalettas, soups, salads, and specialty sandwiches. Try the 1904 World's Fair Chili Dog, the 7th Street Sicilian, or the St. Louie Primo. Open Monday through Saturday, 11 a.m. to 4 p.m. On Thursdays, the deli is open until 8 p.m. to accommodate the weekly House Party, featuring beer specials and an acoustic blues jam. Live music every Saturday afternoon. Closed Sunday.

BREVÉ ESPRESSO COMPANY $

One SBC Center
909 Chestnut Street
(314) 231-2326
www.brevecoffee.com

Brevé is more than yet another espresso/coffee

place. Locally owned Brevé Espresso Company opened its first espresso bar in 2001 and has grown to include four locations in the metropolitan area. In addition to the usual list of lattes and handcrafted coffee blends, Brevé's serves up tasty sandwiches, soups, salads, pastries, and excellent grilled panini sandwiches. The staff is friendly and helpful—no coffee snobs here—and the atmosphere is relaxed and extremely comfortable. The cafe adjoins the 10th Street Loft building, whose lobby area serves as a sort of clubby annex to the cafe. The cafe is wheelchair accessible and a smoke-free environment. Open Monday through Friday.

THE EDIBLE DIFFERENCE $
615 Pine Street
(314) 588-8432
Conveniently located among the high-rise office buildings in downtown St. Louis, the Edible Difference is within walking distance of most downtown-area businesses, hotels, and tourist attractions. The eatery is open for breakfast and lunch on weekdays, and the menu includes fresh homemade muffins, pastries, bagels, deli sandwiches, homemade soups, quiche, and salads.

ROOSTER $
1104 Locust Street
(314) 241-8118
www.roosterstl.com
Rooster is a European-style cafe that features unique twists on traditional sandwiches, soups, salads and fresh crepes. Try the open-faced egg salad sandwich made with chunks of eggs, pickles, crunchy celery, and a tasty Asian dressing with just a hint of curry. You can also dive into the roasted sirloin crepe with asiago cheese, mushrooms, and caramelized onions. There are a number of items to suit both vegetarians and carnivores. Breakfast and lunch is available Monday through Friday mornings, and brunch is served on Saturday and Sunday. A tempting selection of dessert crepes and specialty coffees are also available.

Seafood/Steak

MIKE SHANNON'S STEAKS & SEAFOOD $$–$$$
620 Market Street
(314) 421-1540
www.mikeshannonssteaksandseafood.com
For lunch—or at the bar—Shannon's offers generously sized steak sandwiches, soups, salads, and appetizers in a clubby, sports-themed atmosphere. Owned by former Cardinals player and current team broadcaster Mike Shannon, the eatery is a popular pre- and post-game gathering spot. At night the sports theme stays the same, but the dinner menu expands to include pastas, seafood, steaks, grilled chicken, and chops in a slightly more sophisticated atmosphere. Or you can keep it casual and hang out in the bar area to watch a game—Shannon himself is likely to wander in when you least expect it. Reservations are recommended for dinner. Open daily.

CENTRAL WEST END

After-Dinner Delights

BISSINGER'S: A CHOCOLATE EXPERIENCE $
32 Maryland Plaza
(314) 367-7750, (800) 325-8881
www.bissingers.com
More than just a candy counter, Bissinger's has created the concept of the "chocolate lounge," which is also known as "Chocolate Heaven." The relaxing sanctuary features fine chocolates in various forms, decadent desserts, fine wines and premium liqueurs. Bissinger's is a European-style chocolatier with a history dating back to the 17th century, and it's one of the few places you can still find handmade chocolates. The new "experience" offers a way to immerse yourself in a world of delicious, sinful chocolates. Open daily.

NADOZ CAFE $
3701 Lindell Boulevard
(314) 446-6800
www.nadozcafe.com
Located inside the beautifully restored Coronado

on Lindell, Nadoz Cafe serves up a varied selection of European-style pastries, confections, and candies, as well as other handcrafted desserts. Specialties include the lemon chibouze cake, seasonal fruit tarts, white chocolate cheesecake, tiramisu, truffles, chocolate praline torte, and assorted cookies. The choices change daily, so you may need to make more than one trip! A second location has opened at The Boulevard shopping center in mid-county (#12 The Boulevard; 314-726-3100), across from the Saint Louis Galleria. Open daily.

American

DUFF'S RESTAURANT $–$$
392 North Euclid Avenue
(314) 361-0522
www.dineatduffs.com
Located in the Central West End since 1972, Duff's offers fine dining in a casual atmosphere. The eclectic menu changes seasonally, but you can usually find an assortment of lunch and dinner options that include salads and appetizers such as hummus and pâté, along with sandwiches and pizzas. Lunch and dinner entrees range from strawberry duck and New York pepper steak to pasta Peking primavera and shrimp Aphrodite, as well as a number of vegetarian entrees. There's also a good selection of wines available, and a brunch is offered on Saturday and Sunday. Duff's patrons receive one hour of validated parking at the McPherson and North Euclid Avenue parking lots. Open daily.

EAU BISTRO $$$
Chase Park Plaza Hotel
212 North Kingshighway
(314) 633-3200
www.chaseparkplaza.com
To some, a bistro represents an informal dining experience. This isn't the case at Eau Bistro in the swanky Chase Park Plaza Hotel. The beautiful decor provides a hint as to what kind of dining experience one can expect, and the menu doesn't disappoint. Eau Bistro specializes in New American cuisine, featuring fresh seafood and

meats from select sources around the country, along with a 300-bottle wine list. Open daily. Brunch is served on Sunday.

LILUMA $$–$$$
236 North Euclid Avenue
(314) 361-7771
www.liluma.com
Liluma is still one of the Central West End's hot spots, and this Parisian-style bistro features a menu that stretches from one culinary extreme to the other. On the simpler side, there's the burger with Nana's slaw, served with hand-cut french fries. For the more sophisticated palate, the braised Arkansas rabbit with gnocchi, kalamata olives, and capers might be a better choice. There's also a litany of soups, salads, and pastas that fall somewhere in the middle, and the prices for all are very reasonable. Closed Sunday; reservations are recommended.

WILDFLOWER RESTAURANT & BAR $$–$$$
4590 Laclede Avenue
(314) 367-9888
www.wildflowerdining.com
Wildflower offers gourmet food in a casual, contemporary atmosphere. If the weather is nice and tables are available, be sure to dine alfresco at this charming Central West End restaurant. People-watching is half the fun, but the eclectic cuisine is what brings in the crowds. Wildflower's lunch menu offers an array of contemporary menu options ranging from soups and salads to sandwiches like the grilled eggplant mozzarella, and the house-cured salmon with avocado salsa and pepper bacon on Italian bread with caper-artichoke tartar sauce. Dinner entrees feature beef, chicken, pork, and seafood, as well as a few off-the-menu specials. The list of wines and cocktails is impressive. Open daily.

Continental

MOXY CONTEMPORARY BISTRO $$–$$$
4584 Laclede Street
(314) 361-4848
www.moxybistro.com

Chef Eric Brenner turned a tiny storefront into one of the most unique restaurants in St. Louis. Moxy's offerings combine a number of ethnic influences, including Asian, Italian, and French, and even blends them with comfort food. Even the appetizers are good enough to be an entree. The rope-shaped strozzapreti pasta in the Portobello and porcini mushroom sauce is excellent, and the buttermilk-marinated fried chicken (free-range, of course) will make those who fear nouveau cuisine feel right at home. The wine list has a select number of moderately priced options, and the coffee and dessert menu offers a number of exotic treats. Lunch and dinner are served Monday through Friday; dinner only on Saturday. Closed Sunday.

i If you're looking for a specific type of restaurant but don't know where to turn for advice, check out www.sauce magazine.com. The Web site and Sauce—the free monthly tabloid—can offer suggestions of places to eat by cuisine, location, and ambience. The printed piece isn't as extensive as the Web site, but it can be found at a variety of hotels, restaurants, bars, and shops throughout the area.

THE SCOTTISH ARMS $–$$
6–10 South Sarah Street
(314) 535-0551
www.thescottisharms.com
The Scottish Arms is a casual neighborhood restaurant and bar that features authentic Scottish cuisine that ranges from haggis and hummus to Celtic crisps and Scotch eggs. Entrees include Guinness stew, fish and chips, steaks, pheasant, shepherd's pie, and one of the pub's most popular dishes, Cock A Leekie. This casserole-type dish is made with slow-simmered chicken breast, leeks, cream, and a special secret seasoning. Surprisingly, the menu includes a number of vegetarian options, and the kids' menu features the ever-popular chicken tenders along with the more adventurous bangers and mash. The

interior space is divided into two sections—the bar and the restaurant—and smoking is allowed on the bar side only. Outside, a new wooden patio area is set up with a dozen large tables with oversize umbrellas and lots of greenery, and is surrounded by tall wooden fencing. Open Tuesday through Saturday for lunch and dinner; Sunday and Monday for dinner only.

Italian

BAR ITALIA RISTORANTE & CAFE $$
13 Maryland Plaza
(314) 361-7010
www.baritaliastl.com
Outstanding authentic Italian food is the draw to this casual yet fashionable Central West End eatery, and its outdoor dining area adds to the European feel of the place. Some of Bar Italia's signature dishes include tortellini in cream sauce, and chicken with almonds and raisins, in addition to other pasta dishes and Mediterranean fare. The restaurant also features a very good wine list, and a full cocktail menu is available. Open daily.

i Toasted ravioli was accidentally created at Oldani's Restaurant on the Hill in 1947 and quickly became a tasty tradition. Legend has it that this specialty was created accidentally when a cook knocked some ravioli into the deep fryer.

Pub Food

CULPEPPERS $
300 North Euclid Avenue
(314) 361-2828
www.culpeppers.com
Known for world-famous spicy chicken wings, Culpeppers serves up a hearty menu of bar food designed to complement its extensive cocktail menu. Soups, salads, sandwiches, and burgers make up most of the menu, along with some hearty entrees and mouthwatering desserts. Specialties include Culpeppers Barbecued Ribs, sweet bourbon salmon, and blackened chicken Alfredo. Open daily.

LLYWELYN'S PUB $
4747 McPherson Avenue
(314) 361-3003
www.llywelynspub.com

The Central West End location of this Celtic pub has plenty of places to hang out, from the main bar to the loft to the patio or the beer garden. Llywelyn's serves up a menu of traditional Irish food as well as the usual lineup of American pub grub and several lighter-fare items. Traditional specialties include fish and chips, corned beef and cabbage, Finnagan's Fish Pie, and a rosemary and citrus chicken casserole. Be sure to try the Welsh Potato Chips. There are two other locations in the area, including one in Soulard (1732 Ninth Street; 314-436-3255) and one in Webster Groves (17 Moody Street; 314-962-1515). Open late, seven days a week.

TOM'S BAR & GRILL $
20 South Euclid Avenue
(314) 367-4900
www.tomsbarandgrill.com

Tom's Bar & Grill is a friendly and casual gathering spot located just east of the Chase Park Plaza in the Central West End neighborhood. A large picture window and the liberal use of gorgeous dark wood help give the bar a warm and cozy feel, even on the dreariest of days. The menu offers the usual lineup of bar food, with special praise for its burgers, fries, and steaks. Open daily.

Sandwiches

KOPPERMAN'S SPECIALTY FOODS $
386 North Euclid Avenue
(314) 361-0100

Kopperman's has been around since the 1880s, and this old-school deli and specialty food mart continues to please. Whether you want a quick bite for breakfast or plan to spend a leisurely morning enjoying one of Kopperman's "eggstravaganzas," the food is excellent. The deli offers a variety of kosher meats, salads, soups, and pastas, and the overstuffed sandwiches definitely live up to their name. Specialty coffee drinks and cocktails are available, along with bottles of wine sold at retail price (corking fee). Open daily.

THE HILL

Italian

CUNETTO HOUSE OF PASTA $-$$
5453 Magnolia Avenue
(314) 781-1135
www.cunetto.com

Cunetto's is one of the best Italian restaurants on The Hill—and that's saying a lot. This family-owned and -operated eatery offers authentic Italian cuisine in an atmosphere that's classy, but it's still very casual and extremely family-friendly. The house salad is worth a trip by itself, but the extensive menu options are too good to pass up during the visit. All of the pasta dishes are fabulous, and be forewarned that all of the bistecca, petto di pollo, and pesce (steak, chicken, and fish) entrees come with a "side order" of pasta with red or white sauce and a glass of house wine. These sides could easily serve as a meal for any adult with a normal appetite. Cunetto's is open for lunch and dinner Monday through Saturday. Expect to wait a while on Friday and Saturday nights, or make plans to get to the restaurant at 5:00 p.m. on Saturday, when it opens for the dinner crowd. Closed Sunday.

> **i** Missouri Baking Company, a tiny bakery located on The Hill (2027 Edwards Street, 314-773-0468) offers fresh, delicious handmade Italian cookies, biscotti, and cannoli. The bakery, which opened in 1924, also makes some of the best pound cake, stollen, baklava, danishes, and pies in town. Closed Sundays after 12 noon and all day Monday.

GIAN-TONY'S ON THE HILL $$
5356 Daggett Avenue
(314) 772-4893

Chef/proprietor Tony prepares your meal personally, and what a meal it is. Gian-Tony's offers gourmet Italian food without the gourmet price. In addition to a tremendous selection of veal, beef, chicken, and seafood dishes, the restaurant has the best cavatelli con broccoli in town. The cream sauce is as light (tasting) as air, and it will spoil you for all other cream sauces. Gian-Tony's features a full bar and a good wine list—and if you go on the weekend, you will probably spend some time in the bar waiting for a table. Reservations are accepted on weeknights only. The restaurant's old-world-style ambience lends itself equally well to romantic dinners and family get-togethers. Gian-Tony's is one of the few Italian restaurants on The Hill that is open daily.

GIOVANNI'S ON THE HILL $$-$$$
5201 Shaw Avenue
(314) 772-5958
www.giovannisonthehill.com

Giovanni's on the Hill is widely regarded as one of the best Italian gourmet restaurants in the St. Louis area and features a wonderful menu of authentic southern Italian dishes. The restaurant's dining room has played host to a number of celebrities over the years, including former Beatle Paul McCartney and his late wife, Linda, when they were in town for a concert in the early 1990s. Giovanni's is definitely an upscale dining experience, and its food is as inviting as the ambience. Reservations are required; the restaurant is closed Sunday.

RIGAZZI'S $-$$
4945 Daggett Avenue
(314) 772-4900
www.rigazzis.com

Open since 1957, Rigazzi's offers casual Italian dining and a menu of more than 200 dishes in a family-friendly atmosphere. In addition to its award-winning St. Louis–style pizza, Rigazzi's is renowned for being the "Home of the Frozen Fishbowl," which is a frozen goblet-style glass that is usually filled with draft beer, soda, or the occasional frozen daiquiri. Reservations accepted. Open for lunch and dinner. Closed Sunday.

ZIA'S ON THE HILL $-$$
5256 Wilson Avenue
(314) 776-0020
www.zias.com

Zia's is an ideal place for a big family gathering or an intimate dinner for two. The atmosphere is casual, and the wait staff is informative and friendly. The food ain't bad either. Zia's serves excellent gourmet and St. Louis–style Italian cuisine at reasonable prices, along with an impressive wine list that includes various Italian wines. Open for lunch and dinner, Zia's offers steak, chicken, fish, and pasta dishes, as well as sandwiches and burgers for the "less mature" taste buds at the table. Be sure to try the tiramisu or New York–style cheesecake. Closed Sunday.

Sandwiches

ADRIANA'S $
5101 Shaw Boulevard
(314) 773-3833

This tiny Italian deli is only open Monday through Friday for lunch, but it offers excellent sandwiches, salads, and pasta dishes for those fortunate enough to make it to The Hill during the middle of the day. Hearty Italian subs like the Charlie's Special (mozzarella and provolone cheese, lettuce, tomato, onions, black olives, and Italian dressing) are served on toasted bread, and a full sandwich can easily serve two people. Daily specials include the option to order half a sandwich and a side order of pasta, salad, or soup, which is an economical way to sample a couple of Adriana's specials at one sitting. The line to order may be long, but it moves quickly, and the tables turn over relatively fast

Spanish

MODESTO TAPAS BAR AND
RESTAURANT $$
5257 Shaw Boulevard
(314) 772-TAPA
www.modestotapas.com

Modesto offers a contemporary taste of the Mediterranean in the middle of a historic Italian neighborhood. The walls are painted the earthy reddish-yellow colors of southern Spain, and the decor blends well with the acoustic sounds of flamenco guitar music. Modesto offers a full menu of authentic Spanish cuisine, such as Paella Valenciana, Gambas al Modesto (sautéed shrimp with peppers), and Filete Salteado (beef tenderloin sautéed with garlic, parsley, and Idiazabal cheese). All the ingredients used at Modesto are exclusively Spanish, from the wines and the cheeses to the olive oil. Try the Aceitunas a la Sevillana—marinated Spanish olives with red peppers, garlic and thyme. Open Monday through Saturday for dinner only. The Spanish Fly, Modesto's late night happy hour with guest DJs, food and drink specials, takes place Wednesdays starting at 10 p.m.

MAPLEWOOD

American

MIHALIS CHOP HOUSE $$$$
1603 McCausland Avenue, Maplewood
(314) 333-3301
www.mihalischophouse.com
If you like steaks and chops, then this upscale, contemporary steak house is sure to feed your need. In addition to hand-cut steaks and chops, the menu includes various salads and seafood and pasta dishes. Specialties include shrimp and crab fettuccine, lamb osso buco, fennel-encrusted ahi tuna, and the Mihalis Harvested Salad, made with field greens, grilled beef tenderloin, and roasted baby beets with wild mushroom vinaigrette. They also have an extensive wine cellar—more than 1,800 bottles—and offer approximately 20 wines by the glass. Open Monday through Saturday for dinner only. Reservations are recommended.

SCHLAFLY BOTTLEWORKS $-$$
7260 Southwest Avenue, Maplewood
(314) 241-BEER
www.schlafly.com
Schlafly Bottleworks features a full-service restaurant, an indoor bar, a retail shop, and an outdoor beer garden. The menu is extensive, and it offers a lot more than typical bar food. There are numerous vegetarian items available, along with dozens of soup, salad, and sandwich options, as well as some creative pizzas and calzones. Entrees are in abundance as well, with heartier fare like the Hoisin Glazed Short Ribs, Gluten-Free Chicken Pesto Pasta, and pretzel-encrusted chicken. Desserts are huge—big enough for at least two people—but well worth the calories. Oh, and they make their own beer here, too. Try one of the regular beers or get a little adventurous and sample some of the seasonal brews. Open daily.

Continental

MONARCH $$$-$$$$
7401 Manchester Road, Maplewood
(314) 644-3995
www.monarchrestaurant.com
The contemporary atmosphere and "global fusion" menu quickly made Monarch a favorite destination for sophisticated palates throughout St. Louis. There are two dining areas—the bistro and the main dining room—as well as two menus for each room for both lunch and dinner. Both feature soups, salads, and appetizers, with the entrees serving as the big difference. Monarch offers haute cuisine made with French overtones such as Grilled Orange Nairagi, Pistachio Encrusted Lamb Chops and a six-course vegetarian menu. Wine list features more than 450 varieties, with 30 available by the glass. Open for lunch and dinner Tuesday-through Friday, dinner only Monday and Saturday.

Greek/Mediterranean

OLYMPIA KEBOB HOUSE AND
TAVERNA $-$$
1543 McCausland Avenue, Maplewood
(314) 781-1299
Olympia Kebob House and Taverna is an unassuming neighborhood tavern and eatery that offers an assortment of unique beverages and authentic Greek cuisine at reasonable prices. Steeped in Greek culture and a casual ambience, Olympia serves up a host of dining and drinking options. The hummus is stellar, as well

as the spanikopita (spinach pie), traditional and vegetarian gyros, baba ghanoush, and a selection of Greek wines and, of course, ouzo. The daily specials nearly double the overall menu, and the baklava itself is worth the trip. Open daily.

Mexican

MAYA CAFE $–$$
2716 Sutton Boulevard, Maplewood
(314) 781-4774

Maya Cafe is the reincarnation of a Central West End restaurant that was popular in the 1970s. Relocated to the hip and funky Maplewood area, Maya is a welcome addition to the diverse neighborhood. The dual-storefront restaurant is filled with neat tables and chairs and a small but well-stocked bar and is accented with numerous eccentric pieces of colorful artwork. Margaritas and sangria are excellent ways to start off the meal, along with the (complimentary) warm tortilla chips and a chunky, spicy salsa. Daily specials spice up a somewhat small menu, but everything served is delicious. There are paella, fish tacos with saffron rice, chimichangas, enchiladas, and a tasty salad of black and green olives marinated in olive oil and vinegar with slices of celery and onions. Open daily.

THE LOOP

After Dinner Delights

IN SPOT DESSERT BAR & LOUNGE $
5854A Delmar Boulevard
www.inspotlounge.com

In Spot is the place to satisfy your sweet tooth in a hip lounge atmosphere. In fact, it's so hip—there's not even a telephone number! The dessert bar offers a variety of specialty items from bakeries and pastry chefs around the country, as well as a menu of appetizers, coffee drinks, and cocktails.

American

BLUEBERRY HILL $
6504 Delmar Boulevard
(314) 727-0880
www.blueberryhill.com

A St. Louis landmark filled with rooms of pop culture memorabilia, Blueberry Hill is one of St. Louis's best—and hippest—places to eat. A regular winner of the best burgers (and fries) in town distinction, the eatery's menu also offers Jamaican jerk chicken, trout almandine, soups, salads, sandwiches, and a number of vegetarian options like the spicy Mexicali rice, Greek pasta salad, and even a veggie burger for the non-carnivorous among us. Blueberry Hill's beer selection includes more than 60 bottled domestic and imported beers, plus 18 brands on tap. Open daily.

BRANDT'S MARKET & CAFE $$
6525 Delmar Boulevard
(314) 727-3663
www.brandtscafe.com

Brandt's is an eclectic, European-style cafe that offers full menus for lunch and dinner, as well as a breakfast buffet and Bloody Mary bar each Saturday and Sunday morning. Lunch options include soups, salads, crab cakes, sandwiches wraps, and the chef's specialty, Vietnamese spring rolls with sweet chile sauce. For dinner the lineup includes braised duck with cherry sauce, sautéed pork chops, lobster ravioli, and a variety of pastas and vegetarian dishes. Wine connoisseurs and beer lovers will find plenty to cheer about here, with extensive selections of domestic and imported libations. Brandt's is a favorite for outdoor dining as well. Open daily.

DELMAR RESTAURANT AND LOUNGE $–$$
6235 Delmar Boulevard
(314) 725-6565

The atmosphere at the Delmar is classy and swanky, and it looks a lot like the cocktail lounges of the 1950s and '60s. This upscale eatery is known for its contemporary American fare, and the house specialties include portobello-stuffed ravioli, crawfish-stuffed beef tenderloin, seared jumbo scallops, and an eclectic selection of martinis and specialty cocktails. Or, just hang out and listen to some great live jazz or people-watch on the patio—the Delmar is a relaxing place to spend an evening. Open daily.

FITZ'S AMERICAN GRILL AND
BOTTLING WORKS $
6605 Delmar Boulevard
(314) 726-9555
www.fitzsrootbeer.com

Microbreweries are prevalent in St. Louis, but Fitz's is a little different than most. It's a root beer brewpub where you can see the brew being bottled, and it uses a legendary recipe from 1947 that includes roots, herbs, bark, and cane sugar. Plus, it's really good. Even people who say they don't usually like root beer like Fitz's brew. In addition to a full lineup of soda options (including orange pop, cream soda, grape pop, Hip Hop Pop, ginger ale, and diet root beer), the menu features a variety of appetizers and entrees with a decidedly American–Cajun–Tex-Mex–Asian flair. All sorts of pizzas and burgers are available, including the Elvis Burger (topped with slaw and barbecue sauce), a homemade veggie burger, and the Milan Pizza, made with sweet roasted-garlic tomato sauce. Open daily.

PAM'S CHICAGO STYLE DOGS AND MORE $
6016 Delmar Boulevard
(314) 721-7267
www.pamscsd.com

The tiny eatery in The Loop features "the real deal" for fans of Chicago-style hot dogs. Pam's versions are served on steamed poppy seed buns and include yellow mustard, neon relish, onions, tomato, sport peppers, a pickle spear, and the all important dash of celery salt. The menu also includes gyros, burgers, salads, sandwiches, veggie dogs and burgers, breakfast items, and the beloved deep-fried Twinkie. Open daily.

RIDDLE'S PENULTIMATE CAFE &
WINE BAR $$
6307 Delmar Boulevard
(314) 725-6985
www.riddlescafe.com

Riddle's looks like just another bar and grill along the Delmar Loop, but don't let that keep you from venturing inside. Instead of boring bar food and cheap draft beer, the restaurant serves up an ever-changing menu that includes hearty homemade soups and an assortment of vegetable dishes along with pasta, steak, and seafood entrees. The wine menu is just as impressive, as is the list of homemade desserts that take advantage of the freshest in-season fruits. Open Tuesday through Sunday for lunch and dinner, with live music nightly.

Asian

609 RESTAURANT & U LOUNGE $
609 Eastgate Avenue
(314) 721-9168
www.609u.com

The contemporary Asian menu changes seasonally and features an assortment of exclusive wines. Specialties include dishes like pan-seared mahi-mahi with jasmine rice in a cilantro pesto sauce, Panang Curry Chicken, and Asian Eggplant. Open for lunch and dinner Monday through Saturday.

MODAI SUSHI LOUNGE $–$$
6100 Delmar Boulevard
(314) 725-8330
www.modailounge.com

Modai is equal parts sushi restaurant and contemporary lounge, serving fresh, delicately prepared sushi in a hip, contemporary environment. Dinner is served Tuesday through Saturday only, but the lounge is open nightly.

SEKI JAPANESE RESTAURANT $–$$
6335 Delmar Boulevard
(314) 726-6477

Seki offers fine Japanese cuisine, including sushi, sashimi, and a full menu of appetizers and entrees in a casual, contemporary atmosphere. Reservations are encouraged, but the eatery's vibe is comfortable. Open for lunch and dinner daily except Tuesday.

Middle Eastern

AL-TARBOUSH DELI $
602 Westgate
(314) 725-1944

Al-Tarboush keeps a steady supply of Middle

Eastern delicacies like hummus, tabouleh, olives, and feta cheese for appetizers, as well as spinach pie, falafel, and shawarma (marinated beef) sandwiches served in pita bread with tahini and cool veggies. And don't forget the baklava. They have five different shapes, sizes, and flavors of baklava, so if you can't decide which one to get, get the sampler and discover your new favorite. Eat in or grab some stuff to go and head over to Forest Park for a picnic. Open daily.

SALEEM'S $$
14560 Manchester Road, Manchester, MO
(636) 207-1368
www.saleemswest.com
Saleem's, "Where Garlic Is King," definitely lives by its motto. The restaurant's owner is primarily responsible for introducing Middle Eastern fare to St. Louis more than 30 years ago, and it offers area diners a great resource for exploring new culinary territory without being too exotic. Saleem's offers some of the best hummus in town, along with feta cheese and olives as a starter. There are also crisp salads, authentic shish kebabs, falafel, and an excellent baklava. Try the Turkish coffee, which is served with fragrant cardamom rather than packets of sugar or artificial sweeteners. And don't forget a breath mint. Saleem's is open for dinner only, Monday through Saturday, and reservations are recommended.

Sandwiches
SALVATO'S CAFE & DELI MARKET $
6227 Delmar Boulevard
(314) 727-4680
Salvato's is a European-style deli and cafe that is renowned for its hearty Italian, kosher, and vegetarian sandwiches. In addition to a host of American-style sandwiches and beverages, the deli serves as an Italian specialty food market that features wine, beer, and liquors. Salvato's offers indoor and outdoor seating and boasts it has the "Best Sandwich in the World." Open daily.

CLAYTON
American
CARDWELL'S RESTAURANT $$
8100 Maryland Avenue, Clayton
(314) 726-5055
www.cardwellsinclayton.com
Cardwell's is an upscale restaurant that works well for business lunches and special dinners. The dinner menu is extensive and features lots of fresh fish, wood-grilled meats, pastas, and seasonal game. The lunch menu features somewhat lighter fare, including a variety of salads, soups, and sandwiches, along with a half-dozen entrees from the grill. At dinner there's a "casual fare" menu that includes items like Chinese barbecue chicken salad, portobello-filled tortellini in a porcini mushroom broth, and grilled sirloin burger, as well as roasted rack of lamb, grilled veal chops, and a roasted Tuscan vegetable plate. An excellent wine list and some truly decadent desserts round out the stellar menu. Reservations recommended. Closed Sunday.

J. BUCK'S $$
101 South Hanley, Clayton
(314) 725-4700
www.jbucks.com
J. Buck's is a popular area restaurant that is named for the Buck family broadcasters, including the late Jack Buck of KMOX, his son Joe Buck of Fox Sports, and his daughter Julie, who works in local radio. The Clayton location has proved to be so popular that the Bucks decided to open one downtown (1000 Clark Street; 314-436-0394). The eateries may have been "built" on the sports theme, but J. Buck's is far from being a sports bar. In addition to being a popular meet-and-greet spot for young professionals, it offers a casual atmosphere that has been decorated with lots of wood, stone, and warm lighting. The menu features a variety of steaks, chops, sandwiches, salads, gourmet pizzas, fresh fish, and free-range chicken, as well as a list of delectable desserts. There's also a kids' menu and a lengthy martini menu for grown-ups. Open daily for lunch and dinner.

Asian Fusion

MISO ON MERAMEC $$

16 North Meramec Avenue, Clayton
(314) 863-7888
www.misolounge.com

The menu at Miso fuses Thai, Chinese, Japanese, and Vietnamese cooking styles for an eclectic lineup of dinner options. In addition to the extensive sushi menu, there's a variety of soups, salads, small and large plates. Enjoy Asian-fused tapas like grilled teriyaki salmon (served on a bed of jasmine rice and grilled asparagus) and beef tenderloin (with a red wine sherry sauce and served with mashed taro root and fried leeks). Cocktails offered include specialty drinks made with sake, like the Rising Sun Martini, which is a mixture of plum sake, orange juice, and a splash of grenadine. Or try some Asian Firecrackers—cherries soaked in Bacardi 151. Closed Monday.

Mediterranean

PORTABELLA RESTAURANT $$

15 North Central Avenue, Clayton
(314) 725-6588
www.portabellarestaurant.com

Portabella is one of Clayton's premier restaurants, and its rustic Mediterranean cuisine has won rave reviews from area critics and diners. The lunch menu features upscale versions of the usual midday meal fare, such as a tilapia BLT, pasta dishes, shrimp or prosciutto pizza and a griddled ham and Gruyère sandwich. For dinner, the specialties include the pan-seared rainbow trout, grilled smoked pork tenderloin, and duck confit white bean and foie gras cassolette. The wine selection is vast, and it includes selections from top-name wineries in California, Italy, and France. Open Monday through Friday for lunch and dinner; dinner only on Saturday and Sunday. Reservations are recommended.

REMY'S KITCHEN & WINE BAR $$–$$$

222 South Bemiston Avenue, Clayton
(314) 726-5757
www.remyskitchen.net

Remy's is an upscale, comfortable eatery that offers customers a cross-cultural menu that is heavily influenced by the tastes of the Mediterranean and an award-winning wine list that offers three dozen wines by the glass. For lunch diners can sample three different items for less than $10 by choosing one of the Mediterranean Grazings sampler plates. The Quick and Healthy plate offers a cup of soup, a small grilled beef tenderloin salad, and a substantial sample of the house specialty: hummus. Other tri-course options are also available. At dinner the menu expands to include Remy's Orecchiette Aglio e Olio pasta (with Volpi pancetta, broccolini, chile flakes and parmesan cheese), grilled beef tenderloin, and Grilled Eggplant Napoleon (with mozzarella cheese, capers, pine nuts, tomato coulis and topped with fried spinach). Remy's is open for lunch and dinner Monday through Friday, and for dinner on Saturday. Reservations are recommended for dinner.

SOUTH/SOUTHWEST

After-Dinner Delights

ABSOLUTLI GOOSED $–$$

3196 South Grand Avenue
(314) 772-0400
www.absolutligoosed.com

When it comes to after-dinner cocktails, Absolutli Goosed has a menu that isn't to be believed. Yes, it's a martini bar—but if you like a little something sweet to close out the night, try one of the drinks at the Goose. Dessert 'tinis like the Three Musketeers (sweet, creamy, and smooth), Gin Berry Blossom (fruity and tart), and the Halle Berry (chocolate-strawberry) are quite tasty, along with coffee drinks like the chocolate mint and the raspberry mocha. More traditional desserts are available as well, including the lemon cake with blueberry mousse, white chocolate blackberry cheesecake, and various seasonal selections. There is also a selection of beers and wines. Enjoy your drinks on the cozy patio. Open daily.

CRAVINGS $
8149 Big Bend Boulevard, Webster Groves
(314) 961-3534
www.cravingsonline.com
Cravings is where St. Louisans go when they really want dessert. Oh sure, they serve lunch and dinner, but it's the desserts that will make the locals get in their cars and head to Webster Groves for something sweet. Specialties include the lime-blueberry bombé (a dome of chewy brownie crust filled with lime, white chocolate mousse, and blueberries), fresh fruit tarts, and layer upon layer of layer cakes. Chocolate lovers will find something to satisfy their cravings as well, with the caramel ganache tart (crust filled with butter pecan caramel and topped with chocolate truffle filling) and the chocolate mousse cake. Call for hours. Closed Sunday and Monday.

i Looking for a late-night bite? In addition to the usual fast-food suspects, there's the Courtesy Diner on the near south side (3155 South Kingshighway; 314–776–9059). The 1950s diner and drive-in is a tradition in St. Louis, and it serves up breakfast and burgers with equal aplomb. Try the Slinger, a signature dish consisting of a hamburger patty, fried eggs, and hash browns covered with chili. There's a second location nearby (1121 Hampton Road; 314–644–2600) that's shinier, newer, and, well . . . cleaner, but the menu is the same at both places. Open 24/7.

MURDOCH PERK $
5400 Murdoch Avenue
(314) 752-9126
www.murdochperk.net
Located in the Southampton neighborhood of St. Louis, Murdoch Perk is a cozy, comfortable cafe that serves delicious desserts, smoothies, granitas, and specialty coffees. The menu includes such specialties as the Fall Harvest Crepe (warm apples layered with cinnamon, brown sugar, and toasted almonds), a flourless chocolate cake, the Murdoch Perk cheesecake, and a sugar-free apple dumpling. In addition to sweets, the eatery offers sandwiches, salads, and breakfast crepes and quiches. Closed Monday.

TED DREWES FROZEN CUSTARD $
6726 Chippewa Street
(314) 481-2652
www.teddrewes.com
A St. Louis tradition since 1929, Ted Drewes offers the absolute best frozen custard. Called "concretes," these shakes are so thick that you can turn them upside down and not lose a drop. Create your own shake from a menu of cookies and other goodies, or choose from the existing favorites. The sundaes and concretes come in six sizes, but the "mini" or regular size is usually big enough for one person. Closed during January and February. Open daily.

French

CAFE PROVENÇAL $$–$$$
427 South Kirkwood Road, Kirkwood
(314) 822-5446
www.cafeprovencal.com
Cafe Provençal features a light brand of French cooking, concentrating on the foods and culture of the country's Provençal region. The menu is subject to change due to the chef's commitment to using fresh ingredients, but there are a number of items that are almost always available. Appetizers like the salmon pâté and escargots in garlic butter and entrees such as the mahi-mahi grille and the roasted pork with mushrooms have become favorites for restaurant regulars. Entrees include specialties like Choucroute Garni (sausages, pork chop, sauerkraut and potatoes), Poulet DeBergerac (chicken breast in puff pastry), and Saumon a la Moutard de Pemmerey (salmon with coarse grained mustard). Open Tuesday through Friday for lunch and dinner; dinner only on Saturday.

Italian

ONESTO PIZZA AND TRATTORIA $$–$$$

5401 Finkman Street
(314) 802-8883
www.onestopizza.com

Located in the Southampton neighborhood nicknamed SoHa, Onesto's gourmet pizza is worth the trip alone. The eatery also features a variety of pasta dishes—including an excellent fettuccine alfredo and sweet potato gnocchi—along with sandwiches, calzones, Stromboli, and some of the best Tiramisu in town. One of Onesto's specialties is the Arancini, a large breaded and deep fried rice ball stuffed Parmesan cheese, tomato sauce, ground beef, and peas. Open for lunch and dinner on Monday and Wednesday through Saturday; dinner only on Sunday. Closed Tuesday.

Mexican

PUEBLO SOLIS $–$$

5127 Hampton Avenue
(314) 351-9000
www.pueblosolisstl.com

This friendly, family-owned restaurant specializes in traditional dishes from northern Mexico. In addition to excellent hand-crafted margaritas, freshly prepared guacamole, fajitas, burritos, and quesadillas, the menu includes Filet Solis (beef medallions served over Mexican Russet Potatoes with mole sauce) Mexican Salmon, and Shrimp Diablo. Open for dinner nightly.

WEST COUNTY

American

ANNIE GUNN'S AND
THE SMOKEHOUSE MARKET $$–$$$

16806 Chesterfield Airport Road, Chesterfield
(636) 532-7684
www.anniegunns.com

Situated inside a building (circa 1937) that once housed a country market, Annie Gunn's is one of the most popular places to eat in the county. The menu features soups, salads, steaks, burgers, and sandwiches for lunch and dinner. Lunch entrees include chicken-fried steak, braised pork shank, fettuccine with house-made chicken meatballs, and grilled meat loaf and gravy. The dinner menu expands to include entrees like grilled tenderloin, crispy duck confit, jumbo shrimp, braised veal cheeks, grilled scallops, and roasted chicken. Appetizers range from foie gras and grilled Muscovy duck on pumpernickel to Kobe beef carpaccio and soft pretzels with house-made sausage, cremini mushrooms, and horseradish mustard. The kids' menu is just as extensive, with burgers, chicken tenders, sandwiches like Liam's Smoosh (peanut butter and marshmallow cream on white bread), and buttered noodles with Parmesan cheese. The restaurant is regularly awarded the Award of Excellence by *Wine Spectator* magazine, thanks to its wine list that features more than 700 varieties. Closed Monday.

DIERDORF & HART'S STEAK
HOUSE $$$–$$$$

323 Westport Plaza
(314) 878-1801
www.dierdorfharts.com

The upscale Dierdorf & Hart's is owned and operated by former St. Louis (football) Cardinals Dan Dierdorf and Jim Hart. The menu includes a variety of oversized steaks and chops, as well as seafood, salads, and fine wines in a comfortably elegant atmosphere. Open for dinner only, Monday through Saturday. Reservations suggested.

VINTAGE RESTAURANT AT STONE
HILL WINERY $$

1110 Stone Hill Highway, Hermann
(573) 486-3479, (800) 909-9463
www.stonehillwinery.com

Stone Hill Winery, located in the heart of Missouri Wine Country, is a family owned and operated vineyard, winery, and restaurant in Hermann, Missouri. The restaurant is located in the winery's restored carriage house and horse barn, serving German cuisine, steaks, American dishes, and Stone Hill wines. Open for lunch and dinner. Hours vary by season, so it's best to call ahead. Reservations recommended.

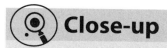 **Close-up**

Holey Rollers

Back in the day, before fat grams and "carbophobia" took over America, doughnuts were a regular taste treat for many Americans. The neighborhood doughnut shop churned out dozens of exotic delicacies, and you would be hard-pressed to find a doughnut anywhere else. You went to the bakery for cakes, cookies, or bread, but you went to the doughnut shop for something really special.

For whatever reason, these throwbacks to the past are still thriving in at least one section of St. Louis. The southern/southwestern neighborhoods of the city are home to numerous shops that specialize in the holey pastry, with several shops located within mere blocks of one another. You can watch doughnuts being made the old-fashioned way—no machinery here. Whatever the flavor they eventually become, all doughnuts start out as a pile of dough worked over with an industrial-strength rolling pin, hand-cut and deep-fried. Depending on what's selling best that day, customers can see the evolution of everything from the traditional yeasty glazed version to hearty cake-style or jelly-filled varieties being created.

All of the St. Louis shops have "official" names, but there's usually only one sign that's visible—the one that reads DONUTS (or, in some cases, DO-NUTS). But, no matter how you spell it, it's definitely worth the trip back in time. So take your own taste test—you can decide for yourself which one has the best "city donut."

Donut Drive-In
6525 Chippewa Street (Route 66)
(314) 645–7714

The Donut House
8500 Morganford Road
(314) 638–5828

O'Fashion Donuts
5120 Southwest Avenue
(314) 772–0398

St. Louis Hills Donut Shop
6917 Hampton Avenue
(314) 481–6050

World's Fair Doughnuts
1904 South Vandeventer at Southwest Avenue
(314) 776–9975

Pub Food

KRIEGER'S PUB & GRILL $-$$
12664 Dorsett Road, Maryland Heights
(314) 878-1517
www.kriegerspub.com
All of the Krieger's locations provide the same casual, family-friendly atmosphere and serve as popular gathering places to watch sporting events on TV. Krieger's, open daily for lunch and dinner, specializes in big burgers and sandwiches, along with award-winning chicken wings, pizzas, salads, and steaks. On Tuesday nights, kids eat free whenever Mom or Dad has an entree.

OZZIE'S RESTAURANT & SPORTS BAR $
645 Westport Plaza, Maryland Heights
(314) 434-1000
www.ozziesrestaurantandsportsbar.com
Former Cardinals shortstop and Hall of Famer Ozzie Smith's namesake eatery is one of the most popular places in town to catch a game. In addition to numerous TVs located throughout the bar, Ozzie's features good food that is a step above the traditional sports bar pub grub. There are numerous burgers and sandwiches on the menu, along with soups, salads, pastas, and desserts. The wine list is minimal, but the lineup of beers available on tap is respectable. This is

a family-friendly sports bar that offers excellent food at reasonable prices. Open daily.

TRAINWRECK SALOON $-$$
314 Westport Plaza, Maryland Heights
(314) 432-7222
www.trainwrecksaloon.com
In addition to a respectable number of domestic and imported beers on the menu, Trainwreck has a wide range of pub-grub options and a kids'

menu for the small fry. Ideal for lunch or dinner, this casual tavern's menu ranges from the usual lineup of soups, salads, and appetizers to not-so-usual burger options (beef, bison, and ostrich). Be sure to try some of the always-tasty seasoned french fries. Trainwreck's desserts are irresistible, and the wine selection includes offerings by the glass and by the bottle. Open daily.

NIGHTLIFE

There are a number of entertainment areas throughout the greater St. Louis area, including three distinct regions within downtown St. Louis.

Laclede's Landing, located on the riverfront, is home to a variety of restaurants, nightclubs, and other entertainment options, and some have a 3:00 a.m. liquor license. It is also home to two casinos—the President casino and the swanky new Lumière Place casino complex.

Just south of downtown is Soulard, a neighborhood of red brick buildings that house private residences, restaurants, bars, and some of the best live blues clubs in town. From locals' favorites like BB's Jazz, Blues & Soups, and the Broadway Oyster Bar to the internationally renowned McGurk's Irish Pub and Restaurant, there's almost always live music somewhere in this neighborhood. Soulard is the site of St. Louis's annual Mardi Gras festivities, which include parades, parties, and lots of live music.

Washington Avenue is still a thriving area, but gone are the days when there was a dance club on every corner. Today the street bustles with a variety of bars, restaurants, shops, and galleries, as well as a handful of lounges. Rue 13 still has something to offer hipsters and club-goers, along with nearby hot spot Pepper Lounge. The Side Bar is a newcomer to Washington, offering live music from local bands and large plasma TVs for sports fans, and Lucas Park Grille is a popular restaurant that serves as a prime place for those on the see-and-be-seen scene. The Flamingo Bowl is a combination bowling alley and martini bar, and Flannery's offers a plethora of flat screen TVs for die-hard sports fans.

Farther west, Lafayette Square and the Central West End (CWE) each offer unique entertainment options. Lafayette Square is home to stylish restaurants and taverns, while the CWE has options ranging from cocktails (and people-watching) al fresco to tripping the light fantastic at the lively Club Viva for a night of salsa music and dancing.

Just west of the CWE, two tiny municipalities are becoming even more popular with those in search of excitement after sundown. The Loop neighborhood features live music at clubs like Blueberry Hill's Duck Room, and Cicero's, as well as a spectacular nightclub/concert venue called The Pageant. Maplewood is quickly becoming a mini bohemian gathering place, complete with trendy (and good) eateries like Maya Cafe, the Schlafly Bottleworks brewpub, and the historic bowling alley/bar known as Saratoga Lanes.

Westport, located in western St. Louis County, includes the Westport Plaza shopping/dining/hotel complex that's home to popular eateries like Ozzie's Restaurant & Sports Bar, Pujols 5 Westport Grill, the Trainwreck Saloon, and the Funny Bone Comedy Club. Other entertainment options nearby include a two-casinos-in-one Harrah's complex and the Verizon Wireless Amphitheater, site of dozens of concerts from top-name entertainers throughout the summer and early fall. (Locals still call it Riverport.)

And, no matter what part of town you're in, you're never far from a sports bar. St. Louis is one sports-crazed town—with good reason—and you can always find a place to watch the game or talk sports. Downtown, Mike Shannon's Steak & Seafood restaurant has an upscale bar area with numerous flat screen TVs nearby Maurizio's Pizza & Sports Cafe offers good pizza in a real "locals'" atmosphere. Maurizio's is a popular stop prior to Rams games for the ultimate "low-maintenance" tailgate fare.

Almost all of the clubs and taverns listed in this chapter still allow smoking in at least some portion of the establishment. The majority of bars in town shut things down by 1:30 a.m., although there are a number of places with 3:00 a.m. liquor licenses. Cover charges are usually minimal or nonexistent on weeknights and vary widely from club to club on weekends.

If you plan to party in St. Louis, make sure you're aware of the most up-to-date liquor laws and drunk-driving penalties. Both Missouri's and Illinois's definitions of legally drunk is .08, and DUI penalties are severe, so if alcohol is part of your evening, make sure that you have a designated driver or plan to cab your way around town. Carrying open containers of alcohol in your car is illegal, and it's illegal to wander through the streets with a can or bottle of booze. Recent changes to Missouri's liquor laws include moving Sunday sales back to 9:00 a.m. (in downtown) to allow for football tailgating. Not all bars in town serve food, so if you're planning to eat, drink, and be merry, make sure that your pub of choice has more to offer than just snack mix.

DOWNTOWN

Bars and Pubs

AL HRABOSKY'S BALLPARK SALOON
800 Cerre Street
(314) 241-6969
www.alhraboskys.admitonevip.com
This downtown sports-bar is owned by former Cardinal pitcher and current team broadcaster Al Hrabosky. Known as "the Mad Hungarian" during his playing days, Hrabosky is a local favorite among baseball fans, and his hangout is a popular pre- and postgame destination. Oversize doors remain open most of the time, allowing for easy access between the indoor bar and to-go food kitchen and the spacious outdoor mingling and seating areas. The menu features burgers and sandwiches like the Big Hrabosky (beef brisket, grilled onions, and mushrooms on toasted bread), the Red Burd (a char-grilled chicken sandwich), and the Mad Hungarian Burger (a half-pound burger on a toasted Kaiser roll), along with snacks and salads. Grab a drink, order some grub, and secure a spot inside or out for some casual socializing or some serious baseball talk with the man himself. Al can often be found chatting with the masses after the game.

FLANNERY'S
1324 Washington Avenue
(314) 241-8885
www.flanneryspub.com
Located in the newly revitalized Loft District, Flannery's is a neighborhood gathering place and one of the best places in town to watch a game. The pub features multiple flat screen TVs, with each tuned to football, baseball, basketball or hockey. Depending on the crowd, the bartenders are usually happy to dial-up whatever game you're looking for—unless you're a Cubs fan—and put it on a screen near you. Flannery's has a full bar and a respectable pub grub menu. Open daily.

HARRY'S
2144 Market Street
(314) 421-6969
Harry's is well known among downtown businesspeople who frequent the restaurant for lingering lunches and after-hours colloquies. The room's towering Palladian windows afford an unparalleled view of the city skyline. A smart, buoyant young crowd converges on Harry's every Thursday, Friday, and Saturday evenings for live music on the expansive patio, which is also a festive place to carouse after a Cardinals, Rams, or Blues victory. In fact, you might even run into some of the players here.

MIKE SHANNON'S STEAKS AND SEAFOOD
620 Market Street
(314) 421-1540
www.mikeshannonssteaksandseafood.com

Former St. Louis Cardinals third baseman and current Cardinals broadcaster Mike Shannon is one of the most colorful characters in the team's rich history and the owner of this sports bar and restaurant, located just a couple of blocks from Busch Stadium. Shannon's has an outstanding collection of sports memorabilia on display. Shannon himself can be found in the bar area after games, and he often does live radio broadcasts from the pub's friendly confines. There are lots of TVs here as well, and all are tuned to local baseball, football, or hockey whenever a game is available. The restaurant and bar's new location allowed the owners to expand "outdoors." On Cardinals game days, the patio bar called "The Outfield" opens for business, and it's a great place to meet before and after games.

MORGAN STREET BREWERY
721 North Second Street
(314) 231-9970
www.morganstreetbrewery.com

Morgan Street Brewery is a warm and inviting place to have dinner or drinks, watch a game, or play some pool. The brewpub's rich architecture and warm interior feature burnished wood, lots of exposed brick, and cozy nooks and corners. The main brewery building and adjacent Lodge, both more than 130 years old, are separated by a brick patio that is ideal for cafe -style dining during the warm-weather months. The kitchen is open late, and the pub serves a variety of domestic and imported beers in addition to its own microbrews, which include Honey Wheat, Golden Pilsner, Dark Wheat, Red Lager, Oatmeal Stout, Cobblestone Steam Lager, Mai-bock, Altbier, and Doppelbock. Try the "coniques," deep fried mashed potato balls—they go great with beer.

PADDY O'S
618 South Seventh Street
(314) 588-7313

On game days, members of Cardinal Nation trek to neighboring Paddy O's for their pre- and post-game celebrations. This comfortable sports bar is a great place to hang out, play some pool, or people-watch, and the outside party scene is as much fun as the party inside. Chances are you'll run into a baseball player or two, as this laid-back watering hole is often a post-game destination for members of the Cardinals and visiting teams.

SCHLAFLY TAP ROOM
2100 Locust Street
(314) 241-2337
www.schlafly.com

The Tap Room microbrewery and brewpub features live music on the weekends and has a diverse selection of handcrafted Schlafly beers that are brewed on-site. The main dining room offers a great view of the brewery's standpipes and other inner workings, and Daniel's Den, a separate bar and game room area, features a jukebox, darts, TVs, pool, and foosball tables. Live bands perform occasionally, usually upstairs in a third bar area. Free parking in adjacent lot.

THE SIDE BAR
1317 Washington Avenue
(314) 621-7376
www.sidebar.admitonevip.com

Sports fans and legal eagles flock to this casually upscale pub in the downtown loft district. Three large plasma TVs and a giant projection screen provide great views of whatever game or sport is being played at the moment, and the bar's atmosphere makes it an enjoyable place to hang out. There's live music on weekends, and the bar is a popular pre- and post-game gathering place for Cardinals, Rams, and Blues games. In addition to a respectable food menu and a selection of cocktails, beers, and wine, The Side Bar offers a variety of seasonal "mixology drinks" that feature muddled fruits mixed with liqueurs. One highlight is the pepper-infused vodka used to make Bloody Marys for Sunday brunch.

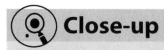 **Close-up**

More Than Just A Beer Town

The Ritz-Carlton hotel's bar (100 Carondelet Plaza, Clayton; 800-241-3333) was one of the region's pioneers in introducing the martini to St. Louis taste buds. The Lobby Lounge's "official" martini menu contains more than 60 varieties, but that's less than a third of the total number of specialty martinis they serve. Today's thirst for the unusual continues to grow, along with the list of atypical ingredients on the bartender's recipe cards. Cosmopolitans still lead the pack as St. Louisans' favorite martini, but there is any number of "martiniesque" concoctions coming in tied for second place. Any talk about martinis with fruity flavors already being on the way "out" on the East and West coasts hasn't proven itself here yet. Seems St. Louis isn't quite as trendy and easily swayed by the beautiful people and media hipsters as previously thought.

The drinks have remained—so popular with St. Louisans that more and more martini bars seem to be opening every day. One of the most popular mainstays of the cocktail craze is Absolutli Goosed (3196 South Grand Avenue; 314-772-0400), a cozy and casual bar in the city's South Grand neighborhood. A regular winner of the Riverfront Times Readers' Poll for Best Martini, the bar serves up dozens of variations on the martini theme. Popular picks include the Razmopolitan (Stoli Razberi, Skyy Citrus, Chambord, cranberry, and lime); Ciroc Lemon Drop (Ciroc vodka and a squeeze of fresh lemon with a sugar rim); Orange Long Island Tea, an orange twist on the original Long Island tea recipe; and a half-dozen versions of the chocolate martini. With a motto that reads "No martini experience required," Absolutli Goosed is a great place for the novice to learn about the various types of 'tinis without feeling like, well—a novice—and a unique place for the veteran imbiber to experiment with a variety of martini options.

Another local favorite that serves up a fine martini is a longtime neighborhood tavern called the Famous Bar (5213 Chippewa, 314-832-2211, www.thefamousbar.com) in South St. Louis. Voted Best Martini in the 2008 Riverfront Times Readers' Poll, their specialty is the original—a classic gin martini. While the knowledgeable bartenders can make you any flavor (or color) you'd like, their strong suit is "the king," also known as the Bombay Sapphire gin martini.

Coffeehouses

ESPRESSO MOD
210 North Ninth Street
(314) 436-3240
www.espressomod.com

Voted "Best Coffeehouse" by St. Louis's ALIVE magazine, Espresso Mod offers a cool, retro atmosphere and serves everything from cappuccinos to fresh brews. They also have breakfast pastries, paninis, sandwiches, and Italian-style gelato ice cream. Open Monday through Saturday.

THE LONDON TEA ROOM
1520 Washington Avenue
(314) 241-6226
www.thelondontearoom.com

Designed to resemble the tea rooms found in the owner's home country, this casual eatery features tea, espresso and coffee. They serve full Afternoon and Cream Teas, as well as fresh-baked pastries, scones, quiches, sandwiches, soups, and salads. Loose teas are available by the ¼ pound. Open Tuesday through Sunday.

MISSISSIPPI MUD HOUSE
2101 Cherokee Street
(314) 776-6599
www.mississippimudhouse.com

This corner cafe in the historic Cherokee Street neighborhood offers gourmet, fresh roasted coffee, local wines, and specialty beers, along with homemade sandwiches, salads, and pastries.

There's a beautiful patio and access to free Wi-Fi. Open daily for breakfast, lunch and dinner daily.

SOULARD COFFEE GARDEN & CAFE
910 Geyer, Soulard
(314) 241-1464

This quaint and comfortable coffeehouse features festively painted walls and lots of exposed brick, combining for a warm and inviting place to enjoy a cup of gourmet coffee or espresso and play one of the many board games kept on hand. The coffeehouse's menu includes a variety of vegetarian and non-vegetarian items, including sandwiches, baked goods, and fruit. There's a patio that's open whenever the weather allows, as well as live acoustic performances. Open until 9:00 p.m. Friday and Saturday.

Concert Venues

ROBERTS ORPHEUM THEATER
416 North Ninth Street
(314) 588-0388
www.robertsorpheum.com

Originally built as a vaudeville palace in 1917, the Roberts Orpheum Theater underwent an extensive renovation a couple of years ago and has been returned to its original "Parisian-style" splendor. Today the venue hosts a variety of events ranging from concerts and live theater and dance productions to corporate awards shows and private parties. The beautiful theater is located in the heart of the revitalized Loft District, just a block south of Washington Avenue and the America's Center convention complex.

SCOTTRADE CENTER
1401 Clark Street
(314) 531-7887
www.scottradecenter.net

Scottrade Center, home ice for the NHL's St. Louis Blues, is a 20,000-seat venue that hosts numerous athletic events, family entertainment shows, and live concerts throughout the year. The most innovative use of the facility is the Concert Club set-up, which essentially cuts the large arena down to a more intimate size of just 4,500 seats. The full-house seating arrangement hosts such big names as Bruce Springsteen, Avril Lavigne, Metallica, AC/DC, Eric Clapton, and the Dixie Chicks, while the Concert Club provides excellent acoustics and sight lines for smaller shows such as Sheryl Crow, B. B. King, and even the Bear in the Big Blue House children's show. Tickets to all shows are available at the Scottrade Center box office (314) 421-4400 and through Ticketmaster (314) 241-1888.

Dancing

EXO
3146 Locust Street
www.EXOstl.com

EXO is downtown St. Louis's newest urban, premium "lifestyle entertainment space" featuring live local and national bands and DJs. The vibe varies nightly, so the featured tunes could be jazz one night, followed by R&B and hip-hop or house music and background lounge music. In addition to a kitchen serving Southern Creole fare, the bi-level venue features a dance floor, VIP area, cigar room, lounge areas, bottle service space, and patio. Open 5 p.m. to 1:30 a.m., Monday through Saturday.

PEPPER LOUNGE
2005 Locust Street
(314) 241-2005
www.thepepperlounge.com

The Pepper Lounge has succeeded in combining warm and comfortable surroundings with a decidedly hip feel. There are actually two bar areas here, each offering somewhat different atmospheres. The front room features a large, speakeasy-type bar, hardwood floors, exposed brick, and subdued lighting. Down a short hallway and tucked behind the kitchen is the Lounge, a Vegas/1950s-style bar-within-a-bar that serves as the music and dancing room. From Thursday through Saturday nights, it's one of the hottest places in downtown.

RUE 13

1313 Washington Avenue
(314) 588-9797
www.rue13stl.com

Rue 13 offers a variety of themed music nights and happy hours throughout the week, ranging from retro rock and hip-hop Wednesdays to '80s Night Fridays and contemporary burlesque on Saturdays. No flashing disco lights or driving bass lines here—the lounge offers excellent sushi, high-end cocktails and good old-fashioned domestic beers in a trendy, contemporary atmosphere. Closed Sunday.

Gay and Lesbian Bars

CLEMENTINE'S

2001 Menard Street
(314) 664-7869
www.clementinesbar.com

Clementine's, St. Louis's oldest gay bar, is open seven days a week and features an adjoining cafe and a patio bar. The restaurant, called the Oh My Darlin' Cafe, is highly regarded throughout the area and features culinary delights from "Chef Bubbles" and "Ms. Connie," including steaks, prime rib, chicken pot pie, and other house specialties. Clementine's features happy-hour pricing from 10:00 a.m. to 7:00 p.m., Monday through Friday.

Live Music

BB'S JAZZ, BLUES & SOUPS

700 South Broadway
(314) 436-5222
www.bbsjazzbluessoups.com

BB's Jazz, Blues & Soups is a funky, eclectic music club that has been around—in various conditions—for more than 30 years. It is one of a handful of St. Louis–area clubs that offer live music every night of the week, as well as bands on weekend afternoons. The kitchen is open until midnight during the week and until 2:00 a.m. on Friday and Saturday. BB's offers a variety of specialty drinks and a large assortment of domestic and imported beers.

BEALE ON BROADWAY

701 South Broadway
(314) 621-7880
www.bealeonbroadway.com

Located right across the street from BB's Jazz, Blues & Soups and within shouting distance of the Broadway Oyster Bar, Beale on Broadway is yet another club that showcases St. Louis's finest jazz, blues, and roots musicians. The club opens at 6:00 p.m. nightly, and the music starts almost as soon as the doors are unlocked. The bar has a Louisiana feel, with wood floors and wooden tables and lit by tiny, colored lights. This friendly neighborhood bar is an ideal spot to start the evening or wrap things up after a night on the town. Live music seven nights a week from local and national bands.

THE BIG BANG

807 North Second Street
(314) 241-2264
www.thebigbangbar.com

The Big Bang is a high-energy, rock 'n' roll, sing-along show that features two dueling piano players who keep the place lively with their incredible piano-playing ability and lots of witty banter. There really doesn't appear to be any song that these talented musicians can't play—and even if they do get stumped by an obscure song title, they're very adept at improvising songs on the spot. Good clean fun nightly until 3:00 a.m., but you must be 21 to enter. Closed Monday.

THE FIREBIRD

2706 Olive Street
www.firebirdstl.com

The Firebird is an independent music and events venue specializing in local and underground indie rock, punk, ska, rockabilly, electro, and post-rock touring acts. Shows usually take place Tuesday through Saturday nights, with an occasional Sunday night thrown in. Check the Web site for times, cover charges, and whether a particular show is 18+ or 21.

Looking for live music on a week-night? You can't go wrong at the three clubs that make up the "Blues Triangle" at the southern end of downtown. BB's Jazz, Blues & Soups, Beale on Broadway, and Broadway Oyster Bar are located within shouting distance of one another at the intersection of South Broadway and Cerre Street, and all three have great live blues bands every night of the week.

BROADWAY OYSTER BAR

736 South Broadway

(314) 621-8811

www.broadwayoysterbar.com

Catch local and national bands playing jazz, blues, zydeco, and R&B nightly, and enjoy Cajun, Creole, and American delicacies. With the wonderful ambience of the French Quarter in New Orleans, the Broadway Oyster Bar. There's no better place to enjoy live music on a warm evening than on the colorful patio—you'll feel like you're in New Orleans or along the bayou.

1860S HARD SHELL CAFE & BAR

1860 South Ninth Street

(314) 231-1860

The 1860s Bar offers a full, diverse menu and a great environment to enjoy live music. Live local blues and rock bands play here nightly, plus Saturday from 2:30 to 6:30 p.m. The Courtyard offers a casual, enclosed dining and drinking environment under a permanent tin ceiling, and all of the creature comforts of home. It's an ideal spot for the hot St. Louis nights or chilly fall evenings.

HAMMERSTONE'S

2028 South Ninth Street

(314) 773-5565

www.hammerstones.net

Hammerstone's offers live music by local bands seven nights a week, along with an additional set on Saturday and Sunday afternoons. The crowd at this casual watering hole is a mixture of neighborhood residents and folks from all sides of the production line at "the brewery," which explains

Live Blues

One of the best things about St. Louis is that you can see blues performances in area clubs and neighborhood taverns any night of the week, thanks to a thriving local music scene. In fact, it's an oft-repeated—but hard to prove—declaration by the locals that there are more working blues musicians in the St. Louis area than any other city in the country. The St. Louis Blues Society and the St. Louis Convention & Visitors Commission, who tout this fact most often, are easily considered the most logical experts on the subject, so just take these two reputable organizations at their word and enjoy the music.

Nightly repositories of St. Louis blues music include BB's Jazz, Blues & Soups, Broadway Oyster Bar, Beale on Broadway, and Backstreet Jazz and Blues in Maryland Heights. (For details about these nightspots, see their full listings in this chapter.) Popular local bands and artists who regularly perform throughout the area include Alvin Jett & Phat Noiz Blues Band, Big George Brock & The House Rockers, the Bottom's Up Blues Gang, Kim Massie, Gumbohead, Renee Smith & Solé Blue, the Rich McDonough Band, the Soulard Blues Band, and teen blues phenom, Marquise Knox.

the overwhelming number of Anheuser-Busch products visible on the tables. The bar also serves many other varieties of brews, wines, and a full cocktail menu. The patio at Hammerstone's is one of the best in St. Louis, and it is an ideal spot to enjoy cocktails when the weather cooperates.

The neighborhood tavern is also a lively meeting place before and after Rams, Cardinals, and Blues games, thanks in part to the bar's free round-trip shuttle to the Edward Jones Dome, Busch Stadium, and the Scottrade Center.

> **i** On weeknights most of the live-music clubs don't charge a cover, and on weekends the cover charge is around $10.

MCGURK'S IRISH PUB & RESTAURANT
1200 Russell Boulevard
(314) 776-8309
www.mcgurks.com

For more than 20 years, McGurk's has been the epitome of "Irishness" in St. Louis. From its food menu to the wide selection of beer, wines, and whiskey, the cozy Soulard bar is the closest thing to a real Irish public house this side of Dublin. The big draw for music fans is the nightly performances of traditional Irish music by artists imported from the motherland. According to one *St. Louis Post-Dispatch* reporter who interviewed one of the Irish musicians performing at the pub, McGurk's is to Irish music what New Orleans's Preservation Hall is to jazz.

OFF BROADWAY
3509 Lemp Avenue
(314) 773-3363
www.offbroadwaystl.com

Off Broadway, named for its location downtown and just off Broadway, is one of St. Louis's favorite music clubs, featuring touring national, regional, and local acts such as Ian Moore, Jimmie Dale Gilmore, Wayne the Train Hancock, Jonathan Richman, Two Cow Garage, and the Redwalls. The focus is mainly folk and roots rock, but all types of bands have played the stage here. Voted best concert venue in 2007 by readers of St. Louis Magazine.

OLD ROCK HOUSE
1200 South Seventh Street
(314) 588-0505
www.oldrockhousestl.com

Located off the beaten path between downtown and Soulard, the Old Rock House offers a full schedule of various musical genres. In addition to an acoustic happy hour, ORH features local, national and touring bands Tuesday through Saturday nights, along with a ull menu of lunch and dinner options. The historic building, which is listed on the historic registry, started as a saloon in 1880 and reportedly was a popular spot for steamboat captains, millionaires, and writers such as Mark Twain and Eugene Field.

VENICE CAFE
1903 Pestalozzi
(314) 772-5994

Venice Cafe is a unique watering hole located just a stone's throw from the Anheuser-Busch brewery. Stepping into the bar's Caribbean-inspired patio is like entering a courtyard filled with imagination. The walls are covered with colorful mosaics and you're surrounded by lush greenery and an eclectic mix of artwork. Artists, craftspeople, and fans of the eclectic style come by to exchange ideas, have a drink, and check out the latest additions to the landscape of mosaics, buttons, bottle caps, and "found art." Many even contribute to the growing expanse of funky-cool decor, which makes all involved feel like they have contributed something artistic to "their" bar. The bar has live entertainment almost every night, ranging from a rather avant-garde open-mike night to good old-fashioned house parties on the weekends. The bands that play here are as eclectic as the artwork—and the patrons. Closed Sunday.

MIDTOWN

Concert Venues

CHAIFETZ ARENA
1 South Compton Avenue
(314) 977-5000
www.thechaifetzarena.com

Located on the campus of Saint Louis University (SLU), Chaifetz Arena is a 10,600-seat venue that plays host to approximately 100 sporting and theatrical events each year. In addition to serving as the home court for SLU's basketball and volleyball teams, the venue holds trade shows, commencement ceremonies, and concerts by such artists as Barry Manilow, Stevie Nicks, and Carrie Underwood.

THE FOX THEATRE
527 North Grand Boulevard
(314) 534-1111
www.fabulousfox.com

The Fox originally opened as a vaudeville palace in 1929, and today it presents live entertainment with superstars, Broadway shows, family shows, and concerts. From musicals such as The Music Man and The Full Monty to family-friendly shows such as The Lion King and The Wiggles, the Fox is an excellent place to see a show. Past acts at the Fox have included such performers as Norah Jones, B. B. King, Jackson Browne, Steely Dan, and Kathy Griffin.

THE SHELDON CONCERT HALL
3648 Washington Boulevard
(314) 533-9900
www.sheldonconcerthall.org

Built in 1912, the Sheldon hosts a variety of concerts. The 702-seat hall is the site of more than 300 events each year, including jazz, folk, and classical music from some of the world's finest musicians. The Sheldon also presents family concerts, educational programs, and daytime Coffee Concerts during certain times of the year. Notes from Home is a popular series of weeknight performances that showcases local artists playing all styles of vocal and instrumental jazz, classical,

i In the early 1960s Gaslight Square was born. This thriving art colony and entertainment district, centered around Olive and Boyle Streets, offered more than 40 shops and restaurants, and featured jazz, blues, Dixieland, folk music, comedy, original dramas, and poetry readings. Before it closed down in the 1970s, it was considered comparable to New Orleans's famed Bourbon Street and New York's Greenwich Village.

folk, blues, and gospel. The venue is known for its outstanding acoustics, which some performers have described as "acoustically perfect."

Live Music

JAZZ AT THE BISTRO
3536 Washington Avenue
(314) 531-1012
www.jatb.org

The Bistro, also located in the Grand Center Arts & Entertainment District, is St. Louis's premier jazz venue. The club features a stellar lineup of the finest national and international jazz artists in a charming, intimate setting. The club has hosted such noted performers as Jane Monheit, Jeremy Davenport, Bucky Pizzarelli, Diana Krall, and hometown hero Jeremy Davenport. Open Wednesday through Saturday only, the club offers two sets: one at 8:30 p.m. and a second at 10:15 p.m.

CENTRAL WEST END

Bars and Pubs

CAFE EAU
Chase Park Plaza Hotel
212 North Kingshighway
(314) 454-9000
www.chaseparkplaza.com

Cafe Eau is one of St. Louis's most popular nightspots, and it's known for its top-notch martinis and specialty drinks, as well as an eclectic menu for breakfast, lunch, and dinner. Two of the more popular specialty 'tinis are the Eau Get Up (vanilla vodka, Bailey's, caramel syrup, and a shot of espresso) and the raspberry chocolate martini (Godiva white and dark chocolate liqueurs, vanilla vodka, and Chambord). The bar does feature some live entertainment, but this colorful and contemporary watering hole is more of a "scene" to be seen in than a live-music venue.

DRESSEL'S PUB
419 North Euclid Avenue
(314) 361-1060

This pub has been an anchor of the Central West

End neighborhood for more than two decades and continues to offer a welcome change from the usual bar scene. Its stained-glass windows and decor dedicated to paying homage to famous composers and writers give the place an almost Ivy League feel, and the regulars still like to engage in the ever-dwindling art of conversation. For those seeking further respite—or an impressive selection of single malt scotches—take a trip up the circular wooden staircase and visit the pub-within-a-pub called, appropriately, the Pub Above. Dressel's is open daily, and the Pub Above is open Thursday through Saturday. The pub also hosts live music on occasion.

TOM'S BAR & GRILL
20 South Euclid Avenue
(314) 367-4900
www.tomsbarandgrill.com

Tom's is one of the most comfortable and laid-back establishments in the Central West End. Whether you want to check out the big game on TV or talk sports with friends, this cozy tavern is the perfect place. Part of the charm of this casual eatery is its furnishings. When the bar was built in the mid-1970s, the original Tom went around to old buildings throughout the area and procured the antique wood fixtures and furnishings that make up the restaurant's decor. An extensive menu features burgers, sandwiches, and other great pub grub, along with plenty of ice-cold adult beverages. Open daily.

Dancing

CLUB VIVA
408 North Euclid
(314) 361-0322
www.clubviva.20m.com

Viva, in the Central West End neighborhood, is a spicy, multicultural, and intergenerational addition to the local club scene. Open Tuesday through Saturday, Club Viva offers live Latin, reggae, and hip-hop dance music, as well as a mix of salsa and merengue sounds. Free salsa dancing lessons are offered on Thursday and Saturday.

SOUTH/SOUTHWEST

Bars and Pubs

MILO'S BOCCE GARDEN
5201 Wilson Avenue
(314) 776-0468
www.milosboccegarden.com

Milo's is a neighborhood bar that doubles as a family-friendly restaurant during the day and into the early evening hours. The front room handles the restaurant chores, although the hearty wooden bar anchors almost one entire wall. Behind the bar is a game room where patrons can play foosball, darts, and assorted video games. It's what's in the backyard, however, that makes Milo's different from all the other neighborhood bars in the area: Bocce courts are located on a large enclosed patio area that is about the same size as the entire interior of the bar and restaurant. Bocce, Italian lawn bowling, is fun to watch and easy to play. And, most importantly, you only need one hand to play, which leaves your other hand free to hold your beer. Closed Sunday.

O'CONNELL'S PUB
4652 Shaw Avenue
(314) 773-6600

Located just across the street from The Hill neighborhood, O'Connell's relocated to its current location in 1972. The pub was one of the most popular bars in St. Louis's legendary entertainment district called Gaslight Square. Today, the clubby pub features almost all of the original woodwork and fixtures, including the beveled glass windows and the bell bronze chandeliers that hung in the Belgian exhibition hall at the 1904 World's Fair. Modern day patrons choose from a menu of beers, wines, Irish Whiskeys, and Single Malt Scotch. Open daily.

POP'S BLUE MOON
5249 Pattison Avenue
(314) 776-4200
www.popsbluemoon.com

Pop's Blue Moon hosts live local bands six nights a week, and on Tuesday nights, it's open-jam night for anyone who wants to play. The building that houses the small, family-owned bar has been around since the end of Prohibition, and the current owners have done a nice job of updating it without losing the original charm. Great local blues, folk, and "soul funk" bands play here, so check them out. Friendly service, creative cocktails, and a respectable beer list make this bar a comfortable place to visit. Closed Sunday.

THE ROYALE
3132 South Kingshighway
(314) 772-3600
www.theroyale.com
The Royale is a destination of choice for those who enjoy debating politics, poetry, and policy— or just about any other intellectual endeavor. Specialty cocktails are testaments to St. Louis's political past and present, with many named for some of the city's most recognizable neighborhoods. Try the Forest Park Southeast (Tanqueray, fresh orange and grapefruit juice), the Cherokee Street (tequila, Cointreau, fresh lime juice, a touch of sugar, served straight, with a sugar and salted rim) and the South Side Snob (Maker's Mark, Stolichnaya Orange, triple sec, and a splash of orange). A distinctive food menu draws in the crowds as well. Open daily.

Concert Venues
FOCAL POINT
2720 Sutton Avenue, Maplewood
(314) 781-4200
www.thefocalpoint.org
Focal Point showcases traditional and original folk music concerts, with 55 to 60 concerts held a year. On non-concert evenings, dancers take to the venue's maple hardwood floor for lively nights of swing, Cajun, and zydeco dancing, along with special nights dedicated to Argentine tango or English country dance groups. The venue also hosts a number of acoustic jams, poetry nights and improvisational theater presentations throughout the year.

Dancing
CLUB LA ONDA
4920 Northrup Avenue
(314) 772-0877
www.myspace.com/clublaonda
Located on The Hill, La Onda offers hot Latin sounds and a variety of world music. The club serves up Viernes Calientes every Friday night with Mexican music from local DJ La Raza. On Saturday nights it's Musica Nortena en Vivo, live, authentic Mexican music. Open Friday and Saturday only. Eighteen and up to enter.

Live Music
CASA LOMA BALLROOM
3354 Iowa Avenue
(314) 664-8000
www.casalomaballroom.com
For more than 70 years, the Casa Loma has been a landmark of live entertainment, including music and dancing. From the early days with Glenn Miller, Benny Goodman, and Frank Sinatra, this unique ballroom has been the place to go and dance in St. Louis. Today the ballroom features some touring groups, along with top-name bands from throughout the area. Dances and dancing lessons range from ballroom and rock 'n' roll to old-school Imperial swing dancing, and the venue features a calendar of special events including Mardi Gras balls, salsa dances, and private parties.

THE FAMOUS BAR
5213 Chippewa Street
(314) 832-2211
www.thefamousbar.com
Located in a mostly residential area on Chippewa Street, the Famous Bar is continuing a neighborhood tradition. Its location has been a tavern of one type or another for more than 70 years, so the current "loungey" version is also stocked with lots of history and charm. On Friday and Saturday nights, there's live music from local bands, and you can usually join in a game of pool. In addition to its signature Bloody Marys, the bar stocks

an extensive selection of imported and domestic beers, along with an assortment of wines. Open until 1:30 a.m., Monday through Saturday.

LEMMONS BASEMENT BAR
5800 Gravois Avenue
(314) 481-4812
www.myspace.com/lemmons

If you like your rock 'n' roll as gritty and as basic as it gets, then make sure you catch one of the live shows here. A former southside mainstay eatery, Lemmons has been transformed into one of the best places to catch "no-name" bands making the rounds and paying their dues on the road. The decor is somewhat of a frat house/living room combination, and the place gives new meaning to the phrase "no frills." But it's a great place to hear some barroom rock 'n' roll on Friday and Saturday nights and the pizza ain't bad either. Other events include film "feastivals" (with free pizza buffet), card tournaments, Trivia Nights, and DJ spins. Closed Sunday.

MAPLEWOOD

Bars and Pubs

BOOGALOO
7344 Manchester Road, Maplewood
(314) 645-4803
www.boogaloostl.com

Boogaloo's bar swings—literally. Well, the bar itself is pretty solid, but the bar stools certainly swing. They're hung from sturdy cables in the ceiling, and each "swing" has a pole attached to the underside for a little added support for those who might feel a little uneasy swaying with their cocktails. The eclectic bar and colorful atmosphere makes for a unique experience, but it's one you will enjoy. Boogaloo's DJ spins include everything from reggae and Latin house to soul and dance "oldies" from the '80s and '90s, Tuesday through Saturday nights.

SCHLAFLY BOTTLEWORKS
7260 Southwest Avenue, Maplewood
(314) 241-BEER
www.schlafly.com

Schlafly's brewing and bottling facility, Schlafly Bottleworks, is located in nearby Maplewood, a fun and funky neighborhood that is enjoying a resurgence among artists. The Bottleworks currently includes an indoor bar, retail shop, full-service restaurant, and an outdoor beer garden. There's live music on Friday, Saturday, and Sunday. Brewery tours are available daily. The bar also hosts some unique "movie nights" and film series throughout the year.

THE LOOP/CLAYTON

Bars and Pubs

DELMAR RESTAURANT AND LOUNGE
6235 Delmar Boulevard
(314) 725-6565

Delmar offers upscale, contemporary cuisine in a plush—yet relaxed—setting. The menu includes a host of fine wines, classic cocktails, and specialty martinis, while the musical lineup includes some of St. Louis's finest jazz musicians on Friday, Saturday, and Sunday nights. The restaurant and bar are both open late, with alcohol available until 3:00 a.m. The DJ spins rock during the late-night hours.

HALO BAR
6161 Delmar Boulevard
(314) 726-6161
www.thepageant.com/halo.html

The Halo Bar, tucked beneath The Pageant marquee and between the club's east and west entrance doors, is a sleek and funky neighborhood watering hole that serves as a "holding pen" of sorts for the club's preshow crowds. Even when there isn't a show at the Pageant, the Halo Bar is a top-notch, no-frills cocktail bar. The music selection is as eclectic as the clientele, as it's "bartender's choice." DJ spins take place on Saturday and Sunday from 10:00 p.m. to 2:30

a.m. On show nights, the bar fills up with early arrivals between 6:00 and 7:00 p.m., as patrons are allowed early entry into the adjacent club. Because of the many general-admission shows that the concert club hosts, patrons take advantage of the chance to get in early and get a good seat. Open daily until 3:00 a.m.

i Check out art films, documentaries and classic movies at the Tivoli Theatre (6350 Delmar) in The Loop. Built in 1924, this classically restored theater is equipped with state-of-the-art equipment, three screens, and display cases filled with movie memorabilia. Call (314) 995–6270 for show times.

PIN-UP BOWL
6191 Delmar Boulevard
(314) 727-5555
www.pinupbowl.com

"What size bowling shoes would you like with that martini?" Not your usual bartender banter, but those are two topics of discussion at St. Louis's coolest hot spot. In 2004 Pin-Up Bowl was ranked as one of only 30 bars, clubs, and lounges worldwide to receive the *Condé Nast Traveler* "Hot Nights" award. In addition to pool tables, eight state-of-the-art bowling lanes, and an extensive cocktails menu, the kitschy kitchen serves up everything from Campbell's soup to Pop-Tarts. Open daily until 3:00 a.m. All ages are welcome until 9:00 p.m. After that, you've got to be 21 to roll in this alley.

Concert Venues

THE PAGEANT
6161 Delmar Boulevard
(314) 726-6161
www.thepageant.com

This 33,000-square-foot venue features state-of-the-art lighting and sound systems and excellent sight lines no matter where you choose to watch the show. The 1,500-seat club has become a favorite place to see a variety of regional and national touring acts ranging from folk to rock to hip-hop and jazz. Such diverse headliners as Emmylou Harris, Ludacris, Keb' Mo', the Neville Brothers, and Bela Fleck have played The Pageant.

i Chuck Berry, the "Father of Rock 'n' Roll," still rocks the house each month at The Duck Room. Tickets go fast, so check out www.blueberryhill.com for the latest information.

Gay and Lesbian Bars

ATTITUDES
4100 Manchester Road
(314) 534-0440

This small neighborhood bar caters to lesbians but hosts a C&W night for "the boys" and is straight-friendly. Attitudes features a pub, cafe, conversation area, and dance floor, with karaoke, pool tables, TVs, and special events including the occasional drag show. Closed Sunday and Monday.

COMPLEX
3515 Chouteau Avenue
(314) 772-2645
www.complexnightclub.com

The Complex bar is reputed to be one of the most outstanding "alternative" clubs in St. Louis, and the patrons say the laid-back nature of the bar contributes to a comfortable overall atmosphere for anyone looking to party and who's willing to do so with an open mind and attitude. There are DJs spinning tunes and an expansive dance floor, along with a separate game room and five bars throughout the club. Closed Monday and Tuesday.

NOVAK'S BAR & GRILL
4121 Manchester Road
(314) 531-3699
www.novaksbar.com

Novak's bills itself as a gay and lesbian bar that is straight-friendly, and due to the fact that it is regularly voted one of the top lesbian bars in

St. Louis, it must be doing something right. The casual bar and grill features a menu of burgers and various appetizers, offers karaoke on Wednesday and Sunday nights, and has a regular lineup of live entertainment, including drag shows on Thursday and Saturday nights. Open daily at 4:00 p.m.

Live Music

BLUEBERRY HILL
6504 Delmar Boulevard
(314) 727-0880
www.blueberryhill.com

Blueberry Hill is a St. Louis landmark filled with pop culture memorabilia that is worth a trip in itself. The restaurant/bar is also home to The Duck Room, which hosts regional and national bands almost every night of the week. In addition to such artists as Marc Broussard, Todd Snider, and the Bottle Rockets, Rock 'n' Roll Hall of Famer Chuck Berry plays here monthly and his shows usually sell out fast. Tickets are available via www.ticketmaster.com, or you can buy them from a bartender. Advance tickets are available until an hour before show time and can be purchased "at the door" as you enter the Duck Room.

CICERO'S RESTAURANT AND ENTERTAINMENT PLEX
6691 Delmar Boulevard
(314) 862-0009
www.ciceros-stl.com

Cicero's is a haven for up-and-coming local and touring bands of all genres, seven nights a week. In addition to a late-night food menu full of pub grub, Cicero's stocks more than 100 bottled imported and domestic beers, as well as a staggering 50 beers available on tap. Some shows welcome "all ages," but call first to confirm.

RED CARPET LOUNGE AT BRANDT'S
6525 Delmar Boulevard
(314) 727-3663
www.brandtscafe.com

Located inside Brandt's Market and Cafe, the Red Carpet Lounge features mostly local performers,

including popular songstress Erin Bode, former Gaslight Square regular Jeanne Trevor, Hugh "Peanuts" Whalum, and Latin sensation Javier Mendoza. Occasionally the club will host national artists such as Kirk Whalum, or New Orleans alto sax man Loren Pickford. There's live music on most nights, and a late night food menu as well.

RIDDLE'S PENULTIMATE CAFE AND WINE BAR
6307 Delmar Boulevard
(314) 725-6985
www.riddlescafe.com

Riddle's quite possibly could be the ultimate cafe and wine bar due to its comfortable environment and non-pretentious staff. The cafe's varied food menu seems dwarfed by the number of beer options (more than 50) and wine choices (more than 350). Throw in some free live music from an eclectic array of local bands, and those numbers could quite possibly add up to ultimate status. Bands range from jazz and blues to boogie-woogie, so the entertainment is as diverse as the menu. No cover charge. Closed Monday.

WEST COUNTY

Bars and Pubs

BACKSTREET JAZZ AND BLUES
610 Westport Plaza, Maryland Heights
(314) 878-5800
www.backstreetclub.com

This eclectic music hall seems a bit out of place in the suburbs, but it holds its own when it comes to live music. In spite of an occasional karaoke

i For a complete list of live music and other entertainment options, pick up a copy of the Riverfront Times. The free weekly newspaper, available at most restaurants, hotels, and office buildings throughout the region, features an extensive listing of who's playing where and what time the party starts. Can't locate a copy? Log on to www.riverfronttimes.com.

night, most of the entertainment offered here is top-notch, with many of the area's most popular blues bands and jazz musicians making the trek westward to play at Backstreet. Open 8:00 p.m. to 1:00 a.m. nightly.

OZZIE'S RESTAURANT & SPORTS BAR
645 Westport Plaza, Maryland Heights
(314) 434-1000
www.ozziesrestaurantandsportsbar.com
The former Cardinals shortstop and Hall of Famer's namesake eatery is one of the top places to watch a game in the region. There are two big-screen TVs and numerous other monitors of varying sizes located throughout the bar. In addition to a collection of Smith's Rawlings Gold Glove awards, the bar is decorated with all sorts of pro sports memorabilia from St. Louis teams and others around the world. Ozzie's is a family-friendly sports bar that serves excellent food at a reasonable price and offers a diverse lineup of domestic and imported beers.

PUJOLS 5 WESTPORT GRILL
342 Westport Plaza, Maryland Heights
(314) 439-0505
www.pujols5grill.com
Albert Pujols is the most beloved man in St. Louis these days, so it's only fitting that he have a restaurant named after him. But Albert and his wife, Deidre, are much more than just namesakes of this popular eatery. Both were very involved with creating the menu—Deidre provided her recipes for some of her husband's favorite foods—and Albert provided input on the decor, donating some of his numerous trophies and awards for display. The eatery features a high-tech sports bar with a state-of-the art audiovisual system and 32 LCD and plasma screens, with each table in the bar able to control a screen. Patrons can choose what game they watch, and the table's speaker lets them control the volume of the play-by-play.

Comedy Clubs

FUNNY BONE COMEDY CLUB
614 Westport Plaza, Maryland Heights
(314) 469-6692
www.myspace.com/funnybonestl
The Funny Bone showcases some of the nation's top comics in an intimate club setting. This location, part of the comedy club chain, enjoys a reputation as one of the most successful comedy operations in the country, and it was named one of *USA Today's* top 10 comedy clubs. Weekly shows include a house emcee, an opening act, and a headliner. Touring comics perform Wednesday through Sunday nights, with two shows on Friday and three shows on Saturday. Tuesday is open-mike night. Open nightly.

Concert Venues

THE FAMILY ARENA
2002 Arena Parkway, St. Charles
(636) 896-4200
www.familyarena.com
The Family Arena hosts a number of events each year, the majority of which are designed to appeal to family audiences. In addition to an assortment of ice shows and holiday events, the venue books some country-music artists, such as LeAnn Rimes, Keith Urban, and Phil Vassar, as well as a number of touring rock bands, stand-up comics and special events.

VERIZON WIRELESS AMPHITHEATER
14141 Riverport Drive, Maryland Heights
(314) 298-9944
www.riverport.com
Another popular concert venue that is still referred to by its pre-corporate sponsor name is the Verizon Wireless Amphitheater. Originally known as Riverport Amphitheatre, the outdoor venue brings in all types of live music shows. With 7,000 "covered" seats, the pavilion also has a lawn-seating area that can accommodate up to 13,000 music lovers. Headliners range from James Taylor and Toby Keith to Ozzy Osbourne and the

Dave Matthews Band. Parking fees are included in the ticket price, which should help speed up the parking process at this one-way-in-one-way-out venue, but it's a good idea to allow extra time to get into the show. And don't be in any huge rush to get out afterwards.

ℹ️ Looking to extend the party? Bars on the Missouri side of the river must close by 3:00 a.m., but nightlife on the Illinois side continues. The OZ Nightclub stays open until 5:00 or 6:00 a.m., while Pop's stays open 24/7, with live music from midnight to 5:30 a.m.

Live Entertainment

HOME NIGHTCLUB
1260 South Main Street, St. Charles
(636) 940-3707
www.homenightclubstl.com
Located inside the Ameristar Casino Resort Spa, Home is a lounge/dance club featuring decadent decor, state of the art audiovisual technology, a full bar, dance club, and unique special events that include appearances by celebrity guests. Everyone from Paris Hilton and Benji Madden to Jaime Pressly and DJ AM has mixed and mingled here, and it's a popular party spot even without the imported personalities. Reserve one of the oversized booths with Xbox systems. There's usually a line to get in on weekends.

iBAR HARRAH'S CASINO
777 Casino Center Drive, Maryland Heights
(314) 770-8100
www.stlnightscene.com
The iBAR, situated inside the Island Casino section of the Harrah's complex, features a full-service cocktail bar, stand-up blackjack gaming tables, and live entertainment. Patrons can enjoy nightly performances by the iBAR Dance Revue, which features a choreographed dance troupe and light show, all set to the rhythms of hot dance tunes. Open Thursday through Saturday nights.

TRAINWRECK SALOON
342 Westport Plaza, Maryland Heights
(314) 432-7222
www.trainwrecksaloon.com
Trainwreck Saloon is a popular happy-hour destination for West County workers and residents, along with visitors housed in one of Westport's many hotels. Nightly drink specials, interactive special events, live music, and a good-time atmosphere contribute to Trainwreck's overall inviting atmosphere. Beer lovers will appreciate the number of beer options, with a variety on tap, plus an assortment of domestic, microbrews, and imports, as well as a full bar and restaurant menu available seven days a week.

VOODOO CAFE & LOUNGE
Harrah's Casino
777 Casino Center Drive, Maryland Heights
(314) 770-8100
www.stlnightscene.com
VooDoo Cafe & Lounge is located in the heart of the Harrah's casino complex. The VooDoo features lots of action, including "flair bartenders"—those who put on a show while making your cocktail—live music, and cage dancers on Friday and Saturday nights. The lounge frequently brings in national bands, and has hosted such big names as Bo Diddley, Los Lobos, Martin Sexton, Jefferson Starship, Toots & The Maytals, and, yes, even Air Supply. There are also plasma screens and a 45-foot video screen that let you keep an eye on the big game. Open daily until 1:00 a.m.

OUT OF TOWN

Bars and Pubs

FAST EDDIE'S BON-AIR
1530 East Fourth Street, Alton, IL
(618) 462-5532
www.fasteddiesbonair.com
In 1921 Anheuser-Busch decided to open a drinking establishment in the picturesque river town of Alton, Illinois. A yellow brick building known as the Bon-Air was constructed right on the corner

of three streets at Fourth, Pearl, and Broadway. About 10 years later, Busch was forced to sell the tavern due to a change in the statutes that prohibited breweries from owning drinking establishments. Each weekend, Fast Eddie's features live entertainment, including such regional favorites as Planet Boogie, Spur, and Sable. Fast Eddie's attracts a lively, mostly blue-collar crowd, and the patrons like their beer cold and the music loud. It's usually packed on weekend nights, including Sunday. The bar doubled in size in 2008 and now features a spacious patio area. Live music Thursday through Saturday.

Country and Western Nightclubs

WILD COUNTRY
17 Gateway Drive, Collinsville, IL
(618) 346-6775
www.wildcountrynightclub.com
This dance hall is the area's biggest country and western nightclub, and it features a large dance floor and light show. The local TV show St. Louis Country is taped here on Thursday nights, with live bands playing on Friday and Saturday nights. The rest of the time, it's mainly DJs and dance tunes with a decidedly country flavor. Country line-dancing lessons are available on Wednesday evenings. Must be 18 and up to enter, 21 and over to drink. Closed Sunday through Tuesday.

Dancing

OZ NIGHTCLUB
300 Monsanto Avenue, Sauget, IL
(618) 274-1464
www.oznightclub.com
"The OZ," in nearby Sauget, Illinois, is one of those bars that seems to be just getting started when all of the other places are closing down for the night. For more than two decades, night owls and insomniacs have been sharing the dance floor with hip-hop, techno, and dance music fans from 10:00 p.m. to 6:00 a.m. nightly. (It closes at 9:00 a.m. Friday and Saturday.) In addition to tunes spun by various DJs in its main and VIP rooms, OZ frequently hosts special events.

Live Music

POP'S
1403 Mississippi Avenue, Sauget, IL
(618) 274-6720
www.popsrocks.com
Pop's is a 24/7 rock 'n' roll nightclub located across the river in Sauget, Illinois. This club specializes in live shows by reunited rock bands, local metal groups and tribute bands, but also brings in acts from other genres. Local bands take the stage around midnight Thursday, Friday, and Saturday nights, and DJs spin Top 40 dance mix tunes from midnight to 6:00 a.m. Sunday through Wednesday. Pop's has a large dance floor, two full bars, rows of pool tables, darts, NTN Trivia, Texas Hold 'em and video games to keep the patrons amused at all hours.

CASINOS

Riverboat gaming hit the St. Louis area like a firestorm in the mid-1990s, and while the actual "boat" aspect is mostly implied, casinos have proved to be a popular addition to the local entertainment scene. None of the boats actually cruise anymore—that was one of the original requirements for the facilities on the Illinois side of the Mississippi River—but no one seems to mind too much. Overall, there are six casinos located in the metropolitan area.

The Harrah's casino in west St. Louis County took over its next-door neighbor, the former Player's Casino, and turned the whole complex into one mega-casino with two separate themes. In fact, other than the themes, there are very few real differences in the St. Louis–area gaming facilities. You can find just about all of the same games and machines at all six casinos, and all will claim to have the "loosest slots" or boast the most winners. All the casinos offer free admission. Many of the venues offer restaurant and drink specials, along with a diverse assortment of live entertainment options, as well as free parking for high-rolling—and not-so-high-rolling—customers. So all that's left to do is to ask the big question: Do you feel lucky?

AMERISTAR CASINO ST. CHARLES
1260 Main Street, St. Charles
(636) 949-7777, (800) 325-7777
www.ameristarcasinos.com

The $360 million Ameristar Casino in nearby St. Charles boasts the largest selection of slot machines and table games in the St. Louis market. Docked on the Missouri River, the St. Charles venue features a 130,000-square-foot casino with more than 3,000 slot machines, nearly 100 table games, a live poker room, and Home, a hip and trendy nightclub. The property offers a wide variety of entertainment, dining, and casino gaming amenities, including seven restaurants that provide innovative selections at affordable prices. The Bottleneck Blues Bar hosts such name performers as .38 Special, Joan Jett and the Blackhearts, Bo Bice and Buddy Guy, along with comics Sinbad and Kathleen Madigan. There are also weekly karaoke nights and late-night dancing. Ameristar offers free valet and covered parking.

ARGOSY'S ALTON BELLE CASINO
1 Front Street, Alton, IL
(800) 711-GAME
www.argosycasinos.com/stlouis

Located about 25 minutes from downtown St. Louis, Argosy's is a themed floating casino complex on Alton's historic riverfront. Features include restaurants, lounges, live music, and dockside gaming with unlimited-stakes wagering, 22 hours a day, seven days a week. Gaming options include blackjack, craps, roulette, Caribbean stud, three-card and Let It Ride poker, video poker and keno, and slot machines. The first and third floors of the casino offer a diverse assortment of slot machines ranging from penny slots to $100 machines. The second floor features table games, additional slots, and a full-service bar. Food and beverage options include the Key West Bar, where guests can enjoy tropical drinks and the flavor of the Caribbean, and the Captain's Table Buffet, a multi-themed, all-you-can-eat buffet restaurant. The Captain serves up such specialties as prime rib, barbecue, seafood, and popular American, Italian, Asian, and Mexican delicacies. There's also a soup and salad bar along with fresh fruits, vegetables, pastas, and plates of pies, cakes, cookies, cheesecakes, and other sweet treats. Outfitters Grill is an in-house steak house serving juicy steaks, hamburgers, fish, and pasta dishes, while La Cantina–Snack Bar is a faster-food option for gamers on the go.

CASINO QUEEN
200 South Front Street, East St. Louis, IL
(618) 874-5000, (800) 777-0777
www.casinoqueen.com

On the other side of the river from downtown St. Louis, the Casino Queen offers a host of gaming, dining, and entertainment options. Originally a cruising casino, the facility is now land-based, and the location across from the Gateway Arch provides a spectacular view of the Arch and the St. Louis skyline. In addition to a full-service hotel, Casino Queen has more than 28,000 square feet of casino gaming space over three decks and features more than 1,000 slot and video poker machines. The facility claims to have the most liberal slot payouts and was rated by one Las Vegas newsletter as one of the top 10 casinos in the United States "where you're most likely to win." Those who prefer more interactive activities have plenty to keep them occupied as well, as the Queen offers high-stakes wagering with table limits from $2 to $2,000 on games like blackjack, craps, roulette, Caribbean stud, Let It Ride, and mini-baccarat. On-site restaurants include steaks and seafood at the Royal Table and pizza, sandwiches, snacks, and breakfast items at the Gazebo Cafe. In the Riverview Grill guests can enjoy lunch or dinner in a casual atmosphere, or breakfast, lunch, or dinner in the gardenlike setting of the Queen's Courtyard Buffet. The Casino Queen operates 22 hours a day, 7 days a week, and there's free admission, free parking, free downtown St. Louis shuttles, and no buy-in or wagering limits. There's also a full-service RV park on the property that features pull-through sites, full hookups, and 24 hour security.

HARRAH'S ST. LOUIS
777 Casino Center Drive, Maryland Heights
(314) 770-8100
www.harrahs.com

Harrah's St. Louis casino is actually two casinos in one. The enticing Island Casino reflects a more laid-back atmosphere, complete with waterfalls, giant fish tanks, and plenty of palm trees. Next door, Harrah's has a New Orleans–style casino decorated with beads, masks, and pizzazz galore.

Combined, the facility has more than 120,000 square feet of gaming space that includes 2,800 video poker and slot machines, nearly 100 table games, and a dedicated live poker room with 21 tables. Is all of that gaming making you hungry? You don't have to go far to feed your craving. Harrah's has eight very different eateries to choose from. Harrah's signature Range Steakhouse offers steaks, seafood, and a variety of popular wines in a refined atmosphere. Charlie Gitto's From the Hill serves up Italian-American delicacies from St. Louis's most flavorful neighborhood, and the Eat Up! Buffet includes more than 100 items for breakfast, lunch, and dinner. Moby's Fish Tales reels 'em in with signature dishes such as crab and lobster pasta, chicken Alfredo, southern catfish, and a number of tasty shrimp dishes. Club Aroma offers a selection of specialty coffees, pastries, soups, and hot sandwiches, and Jester's Deli features salads, sandwiches, and breakfast pastries. Ice-cream lovers can get their fix at Ben & Jerry's. In the VooDoo Cafe, guests can enjoy a specialty cocktail mixed by one of the "flair bartenders," grab a bite to eat, or watch the big game on one of the 14 plasma screens or the 45-foot video screen. The VooDoo, open dinner nightly and lunch and dinner on Saturday and Sunday, also features live entertainment on Thursday, Friday, and Saturday nights. The 455-room on-site hotel has 47 luxury suites and frequently offers "Stay & Play" packages that include special room rates, restaurant food comps, and other incentives.

LUMIÈRE PLACE
(314) 531-3030
www.lumiereplace.com

Lumière Place is a single-level, 75,000-square-foot casino featuring 2,000 slot machines, a dedicated 13-table poker room, VIP high-limit area and more than 40 table games. The complex also has seven on-site dining venues, retail shops, a nightclub, concert venue and Missouri's only Four Seasons hotel. The Lumière Link is a secure pedestrian walkway that connects the casino complex with the America's Center convention complex and the Edward Jones Dome. The casino's eateries range from the casual Burger Bar, Kitchen Buffet and Bistro, and Peet's Coffee and Tea to the upscale Sleek Steakhouse, Asia, and House of Savoy. Open all day, every day.

i **The President Casino on Laclede's Landing offers a free shuttle to and from downtown hotels. Check with the concierge or front desk staff for pick-up times.**

PRESIDENT CASINO
St. Louis Riverfront
(314) 622-3000, (800) 772-3647
www.presidentcasino.com
Docked on the Mississippi River at Laclede's Landing, the President Casino is housed in a shiny piece of St. Louis history from the early 1900s. The

Admiral, as it's been known since 1940, was actually built in 1907, and generations of St. Louisans have memories of entertaining days and nights spent aboard the former excursion craft. Today's patrons visit the boat in search of a little different kind of entertainment, and the riverboat gaming facility offers more than 1,000 slot machines, video poker and keno, table games, and a live poker room. In addition to gaming, the President has a daily all-you-can-eat buffet at the on-board eatery called the President's Buffet. There's a different theme each day, and it's open extended hours on the weekend. Another in-house option is the River's Edge Deli, which offers a variety of deli sandwiches, pizza, hot dogs, salads, and desserts. Boarding times for the President are from 8:00 a.m. to 4:00 a.m. on weekdays and around the clock on weekends. Free parking is available.

SHOPPING

St. Louis has always been a destination for those looking to buy, sell, or trade. Pioneers journeying west often stopped for supplies in St. Louis, which started out as a fur trappers' trading post. The city eventually became a regional hub of shopping activity. St. Louis outfitted fashionable Victorian ladies, mountain men, riverboat gamblers, and long lines of wagon trains in the 18th and 19th centuries, and even explorers Lewis and Clark prepared for their historic expedition by buying their supplies in St. Louis.

Today's explorers can find sophisticated styles, bargains, and hard-to-find items throughout the area. From clothes with big-city style to retro fashions, St. Louis probably has a store carrying what you're looking for. A host of one-of-a-kind shops located throughout St. Louis's historic neighborhoods feature beautiful antiques, artsy galleries, and crafty boutiques. Or, you can remember your time in St. Louis by purchasing some jewelry, a botanical treasure, or an abstract piece of art from one of the dozens of museum and attraction gift shops.

Plus, if you like what you eat in St. Louis—and you will—you won't want to go home without some tasty reminders of the good food you'll find here. The Schnucks grocery store chain is a good place to find low prices on a variety of St. Louis–specific goodies, including pasta sauces and salad dressings from some of the popular Italian restaurants in The Hill neighborhood. Beer lovers might want to take home a pack of St. Louis–brewed Schlafly beer, a microbrew that's sold in dozens of area restaurants and bars. You can find Schlafly favorites at area grocery stores as well, along with many of its specialty and seasonal brews.

So, whatever you're looking for, you can find it in St. Louis. Maybe you should bring an empty suitcase with you so your cool souvenirs don't get squashed during the ride home.

ANTIQUES SHOPS

ANTIQUE CENTER OF ST. LOUIS
4732 McPherson Avenue
(314) 367-0588
www.antiquecenterofstlouis.com
The Antique Center is a 10,000-square-foot store—one store, not a mall—that's filled with continental, Italian, French, and English furniture and chandeliers from the 18th, 19th, and early 20th centuries. The owners stock the items they have a penchant for, including bombé chests, armoires, country buffets, English sideboards, and other beautifully appointed furniture pieces and accessories for the home. Nestled in among the grand homes of the Central West End, this store is like a museum of the neighborhood's interiors. Open Monday through Saturday; Sunday by appointment only. The owner lives above the shop and is happy to accommodate visitors.

BRILLIANT ANTIQUES
8107 Maryland Avenue, Clayton
(314) 725-2526
www.brilliantantiques.com
This popular Clayton antiques shop always has a stock of continental and English accessories on hand, including silver, brass, copper, pottery and porcelain decorative items; fireplace tools; candlesticks; picture frames; dresser jars; and antique boxes. Brilliant Antiques carries Majolica, "Blue and White," and Staffordshire items, along with an excellent selection of vintage gifts for the hard-to-buy-for folks on your gift list. The shop offers free gift wrap and can ship your purchases just about anywhere. Closed Sunday.

CENTRAL WEST END NEIGHBORHOOD (CWE)
Euclid and Maryland, McPherson, and
Laclede Avenues
(314) 367-2220
www.thecwe.com

This cosmopolitan neighborhood near Forest Park features fine dining, cafes, galleries, and specialty shops amid turn-of-the-20th-century buildings. It's also a great place to people-watch, and several special events take place here throughout the year (see the Annual Events chapter). There are three main retail areas along the CWE's "main drag," Euclid Avenue. Retro-maniacs and antiques lovers will find an abundance of possibilities in the shops located at the intersections of Euclid and McPherson, Euclid and Maryland, and Euclid and Laclede Avenues.

CHEROKEE ANTIQUE ROW
2125 Cherokee Street
(314) 776-6410
www.cherokeeantiquerow.net

Cherokee Antique Row offers six blocks of shops full of antiques and collectibles of all types. The historic neighborhood, located about 10 minutes south of downtown, has been a shopping hub for treasure hunters since 1965, and the prices here are usually very reasonable. Even if you're not buying, Cherokee Street is a fun adventure that illustrates Americans' obsession with "stuff." The selections at the 30-plus stores range from "fine" to "funky" to just plain funny. There's even a saxophone museum and repair shop.

THE NEON LADY
1926 Cherokee Street
(314) 771-7506
www.neonlady.com

Open for more than 30 years, the Neon Lady carries an assortment of custom and collectible neon lights, antiques, and treasures like chrome art deco telephones and toasters, old metal coolers, lunchboxes, Betty Boop figurines, and Mickey Mouse glasses. An official member of the Anheuser-Busch Collectors' Club (a big deal

around these parts), the store also has a large collection of new, rare, and secondary collectible beer steins.

QUINTESSENTIAL ANTIQUES
4501 Chouteau Avenue
(314) 531-9701
www.antiquesstlouis.com

This family-owned antiques store offers an eclectic array of collectibles, ranging from architectural items and furniture to books and glassware. This comfortable, non-pretentious store also has a variety of exquisite tables, bedroom sets, wardrobes, and bric-a-brac gathered from buying trips across the country. The atmosphere is cordial and cooperative, and the prices are extremely reasonable. Open the first Friday and Saturday of the month or by appointment.

ROTHSCHILD'S ANTIQUES & HOME FURNISHINGS
398 Euclid Avenue
(314) 361-4870
www.rothschildsstl.com

Rothschild's has been a centerpiece of the Central West End neighborhood for decades, and it offers a number of antiques-related services in addition to an extensive collection of stuff. The shop offers quality services in repair, refinishing, and appraisals, as well as a beautiful selection of furnishings and accessories. The diverse inventory includes rustic, Asian, and contemporary pieces, as well as statuary, candles, china, vases, stained glass, chandeliers, and wrought iron.

TFA—THE FUTURE ANTIQUES
3229 Morgan Ford Road
(314) 865-1552
www.tfa50s.com

TFA specializes in furniture and accessories from the '50s to the '70s and keeps a hearty stock of groovy yet affordable lamps, jewelry, wall clocks, vintage clothing and hats. You can also pick up some Austin Powers-inspired barware and retro kitchen items. From avocado-colored princess phones and plastic record players to minimalist vinyl couches and 1950s style dinette sets, TFA has just the right decor for that hipster haven you call home. Closed Tuesday.

BOOKSTORES

BIG SLEEP BOOKS
239 North Euclid Avenue
(314) 361-6100
www.bigsleepbooks.com
Big Sleep carries a variety of fiction and nonfiction works, but the main genres here are mystery, detective, and espionage books. There's also a great collection of new and used soft-cover and hardback books in stock, including rare first editions and signed first printings. A knowledgeable staff stands ready to help you find your favorite authors, or even to suggest a new favorite.

HAMMOND'S BOOKS
1939 Cherokee Street
(314) 776-4737, (800) 776-4732
www.hammondsbooks.com
Hammond's is the ultimate place for out-of-print, rare, and hard-to-find books. The store features a massive collection of reading material stored among reproduction art deco treasures and the always-appreciated espresso bar. Bibliophiles can get lost in the intriguing stacks or take the high-tech approach and search the entire collection via an in-store database. Can't find what you're looking for? Hammond's can search a computerized database that lists thousands of books and bookstores across the country at no charge. Open Tuesday through Saturday.

LEFT BANK BOOKS
399 North Euclid Avenue
(314) 367-6731
www.left-bank.com
A full-service bookstore of new and used books, Left Bank is one of the last independently owned bookstores in the region. In addition to a diverse selection of new fiction and nonfiction titles, the neighborhood bookstore also operates a small art gallery that features local artists. Left Bank hosts frequent book-signing events, including such celebrated authors as Hillary Clinton, Alan Alda, John Danforth, and many others. And, for that obligatory cup of java, the shop also operates Cafe Danielle, a cozy coffee shop that serves various coffee beverages, sandwiches, and other light fare. In 2009, a second 5,500-square-foot location opened in downtown St. Louis at 321 North 10th Street. Open daily.

SUBTERRANEAN BOOKS
6275 Delmar Boulevard
(314) 862-6100
www.subterraneanbookstore.com
From high culture to subculture, this longtime staple of The Loop neighborhood stocks a full range of new, used, and rare books in a comfortable, non-pretentious setting. Due to the ever-changing inventory, you never know what you'll find among the stacks, which include lots of history and pop culture choices, as well as biographies, literature, and science fiction. Open daily.

BOUTIQUES/SPECIALTY SHOPS

20:08 GALLERY SAINT LOUIS
2008 Cherokee Street
(314) 772-2008
www.gallerysaintlouis.com
One of St. Louis's newest and most respected photographic fine art galleries, 20:08 Gallery offers museum-quality landscapes, nature and cityscapes by award-winning artists from the St. Louis region. Open Saturday and Sunday weekly, and on weekdays by appointment.

ALL-AMERICAN COLLECTIBLES
6510 Chippewa Street
(314) 352-7700
www.aac-mo.com
If comics and collectibles are your game, then you'll enjoy a trip to southwest St. Louis for a look at all of the goodies at AAC. There's a large selection of items to choose from, including vintage and current collectible games and comic books, card games, toys, and trading cards. If you're look-

ing for a gift or keepsake for that little boy or girl who never grew up, chances are good that you can find something here. Located two blocks east of Ted Drewes frozen custard stand.

IRON AGE STUDIOS
6309 Delmar Boulevard
(314) 725-1499
www.ironagestudio.com
Looking for something a little more permanent to take home with you from St. Louis? Iron Age Studios, located in The Loop neighborhood, is one of the region's most popular body art studios. In addition to a clean and friendly environment, the colorful shop features male and female tattoo artists and piercers and a complete selection of body jewelry. You must have a photo ID to get tattooed or pierced. Open daily.

PHOENIX RISING
6331 Delmar Boulevard
(314) 862-0609
www.shopphoenixrising.com
Phoenix Rising offers a diverse selection of one-of-a-kind handcrafted jewelry, unusual gemstones, whimsical characters, metal works, and clocks, along with a variety of bath products, candles, books, toys, and cards. It's a great place to find unusual gift items or accessories that will add a splash of color to your home decor. Open daily.

SAXQUEST
2114 Cherokee Street
(314) 664-1234
www.saxquest.com
Located in the Historic Cherokee Antique Row, Saxquest specializes in buying, selling, trading, repairing, and restoring vintage and professional saxophones. Run by a couple of professional musicians, the shop has an on-site master craftsman and features the only dedicated saxophone museum in the U.S.

UMA, URBAN MATERIALS + ACCESSORIES
313 North 11th Street
(314) 241-9990
www.iloveuma.com

UMA is ideally located in the downtown loft district, as its furniture and lifestyle accessories are a perfect match for the sleek, contemporary loft developments all around the store. In addition to various gifts, spa products, and designer handbags, UMA offers lighting options, vases by Jonathan Adler, candles from the Frank Lloyd Wright collection, and the increasingly popular Chilewich floor coverings. Open Monday through Saturday year-round, plus Sundays during December.

CLOTHING STORES

BEVERLY'S HILL
1309 Washington Avenue
(314) 621-1633
www.123underwear.com
One of the new unique boutiques that have popped up in St. Louis's newly revitalized downtown, Beverly's Hill showcases the latest in Paris fashion, women's intimates, swimwear, and activewear. Closed Sunday.

BOUTIQUE CHARTREUSE
8135 South Big Bend Boulevard
(314) 458-2410
www.boutiquechartreuse.com
This Webster Groves-based shop, the only eco-fashion boutique in the area, offers "green" and sustainably-made clothing and accessories for the fashion-conscious woman. The shop features items from such designers as Eco-Ganik, Passenger Pigeon, Del Forte, Habitude, and many more. Closed Sunday.

LEE J.
1000 Washington Avenue
(314) 241-0440
www.leejfashions.com
This trendy and comfortable boutique features dressy and casual clothing, shoes, and accessories for men and women. In addition to offering brands such as Kenneth Cole, Coogi, French Connection, Gucci, and Calvin Klein. Lee J. and his staff are always willing to help customize your own hot look and keep you apprised of the latest worldwide fashion trends. Lee J. is one of the

latest additions to the hip and chic shops in the Loft District, aka Washington Avenue.

NCJW COUNCIL SHOP
8612 Olive Boulevard
(314) 692-8141
www.ncjwstl.org

The National Council of Jewish Women's resale shop offers new and gently used clothing and accessories for men, women, and children, along with household items and electronics. Options range from bridesmaid dresses and giftware to chandeliers and handbags. Additionally, the store features a number of special sales and preview events throughout the year, such as its popular Couturier Sale, which features designer merchandise at bargain prices. Closed Sunday.

SCHOLARSHOP
8211 Clayton Road
(314) 725-3456;
7930 Big Bend Boulevard, Webster Groves
(314) 961-2525
www.scholarshopstl.org

The ScholarShops are upscale resale shops chock-full of clothing and accessories for men, women, and children. Thanks to the Clayton Road store's location on the fringe of Ladue, one of St. Louis's toniest suburbs, it gets a regular influx of high-end castoffs from the area residents. Here you'll find everything from designer sportswear to formal wear and ball gowns. The shop on Big Bend Boulevard also benefits from its location in the upper middle class suburb of Webster Groves. Proceeds from both of the shops' sales go to a scholarship foundation for less fortunate students in the area.

TANTRUM
6370 Delmar Boulevard
(314) 783-0527
www.tantrumstl.com

Tantrum brings in trendy—yet affordable—men's and women's fashions from international designers such as French Connection, Itsus, Silver Jeans, JLo, Fire Crown, and TankFarm. The store also offers the latest West Coast styles and assorted upscale fashions for those who strive to dress to impress.

CHILDREN'S CLOTHING

CITY SPROUTS
6354 Delmar Boulevard
(314) 726-9611
www.citysprouts.com

Located in the über-hip University City area called The Loop, City Sprouts is "cootchie-cool" in its approach to clothing, furniture, bedding, toys, and gear for newborns, babies, and kids up to age six. The shop, recently named one of *Child* magazine's Top 100 Children's Stores in the country, features contemporary kids' wear from clothing lines such as Wry Baby and Tea, furniture by Nursery Works, and the popular European wooden toys by Haba. There's also a selection of gear for mom and dad, including "masculine" diaper bags from Diaper Dude. Open daily.

JILLYBEAN CHILDREN'S BOUTIQUE
9208 Clayton Road, Ladue
(314) 872-2988
www.jillybeanboutique.com

This fashionable shop specializes in stylish boys and girls fashions from Europe and various East and West Coast designers. In addition to dresses, pants, skirts, jeans, coats, and swimsuits in sizes newborn to 14, Jillybean features an assortment of baby gifts, diaper bags, infant bedding and clothing, hair accessories, shoes, and more. Closed Sunday.

ROBERTS BOYS SHOPS
9733 Clayton Road, Ladue
(314) 997-1770
www.robertsboysshop.com

Roberts Boys Shops (although there is only one location) is a family-owned clothing store that has been in St. Louis since 1947. The upscale shop features pricey—but very good quality—dress shirts, ties, jackets, pants, and footwear, along with casual clothing such as jeans, sweaters, and polo-style shirts. They carry slim, regular, and husky sizes 4–24, and feature prominent designers like Europa, Tommy Hilfiger, Mezzanote, Calvin, Perry Ellis, Nicole Miller, and Nautica. Alterations are free, and the staff makes sure that the young gentlemen leave their shop with properly fitted attire that will last—at least until they grow out of it. Open Monday through Saturday year-round and Sundays, September through April.

MEN'S CLOTHING

DEAN'S CLOTHIERS FOR THE BIG & TALL
1757 Clarkson Road, Chesterfield
(636) 532-1771
www.deansclothiers.com
This store, which specializes in casual wear and business attire for big and tall men, carries a variety of popular brand names, such as Cutter & Buck, Gant, Polo Ralph Lauren, Gitman Bros., Tundra, Burberry, and many others. Dean's Clothiers also carries Allen-Edmonds shoes, extra-long neckties, and a selection of business casual items and offers a variety of custom clothing services. Open daily.

SAVILE ROW CUSTOM CLOTHIERS
9727 Clayton Road
(314) 567-8500
Recognized as one of the country's top custom clothing businesses by *Town & Country* and *Cigar Aficionado* magazines, Savile Row specializes in fine men's clothing, including custom-made shirts, suits, and business and casual wear. Closed Sunday.

WOODY'S MEN'S SHOP
10411 Clayton Road, Frontenac
(314) 569-3272
This family-owned specialty shop promises to outfit a man with everything he needs, from custom-made suits and sport coats by Coppley to designer socks and Zenga shirts. From traditional to funky, this men's store has something for every personality and offers a selection that runs the gamut of tastes, styles, and quality. Woody's, the largest distributor of Robert Talbot ties and shirts

in the area, only deals with single-owner, non corporate suppliers, so their unique stock doesn't look like every other "off-the-rack" men's store. Plus, they're really a fun group. Enjoy a glass of wine or a beer while you shop—they frequently host tastings for their customers.

VINTAGE CLOTHING

ALICE'S VINTAGE CLOTHES
6370 Delmar Boulevard
(314) 361-4006
If you're in the market for vintage clothing, jewelry, purses, and other accessories from the 1920s to the 1970s, Alice's could have just what you're looking for. One of the few vintage stores that carries a large selection of clothing in a broad range of sizes, it specializes in threads from the '40s and '50s but has items from all six of the "official" retro decades. In addition to duds, the shop offers an extensive stock of antique hats and buttons, as well as one of the best selections of vintage jewelry in St. Louis. This is a place where vintage fanatics can easily lose an entire afternoon.

RAG-O-RAMA
6388 Delmar Boulevard
(314) 725-2760
www.ragorama.com
This vintage clothing shop is regularly voted "Best Place to Buy Used Clothing" in local readers' polls. Rag-O-Rama buys, sells, and trades current, classic, and vintage styles for men and women, as well as one-of-a-kind accessories, wigs, handbags, jewelry, sunglasses, and costumes. Open daily.

TAG
6314 Delmar Boulevard
(314) 721-1370
www.tag-stl.com
Timeless Authentic Garments (tag) offers a variety of men's and women's vintage fashions, ranging from T-shirts to formal wear. The shop offers vintage merchandise with a modern shopping experience and the owners are skilled at creat-

ing unique, fashionable outfits that incorporate something old with something new.

WOMEN'S CLOTHING

DAISY CLOVER
8146 Big Bend Boulevard, Webster Groves
(314) 962-4477
www.daisy-clover.com
This boutique's mantra is "Fashion; the best we can find, in sizes to fit the average woman," which happens to be misses sizes 2 through 12. Daisy Clover offers a variety of contemporary clothing, accessories, denim, outerwear, and footwear from designers including L.A.M.B., Big Buddha, Lilla P, Seychelles, JW Los Angeles, and Citizens of Humanity. In 2006 the shop was voted Best Women's Boutique by the readers of St. Louis Magazine. Open daily.

FEMME
7270 Manchester Road, Maplewood
(314) 781-6868
This trendy women's boutique features the hottest and hippest fashions from both coasts and Paris. In addition to its fresh styles, Femme offers a distinct collection of unique jewelry, purses, and accessories, along with assorted French soaps and lotions. Closed Sunday.

LAURIE SOLET
8228 North Forsyth Boulevard, Clayton
(314) 727-7467
www.lauriesolet.com
"Hometown girl goes Hollywood then returns to her roots to bring high style and fashion to St. Louis." That's basically the story of Laurie Solet, the founder of this fashionista hot spot. Her boutique offers high-quality clothing, beauty products, and accessories that are straight out of the pages of trendsetter mags like *InStyle, Lucky,* and *Vogue.* She includes togs from top name designers and up-and-coming design stars in her inventory, and features many lines that may be hard to find here in "fly-over country." Closed Sunday.

MACROSUN INTERNATIONAL
1310 Washington Avenue
(314) 421-6400
www.macrosun.com
MacroSun International offers fashion with a mission. The store earmarks a portion of its profits for Third World relief efforts and imports all of the handmade items from South Asia. The store's clothes target a more mature fashionista who still craves styles that are colorful as well as flattering. Fashion mavens are sure to find unique outfits and accessories, from vintage silk sundresses and mantra scarves to Chinese wrap pants and Burmese backpacks. There's a second location in The Loop (6273 Delmar; 314-726-0222). Closed Sunday.

MERLE FREED
9723 Clayton Road
(314) 997-3300
This upscale shop specializes in cutting-edge designer fashions. Merle Freed prides itself on having all of the hot new looks from catwalks around the world before they even make it to the department stores. Whether you're looking for something striking and casual or elegant and dressy, the shop will do whatever it takes to get you the clothes you need. It even offers after-hours appointments if the store hours don't mesh with your schedule, and it delivers to area hotels. Closed Sunday.

ZIEZO
6354 Delmar Boulevard
(314) 725-9602
www.myspace.com/ziezo
You'll find cutting-edge, up-to-the-minute fashions as well as accessories, shoes, and gifts here. Brand names include Triple 5 Soul, Miss Sixty, To The Max, Urban Outfitters, and the sporty-chic fashions by Forarina. Ziezo also carries a collection of decorative items, including trinkets from Asia, retro decor reminiscent of '50s-style Americana, and whatever else the hip thing is to have or to wear at the moment.

FARMERS' MARKETS

CLAYTON FARMERS' MARKET
North Central Avenue between Forsyth and
Maryland Avenues, Clayton
(314) 645-5807
www.ci.clayton.mo.

From June through October each year, the Clayton market brings a taste of country living to this St. Louis suburb every Saturday from 8:00 a.m. to noon. Located in the city's central business district, the market offers an array of locally grown fruits, vegetables, herbs, nuts, flowers and plants, as well as beef, lamb, and pork raised on sustainable farms. Activities include chefs' demonstrations, tours of farmers' booths and lectures about sustainable farming, and booths serving dishes made from the eggs, produce, and meat sold at the market.

MAPLEWOOD FARMERS' MARKET
Schlafly Bottleworks
7620 Southwest Avenue, Maplewood
(314) 241-BEER
www.schlafly.com

Every Wednesday from mid-May through late October, the Maplewood Farmers' Market takes place in the parking lot adjacent to the Schlafly Bottleworks. Vendors include area farmers who produce organic fruits and vegetables, free-range meat and poultry, seasonal herbs, and plants and flowers. You can also pick up homemade goodies like apple butter and jams. Open 4:00 to 7:00 p.m. only.

SOULARD FARMERS MARKET
Lafayette and Seventh Streets
(314) 622-4180
www.soulardmarket.com

Soulard Farmers Market is the last survivor of the once-numerous public markets in St. Louis. Established in 1779, the Soulard Market has evolved from just selling foodstuffs and become an enjoyable destination shopping experience. From Wednesday through Sunday of each week, neighborhood residents and out-of-town visitors can wander the aisles of the open-air market, gazing upon myriad bakery goods, meats, cheeses, produce, nuts, flowers, and more. Specialty goods range from apparel, spices, and soaps to souvenirs, crafts, incense—and maybe even a litter of puppies. This colorful and affordable outing will no doubt lead to a purchase of some sort—even if it's just a bite to eat or a cup of fresh-brewed coffee. Open year-round.

GARDEN SHOPS

THE BUG STORE
4474 Shaw Boulevard
(314) 773-9251

Located just down the street from the Missouri Botanical Garden is the Bug Store, a quaint and charming shop that sells a variety of outdoor accessories and whimsical gifts for gardeners and nature lovers. Oh yeah, and it sells bugs, too—but these bugs are actually beneficial to your lawn and garden. There are 30 types of insects for sale at the store, along with information and guidance on what types of bugs will work the best for your particular problem. The staff will also help you choose a custom "Bugscription," which includes the right assortment of bugs for use throughout the growing season. Open daily.

GARDEN GATE GIFT SHOP
4344 Shaw Boulevard
(314) 577-5137
www.mobot.org

The Missouri Botanical Garden has an on-site gift shop that offers all sorts of plant- and garden-related books, gifts, tools, and accessories for the avid gardener or casual flower enthusiast. There is a good selection of plant- and gardening-themed toys, experiments, and projects for the budding enthusiast, along with a seemingly endless collection of wind chimes, indoor and outdoor decorative items, and accessories designed to make gardening easier and more productive. There are also plenty of plants on sale, and the gift shop frequently hosts special seasonal plant sales. Open daily.

GIFTED GARDENER

8935 Manchester Road
(314) 961-1985
www.thegiftedgardener.com

This shop is more about gifts than actual gardens—there aren't a lot of green things growing and blooming around here—but there are plenty of gardening-related items on hand. And speaking of hands, the store offers various soaps and lotions designed to soothe that green thumb when necessary, along with gardening clogs, hand tools, and books on gardening. There's plenty of pretty garden-related stuff, too, like fountains, urns, porcelain and ceramic pots, sundials, shadow boxes, welcome mats, rain gauges, and outdoor thermometers. Open daily.

GRINGO JONES IMPORTS

4470 Shaw Boulevard
(314) 664-1666
www.gringojonesimports.com

A green-thumb neighbor to the Missouri Botanical Garden, Gringo Jones offers a variety of stone and metal yard ornaments, knickknacks, Talavera pottery, wrought-iron furniture, and items from Mexico. The store has inexpensive options to fully furnish a garden area or sun-room, including such unusual furnishings as a 9-foot-tall suit of armor and a Statue of Liberty light post. Open daily.

MUSIC STORES

EUCLID RECORDS

601 East Lockwood, Webster Groves
(314) 961-8978
www.euclidrecords.com

For more than 25 years, Euclid Records has filled a niche for music lovers who love nothing better than to spend an afternoon digging through stacks of records for "hidden treasures." The shop has expanded past its LP days and—in addition to new and used vinyl—now offers more than 6,000 square feet of new and used CDs, DVDs, books, and accessories, and feature rare and out-of-print records. Euclid's knowledgeable staff can answer almost any music-related question you can ask, and they offer great advice on essentials for your music collection. Open daily.

RECORD EXCHANGE

5320 Hampton Avenue
(314) 832-2249
www.recordexchangestl.com

Record Exchange is a haven for those who love to sort through used LPs, DVDs, cassette tapes, and CDs. The store, which occupies a building that formerly served as a branch of the St. Louis Public Library, buys and sells everything musical, and also stocks an impressive number of used VHS videotapes and books related to the worlds of music, movies, and TV. It's a great place to spend a rainy afternoon—or any afternoon for that matter. Open daily.

STREETSIDE RECORDS

10865 West Florissant Road
(314) 521-7610

Streetside Records, part of the Trans World Entertainment Corporation, features new/used CDs and DVDs, cassettes, concert tickets, accessories, and an opportunity to "try it before you buy it" at its various listening stations. Open daily.

VINTAGE VINYL

6610 Delmar Boulevard
(314) 721-4096
www.vintagevinyl.com

A locally owned, independent record store that boasts "America's largest collection of new/used CDs, LPs, and DVDs," Vintage Vinyl has more than 7,000 square feet of music and music-related T-shirts, posters, and accessories. The shop was voted "One of America's 10 Best Record Stores" by *Rolling Stone* magazine, and it is a perennial favorite among local voters in the annual weekly and daily newspapers' readers' polls. Vintage Vinyl also holds a number of CD-release concerts, signings and live music events, as well as other in-store activities that draw the crowds. Open daily.

OUTFITTERS/SPORTS SHOPS

ALPINE SHOP
440 North Kirkwood Road, Kirkwood
(314) 962-7715

1616 Clarkson Road, Chesterfield
(636) 532-7499
www.alpineshop.com

The Alpine Shop has been outfitting area climbers, backpackers, hikers, campers, paddlers, cyclists, snowboarders, and alpine and cross-country skiers for more than 30 years. Both locations carry every brand of gear imaginable—from Alps Mountaineering to Motorola to Yakima—and they offer how-to classes for beginner and intermediate recreationalists. In addition to a full-service bike shop, the stores offer a number of repair and fitting services, like ski and snowboard tuning, custom footbed fitting/production, and seasonal gear rental for skiing, snowboarding, and camping. Open daily.

BASS PRO SHOPS SPORTSMAN'S WAREHOUSE
1365 South Fifth Street, St. Charles
(636) 688-2500
www.basspro.com

The mother lode of sports gear for hunters and fishers, the Bass Pro Shop has more than 70,000 square feet of outdoor gear. From fishing (including saltwater and fly fishing) and hunting to all the latest boating and camping supplies, Bass is heaven to those who love the great outdoors. There's an abundance of outerwear, footwear, and gifts, as well as all the accoutrements for life in the great outdoors, and there's even a supply of hunting- and fishing-themed home decor items. The national chain features a number of in-store activities and promotions throughout the year, including the Outdoor Skills Workshops, and special events like the Camping and Boating Classic and Turkey Week. Open daily.

BIG RIVER RUNNING COMPANY
5352 Devonshire
(314) 832-2400
www.bigriverrunning.com

The tiny shop in the Southampton neighborhood offers a full-line of top name running and walking shoes along with shorts, shirts, pants, and a large selection of accessories. The staff is knowledgeable and very helpful in determining the right type of shoes you need for your personal foot strike and at prices that are very reasonable. Big River also has a selection of sunglasses, watches, books, DVDs, orthotics, reflective gear, training logs, GPS units, singlets, racing shorts, racing flats, and a line of track and cross country spikes. A second location is located at 14059 Manchester Road (636) 394-5500 in West St. Louis County. Both are open daily and both schedule a number of weekly "group runs."

REI
1703 South Brentwood Boulevard
(314) 918-1004
www.rei.com

The St. Louis location of the popular outdoor recreational store chain offers a great selection of quality outdoor gear and clothing, as well as everything you'll need for camping, climbing, cycling, or paddling. There are a variety of energy bars, books and maps for sale, along with outdoorsy apparel and footwear for men, women, and kids. There's even a 24-foot climbing wall inside the store, along with a water filter test station and a footwear test trail. Open daily.

SOUVENIR SHOPS

In addition to the excellent selections available at area museums, attractions, and cultural institutions, here's a list of likely locales for that ever-important St. Louis souvenir. Another one-stop-shopping location to consider is the historic train station–turned–entertainment marketplace, St. Louis Union Station (see the Attractions chapter for details), which has a variety of stores that offer St. Louis–and Missouri–related gifts and remembrances.

ANHEUSER-BUSCH BREWERY GIFT SHOP

1127 Pestalozzi Street

(314) 577-2297

www.budweiser.com

The best place to get Anheuser-Busch memorabilia and souvenirs is—where else—at the Anheuser-Busch headquarters in St. Louis. The shop stocks logoed merchandise ranging from screen savers and swimsuits to clothing and coolers, all with the different brands from the A-B family of products (Budweiser, Bud Light, Michelob, Michelob Light, Busch, Busch Light, etc.). This is also a great place to pick up collectible beer steins, sporting goods, neon beer signs, and anything related to the world-famous Clydesdales. The store also carries merchandise representative of its family entertainment entities, including stuffed animals, clothing, and accessories from Sea World and Busch Gardens. Open daily.

THE BEST OF ST. LOUIS

St. Louis Union Station, first level

(314) 231-2729

www.stlouisunionstation.com

This eclectic souvenir shop includes a variety of regionally themed gifts, apparel, and collectibles, along with a large selection of books about Missouri, St. Louis, and the Lewis & Clark expedition. The Best of St. Louis also features samples of salad dressings and other tasty products that can be found in various St. Louis restaurants. Open daily.

BUD SHOP

St. Louis Union Station, first level

(314) 436-0191

www.stlouisunionstation.com

Another convenient location for all sorts of beer-related merchandise, the Bud Shop stocks glassware, coasters, bar signs, neons and mirrors emblazoned with logos from Anheuser-Busch brands. In addition to Bud-related apparel, hats, and T-shirts, the shop features collectible beer steins and figurines.

CARDINALS OFFICIAL TEAM STORE

Seventh and Clark Streets, Busch Stadium

(314) 421-3263

www.buschstadiumteamstore.com

Located inside Busch Stadium, the official Cardinals gift shop is open year-round. As you would expect, the shop has the largest selection of Cardinals merchandise anywhere, including authentic jerseys, caps, jackets, sweatshirts, T-shirts, posters, and prints. There are also enough Christmas ornaments, stuffed toys, books, and home decor items to keep Cardinals fans of any age happy. The store also has a good stock of official 2009 All-Star Game merchandise. Open daily.

LOGOS & LABELS

St. Louis Union Station, first level

(314) 621-0702

www.stlouisunionstation.com

The shop offers high quality gifts and apparel with a variety of St. Louis brands and trademarks, including the NFL's Rams, NHL's Blues, and MLB's Cardinals merchandise. It's also a great place to pick up a variety of St. Louis souvenirs featuring the Arch, Budweiser, and other "only in St. Louis" locales.

SPECIALTY FOOD STORES

BISSINGER'S: A CHOCOLATE EXPERIENCE

32 Maryland Plaza

(314) 367-7750

www.bissingers.com

Bissinger's is one of the last handcrafted chocolatiers in the world. Serving chocolate to Americans since 1863, the family-owned candy company makes more than 900 different confections. Bissinger's candy orders are still made in the St. Louis kitchen, and most still use the original recipes from the family cookbook, dated 1899. No high-tech machinery here—the candy makers personally oversee the production of each piece. Hand-dipped and hand-decorated, the confections are still made in copper kettles, then cooled on marble slabs.

Schnucks Locations

There are dozens of Schnucks grocery stores located throughout the metro area, but here's a short list of some locations closest to downtown, Clayton, and the Mid-County area:

5055 Arsenal Street, The Hill
(314) 771–5008

7651 Clayton Road, Clayton
(314) 721–8975

Interstate 55 and Loughborough Avenue
(314) 752–5333

8800 Manchester Road, Brentwood
(314) 961–5454

6920 Olive Boulevard, The Loop
(314) 726–2373

10275 Clayton Road, Frontenac
(314) 991–0510

i Looking for inexpensive Cardinals, Rams, or Blues souvenirs? Schnucks supermarkets and area Target stores usually have a small selection of T-shirts, sweatshirts, and caps at reasonable prices.

DIGREGORIO'S ITALIAN FOODS
2232 Marconi
(314) 776-1062
www.digregoriofoods.com
DiGregorio's is a neighborhood tradition on The Hill. You can get a variety of imported Italian foodstuffs, meats, spices, wines, cheeses, and olive oils, as well as homemade pasta, sausage, and assembled Italian food baskets. The expanded deli area features an overwhelming number of options, including several varieties of olives, fresh bread, and homemade specialties. Closed Sunday.

JOHN VIVIANO & SONS GROCERY CO.
8935 Shaw Avenue
(314) 771-5476
www.shopviviano.com
Viviano's is a classic, old-world Italian grocery store that has been open at its current location since 1949. The family-owned and operated business continues to offer the best imported cheeses, spices, sauces, and myriad Italian specialties to customers from throughout the bi-state area. Pick up a bottle of olive oil, some pesto sauce, a pound of prosciutto, or some fresh grated Parmesan and Romano cheese, along with some wine or a favorite liqueur—you won't be disappointed. Closed Sunday.

SCHMITZ SPICE SHOP
730 Carroll Street, Soulard Farmers Market
(314) 241-5369
Schmitz's offers cheese, salami, olives, baking mixes, pasta, and spices from around the world. Whether your recipe calls for Cajun-style seasoning or a unique blend of herbs, Schmitz's friendly staff can help you find everything from adobo to za'atar. Specialty coffees and herbal teas are also available. Open Wednesday through Saturday.

33 WINE SHOP & TASTING BAR
1913 Park Avenue
(314) 231-9463
www.33wine.com
This intimate neighborhood wine and beer bar offers more than 300 wines from around the world, as well as an assortment of 30-plus global brews—and most are available by the glass or by the bottle to go. The proprietor, Jake, seems to always be on duty, and he loves nothing more than introducing new wines to his patrons. Open Tuesday through Saturday.

SQWIRES URBAN MARKET & COFFEE SHOP
1415 South 18th Street
(314) 865-3522
www.sqwires.com/urbanmarket
Located adjacent to SqWires Restaurant, this cozy Lafayette Square market features an assortment

of gourmet foods, wines, deli items, fresh seafood, and microbrews. The shop, located inside SqWires restaurant, offers fresh-baked breads, bagels, muffins, and pastries, as well as fresh veggies and fruits, imported and domestic cheeses, and groceries. The market's chef prepares and packages entrees and side dishes for diners on the go.

URZI'S BLUE RIDGE ITALIAN MARKET
5430 Southwest Avenue
(314) 771-5542

Urzi's has been around for more than 60 years, and it has a veritable feast of imported wines, cheeses, specialty foods, and the most reasonably priced spices you'll find. From homemade pizza shells and fresh bread from the neighborhood bakeries to hard-to-find Italian specialties and an excellent deli, Urzi's is a great spot for gourmets, amateur chefs, and foodies of all types. Cash only. Closed Sunday.

THRIFT SHOPS

GOODWILL INDUSTRIES STORE
4140 Forest Park Boulevard
(314) 535-3945
www.goodwill.org

Located directly across the street from the Society of St. Vincent de Paul's thrift store, this Goodwill store offers a fairly good selection of housewares, books, and furniture. Clothing is the main draw here, and the selection is usually varied and extensive. Women's and children's clothing dominate the selection, with a smaller section devoted to men's apparel. Additional retail stores are located at 7575 Olive Street, (314) 727-9280; 9116 Manchester Road, (314) 918-7804; and 10570 Baptist Church Road, (314) 842-9114.

SOCIETY OF ST. VINCENT DE PAUL OF ST. LOUIS
4127 Forest Park Boulevard
(314) 531-9364
www.svdpstl.org

This local thrift store, operated by the Archdiocese of St. Louis for the benefit of lower-income families, has a revolving stock of used furniture, household items, and affordable clothing and accessories for men, women, and children. If you're willing to dig through the racks and stacks of stuff, you might happen across an actual antique or other buried treasure.

ATTRACTIONS

The St. Louis area is home to a diverse collection of attractions and activities that are well suited to families, couples, and kids of all ages. The attractions are presented under self-explanatory subject headings, such as Amusements and the Zoo; Boat, Train, and Helicopter Rides; Farms and Gardens; etc. Many of the main attractions—including the history museum, art museum, zoo, and science center—are easily accessible by riding MetroLink, St. Louis's light-rail system. MetroLink has 30-plus stations and stretches more than 46 miles, serving a number of municipalities throughout St. Louis and into Illinois.

This chapter also includes a listing of places to go and things to see on the "other side" of the Mississippi River, in the area often referred to by locals as the Metro East. Illinois has a number of fun and exciting places to visit, and included here is a list of the most popular.

Price Code

Admission to many of the most popular attractions is free, so St. Louis is an economical place to visit. Even those attractions that charge admission are reasonably priced, so checking out all there is to see and do won't break your bank account. The following price codes are based on admission for one adult, but keep in mind that most attractions offer discounted admission fees for children and senior citizens.

$	$12 or less per person
$$	$13–$20 per person
$$$	$21–$30 per person
$$$$	More than $30 per person

AMUSEMENTS AND THE ZOO

DEMOLITION BALL $-$$
1875 Old Highway 94, St. Charles
(636) 940-7700
www.demolitionball.com
This family-style amusement center offers a unique activity that combines hockey, football, polo, and basketball into bumper cars. The object of the game, which is played in a supercharged bumper car on courts with two five-player teams, is to shoot a wiffle ball through a 16-inch circular goal using a track ball scoop. It's a high-energy activity for both kids and adults, but it might not be suitable for younger children. The facility also includes video games, foosball, pool, and the Adrenaline Zone laser-tag arena. Open daily.

MARYLAND HEIGHTS AQUAPORT $-$$
2344 McKelvey Road, Maryland Heights
(314) 434-1919
www.marylandheights.com
This 8,000-square-foot family fun pool includes the 740-foot-long Lazy River, five slides, a body flume, tube rapids, and racer slides. Smaller kids (48 inches and under) can play in the Wacky Water play area and enjoy a variety of bubblers, sprinklers, and fountains. There's a spacious deck area for those who are more interested in soaking up a little sun, along with changing areas, a snack bar, and free parking. Open Memorial Day through Labor Day.

RAGING RIVERS WATERPARK $$
100 Palisades Parkway, Grafton, IL
(618) 786-2345
www.ragingrivers.com
This giant water park has wet and wild attractions such as a giant wave pool, swirling flumes and slides, and a network of crawl tunnels and rope pulls at Treehouse Harbor. For smaller kids, Itty Bitty Surf City has pint-size waterslides and splash

pools, a rain tree, tunnels, and the Fountain Mountain family interactive area. Raging Rivers is located about 40 minutes from St. Louis on the Great River Road (Illinois Highway 100). Open Memorial Day through Labor Day. Children under two are admitted free.

SIX FLAGS ST. LOUIS $$$
Interstate 44, exit 261, Eureka
(636) 938-4800
www.sixflags.com

Six Flags has lots of kiddie rides and family entertainment options such as Miss Kitty's Saloon Revue, the Palace Theater, the Empire Theater, and "Merlin's Magicademy" at Sound Stage #2. There is also an abundance of thrill rides, including Tony Hawk's Big Spin, the Evel Knievel roller coaster, Batman the Ride looping super coaster, the Ninja steel coaster, Mr. Freeze, and the Screamin' Eagle. Visitors can cool off at Thunder River's seven acres of the white-water rapids, at Hurricane Harbor water park, or on the Tidal Wave ride as a 20-person boat drops over a 50-foot waterfall into 300,000 gallons of water. There's also the Colossus Ferris wheel, the Log Flume, Highland Fling, Rush Street Flyer, River King Mine Train, Tom's Twister, the Joker, and Shazam!—to name a few. The popular Scooby-Doo! Ghostblasters ride takes thrill-seekers through a scary swamp adventure. Other attractions include rides such as Dragon's Wing, the Rock Wall Climb, and Speed O'Drome Go-Karts. During the summer months, this Six Flags location hosts a number of live pop and country music concerts at the Old Glory Amphitheater located on-site. Tickets to the shows are an additional fee to the park admission price. Beginning in 2009, visitors can experience The Wahoo Racer, a six-lane water slide that propels riders along 262-feet of steep drops and rolls. After the sun sets, Six Flags lights up the night with Glow in the Park, a nighttime parade featuring six custom-designed floats, mobile units, and 65 light-adorned drummers, puppeteers, singers, dancers and stilt walkers.

St. Louis offers more free attractions than any area outside of the nations' capital. Popular freebies include the Missouri History Museum, St. Louis Zoo, Anheuser-Busch Brewery, Saint Louis Art Museum, Grant's Farm, Purina Farms, the Gateway Arch's Museum of Westward Expansion, Saint Louis Science Center, Old Courthouse, Cathedral Basilica of St. Louis, and Laumeier Sculpture Park.

ST. LOUIS CAROUSEL $
Faust Park
15185 Olive Street Road, Chesterfield
(636) 537-0222
www.co.st-louis.mo.us/parks

The St. Louis Carousel, with its more than 60 hand-carved horses, deer, and chariots, was made by the Dentzel Company of Philadelphia around 1920. It was first installed by a family restaurant to attract public interest, along with other carnival rides. The business eventually became the Forest Park Highlands Amusement Park. A trip to the Highlands—and a ride on the carousel—was a beloved tradition for school picnics and family outings for generations of St. Louis children. The carousel consists of 61 horses and two wooden chariots, and is one of only five 1920s Park-type-four-bank Dentzel carousels still in operation. Closed Monday.

SAINT LOUIS ZOO $
Forest Park
(314) 781-0900
www.stlzoo.org

With its natural-habitat exhibits and more than 11,000 animals, the St. Louis Zoo is regularly voted one of the best zoos in the country. Some of the highlights include the Antelope Area, which also has zebras, giraffes, and camels; Big Cat Country; and the Bird House, Flight Cage, and Bird Garden. This was the very first zoo exhibit, left over from the 1904 World's Fair Flight Cage. In the Bird House, thin piano wire separates you from birds from around the world, and in the Bird Garden you'll have the chance to see a bald eagle up close and personal. At the Bear Pits, you can see polar bears play in their pool, and the Children's Zoo allows kids to feed a lorikeet and see river otters swimming in their pool. At the Herpetarium, there are venomous snakes, colorful frogs, giant tortoises, and lazy crocodiles on display in replicas of their wild habitats, while the Insectarium, an interactive exhibit with more than 100 species of insects and invertebrates, features butterflies, damselflies, and katydids in a beautiful walk-through flight dome. The Jungle of the Apes exhibit has gorillas, chimpanzees, and orangutans, and the Primate House allows visitors to watch as social groups of monkeys and lemurs swing from branch to branch. The River's Edge allows you to immerse yourself in nature, without visible barriers or buildings, as you follow a waterway to see how animals all over the world live at the river's edge. The exhibit includes Asian elephants, cheetahs, hyenas, hippos (with underwater viewing), rhinos, and capybaras. The Cypress Swamp exhibit, features aquatic birds that live in swamps along the Mississippi River. Swamp-loving ducks, egrets, herons, and other feathered friends are featured in this wetlands habitat. The Wild features cold-weather animals such as penguins, puffins, and polar bears, as well as grizzlies and black bears, and the ZOOmagination Station offers interactive activities that encourage kids to explore and investigate life in the animal world. While general admission to the zoo is free, the Children's Zoo and other special exhibits/attractions charge a nominal fee. However, admission to the Children's Zoo is free every day from 9 a.m. to 10 a.m.

SWING-A-ROUND FUN TOWN $–$$
Highways 141 and 30, Fenton
(636) 349-7077

3541 Veterans Memorial Parkway, St. Charles
(636) 947-4487
www.sarfun.com
Swing-A-Round Fun Town offers a variety of games and activities for families, including three miniature golf courses, go-karts, bumper boats, batting cages, "Bowlingo" Bowling Lanes, and an arcade with more than 80 games. Food concessions and snacks are available for purchase on-site.

i St. Louis Walking Tours offers two-hour historic Art and Architecture tours through downtown twice a day. The morning tour starts at Union Station, and the afternoon version steps off from the America's Center convention complex. Call (314) 368–8818 for more information.

BOAT, TRAIN, AND HELICOPTER RIDES

FOREST PARK BOATHOUSE $
Government Drive
(314) 367-3423
www.boathouseforestpark.com
This is a great family spot and a fun way to step back in time and enjoy a "human-powered" boat ride. Boat rentals and gondola cruises are available, as well as lakeside patio dining, live music and a full-service restaurant. The menu is family-friendly and includes Angus burgers, soups, stews, chili, hand-tossed pizzas, and salads, along with signature dishes such as flank steak rarebit and salmon BLTs. Warm up with a glass of wine or a hot toddy around the stone, wood-burning fireplace during cold weather months.

GATEWAY AIR TOURS $$$$
St. Louis Riverfront
(314) 393-2665
www.gatewayarch.com
From Memorial Day through mid-September, visitors to the St. Louis Riverfront can enjoy helicopter tours that take off from a barge docked on the mighty Mississippi River. Two versions are available for those looking for a bird's-eye view of the Gateway City. The St. Louis Skyline tours offer a quick 5- to 6-minute look at the riverfront and immediate downtown area, while the Explore St. Louis tour lasts about 15 minutes and includes downtown, the riverfront, a flyover of Forest Park, and a jaunt out to the confluence of the Missouri and Mississippi Rivers.

GATEWAY ARCH RIVERBOATS $

St. Louis Riverfront

(314) 923-3048, (877) 982-1410

www.gatewayarchriverboats.com

Join Gateway Arch Riverboats for one of its spectacular Mississippi River sight-seeing cruises. Narrated by seasoned riverboat captains, these scenic cruises recapture the vibrant life on the river at the peak of the steamboat era. Historic ports of call along the Mississippi's banks, lively river characters from Mark Twain to Louis Armstrong, and famous river tales are all brought to life in the course of an hour-long journey up the river and back through time. Nighttime cruises include dinner cruises and entertainment cruises with live bands and DJs. on board.

WABASH FRISCO AND PACIFIC
STEAM RAILWAY $

Old State Road and Washington Street, Glencoe

(636) 587-3538

www.wfprr.com

Kids and adults can have fun and enjoy an old-fashioned train ride aboard the Wabash Frisco and Pacific Steam Railway on Sundays from May through October. Trains start scheduled departures from the station around 11 a.m., with the final train leaving at 4:15 p.m. The ride lasts about 30 minutes and travels along the scenic Meramec River. Children three and under ride free.

FARMS AND GARDENS

GRANT'S FARM $

10501 Gravois Road

(314) 843-1700

www.grantsfarm.com

Grant's Farm is a 281-acre wildlife preserve and historical site that is home to hundreds of exotic animals from around the world. In addition to live animal shows, a petting area, and a tram ride through the wildlife preserve, the farm includes the Bauernhof, the first building constructed on the Busch family estate. Built in 1913, the building currently houses the family's world-renowned antique carriage collection. The facility surrounds a beautiful courtyard and is typical of a 19th-century Bavarian farm, complete with stables, a carriage house, and offices and quarters for those who live and work on the farm. This is also home to the famous Budweiser Clydesdale horses. More than 40 Clydesdale mares, stallions, geldings, and foals call Grant's Farm home, along with an amazing variety of animals that perform in the Tier Garden Amphitheater. Visitors can pet and hand-feed some of the animals or attend the elephant, parrot, and bird of prey shows. A stop at the Small Animal Area includes an opportunity to feed and pet the farm's pygmy goats. A slightly larger resident on hand is Bud, a 7,000-pound African elephant. The farm takes its name from the 18th president of the United States, Ulysses S. Grant, who farmed a portion of the acreage in the 1850s. The land later became the ancestral home of the Busch family. Open weekends only April through October. Closed November through March. Admission is free, but there is a per car parking fee of $10.

JEWEL BOX FREE

Forest Park

(314) 289-5389

www.stlouis.missouri.org/citygov/parks/jewelbox

Listed on the National Register of Historic Places, the Jewel Box, located on 17 acres in Forest Park, was built by the City of St. Louis in 1936. The facility hosts special flower shows throughout the year, including an annual poinsettia show at Christmas. Other popular shows are held at Easter and around Mother's Day, and there is a summer show and a chrysanthemum show in the fall. (These shows charge a nominal admission fee.) A popular spot for weddings, the Art Deco–style Jewel Box is filled with tropical trees, plants, and flowers year-round, with a main display room that is 50 feet high, 55 feet wide, and 144 feet long.

MISSOURI BOTANICAL GARDEN $

4344 Shaw Boulevard

(314) 577-9400, (800) 642-8842

www.mobot.org

The Missouri Botanical Garden was created by Henry Shaw, a prominent St. Louis businessman who opened his garden to the public in 1859. Inspired by the gardens of his native England, Shaw intended his garden to be a center for education, scientific research, and horticultural display. Today the Missouri Botanical Garden is a National Historic Landmark and maintains one of the world's leading programs in botanical research. One of the garden's most popular attractions is the 14-acre Japanese Garden, the largest Japanese strolling garden in the Western Hemisphere. The four-acre lake is complemented by waterfalls, streams, water-filled basins, stone lanterns, and dry gravel gardens that are raked into beautiful rippling patterns. Four islands rise from the lake to form symbolic images, and several Japanese bridges link the shorelines. Kids love to feed the giant, colorful koi (Japanese carp). The garden also contains cherry blossoms, azaleas, chrysanthemums, peonies, lotuses, and other Oriental plantings. Other attractions include the Ottoman Garden, complete with exotic Turkish plantings and fountains; an English woodland garden; a Strassenfest garden; a Nanjing Friendship Chinese Garden; the Kemper Center for Home Gardening, which features 23 residential-scale gardens within an eight-acre design and is a great place to learn about vegetable gardening, flower growing, planting ornamental shrubs, landscaping, and indoor plants; and the Climatron, a stunning geodesic-domed conservatory that houses a tropical rain forest display, including streams, waterfalls, and more than 1,200 species of plants in a natural setting. About half of the plants in the Climatron were collected in the field, which gives them more scientific value than plants raised in a greenhouse, and the facility is home to representatives of numerous endangered species. The Doris I. Schnuck Children's Garden: A Missouri Adventure is two acres of interactive fun. Kids can explore wetlands, climb in a tree house, check out a limestone cave, and visit a Midwestern prairie village as they explore the world of Mother Nature (there is a small additional charge for this attraction). Children 12 and under are admitted free.

PURINA FARMS · FREE

200 Checkerboard Drive, Gray Summit
(314) 982-3232
www.events.purina.com/dogs/farms

The Purina Farms visitor center includes a variety of activities centered on animals that kids of all ages are sure to enjoy. At the Barn and Play Area, visitors can pet and interact with many domestic animals found on a typical working farm, play in the hayloft, swing on a rope, or even milk a cow. (Milking demonstrations are held throughout the day.) A petting ring in the Barn's nursery area allows children to get up close and personal with baby bunnies, chicks, and piglets. The Pet Center is home to the dozens of dogs and cats that call Purina Farms home, and the key attraction here is a 20-foot-tall, multilevel cat house, complete with windows, stairways, rocking chairs, and other feline-focused furnishings that combine to create a cat's idea of paradise. (A staircase surrounding the structure provides an eye-level view of the cat house's inhabitants.) Open from mid-March to mid-November. Reservations are required.

i At the Pet Center at Purina Farms, there's a unique display that lets you experience the scents a dog's sensitive nose perceives while walking through a field. P-U!

SHAW NATURE RESERVE · $

Highway 100 and I–44, exit 253,
Gray Summit
(636) 451-3512
www.shawnature.org

Shaw Nature Reserve, an extension of the Missouri Botanical Garden, includes 2,500 acres of natural Ozark landscape and managed plant collections. Located 35 miles southwest of St. Louis, the nature reserve includes the Pinetum, a 55-acre park like expanse of meadows studded with conifers from around the world; and the Whitmire Wildflower Garden, a five-acre concentration of Missouri and eastern U.S. native wildflowers, accented by native grasses, shrubs, and trees. The Shaw Nature Reserve also contains 13 miles of hiking trails through a full array of Ozark Border landscapes, including floodplain forest, oak-hickory woods, glades, bluffs, tall-grass prairie, savanna, and marsh wetlands. The Joseph H. Bascom Manor House, an elegant brick mansion built in 1879, contains a variety of exhibits called People on the Land, which illustrates the broad environmental and conservation themes of the nature reserve's mission. The Nature Reserve is open to hikers daily but the Visitor Center and Bascom House are closed on some major holidays. Children 12 and under are admitted free.

HISTORIC SITES AND HOUSE MUSEUMS

CAHOKIA MOUNDS STATE HISTORIC SITE AND INTERPRETIVE CENTER   FREE

30 Ramey Street, Collinsville, IL
(618) 346-5160
www.cahokiamounds.com

The site of the largest prehistoric Indian city north of Mexico, Cahokia Mounds is the remnants of the Mississippians' central city—now known as Cahokia—for the Indians who lived nearby in the late 1600s. The mounds are preserved within the 2,200-acre tract that is the Cahokia Mounds State Historic Site, located just 8 miles east of downtown St. Louis. The Cahokia Mounds Interpretive Center offers a fuller understanding of what daily life was like there from 800 to 1400 AD, and it also has a life-size diorama of Cahokia as it looked 900 years ago. Other attractions include a reconstructed thatched-roof house with daub construction, a garden of representative plants from the era, and a reconstructed Woodhenge solar calendar. Closed Monday and Tuesday.

CAMPBELL HOUSE MUSEUM $

1508 Locust Street
(314) 421-0325
www.stlouis.missouri.org/chm

Built in 1851, this three-story town house, with its carriage house, rose garden, and gazebo, is a showcase of Victorian furnishings and decorative arts. Ninety percent of the furnishings are original to the family who lived here from 1854 through 1938. The estate is the sole survivor of a once-elegant neighborhood of aristocratic family homes called Lucas Place. The Campbell House Museum collection includes classic Rococo Revival Victorian furniture, portraits, textiles, silver, gold-leaf frames and cornices, faux-grained woodwork, and other examples of decorative arts. Children under 12 are admitted free. Closed Monday and Tuesday.

CATHEDRAL BASILICA OF SAINT LOUIS (NEW CATHEDRAL)   FREE

Lindell Boulevard at Newstead Avenue
(314) 373-8242
www.cathedralstl.org

Archbishop John Glennon began building this beautiful cathedral in 1907. Its unique design combines architecture of the Romanesque style on the exterior with an amazingly beautiful Byzantine-style interior. This "New Cathedral," as it's called by the locals, contains the largest mosaic collection in the world; it was created by 20 different artists and covers 83,000 square feet. The installation, which contains almost 42 million pieces of glass tesserae in more than 7,000 colors, began in 1912 and was completed in 1988. In the narthex (vestibule) the mosaics depict the life of Saint Louis IX, King of France, and provide a preview of the beauty yet to be discovered in the main body of the church. The great center dome and the two smaller domes, together with the arches, reveal the story of the Catholic faith, from creation to the last judgment, in mosaics. Portraying scenes from both the Hebrew and Christian scriptures, the mosaic works picture men and women of Judeo-Christian history as well as illustrate the more recent development of the Catholic Church in North America and particularly in St. Louis. The Mosaic Museum, on the lower level of the cathedral, provides additional information on the church's construction and the installation of the artwork. The Cathedral Shop, located on the west side of the vestibule, stocks postcards and books that provide detailed information on the history of the church. Visitors are encouraged to tour the cathedral on their own whenever there is not a service or ceremony in progress.

CHATILLON-DEMENIL MANSION AND MUSEUM $
3352 DeMenil Place
(314) 771-5828
www.demenil.org

This Greek Revival mansion was built in two sections by families with very different lifestyles. Henri Chatillon, a hunter and guide for the American Fur Company, built a four-room brick structure in 1848. He sold the "farmhouse" in 1856 to Dr. Nicolas N. DeMenil, a distinguished physician and wealthy Frenchman who came to St. Louis in 1834 and married Emile Sophie Chouteau, a descendant of St. Louis's founding family. In 1861 the DeMenils added the Greek Revival façade and extra rooms that form the principal part of the mansion. The ceiling medallions, marble mantelpieces, plaster decorative elements, hall chandelier, and parquet floor are original to the house, while most of the furniture is dated from 1830 to 1880. The house also features a collection of more than 1,200 items from the 1904 World's Fair. It is one of the largest exhibits of its kind in the country. There is an on-site restaurant that is open for lunch. Open Tuesday through Saturday.

DANIEL BOONE HOME AND BOONESFIELD VILLAGE $
1868 Highway F, Defiance
(636) 798-2005
www.lindenwood.edu/boone

The Historic Daniel Boone Home is a four-story structure built between 1804 and 1810 in the Femme Osage Valley of St. Charles County. It was the last permanent residence of Daniel Boone and his wife, Rebecca, and was where Boone died in 1820. The adjoining Boonesfield Village is a collection of more than a dozen historic buildings from throughout Missouri that have been reconstructed to form a living-history village. The village includes a schoolhouse (circa 1831); a milliner's shop (1840); woodworker's shop (1837); the Peace Chapel (circa 1840–60), complete with

a reconstructed 28-stop Wicks pipe organ; the Stake House (circa 1828–40); and the Sappington-Dressel House (1807). Open daily.

EUGENE FIELD HOUSE AND ST. LOUIS TOY MUSEUM $
634 South Broadway
(314) 421-4689
www.eugenefieldhouse.org

This is the childhood home of Eugene Field, the "children's poet," who authored the popular poem "Wynken, Blynken, and Nod," and his father, Roswell Field, the lawyer who represented Dred Scott in his historic slavery trial. The house, an early Victorian jewel, reflects the era in which Roswell, Frances, and Eugene Field lived within its walls, and it has been turned into a museum that has exhibits and artifacts from Eugene's personal collections. The museum features a number of changing exhibitions each year, ranging from collections of antique dolls or rare teddy bears to games and quilts. Children under age three are admitted free. Open Wednesday through Sunday; open in January by appointment only.

FIRST MISSOURI STATE CAPITOL STATE HISTORIC SITE $
200–216 South Main Street, St. Charles
(636) 940-3322, (800) 334-6946
www.mostateparks.com/firstcapitol.htm

Missouri's first legislators met in the buildings of the First Missouri State Capitol State Historic Site to reorganize Missouri's territorial government into a progressive state system. From 1821 to 1826 heated debates of state's rights and slavery filled the rooms of the temporary capitol. The second floor of two adjoining Federal-style brick buildings was divided and used as Senate and House chambers, an office for the governor, and a small committee room. The second building belonged to the Peck brothers, Charles and Ruluff. The first floor of the Peck brothers' building housed a general store and Ruluff Peck's family residence, and a carpenter shop occupied the first floor of the adjoining building. A variety of shops, restaurants, and other historic attractions are housed in original 18th- and 19th-century buildings in the area.

GATEWAY ARCH JEFFERSON
NATIONAL EXPANSION MEMORIAL $–$$
St. Louis Riverfront
(314) 655-1700
www.gatewayarch.com

At 630 feet tall, the Arch is the tallest man-made monument in the United States. There are plenty of exciting activities here: see a giant-screen movie, a documentary film on the building of the Arch; visit the Museum of Westward Expansion; and, of course, make the "Journey to the Top," where you can get a bird's-eye view of the St. Louis region. A warning to those who are seriously claustrophobic: The tram ride to the top takes place inside a very small "capsule" that feels about as big as a clothes dryer. Up to five people are plugged into this tiny space, and the ride itself takes about four minutes. There isn't any other way to the top—or back down—so if you are afraid of tight spaces, this may not be a good idea for you. The trams run from the south and north legs of the Arch, and each area offers a glimpse into the Arch grounds' past. The south leg features the era in the 1800s when St. Louis's riverfront was bustling with steamboats, fur traders, and merchants. The north leg area transports visitors back to 1965, when construction workers wedged the last triangular section into place at the landmark's apex. The Museum of Westward Expansion (which has free admission) is an excellent way to spend time waiting for your appointed tram ride—or to wait it out while others in your group go to the top. From rare Indian Peace Medals and weapons of survival to an actual tipi and a covered wagon, the collection provides a three-dimensional glimpse into what life was like for the region's earliest settlers. A variety of exhibits include information and artifacts from the Lewis & Clark expedition from St. Louis into lands where buffalo and Native Americans ruled. Life-like animatronic figures retell the history and explain what life was like in the early days of the frontier. The Odyssey Theatre hosts a variety of touring big-screen features, which are shown on a four story-tall screen and fortified with explosive THX sound. A permanent film feature at the museum is the award-winning documentary Monument to the Dream, which provides an up close and personal look at the construction workers who built the Arch from the ground up. During the high-traffic months (May–September), it's best to try to schedule your visit to the Arch early in the day, when crowds are smaller and waiting times shorter. You can order your tram ride and movie tickets in advance by logging on to www.gateway.com.

HISTORIC CHRISTOPHER HAWKEN HOUSE $
1155 South Rock Hill Road, Webster Groves
(314) 968-1857

The Hawken House was built in 1857 by Christopher Miller Hawken, a descendant of the Hawken rifle smiths. This elegant Federal/Greek Revival–style farmhouse is maintained and operated by the Webster Groves Historical Society, and it is furnished entirely in the Victorian decor of the 1800s. Closed Monday.

HISTORIC SAMUEL CUPPLES HOUSE $
Saint Louis University Mall next to
Pius XII Library
(314) 977-3575; (314) 977-3570 (recording)
www.slu.edu/the_arts/cupples

In 1888 a wealthy St. Louis entrepreneur named Samuel Cupples commissioned a prominent architect to design a home for him. The result is this three-story house made of purple Colorado sandstone, complete with limestone gargoyles and other elaborate architectural details. It is a rare example of Richardsonian Romanesque architecture in St. Louis. Inside the home there are various collections of china, glass, and functional objects from the 19th century within its 42 rooms. The house is filled with five centuries' worth of fine and decorative art, including Northern and Italian Renaissance paintings and 19th-century landscape paintings, as well as a number of stained- and leaded-glass windows designed in the Tiffany style. The decorative-art collection includes examples of Meissen and Staffordshire porcelain, English silver, and American and European textiles. Closed Sunday and Monday.

HISTORICAL VILLAGE $
Faust Park
15185 Olive Street Road, Chesterfield
(636) 532-7298
www.stlouisco.com/parks/faust_home.html
Faust's Historical Village includes ten structures representing a variety of styles, from log to brick. Spanning a period from 1840 to 1888, the village illustrates differences in lifestyle resulting from both technological developments and special needs. Blacksmithing, spinning, weaving, natural dyeing, and other antique arts are all demonstrated with historical re-enactors from the spring through the fall months. The village can be toured year-round, but guided, interior tours are available on the last two weekends in May, June and July. The festivities include historical re-enactors in period costume and a variety of demonstrations.

LEWIS AND CLARK STATE
HISTORIC SITE FREE
1 Lewis and Clark Trail, Hartford, IL
(618) 251-5811
www.campdubois.com
The 14,000-square-foot visitor center is located at the confluence of the Missouri and Mississippi Rivers and the site of Camp DuBois, where explorers Lewis and Clark wintered before embarking on their trek through the Northwest. The center features a 12-minute orientation film, At Journey's Edge, which provides a good overview of the expedition, and a life-size replica of the 55-foot keelboat that was used on the journey. The "misquitors" exhibits quote extensively from the journals of the two explorers—neither of whom was a spelling champion. Other exhibits include information on the Louisiana Territory and the Native Americans who lived there, the Corps of Discovery's preparations for the trip, and the impact and legacy of the expedition.

OLD CATHEDRAL—BASILICA OF
SAINT LOUIS, KING OF FRANCE FREE
209 Walnut Street
(314) 231-3250
www.psichurch.com/churches/140stlouis
The Old Cathedral was St. Louis's earliest church and the first Catholic cathedral west of the Mississippi River. The Old Cathedral Museum, located on the west side of the cathedral, contains many religious artifacts and relics from the early days of the Catholic Church in the city, as well as historical information. The first Catholic church in St. Louis was built on this site in 1770, and the original church bell can be seen in the museum. The present structure is more than 160 years old and has been declared a national monument. The cathedral conducts daily mass and is a popular spot for weddings.

OLD COURTHOUSE FREE
11 North Fourth Street
(314) 655-1700
www.nps.gov/jeff/courthouse.html
Built in 1828, the Old Courthouse was the location of the historic Dred Scott slavery trial. Galleries depict the history of St. Louis from its French and Spanish roots to its role in westward expansion. Visitors can walk through a restored courtroom from the 1860s, view exhibits tracing the history of the city's famed riverfront, and see murals depicting historic events such as the bloody attack on St. Louis by the British during the Revolutionary War. The building is also listed on the National Park Service's National Underground Railroad "Network to Freedom." The Old Courthouse frequently hosts trial reenactments and other historical presentations and serves as the site for naturalization ceremonies for new U.S. citizens. The facility also has drawings on display from the architectural finalists who competed for the right to design the official Jefferson Expansion Memorial landmark, today known as the Gateway Arch. The Old Courthouse hosts a number of changing exhibits throughout the year, including an annual observation of Black History Month.

SCOTT JOPLIN HOUSE STATE
HISTORIC SITE $
2658 Delmar Boulevard
(314) 340-5790
www.mostateparks.com/scottjoplin.htm
This restored post-Civil War structure was once the home of Scott Joplin, known as the Father of

Ragtime. In this modest walk-up flat, Joplin and his wife, Belle, began their life in St. Louis around the turn of the 20th century. Their home was located on what was then called Morgan Street, a busy, densely populated, blue-collar district of African Americans and German immigrants. Located nearby were the honky-tonks and dives of the notorious Chestnut Valley and Targee Street, which today is the site of Scottrade Center, home ice for the St. Louis Blues NHL team. Lit by gaslight and appropriately furnished for 1902, the Joplin flat is where many ragtime classics were composed. The rest of the building, which has been declared a National Historic Landmark, has exhibits interpreting Joplin's life and work and explores St. Louis during the ragtime era. There's even an antique player piano that plays Joplin tunes. Open Tuesday through Saturday, November through February; and Monday through Saturday, March through October.

THORNHILL FARM AND HISTORICAL VILLAGE $
Faust Park
15185 Olive Street Road, Chesterfield
(636) 532-7298
www.stlouisco.com/parks/Thornhill.html
At Thornhill, home to Missouri's second governor, Frederick Bates, visitors can relive some of Missouri's pioneer history. The Thornhill farm includes the home and utility buildings of the Bates family and shows what life was like on the frontier in the early 1800s. The site includes an 1820s home, barn, reconstructed summer kitchen, ice and smoke houses, orchard and herb garden, and family cemetery. The home has been restored and partially furnished to look as it did when Governor Bates and his family lived there. Thornhill tours by appointment only.

WHITE HAVEN $
Ulysses S. Grant Historic Site
7400 Grant Road
(314) 842-3298
www.nps.gov/ulsg
Tours of Grant's former home include the two-story house, a stone summer kitchen, icehouse, barn, and chicken house. A visitor center is located in the barn, complete with a number of exhibits about Ulysses and his wife, Julia, a St. Louis native. The center also includes information about the White Haven site and a library with books and other Grant-related items for sale. During the holiday season, the site is decked out in traditional 1850s Christmas decorations and features activities such as caroling, antebellum dancing, and craft making.

MUSEUMS

AMERICAN KENNEL CLUB MUSEUM OF THE DOG $
1721 South Mason Road
(314) 821-3647
www.museumofthedog.org
The American Kennel Club Museum of the Dog, located in beautiful Queeny Park, is home to the world's finest collection of canine art. The 14,000-square-foot facility includes the historic Jarville House, built in 1853, and displays more than 500 original paintings, drawings, watercolors, prints, sculptures, and a variety of decorative art objects. There are special exhibits and educational programs as well. The museum is open year-round, but oddly enough, no dogs are allowed in the house. The museum's gift shop offers a variety of gift items for you and your canine companion, including tapestry pillows, ceramic and jeweled dog dishes, books, jewelry, and some one-of-a-kind objects—just like Fido himself. Closed Monday and holidays.

BIGFOOT 4X4, INC. FREE
6311 North Lindbergh Boulevard
(314) 731-2822
www.bigfoot4x4.com
This is the home of the original monster truck, along with the world's largest collection of memorabilia tracing the history of the Bigfoot phenomenon. Get up close and personal with Bigfoot 1, the legendary Ford pickup truck that started it all, as well as Bigfoot 5, the world's tallest, widest, and heaviest pickup truck. Truck lovers can also check out the world's only monster-truck

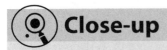

Close-up

City Museum's World Aquarium

In addition to all of the other unique things you'll find here, the City Museum features a 13,500-square-foot World Aquarium. The attraction-within-an-attraction has more than 10,000 animals in 125 living exhibits and offers numerous hands-on, educational, and interactive programs to discover. Visitors to the watery world can pet sharks and stingrays, touch starfish, crawl through giant waterfalls, and play on a sand-castle beach. The exhibits help kids and adults learn more about the aquatic ecosystems of the world.

Exhibits include Sharks in the City, where visitors can get up close and personal with a variety of sharks, and Stingray City, where the hands-on activities include petting and feeding the speedy creatures. Kids can crawl through specially designed lighted caves for a unique peek at these creatures in their underwater habitat. On Sand Castle Beach, visitors explore tide pools and the many life forms and coral forests that make themselves at home in the sea.

A study of marine life a little closer to home can be found in the Rivers of the World section, where comparisons between the Mississippi and Amazon Rivers are displayed, along with the colorful ecosystems of Asia, Africa, and Australia. Additional exhibits include The Water Cycle, which explores the relation of water from the top of the mountains to the bottom of the oceans, and Structure, Function and Color, featuring myriad colors and activities of the animal kingdom. Prehistoric Alley sizes up giant creatures of the deep and jumping fish of the Amazon and displays details of the Jurassic era.

The Conservation Classroom explains classifications, ecosystems, and biodiversity with hands-on activities that utilize a variety of scientific devices and exploration tools. There is an additional admission fee to explore the World Aquarium, but it's well worth it. You can save a couple of bucks by purchasing a combination ticket that allows entrance to both the museum and the aquarium at a reduced rate. For more information log on to www.worldaquarium.net or call the City Museum at (314) 231–CITY.

shop, where the Bigfoot trucks are built and kept race-ready, or just sit back and watch the latest monster-truck videos or videos from Bigfoot's early days. There's also the world's largest collection of monster-truck memorabilia, which covers three decades of "Big Footedness." Kids can play in the Ride & Race Trax play area, which features

Bigfoot, the first monster truck, had its start in 1975 when Bob Chandler, a St. Louis construction contractor, started tinkering with his Ford four-by-four pickup truck, adding new parts to make the truck bigger and better. Bigfoot made its first public appearance at a Denver car show in 1979, and its popularity lead to appearances at truck pulls and stadiums across the country.

remote-control monster trucks, battery-powered ride-on vehicles, video games, and more.

THE GRIOT MUSEUM OF BLACK HISTORY AND CULTURE $
2505 St. Louis Avenue
(314) 241-7057
This museum features life-size likenesses of famous African Americans from throughout the state of Missouri, including inventor George Washington Carver, Dred and Harriett Scott, and jazz musician Clark Terry. Special exhibits rotate in and out of the museum frequently, and topics highlighted range from events of the civil rights era to the history of black hairstyles and fashions. The gift shop includes art and clothing from Africa and a variety of Afro-centric items. Closed Sunday and Monday.

CITY MUSEUM $
701 North 15th Street
(314) 231-2489
www.citymuseum.org

Explore the unexpected at this exciting museum for children and adults. Art, science, history, and fun are woven together in this one-of-a-kind downtown attraction that includes a waterfall and crab pond; the Enchanted Caves; Art City; 4,000 square feet of man-made caves and tunnels; an Enchanted Forest with sky tunnels overlooking fish and turtle dwellings in a giant aquarium; a working shoelace factory; a collection of artisans who might be weaving, throwing pottery, blowing glass, or performing magic; and circus performances by the everyday circus troupe. On the adjacent parking lot, MonstroCity features a monstrous climbing gym made from two Saber 40 aircraft fuselages, a 25-foot cupola, and 4-foot-wide Slinkies. Located within the City Museum, the St. Louis Architectural Museum has a collection of items salvaged from area buildings and construction sites, such as a hoist made with salvaged parts of what once was the world's largest windmill, gargoyles from demolished buildings, and other architectural artifacts.

A fascinating exhibit at this ever-changing facility is the World Aquarium at City Museum (see Close-up), featuring all sorts of hands-on exhibits and interactive programs. Visitors can (safely) pet sharks and stingrays, touch starfish, crawl through waterfall displays, play in a giant sand-castle beach, and learn about the world's aquatic ecosystems among the giant shell columns and jumping jets of water that make you feel like you're swimming or flying through the exhibits. There is an additional admission fee.

Another unique feature—this one specifically for adults—is the Cabin Inn the City. This 19th-century two-story log cabin has been transformed into a cozy beer and wine bar, complete with a brick patio and fire bowl.

On Friday and Saturday nights, the City Museum is open late (1:00 a.m.), with the added benefits of music and cocktails. The kids can still explore and climb to their heart's content, while grown-ups enjoy the libations and the scenery—artistic and otherwise.

CONTEMPORARY ART MUSEUM
ST. LOUIS FREE
3750 Washington Boulevard
(314) 535-4660
www.contemporarystl.org

At this art museum, visitors can learn about contemporary art and its place in the continuum of artistic development. The annual schedule of exhibitions incorporates a broad range of media, topics, and artists, with the goal of engaging people of all ages in the appreciation and interpretation of contemporary art and ideas. The 27,000-square-foot museum has space for paintings, installations, and sculpture along with video art, photography, and performance art. The Contemporary Art Museum presents a yearly schedule of six to ten exhibitions and various programs throughout the year. Self-guided iPod and mp3 player tours of the galleries are available. Visit the museum's Web site and download the podcasts or borrow one of the players available at the Visitors Services Desk.

FOUNDRY ART CENTRE FREE/$
520 N. Main Street, St. Charles
(636) 255-0270
www.foundryartcentre.org

Located in nearby St. Charles, just north of the city and overlooking the Missouri River, the Foundry is dedicated to contemporary visual and performing arts. The four main galleries feature an on-going rotation of special touring exhibits, and juried competitions devoted to photography, pottery, painting, metalwork, glass art, fabric art, and more. There is also an art gallery and studio designed especially for children and families. The galleries are free, as is observing the artists-in-residence at work in their studios. Some exhibitions charge admission, usually $5 or $6 per person, and children under 12 are free. Open Tuesday through Sunday, closed Monday.

HOLOCAUST MUSEUM AND
LEARNING CENTER   FREE
12 Millstone Campus Drive
(314) 432-0020, ext. 3711
www.hmlc.org

The Holocaust Museum and Learning Center (HMLC) is a 5,000-square-foot exhibition center that provides a chronological history of the Holocaust, including personal accounts of survivors who emigrated to St. Louis. Photographs, artifacts, text panels, and audiovisual displays guide visitors through pre-WWII Jewish life in Europe, the rise of Nazism, and events during the Holocaust. The museum also traces postwar events, including the Nuremberg Trials and Jewish life after the Holocaust. HMLC also features changing exhibits, lectures, a monthly film series, teacher-training workshops, and an annual Yom HaShoah community commemoration. There is a comprehensive video library with more than 500 titles and an oral-history project with more than 150 testimonies that is available to educators and the general public. The museum's bookstore stocks a variety of books for sale. Closed Saturday.

JAMES S. MCDONNELL PROLOGUE
ROOM   FREE
Building 100 at McDonnell Boulevard and Airport Road
(314) 232-6896
www.boeing.com/prologueroom

The James S. McDonnell Prologue Room: An Air and Space History Exhibit has more than 300 models of aircraft on display, including the F-15 Eagle, F/A-18 Hornet, AH-64 Apache helicopter, Air Force One, and full-size engineering mock-ups of the Mercury and Gemini spacecraft. A scale model of Sky Lab hangs (securely) from above, along with the Space Shuttle, the International Space Station, and a Harpoon radar-guided missile. Dioramas, photos, and paintings tell the tales of historic milestones in aviation history, such as the first flight around the world in 1924 and the first jet fighter takeoff from a U.S. Navy carrier in 1946. The exhibit tells a panoramic story of nearly a century of aviation progress, from biplanes to space travel.

The facility is designed for self-guided tours, and it is open Monday through Saturday, June through August only. Reservations required.

LAUMEIER SCULPTURE PARK   FREE
2580 Rott Road (at Geyer Road)
(314) 821-1209
www.laumeier.com

One of the major sculpture parks in the country, Laumeier offers year-round exhibitions of modern and contemporary sculpture and installations, as well as drawings, paintings, ceramics, and photography. The museum draws internationally known sculptors and artists to the region to create and install their work, both indoors and outdoors. The pieces represent current and unique approaches to art in a natural environment. Laumeier hosts various special events throughout the year, including the annual three-day Laumeier Art Fair, which takes place during Mother's Day weekend. Visitors can rent iPods and take an audio tour that highlights more than 20 sculptures, with additional works to be added on a regular basis. Closed Monday.

LEWIS AND CLARK BOAT HOUSE AND
NATURE CENTER $
1050 Riverside Drive, St. Charles
(636) 947-3199
www.lewisandclarkcenter.org

The Lewis and Clark Boat House and Nature Center interprets the expedition through exhibits, literature, and educational programs that focus on the unique role St. Charles and its townspeople played in its success. Other exhibits include information about the members of the expedition, the tools they used, the journals they kept, and the many Indian cultures they encountered. Detailed dioramas show the explorers traveling the entire length of the Missouri River, crossing the Rocky Mountains, and proceeding to the Pacific Ocean. This certified site on the Lewis and Clark National Historic Trail is located in historic St. Charles near the 1804 campsite of the Corps of Discovery.

THE MAGIC HOUSE, ST. LOUIS
CHILDREN'S MUSEUM $
516 South Kirkwood Road
(Lindbergh Boulevard), Kirkwood
(314) 822-8900
www.magichouse.org

The Magic House is a nationally acclaimed children's museum that offers more than 100 hands-on educational exhibits for kids of every age. In 2008, the popular museum doubled its size, creating more opportunities for exhibits, exploration, and fun. This addition will include improvements to all aspects of the museum experience, including new galleries and permanent exhibits, interactive Play Garden and a Rooftop Garden complete with a grand spiral staircase that leads to a Fairy Tale Tower—the perfect spot for imagination to take flight. Explore the Children's Village, Math Path, and a three-story slide in this participatory museum that is both fun and educational. Other popular exhibits include A Little Bit of Magic, designed exclusively for kids ages one to seven, and an area just for infants, toddlers, and parents called For Baby & Me. First Impressions, an exhibit that contains more than 75,000 plastic rods and is more than 8 feet tall, allows kids to make an impression of their hands, their head, or their whole body. There's also a Lewis and Clark Adventure, a Water Works exhibit, and Air Power, where kids can experiment with various blasts of, well, air power. Recently, the Magic House was voted the No. 1 national attraction in terms of "child appeal" by Zagat U.S. Family Travel Guide. Children under two are admitted free.

MILDRED LANE KEMPER
ART MUSEUM FREE
Washington University
Forsyth and Skinker Boulevards
(314) 935-4523
www.kemperartmuseum.wustl.edu

The Mildred Lane Kemper Art Museum is considered one the finest university collections in the country. The museum exhibits works from the Washington University permanent collection, special loan exhibitions, and student and faculty shows. The permanent collection includes significant holdings of 19th- and 20th-century American and European paintings, sculptures, and prints as well as major contemporary works. Artists represented in the collection include George Caleb Bingham, Thomas Cole, Pablo Picasso, Max Ernst, Alexander Calder, Jackson Pollock, Edgar Degas, Edouard Manet, and Jean-François Millet. Closed Tuesday and university holidays.

MISSOURI HISTORY MUSEUM
(MISSOURI HISTORICAL SOCIETY) $
Forest Park, Lindell Boulevard and
Skinker entrance
(314) 746-4599
www.mohistory.org

The Missouri Historical Society's History Museum has a number of changing exhibits, as well as Seeking St. Louis, a time capsule of the city's history. Visitors to Seeking St. Louis explore the past and its impact upon the present and the future through three galleries: A Place in Time, which explores the mysterious, now-vanished Mississippian Indian civilization and the great urban center known as Mound City; Currents, which takes visitors into the lives of the city's 18th- and 19th-century inhabitants as they led St. Louis from a frontier village to a major industrial and commercial center; and Reflections, which examines the decades that followed the 1904 World's Fair, including Charles Lindbergh's triumphant return from his historic flight, the city's rise as an industrial center and its mobilization for World War II, the struggle for civil rights, and the building of the Gateway Arch. History unfolds in each gallery through state-of-the-art displays, interactive exhibits, and thousands of artifacts, including a replica of Lindbergh's The Spirit of St. Louis. The replica, acquired by the Missouri Historical Society in 1962, has been fully restored and now hangs in the center of the Grand Hall. General admission to the museum is free, but some exhibits charge admission fees. On Tuesdays, admission is free to all special exhibits.

MUSEUM OF TRANSPORTATION $

3015 Barrett Station Road
(314) 965-7998
www.museumoftransport.org

If it rolls, flies, or floats, chances are that you can find it here. The Museum of Transportation has 27 diesel or other internal-combustion locomotives, one gas-turbine and 10 electric locomotives, 45 freight cars, and 31 passenger train cars, plus street, interurban, and rapid-transit cars. The collection of steam locomotives is the largest in North America and includes an example of almost every major type made. Automobiles on display range from a 1901 steam-powered delivery truck to a 1912 Overland seven-passenger touring car to the incredibly rare 1963 Chrysler Turbine Car. There's even a tugboat that visitors can walk aboard and explore. All totaled, there are more than 300 transportation pieces at the museum, including locomotives, passenger cars, automobiles, streetcars, buses, and aircraft. A more recent feature is a semi-permanent exhibit about one of St. Louis's most well-known Route 66 landmarks, the Coral Court Motel. The motel was popular with travelers on the route as they passed through town on "the Mother Road." The exhibit features the Streamline Moderne façade of one of the motel bungalows, which was built in 1941 of glazed brick and glass blocks and is constructed from original materials removed when the motel was torn down in 1995. The Earl C. Lindburg Automotive Center, which looks like a contemporary auto dealership, Houses a number of unique vehicles, including a 1901 Cadillac, a 1919 panel truck, and the 1960 Bobby Darin "Dream Car." Closed Monday.

i The replica of Charles Lindbergh's plane, The Spirit of St. Louis, which is in the Missouri History Museum, was built in 1928 by the Ryan Airlines Corporation, the company that built the original plane. It was used in the movie *The Spirit of St. Louis,* starring Jimmy Stewart.

SAINT LOUIS ART MUSEUM (SLAM) FREE

Forest Park
1 Fine Arts Drive
(314) 721-0072
www.slam.org

This museum, located inside the building that served as the Fine Arts Palace of the 1904 World's Fair, is one of the leading art museums in the country. The permanent collection ranges from ancient to contemporary and includes a cross section of works by world-renowned artists. The photography holdings include works by Berenice Abbott, Manuel Alvarez Bravo, Roy DeCarava, Walker Evans, Lorna Simpson, Edward Steichen, and Paul Strand. African art, including face masks, headdresses, household furniture, portraits, and free-standing figures, ranges from naturalistic to abstract styles. The collection of American art includes scenes from the Western frontier by George Caleb Bingham and Charles Wimar, paintings by American Impressionists such as John Henry Twachtman and Frederick Carl Frieseke, works by Abstract Expressionists such as Mark Rothko, and the pop imagery of Roy Lichtenstein and Andy Warhol. The ancient art collection includes Assyrian, Coptic, Egyptian, Greek, Iranian, Islamic, Near Eastern, Persian, Roman, and Syrian works, as well as the mummy Amen-Nestawy-Nakht. The museum also has a spectacular collection of Turkish rugs that ranks among the best in the world, and its Asian collection includes magnificent examples of early Buddhist sculpture, Chinese calligraphy and painting, and a broad range of ceramics and decorative arts. SLAM has several exceptional South Asian sculptures and Tantric Buddhist works, as well as a fine representation of Japanese art. The Decorative Arts and Design collection features Renaissance, Western, and contemporary art, with holdings including furniture, silver, glass, ceramics, metalwork, textiles, weapons and armor, and architectural fragments, as well as 20th-century industrial design examples. The collection also features six period rooms that re-create the European and American interiors of the 18th and 19th centuries. European paintings and sculpture include a selection of paintings representing the major categories of 17th-century Dutch art, and the modern art collection includes more than 40 paintings by Max Beckmann, as well as works by early modern masters such as Paul Cézanne, Amedeo Modigliani, Claude Monet, Pablo Picasso, and Vincent van Gogh. More recent work by American and European artists is represented by Louise Bourgeois, Philip Guston, Ellsworth Kelly, Anselm Kiefer, Franz Kline, Brice Marden, Joan Mitchell, Henry Moore, Martin Puryear, Gerhard Richter, and Frank Stella. The collection of Oceanic and Pre-Columbian pieces is considered among the best in the world and includes works from the American Southwest, Papua New Guinea, and Australia. Some special exhibitions charge admission fees.

SAINT LOUIS SCIENCE CENTER $
5050 Oakland Avenue
(800) 456-7572
www.slsc.org
Explore 700 exhibits on the environment, aviation, and technology, or check out the life-size dinosaurs and the James S. McDonnell Planetarium's Space Station experience. Kids of all ages can enjoy the DNA Zone, where they'll learn about the science of genetics and biotechnology, advances in health and medical technology, agriculture, and forensic science. There are more than 15 hands-on exhibits, activities, and demonstrations that explain how genes make everyone unique. Cyberville features state-of-the-art technology, one-of-a-kind exhibits, and more than 45 hands-on activities to make complex technology user-friendly and easy to understand for all ages (especially adults who still can't figure out their DVR or DVD player). The Flight! Gallery features the designs of the 23 contestants of the X PRIZE space race, and the experience of lift-off of a space shuttle launch on video. The Discovery Room provides hands-on experiences for children ages two to eight. Kids can dress up like surgeons, go back in time and imagine life as a Mississippian Native American, or explore fossils and a cave. You can visit with life-sized animated dinosaurs in the Ecology and Environment Gal-

leries, and see innovative science demonstrations and "Science Goes Splat!" at CenterStage. There are also marble highways, a car ramp, computers, a camera and monitor, magnets, optics, microscopes, and activity boxes to help children focus on the fundamentals of science and technology. Smaller kids enjoy the area featuring a Velcro wall, plastic mirrored walls, a gym mat floor, and age-appropriate toys and books. The Omnimax Theater and some special exhibitions charge a fee, but general admission is free.

SAINT LOUIS UNIVERSITY MUSEUM OF ART $
3663 Lindell Boulevard
(314) 977-3399
http://sluma.slu.edu
This four-story, historic French Revival mansion on the Saint Louis University campus houses the university's extensive art collection, including works by Dale Chihuly, Joachim Probst, Miguel Martinez, Joan Miró, Renato Laffranchi, and Charles Lotton. The collection also includes modern and contemporary art by Richard Serra, Ernest Trova, Serge Poliakoff, and Arnoldo Pomodoro, and more than 2,000 pieces of memorabilia and fine art donated to the university by the Cartier family, of the internationally renowned Cartier Jewelers. Open Wednesday through Sunday.

SHELDON CONCERT HALL, BALLROOM AND ART GALLERIES FREE
3648 Washington Boulevard
(314) 533-9900
www.sheldonconcerthall.org
Built in 1912, this building hosts a wide variety of concerts, and it also houses six art galleries. The galleries feature changing exhibits in five categories: photography, architecture, St. Louis artists and collections, jazz history, and children's art. The galleries offer more than 20 yearly exhibitions, and the museum collaborates with local, national and international institutions and individuals in the art world. In addition to the free exhibits, the Sheldon offers a number of educational programs such as Tuesday Evening

Gallery Talks, Lunchtime Lectures in Architecture and Master Class Workshops for children, Closed Sunday and Monday.

SOLDIERS MEMORIAL MILITARY
MUSEUM   FREE
1315 Chestnut Street
(314) 622-4550
http://stlouis.missouri.org/government/
solmem.html
Dedicated in 1936 to St. Louis's veterans and war dead, this museum has exhibits that include uniforms, photographs, weaponry, war souvenirs, and regalia. Located between Market, Pine, 13th and 14th streets in downtown, it is the first of two war memorials in St. Louis that were built to honor World War I veterans. Notable features include the massive stone columns with carved stone panels between the columns that bear the faces of war veterans, and large stone statues of winged horses and military men and women, representing courage, loyalty, vision, and sacrifice.

i   The St. Louis Cardinals Hall of Fame Museum is relocating and will be closed until sometime in 2010. Check out the Cardinal's Web site for more information (www.stlouis.cardinals.mlb.com).

ST. LOUIS FIRE DEPARTMENT
MUSEUM   FREE
1421 North Jefferson Avenue
(314) 289-1933
Housed within the City Fire Marshall's offices, the display includes photos taken at some of the city's most famous fires; a life-size statue of Florian, commander of the Roman Army and patron saint of firefighters; and more than 700 artifacts on permanent loan to the museum from the Missouri Historical Society. This collection of historical fire-fighting equipment and memorabilia includes items such as fire helmets, glass hand-grenade fire extinguishers, badges and medals, a collection of toy fire trucks, as well as fire plates, leather water buckets, and an extensive collection of fire marks, emblems, and plaques from around the world dating from the 1700s. Call for hours.

i   Log on to www.bigthankyou.org to get free or discounted admissions to workshops at and performances by some of St. Louis's most popular attractions and arts organizations, including Dance St. Louis, Saint Louis Symphony, St. Louis Zoo, Sheldon Concert Hall, Jazz at the Bistro, The Magic House, Center of Creative Arts, The Black Rep, Saint Louis Science Center, and many others.

TOURS

ANHEUSER-BUSCH BREWERY TOURS   FREE
Interstate 55 and Arsenal Street
(314) 577-2626
www.budweisertours.com
Tours of the historic brewery include stops at the Brew House, Budweiser Clydesdale stables, lager cellar, packaging plant, hospitality room, and Bud World gift shop. Visitors get to follow the making of Budweiser from its raw natural ingredients, such as barley malt, rice, hops, yeast, and water, to final packaged bottles and cans of "the king of beers." The tour includes stops inside the buildings that house the stainless-steel mash tanks where the brewing process begins. Visitors then see the ground barley malt being mixed with water and boiled rice, which is then transferred into the fermentation tanks. Like the product itself, the tour wraps up on the packaging lines, where the finished product is packaged into bottles, cans, and draft kegs, with the lines capable of filling up to 2.6 million 12-ounce cans or 1.4 million 12-ounce bottles per day. At the conclusion of the tour, visitors of legal drinking age are treated to complimentary Anheuser-Busch products in the tour center's hospitality room.

BUSCH STADIUM $
Clark and Seventh Streets
(314) 345-9565 (tours);
(314) 345-9000 (tickets)
www.stlcardinals.com
When the new Busch Stadium opened its doors in 2006, baseball fans didn't have to learn any

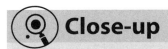

Close-up

Home of the Cardinals: Busch Stadium

In 2006 "the best fans in baseball" celebrated the inaugural season of a new "nest" for the St. Louis Cardinals. The current Busch Stadium, located next door to the location of the old Busch Stadium, is a retro-looking ballpark that reflects the city's rich baseball tradition and its love of red brick.

The state-of-the-art facility was designed by the architecture firm HOK Sport and features a seating capacity of more than 43,975. Including the number of standing room only spaces and additional suite and party room tickets available, the total capacity is 46,861. Ticket prices range from $20 to $25 for bleacher seats to $70 for tickets to the Redbird Club behind home plate. The Redbird Club offers great views, indoor and outdoor viewing options—including TVs—and food and beverage options that are a cut-above the usual ballpark fare. Single game tickets can be purchased in advance by calling (314) 345-9000 or via www.stlcardinals.com.

This version of Busch Stadium—there were two previous stadiums named for the Busch family—includes all of the modern amenities, including luxury suites, party rooms, two full-service cocktail bars, and more than a dozen themed concession stands featuring everything from the usual ballpark favorites like burgers, hot dogs, and nachos to pizzas, fajitas, and barbecue. In addition, the four-level facility includes elevators and escalators, family restrooms, six ATMs, the Cardinals Team Store, and even a Build-Your-Own-Fredbird shop. For the serious fan, a visit to the Cardinals Authentics store is a must for game-used baseballs, bases, and other equipment. The stadium's Family Pavilion, located on Level 1 between Gate 6 and Gate 1, opens two hours prior to each game and continues operation until a half hour after the game is completed. High-energy baseball fans can work off some energy before and during the game in the batting cage or speed-pitch areas, T-Ball cages, or Soft-Play play area. All guests with a day-of-game ticket are admitted to this area free of charge; however, there are fees associated with playing the games and activities. There are two rows of tables and chairs available so you can watch the game from this vantage point for up to two innings.

Stadium tours are offered daily year-round, except when there's a day game and on select holidays. The tour includes stops at the Cardinals dugout, the warning track, the press box, the Family Pavilion, Redbird Club, and Cardinals Club. Call (314) 345-9565 for more info, or e-mail stadiumtours@stlcardinals.com.

new routes to find the ballpark. St. Louis's favorite boys of summer play their home games at the retro-styled stadium that is located immediately adjacent to where the old Busch Stadium was built. The Cardinals' new roost, a beautiful red brick venue that features an incredible view of the city skyline beyond the outfield wall, has all of the modern amenities that fans have come to expect in modern ballparks. Stadium tours are available year-round with the exception of a few major holidays and anytime there's a day game. Tours depart from Gate 5 at 9:30 a.m., 11:00 a.m., 12:30 p.m., and 2:00 p.m. daily, and they include

visits to the Cardinals dugout, the press room, onto the warning track, and to the Redbird Club, Family Pavilion, and one of the party rooms available for rent. (See Close-up on next page for more details.)

Baseball fans attending games at Busch Stadium are permitted to carry in backpacks, purses, diaper bags, fanny packs, and soft-sided coolers that do not exceed a maximum size of 16 x 16 x 8 inches. Snacks and nonalcoholic beverages, including water and soda in open cups or clear plastic bottles no larger than two liters, are allowed into the stadium. This allows fans on a budget to save some cash by not having to rely on the concession stands for all of their food and drink needs. Alcohol, bottles, cans, thermoses, hard-sided coolers, and hard plastic cups/mugs are not permitted.

THE FOX THEATRE $
527 North Grand Boulevard
(314) 534-1111
www.fabulousfox.com

Opened in 1929 as a vaudeville palace, the Fox continues to present live entertainment, including touring Broadway shows and music, dance, and comedy concerts. Throughout the years the "Fabulous Fox" has been a showcase for movie premieres, great stage attractions, special events, and many of the famous personalities of show business. The incredibly ornate theater has been restored to its original splendor and its Siamese-Byzantine decor. Even without a show on the stage, this facility is a destination in itself. Tours are offered Tuesday, Thursday, and Saturday at 10:30 a.m.

WINERIES

LOUIS P. BALDUCCI VINEYARDS   FREE
6601 Highway 94 South, Augusta
(636) 482-VINO
www.balduccivineyards.com

Louis P. Balducci Vineyards is the latest addition to Missouri's wine country. In addition to the beautiful surroundings and breathtaking views, the Balduccis produce 11 wine varieties and offer up a menu of salads, pizzas, pastas, entrees, and dessert specials. Located 3.5 miles west of Augusta, the winery hosts a number of special events throughout the year, including live music on Saturdays from April through October.

MOUNT PLEASANT WINERY   FREE
5634 High Street, Augusta
(636) 482-WINE
www.mountpleasant.com

In addition to great wine and food and top entertainment, Mount Pleasant Winery offers stunning views of the rolling hills and lush green flatland that connect the hill country to the Missouri River. Voted Favorite Winery in the 2008 Sauce magazine readers' poll, Mount Pleasant offers free tours of the facility on weekends and a tasting room with indoor and outdoor seating. You can grab a bite to eat with your wine from the Augusta Grocery, which stocks assorted cheeses, fruit, crackers, and deli meats, or at the Mount Pleasant Grill, which offers salads, sandwiches, veggie wraps, and the house specialty—flatbread baked with sun-dried tomatoes and Fontina cheese and served with a basil pesto dipping sauce. During October, Mount Pleasant joins the other Missouri wineries for a month-long Oktoberfest celebration that includes popular local bands and harvest-related activities, such as grape stomping. Admission may be charged for special events.

STONE HILL WINERY AND
VINTAGE RESTAURANT   FREE
1110 Stone Hill Highway, Hermann
(573) 486-2221
www.stonehillwinery.com

Stone Hill is Missouri's largest winery, and it began making wine around 1847. Today, perched dramatically on a hill overlooking the lovely German town of Hermann, Stone Hill welcomes thousands of visitors to enjoy its award-winning wines and the region's Old-World hospitality. Other activities available include tours of the underground cellars, wine tastings, live music, and wine-related special events throughout the year. Stone Hill also offers features the Vintage Restaurant, situated on the winery grounds in a restored carriage house and horse barn. The menu features German cuisine, steaks, and a variety of American dishes. Admission may be charged for special events.

OTHER ATTRACTIONS

BONNE TERRE MINE/WEST END
DIVING $$–$$$
39 Allen Street, Bonne Terre
(314) 731-5003
www.2dive.com

Bonne Terre Mine, a National Historic Site, is the world's largest freshwater dive resort and offers walking, boat, or scuba tours of world's largest man-made caverns and lake. Scuba classes are also available. Water conditions remain constant, with more than 100-foot visibility year-round. Sights include mammoth architecture, oar carts, scaffolding, grating, staircases, pillars, slurry pipes, the famed elevator shaft, and more. A National Geographic "Top 10 Adventure," Bonne Terre/ West End Diving is one of the most unusual, beautiful, and relaxing full-service dive resorts anywhere. Bonne Terre was an active mine for more than 100 years, and the resort location was filmed by legendary oceanographer Jacques Cousteau. Prices vary by activity.

BUTTERFLY HOUSE $
Faust Park
15193 Olive Boulevard, Chesterfield
(636) 530-0076
www.butterflyhouse.org
This cultural and educational attraction allows visitors a chance to see thousands of butterflies in flight and to witness the mystery of metamorphosis. Changing exhibits are housed in the Grand Hall, which is also home to a variety of plants and animals. The Butterflies of the World exhibit features preserved specimens and provides an introduction to more than 18,000 species. The Butterfly Conservatory is the heart of the Butterfly House, housing more than 1,000 tropical butterflies in free flight. As many as 60 butterfly species and 150 tropical plant species are exhibited, and hundreds of chrysalides from around the world are on display. Butterflies literally emerge before your very eyes—it's fascinating for kids and adults. There are a number of classes and activities for kids of all ages that are offered throughout the year. Closed Monday except Memorial Day through Labor Day. Children three and under are admitted free.

ECKERT'S COUNTRY STORE AND FARMS $
951 South Greenmount Road, Belleville, IL
(618) 233-0513

2719 Eckert Orchard Lane, Millstadt, IL
(618) 476-3260

20995 Eckert Orchard Road, Grafton, IL
(618) 786-3445
www.eckerts.com
Started as a simple roadside stand in 1910, Eckert's is the largest pick-your-own orchard operation in the United States. The combination fruit orchards/family entertainment centers feature a variety of family-friendly activities and special events throughout the year. In addition to riding the wagons out into the fields to pick your own fruits, vegetables, or Christmas tree, seasonal activities include hayrides, craft making, wreath making, and photo contests. Open February through December; hours vary by season. Prices vary by activity.

FOREST PARK FREE
Kingshighway, Lindell, Clayton and I–64
(314) 289-5300
www.stlouis.missouri.org/citygov/parks/forestpark
Forest Park is one of St. Louis's most treasured resources. Located within easy access of most of the region, the 1,370-acre park is the nation's seventh-largest urban park and one of the region's premier attractions. The park's annual attendance is estimated at about 12 million people, which includes those who visit the cultural institutions, participate in recreational activities, attend special events, or just enjoy sitting under a tree and watching the world go by. The park officially opened to the public on June 24, 1876. In 1904 the Louisiana Purchase Exposition, also known as the St. Louis World's Fair, drew more than 19 million visitors from around the world to Forest Park, and the event dramatically changed the appearance of its western half. Today the zoo, art museum, Municipal Opera (Muny), science center, history museum, and the Jewel Box

greenhouse share the park with golf courses, tennis courts, an archery range, ball fields, handball courts, a skating rink, biking and hiking trails, and lakes for fishing and boat rides.

The park also has an "inclusive public playground," designed for use by able-bodied children as well as those with disabilities. The playground is located between the Missouri History Museum and the Dennis and Judith Jones Visitor and Information Center. Visitors can also access a free, self-guided iPod Walking Tour that offers a 30- to 50-minute audio tour introduction/overview of Forest Park and the Grand Basin, Art Hill, Picnic Island, the Boathouse, and the park's recent and not-so-recent history. The tour, which is free, requires a credit card number as a refundable deposit for the listening device. It is available to check out daily from the visitor center on a first-come, first-served basis, and it can be kept overnight and returned the next day. Or you can download the audio tour narrative onto your own MP3 player at the Forest Park Forever Web site (www.forestparkforever.org) along with The Journey of Forest Park brochure.

One of the greatest things about Forest Park is that admission to all of its attractions is free. Most of the institutions host special exhibitions throughout the year that require an admission fee, but these prices are usually reasonable. Each institution also has special free-admission days or times during the week when access to the special exhibits is free as well. Check with the individual museum or institution for details on when free access is available to the touring exhibits.

MERAMEC CAVERNS $$
I–44, exit 230, Stanton
(800) 676-6105
www.americascave.com

Nestled beneath the foothills of the Ozarks, Meramec Caverns showcases more than 400 million years of history. Local tribes of Indians once used it as shelter, and local legend says that the cave was used as a station on the Underground Railroad to hide escaping slaves. In the early 1870s, outlaw Jesse James and his band used the cavern

as a hideout for both men and their horses after train and bank robberies. In 1933 a noted caveologist discovered the seven upper levels of the caverns, and further exploration revealed more than 25 miles of underground passages. Meramec Caverns was opened to the public in 1935 as a tourist attraction, and its complex and colorful mineral formations continue to amaze visitors today. Rangers lead tours through the myriad stalagmites and stalactites that took thousands of years to grow and explain how Mother Nature built an ancient limestone "Wine Table," an entire seven-story mansion, and the rarest and largest cave formations in the world. It's located one hour west of St. Louis, and a motel, campgrounds, a gift shop, a restaurant, boat rides, and canoe rentals are available nearby. Children under four are admitted free. No strollers permitted on the tour.

NATIONAL SHRINE OF OUR LADY OF THE SNOWS FREE
442 South DeMazenod Drive, Belleville, IL
(314) 241-3400, (618) 367-6700
www.snows.org

The National Shrine of Our Lady of the Snows is one of the largest outdoor shrines in North America. Owned and operated by the Missionary Oblates of Mary Immaculate, the shrine blends spirituality, unique architecture, and imaginative landscaping to create a serene setting. In addition to offering daily masses, there are nine devotional areas throughout the grounds for all faiths and denominations. Each year, between Thanksgiving Day and January 6, the shrine comes alive with more than one million white lights along a mile-and-a-half stretch that winds through the grounds. Visitors drive through a collection of electro-art sculptures and life-size figures depicting the Christmas story, then can stop at the visitor center and Christmas Village for storytelling, coloring, and face painting, along with activities at the Children's Theatre, caroling, and a live-animal display. The shrine is open year-round and has a restaurant, gift shop, and motel on-site as well.

ROUTE 66 STATE PARK FREE
I–44 at Lewis Road, exit 266, Eureka
(636) 938-7198
www.mostateparks.com/route66.htm
Route 66 State Park showcases the history and mystique of the highway that has been called "The Main Street of America" and has come to represent American mobility, independence, and a spirit of adventure. Located along the original Route 66 corridor, the 419-acre park is a boon to visitors who want to enjoy nature and see interesting historical displays showcasing Route 66. Bridgehead Inn, a 1935 roadhouse, serves as the park's visitor center and houses a collection of artifacts from the Mother Road. The park also offers road-weary travelers a place to picnic, exercise, bird watch, or just enjoy nature. There are also a number of walking, bicycling, and equestrian trails throughout the park.

SOULARD FARMERS MARKET FREE
Seventh and Lafayette Streets
(314) 622-4180
www.soulardmarket.com
Established in 1779, the Soulard Market has more than 140 stalls filled with farm-fresh and imported produce, meats, herbs, flowers, spices, fresh seafood, and just about everything else you can imagine. Today's Soulard Market is a lone survivor, but it was once one of many markets in the city. Open year-round Wednesday through Sunday. (See the Shopping chapter for more information.)

ST. LOUIS ARTISTS' GUILD FREE
Two Oak Knoll Park, Clayton
(314) 727-9599
www.stlouisartistsguild.org
Located in a restored 1920s mansion, the St. Louis Artists' Guild hosts exhibitions that highlight artistic excellence, cultural diversity, and social concerns. Exhibits range from national, regional, and local competitions to national traveling shows, curated shows, and collaborative and exchange exhibitions with other arts organizations. In addition to classes and art studios, the guild also offers resources that include the Messing Library

and its extensive collection of books on art techniques, art history, and artists; a state-of-the-art printmaking studio, complete with an inking room and pressroom; and a photographic darkroom. Closed Monday and holidays.

ST. LOUIS UNION STATION FREE
Market Street, between 18th and
20th Streets
(314) 421-6655
www.stlouisunionstation.com
St. Louis Union Station, once one of the largest and busiest passenger rail terminals in the world, is now one of America's great marketplaces and boasts more than 90 shops and restaurants, including The Body Shop, Cardinals Clubhouse, the Fudgery, Dog On It, the Bud Shop, Beatles for Sale, and St. Louis's Hard Rock Cafe. Union Station first opened in 1894 but ceased operation as an active train terminal in 1978. It reopened in August 1985 as the largest adaptive reuse project in the United States. Today this National Historic Landmark of unmatched beauty and elegance has been dramatically restored and redeveloped as a dynamic mixed-use project that includes shopping, dining, and entertainment options. St. Louis Union Station also houses a Marriott hotel; luxury offices; four active train tracks; the Train Shed which serves as a plaza for festivals, concerts, and other special events; and even its own lake. The station's architecture is an eclectic mix of Romanesque styles. From its magnificent 65-foot, barrel-vaulted ceiling in the Grand Hall to its Victorian-engineered train shed totaling more than 11 acres, St. Louis Union Station

i One interesting feature of St. Louis Union Station's Grand Hall is the Whispering Arch, the station's entryway. Due to its design, one person can stand at one side of the entry and whisper something that can be heard by another individual standing at the opposite end of the arch. The sound travels up and over the heads of the participants, instead of across the room.

remains one of the nation's true architectural gems. The free "Memories Museum" features personal accounts from people who visited the station during its heyday.

ST. LOUIS WALK OF FAME   FREE
6500 block of Delmar Boulevard
(314) 727-STAR
www.stlouiswalkoffame.org

Embedded in the sidewalk along Delmar Boulevard in an area known as The Loop are more than 110 brass stars honoring individuals from the St. Louis area who have made major contributions to our cultural heritage. Every star is accompanied by a bronze plaque that sums up the achievements of an extraordinary man or woman who is associated with St. Louis. You'll find such familiar names as Nelly, Bob Costas, Ulysses S. Grant, Maya Angelou, Tina Turner, Lou Brock, Chuck Berry, Tennessee Williams, Charles Lindbergh, Scott Joplin, and Redd Foxx, along with some not-so-familiar names like Susan Blow (who created the first public kindergarten) and Pierre Laclede (founder of St. Louis). The informational plaques help make this walk of fame educational as well as enjoyable, because the knowledge gained from the plaques allows visitors to gain insight into the individual and his or her accomplishments. The Walk of Fame is open daily year-round, 24 hours a day.

TURTLE PLAYGROUND   FREE
Oakland and Tamm Avenues
www.stlouis.missouri.org/citygov/parks/
forestpark/turtle.html

Giant turtle sculptures that were built with kids in mind are the highlight of this playground. These turtles were designed to be climbed on, and no kid can resist them. It's a great way to use up some of that extra energy kids always seem to have! The playground is open year-round and overlooks Forest Park and I–64.

WORLD BIRD SANCTUARY   FREE
125 Bald Eagle Ridge Road, Valley Park
(636) 225-4390
www.worldbirdsanctuary.org

The World Bird Sanctuary is a bird facility like no other in the world. Visitors are able to view eagles, owls, hawks, and other creatures in a majestic park setting. There are also a variety of educational programs, nature trails, and displays that help visitors understand the relationship between birds, their environment, and humans. Naturalists are on hand to discuss the birds' role in the world and the problems they face, with many of the "teacher" birds on display for up-close viewing. Open daily.

KIDSTUFF

Lots of cities claim to be "family-friendly" or "kid-centric," but St. Louis means it. Not only are there plenty of activities and attractions geared toward kids of varying ages, but many of the attractions are free, which makes St. Louis a budget-friendly destination for families. The attractions that charge admission have a lot to offer as well, and many of these are great places to go when it's a rainy day and the kids need to use up some of that excess energy that little ones always seem to have.

The listings in this chapter have been organized under the following subject headings: Artsy Stuff, which includes art museums as well as artistic and cultural attractions and organizations; Fun Stuff, a listing of amusement and water parks as well as other select outdoor or more active attractions; Furred, Finned, and Feathered Stuff, which features places where kids of all ages can get up close and personal with animals; Smart Stuff, which includes museums, historic sites, and the like; Tasty Stuff, a listing of restaurants in the area that are especially kid-friendly; and Wacky Stuff, which covers pretty much everything else.

Price Code

The following price codes are based on what it costs for one adult to get into one of these cool places. (After all, the grown-ups are the ones with the bank accounts, right?) Almost all of the attractions and destinations listed in this chapter offer discounted pricing for kids and senior citizens.

$...........$15 or less per person
$$ ....$16–$25 per person
$$$ ....$26–$35 per person
$$$$ ... More than $35 per person

ARTSY STUFF

The following is a list of many of the area's arts and culture organizations that have programs and classes for children as well as adults. Many offer family-centric theater and special event options, daytime performances, and various special events.

CENTER OF CREATIVE ARTS (COCA) $
3750 Washington Boulevard
(314) 535-4660
www.cocastl.org
COCA's Family Theatre Series offers a broad range of performances for kids and adults. Past performances have run the gamut from the juggling and wisecracking Flaming Idiots to the crazy costumes and dance moves of the Frogz dance troupe. The center features educational classes, camps, and workshops for all ages—including adults—as well as numerous contemporary art exhibits in the Millstone Gallery. Admission to the center is free on Thursday. Closed Sunday.

DANCE ST. LOUIS $–$$$$
634 North Grand Boulevard, Suite 1102
(314) 534-6622
www.dancestlouis.org
Dance St. Louis produces a variety of dance performances, including classical ballet, modern dance, and traditional dance, as well as a number of educational and outreach programs for

local dancers and students. The organization also hosts Young People's Performances, live professional dance performances that have been tailored to suit young audiences.

THE IMAGINARY THEATRE COMPANY $
130 Edgar Road
(314) 968-4925
www.repstl.org
This kid-centric theater group sponsored by the St. Louis Repertory Theatre presents a variety of local touring productions, such as My Father's Dragon, Puss 'n Boots, Robin Hood and The Velveteen Rabbit. The Rep produces a full season of main stage and studio theater performances, as well as educational programs at the Loretto-Hilton Theatre. The Imaginary Theatre Company also stages special public Mainstage performances during the winter holidays and in the spring.

MUNICIPAL OPERA ASSOCIATION
(THE MUNY) $-$$
Forest Park
(314) 361-1900
www.muny.org
The oldest and largest outdoor theater in the country, the Muny hosts a number of popular musicals each summer. In addition to live theatrical performances, the Muny Kids and Teens Performing Troupes serve as a community outreach program of the Muny Opera in Forest Park. The troupes perform year-round at special events held throughout the area and help serve as a training ground for talented youngsters.

OPERA THEATRE OF ST. LOUIS $$-$$$
Loretto-Hilton Center at Webster University
Big Bend and Edgar Roads, Webster Groves
(314) 961-0644 (box office),
(314) 961-0171 (office)
www.experienceopera.org
The Opera Theatre of St. Louis produces a mix of familiar and unconventional presentations, sung in English and accompanied by members of the

Saint Louis Symphony Orchestra. Opera Theatre also offers professionally staged opera productions performed by young people for audiences of all ages, usually during the fall term. A young cast from across the St. Louis area works in a professional setting with experienced conductors, directors, and designers.

SAINT LOUIS SYMPHONY
ORCHESTRA $-$$$$
718 North Grand Boulevard
(314) 533-2500 (general info),
(314) 534-1700 (box office)
www.slso.org
The Saint Louis Symphony is a world-renowned ensemble that performs a broad musical repertoire and offers a number of live performances geared to younger audiences.

Hour-long Family Concerts take place on select Sunday afternoons and "come as you are" attire is encouraged. Kinder Konzerts are performances that incorporate instruction and music for kids in kindergarten to grade three, while the Young People's Concerts target children in grades four through six. The Young Adults Concert Series is geared to older students. The critically acclaimed orchestra has received six Grammy Awards and more than 50 Grammy nominations. The orchestra features performances by such world-renowned musicians as Yo-Yo Ma, Itzhak Perlman, and Wynton Marsalis.

SAINT LOUIS SYMPHONY YOUTH
ORCHESTRA $-$$$$
718 North Grand Avenue
(314) 534-1700
www.slso.org
The Saint Louis Symphony Youth Orchestra consists of nearly 100 talented young performers, ranging in age from 12 to 22. The group rehearses weekly during the school year and presents three programs each season in Powell Symphony Hall under the leadership of Ward Stare, music director and resident conductor director of the Saint Louis Symphony Orchestra.

SOUTH CITY OPEN STUDIO AND
GALLERY FOR CHILDREN $
4255 Arsenal Street
(314) 865-0060
www.scosag.org

Located in a renovated gatehouse in Tower Grove Park, the studio welcomes drop-in visitors as well as students to the ongoing classes offered in drawing, painting, clay, bookbinding, and more. Kids are encouraged to explore art at their own pace and can choose from a variety of hands-on arts activities. An Open Studio Pass offers a one-hour exploration in the medium of their choice under the watchful eye of a qualified SCOSAG art instructor. All materials are included. Prices vary for registration in the ongoing classes held throughout the year. Daytime parent and child classes are also available. Closed Sunday.

FUN STUFF

RAGING RIVERS WATERPARK $$
100 Palisades Parkway, Grafton, IL
(618) 786-2345
www.ragingrivers.com

Located on the Great River Road, this water park is popular during the hot and steamy St. Louis summers. There are several wet and wild attractions to keep the kids occupied here, such as the Giant Wave Pool, Swirlpool tunnel flume, Endless River, Tree House Harbor, and Itty Bitty Surf City for smaller children. Little ones can enjoy their own pint-size water-slides, splash pools, rain tree, tunnels, and the Fountain Mountain family interactive area. Open Memorial Day through Labor Day. Inner tube and locker rentals are available for a nominal fee.

i At Schnucks supermarkets, you can pick up coupons for discounted admission to family-friendly attractions like Six Flags and Raging Rivers Water Park.

SIX FLAGS ST. LOUIS $$$–$$$$
Interstate 44, exit 261, Eureka
(636) 938-4800
www.sixflags.com

Smaller kids have an area full of rides tailored to their tamer tastes. There are ten different rides and attractions, including a fun family coaster, a fun maze, and the Looney Tooter, a pint-size train. Kids will enjoy the Scooby-Doo! Ghostblasters— The Mystery of the Scary Swamp boat ride, as well as bumper cars, go-karts, the 1915 Grand Ole Carousel, and an authentic 25-ton narrow-gauge steam locomotive. There are also plenty of coaster-style thrill rides, including the Boss, Batman the Ride, the Ninja, Mr. Freeze, and the Screamin' Eagle. Tony Hawk's Big Spin, the Evel Knievel roller coaster and the Superman Tower of Power are just a few of the park's most popular thrill rides. Others include Thunder River, a whitewater-rapids ride; the Tidal Wave boat ride; the Log Flume; Rush Street Flyer; and the 18-storytall Ferris wheel, Colossus. New for 2009, The Wahoo Racer is a six-lane water slide that propels riders along 262-feet of steep drops and rolls. There are also plenty of live entertainment shows to let you catch your breath or take a short break, including Miss Kitty's Saloon Revue and the Palace Theater Magic Show. After the sun sets, Six Flags lights up the night with Glow in the Park, a nighttime parade featuring six custom-designed floats, mobile units, and 65 light-adorned drummers, puppeteers, singers, dancers and stilt walkers. Six Flags' admission prices include entry to Hurricane Harbor Water Park. Children age three and under are admitted free. There is a fee for on-site parking.

STEINBERG SKATING RINK $
Forest Park
(314) 361-0613
http://steinbergskatingrink.com

Steinberg Skating Rink has been a wintertime tradition in St. Louis since 1957. As soon as it got cold, everyone headed to the rink for some good old-fashioned ice-skating fun. Today locals and visitors can enjoy skating and entertainment at the rink, including sand volleyball games during the warm weather months, as well as outdoor dining and live music at the cafe on weekends. Summer diners can enjoy a great menu along with food served on a keepsake Frisbee for some warm weather fun. Ice skates are available to rent for a nominal charge.

SWING-A-ROUND FUN TOWN $-$$
Highways 141 and 30, Fenton
(636) 349-7077
www.sarfun.com
Go-karts, bumper boats, miniature golf, and batting cages and the new Bowlingo Bowling Lanes offer great ways to entertain the younger set for a few hours. There's a Kiddie Karts raceway specifically for children three to eight years old, and a 12,000-square-foot indoor arcade with more than 80 electronic and interactive games. The facility also has a number of attractions specifically geared to children eight years old and younger, including Softplay tunnels and slides.

TROPICANA LANES $-$$
7960 Clayton Road, Clayton
(314) 781-0282
www.tropicanalanes.com
Tropicana Lanes, located in nearby Clayton, is a great way to spend a day or evening. With 52 lanes, there's a good chance you won't have to wait to roll a few. The venue offers a number of specials that package bowling, shoe rentals, food and sodas on Tuesday, Wednesday, and Sundays. The game room features pool tables, air hockey, pinball and video games. Prices vary, so call for more information.

TURTLE PLAYGROUND FREE
Forest Park, Oakland and Tamm Avenues
Giant turtle sculptures overlook Forest Park from a large grassy area across Interstate 64/Highway 40. Created by City Museum founder and local artist Bob Cassilly, these oversize turtles beg to be climbed upon by kids of all ages. Open year-round.

FURRED, FINNED, AND FEATHERED STUFF

GRANT'S FARM $
10501 Gravois Road
(314) 843-1700
www.grantsfarm.com
This is the Busch (of Anheuser-Busch fame) family estate that once belonged to Gen. Ulysses S. Grant. Grant married a St. Louis girl, and they made their home here before Grant was called into service by President Abraham Lincoln. Today a motorized tram takes you throughout the whole estate and offers a look at some of the farm's exotic animals. In the Bauernhof area, food and refreshment items are available for purchase, and there are complimentary Anheuser-Busch products to certified grown-ups (21 and older). There are also specialty carts throughout the park that sell tasty items. The Bauernhof, built in 1913, was the first building constructed on the Busch family estate. It is typical of a 19th-century Bavarian farm, complete with stables, a carriage house, and offices and quarters for those who live and work at the farm. In addition, there's a barn full of Clydesdales, as well as a veritable museum of classic carriages on display. There's also plenty of live entertainment, including animal shows that allow the kids to participate, as well as

---

Sledding on Art Hill

At the sight of the first snowflake, locals make plans to meet at the top of Forest Park's Art Hill, the area right in front of the Saint Louis Art Museum. Under the watchful eye of the King Louis statue, sledders take to the gentle slope between the art museum and the Grand Basin. Forest Park also offers numerous other activities, such as biking, hiking, boating, and fishing. For more information call (314) 289-5389, or log on to www.forestparkforever.org.

a petting area. Admission is free but the per car parking fee is approximately $10. Open weekends only, April through October.

PURINA FARMS   FREE
200 Checkerboard Drive, Gray Summit
(314) 982-3232
www.events.purina.com/dogs/farms
Purina Farms is an animal lover's dream. In addition to a full-size barn containing domestic farm animals, a theater, and informational center, the attraction offers a variety of informative pet displays, hands-on activities, animal demonstrations, and holiday-themed events. The barn and play area allow visitors to interact with a variety of animals found on a typical working farm, and kids can romp in the hayloft, swing on a rope, or milk a cow. A petting ring in the barn's nursery area allows kids to get close to baby bunnies, chicks, and piglets. Throughout the day, there are milking demonstrations and performances by herding dogs demonstrating their expertise at corralling farm animals. Reservations are required. Call for hours and activities.

SAINT LOUIS ZOO $
Forest Park, Hampton Avenue and
I–64 entrance
(314) 781-0900
www.stlzoo.org
The St. Louis Zoo, founded by noted wildlife expert Marlin Perkins, is a world-class facility that is voted among the top 10 zoos in the country each year. The facility is home to more than 11,000 animals, many of whom live in natural habitat areas such as Big Cat Country, Jungle of the Apes, and the River's Edge. The Wild section features penguins, puffins, and polar bears, as well as grizzlies and black bears. There's a children's petting zoo, a train ride, an Insectarium, ZOOmagination Station and a variety of special events throughout the year. The Children's Zoo includes an amphitheater that presents live animal shows, and presentations change every hour. Visitors can take in programs such as "Pets and Consequences," "Mystery Animals," or "Let's Play

Ball." There's also storytelling with live animals, puppet shows, and animal demonstrations. The zoo's miniature Zooline Railroad offers a 20-minute narrated tour while weaving through tunnels and past favorite animal exhibits on a 1.5-mile trek. Open daily year-round. General admission is free, but some attractions require an additional fee. There are all-day pass packages that allow access to all of the paid attractions. Admission to the Insectarium and the Children's Zoo is free daily from 9:00 to 10:00 a.m. only.

SMART STUFF

BIGFOOT 4X4, INC.   FREE
6311 North Lindbergh Boulevard
(314) 731-8112
www.bigfoot4x4.com
This is the home of the original "monster truck" and the world's largest collection of memorabilia that traces the 25-plus-year history of the Bigfoot phenomenon. Bigfoot started out as your average, everyday 1974 Ford F250 pickup truck and ended up becoming an icon of American entertainment. Closed Sunday.

THE GRIOT MUSEUM OF BLACK
HISTORY AND CULTURE $
2505 St. Louis Avenue
(314) 241-7057
Here you can see life-size wax likenesses of famous African-American Missourians, including peanut butter creator George Washington Carver, former slave Dred Scott, and jazz musician Clark Terry. Highlights include a replica of quarters on a slave ship, artifacts from a slave's cabin in nearby Jonesboro, and an exhibit on the life of Dr. Martin Luther King Jr. Open Tuesday through Saturday, and Sundays during summer months.

CAHOKIA MOUNDS STATE HISTORIC
SITE AND INTERPRETIVE CENTER   FREE
30 Ramey Street, Collinsville, IL
(618) 346-5160
www.cahokiamounds.com
The site of the largest prehistoric Indian city north

of Mexico, Cahokia Mounds includes an interpretive center that gives a 3-D history lesson in how the Mississippian Indian tribe lived more than 900 years ago. Visitors can walk through a life-size diorama of a Mississippian village that includes the stockade, houses, and other structures, as well as everyday items including stone tools, pottery, objects crafted from shell, and clothes made from natural fibers. There's also a Woodhenge solar calendar and an explanation of how the Indian mounds were created. A variety of themed special events take place throughout the calendar year, so it's best to check in advance to see what would be going on. Open Wednesday through Sunday. Donations are suggested.

CITY MUSEUM $
701 North 15th Street
(314) 231-2489
www.citymuseum.org
True to its slogan, this place really is "Unlike Any Museum You've Ever Seen Before." City Museum is the brainchild of a group of local artists who "rescued" most of the items used in the exhibits and attractions from old and historic buildings, factories, and other structures that were destined for the wrecking ball. Kids can climb in, on, and through many of the exhibits, including a hollowed-out tree-trunk maze, and take a quick ride down the old fashioned roller belt slide. There's even a live circus, an aquarium, underground caves, Toddler Town, Tiny Train Town Model Railroad, the Baby Bob Ball Pit and other interactive activities that delight young and old alike. There's also MonstroCity, an elaborate outdoor jungle gym made from airplane fuselages, giant tubes, and more; the Shoelace Factory; and Art City. Snacks are for sale in Beatnik Bob's Cafe, and there's a collection of "antique" video and pinball games as well. City Museum definitely abides by the saying that one man's trash is another man's treasure.

DANIEL BOONE HOME AND
BOONESFIELD VILLAGE $
1868 Highway F, Defiance
(636) 798-2005
www.lindenwood.edu/boone

This Missouri frontier village centered on Boone's 1810 home includes more than a dozen building, including a one-room schoolhouse; church; general store; gristmill; pottery; printer's, carpenter's, and dressmaker's shops; farmstead; homes; and more. The Daniel Boone home, nearly 200 years old, is four stories tall, and its limestone walls are 2.5 feet thick. The home, where Boone lived until his death in 1820, has seven fireplaces, a ballroom, and a variety of everyday items such as a collection of flintlock long rifles, Mrs. Boone's butter churn and sewing basket, Daniel's writing desk, and the family dishes. Closed December through February.

GATEWAY ARCH JEFFERSON
NATIONAL EXPANSION MEMORIAL $-$$
St. Louis Riverfront
(314) 655-1700
www.gatewayarch.com
The 630-foot-high Gateway Arch is the nation's tallest man-made monument and offers a lot of activities. Underneath the Arch, you can watch a riveting documentary about the making of the Arch or an IMAX movie on the very big screen next door. The museum provides a good look at what the region looked like when St. Louis was founded, and it shows what life was like when explorers Lewis and Clark journeyed west from this region in the 1800s. Crowds are generally smaller and the line for the tram to the top is shorter early in the day. You can even buy tickets in advance online at www.gatewayarch.com.

LEWIS & CLARK BOAT HOUSE AND
NATURE CENTER $
1050 Riverside Drive, St. Charles
(636) 947-3199
www.lewisandclarktrail.com
The center, located in quaint downtown St. Charles, interprets the famed Lewis & Clark expedition through a collection of exhibits, literature, and educational programs. Museum exhibits focus on the role St. Charles played in the expedition, as well as the members of the expedition, the tools they used, the journals they kept, and the

many Indian cultures they encountered. Detailed dioramas show the group's journey along the entire length of the Missouri River, crossing of the Rocky Mountains, and the continued trek toward the Pacific Ocean. Each May the city hosts the Lewis and Clark Heritage Days, a reenactment of the encampment, complete with historically accurate costumed participants, black-powder rifle shoots, and frontier craft demonstrations. There are also three replicas of the boats used by the Corps of Discovery and additional exhibits about the expedition.

LEWIS AND CLARK STATE
HISTORIC SITE   FREE
1 Lewis and Clark Trail, Hartford, IL
(618) 251-5811
www.campdubois.com
The visitor center is located at the former Camp DuBois, where explorers Lewis and Clark wintered before embarking on their great trek westward. This 14,000-square-foot exhibit has displays and multimedia presentations on the Lewis & Clark expedition, including a 55-foot keel boat which is a full-size replica of the Corps of Discovery's vessel. The boat is open on one side, revealing the interior passages, storage compartments, living quarters, and cargo. The center also includes an orientation film and exhibits on the Louisiana Territory and the Native Americans who lived there. Open Wednesday through Sunday.

THE MAGIC HOUSE, ST. LOUIS
CHILDREN'S MUSEUM $
516 South Kirkwood Road/(Lindbergh
Boulevard), Kirkwood
(314) 822-8900
www.magichouse.org
This nationally acclaimed children's museum offers more than 100 hands-on educational exhibits for kids—and adults. Kids love the Children's Village, Math Path, and the three-story slide, while new parents and their little ones enjoy the For Baby and Me area for ages two years old and younger. This special area includes a peek-a-boo house, baby gym, and a toddler-size school bus

---

Biking on the Katy Trail

When the weather's beautiful, a great way to enjoy the great outdoors with the kids is to take a bike ride on the Katy Trail, a 185-mile path that begins in nearby St. Charles and offers some of the region's most beautiful scenery. The grade never exceeds 5 percent, so no matter what your fitness level, you and the kids can enjoy a bike ride through this area. You can rent bikes and helmets at trailheads along the route or from the Touring Cyclist (104 South Main Street, St. Charles; 636-949-9630). For more information log on to www.mostateparks.com/katytrail.htm, or contact the Missouri Department of Natural Resources at (800) 334-6946.

---

they can "drive." Older kids (7–14) love the Fitness Safari, where they can swing on a vine like Tarzan, cross a river of balls by jumping from log to log, and explore a dark diamond mine. There's also an area that uses the science of everyday objects to entertain, including magnets, a wind generator, and various pulleys. The museum doubled its size in 2008, which created more programs, exhibits, learning opportunities and hands-on fun. There's a new interactive Play Garden and a Rooftop Garden, complete with a grand spiral staircase that leads to a Fairy Tale Tower—the perfect spot for imagination to take flight. Children under one are admitted free.

MISSOURI HISTORY MUSEUM $
Forest Park, Lindell Boulevard and
Skinker entrance
(314) 746-4599
www.mohistory.org
The Missouri History Museum offers a variety of

different ways to look back at the region and its history. Tour the Seeking St. Louis permanent exhibit, which features three interactive galleries, A Place in Time, Currents, and Reflections, and see the city's history unfold through state-of-the-art displays and interactive exhibits that feature thousands of artifacts. The museum regularly brings in national touring exhibitions, which range from the history of Sesame Street and the life of Charles Lindbergh to exhibits detailing the lives of such legendary figures as Miles Davis and the explorers Lewis and Clark. Admission to the museum is free, but special exhibitions charge an admission fee. Free admission to all exhibits for kids age five and under, and free admission for everyone on Tuesdays.

MUSEUM OF TRANSPORTATION $
3015 Barrett Station Road
(314) 965-7998
www.musuemoftransport.org

This museum has a collection of more than 300 pieces, including locomotives, passenger cars, automobiles, streetcars, buses, and aircraft. Included in this collection of "big toys" are 27 diesel or other internal-combustion locomotives, 10 electrics, one gas-turbine, 45 freight cars, 31 passenger train cars, plus street, interurban, and rapid-transit cars. The collection of steam locomotives on display is the largest in North America and includes an example of nearly every major type. Visitors are encouraged to climb aboard many of the "exhibits," including the steam locomotives Big Boy, the world's largest, and the Santa Fe #5011. They'll even let you ring the bell. There's also the Missouri River towboat H. T. Pott, where visitors can walk the decks, and a restored 1947 Philadelphia

SAINT LOUIS SCIENCE CENTER $
5050 Oakland Avenue
(314) 456-7572
www.slsc.org

This museum features more than 700 interactive exhibits on the environment, technology, aviation, and more, including life-size dinosaurs, an Omnimax theater, a planetarium, and various traveling exhibitions. Visit with life-sized animated dinosaurs in the Ecology and Environment Galleries, and see innovative science demonstrations and "Science Goes Splat!" at CenterStage. There are also marble highways, a car ramp, computers, a camera and monitor, magnets, optics, microscopes—and more! One of the more popular activities is playing with the radar guns that are set up inside a glassed-in walkway that stretches across I–64/Highway 40. The guns are pointed at eastbound and westbound interstate traffic, so kids can "pull the trigger" and get a real reading of how fast traffic is flying past. In the Discovery Room, children ages two to eight can enjoy a variety of hands-on experiences, including dressing up like surgeons, exploring life as a member of the Mississippian tribe, and checking out fossils. They also enjoy the James S. McDonnell Planetarium, which is one of the nation's leading space-education facilities. The planetarium's 80-foot dome allows visitors to see more than 9,000 stars and planets projected overhead, along with eclipses, meteor showers, and other celestial phenomena. Visitors can go onboard the Boeing Space Station and learn what it's like to live, work, and play in space. The center's Omnimax theater includes a four-story-tall screen in a state-of-the-art domed theater with a 15,000-watt sound system. The films shown are incredible and entertaining journeys that are well suited for such a grand scale and have included such movies as Cirque du Soleil's Journey of Man, Jane Goodall's Wild Chimpanzees, and Space Station. General admission to the majority of the museum exhibits is free, but there is a fee for many of the special exhibits and the Omnimax theater. Special admission packages are available.

ST. LOUIS FIRE DEPARTMENT MUSEUM FREE
1421 North Jefferson Avenue
(314) 289-1933

Here you can see historical fire-fighting equipment and memorabilia that celebrates the history of St. Louis firefighters, as well as their colleagues around the world. The ever-evolving museum started out as a labor of love for one St. Louis Fire Department employee, who set about collecting most of the items that are on display. Plus, you'll probably run into a firefighter or two—the museum is located inside the same building as the City Fire Marshall's Office. Open Monday through Friday.

TASTY STUFF

The following list of dining options includes eateries that are all-around safe bets for families with kids. These restaurants serve good food at reasonable prices—and chances are you'll get more food than you could possibly eat in one sitting. St. Louisans are from the old school when it comes to eating, and they hate to think that anyone would walk away from the table hungry.

ADRIANA'S $
5101 Shaw Boulevard
(314) 773-3833
This casual Italian deli in The Hill area offers excellent soups, sandwiches, and pastas and the perfect take-out food for a picnic in nearby Tower Grove Park. Open for lunch only, Monday through Saturday.

BLUEBERRY HILL $
6504 Delmar Boulevard
(314) 727-0880
www.blueberryhill.com
This St. Louis landmark is a great place to take kids of any age, because there's sure to be something that they'll enjoy seeing, doing, or eating. The menu is full of American favorites, and the shelves and display cases are filled with collections of everything from Beatles memorabilia to The Simpsons characters to World Wrestling Federation figures. The 2,000-plus-song Wurlitzer jukebox is rated one of the best in the country by Cashbox magazine, and Blueberry Hill's burgers are regular winners in the Best Burger category. The Dart Room doubles as an arcade with video games, pinball machines, and—of course—darts.

CHARLIE GITTO'S PASTA HOUSE $-$$
207 North Sixth Street
(314) 436-2828
The Gitto family restaurants are a St. Louis mainstay, and Charlie Gitto's downtown location has been around since 1974. The walls are covered with photos of celebrities who frequent the place whenever they're in town, including baseball players from the National League. The restaurant offers good, traditional Italian food at reasonable prices. The service is fast, and the food is fresh. There's a second location on The Hill, but the ambience there tends to be more formal. Open for lunch and dinner.

COMPANION BAKEHOUSE AND CAFE $
4651 Maryland Avenue, Central West End
(314) 721-5454
www.companionbaking.com
Open for breakfast and lunch (until 5 p.m.), this cafe offers excellent homemade breads, pastries, cookies, coffees, and teas. Lunches include a hearty menu of sandwiches, along with house-made soups, lasagna, and salads.

CULPEPPERS $-$$
312 South Kirkwood Road, Kirkwood
(314) 821-7322
www.culpeppers.com
This Culpeppers location, one of eight in the bi-state region, is only a few short blocks south of the Kirkwood train station and welcomes families with children under 12. (The Central West End location caters more to the bar crowd.) In addition to the usual suspects on the kids' menu, there is a good selection of burgers, soups, salads, sandwiches, appetizers, and desserts. Culpeppers is famous for its spicy chicken wings, but they may be a bit too hot for tender young taste buds.

DAVE AND BUSTER'S $-$$
13857 Riverport Drive, Maryland Heights
(314) 209-8015
www.daveandbusters.com
This 55,000-square-foot restaurant and entertainment complex has as many games to play as it

has things to eat. Kids and grown-ups are drawn to Dave and Buster's for the 300-plus games, including billiards, shuffleboard, video games, simulators, and just about every other electronic diversion you can think of. The food is mostly pub grub but includes other stuff as well.

i Riding the Rails: You can take the train from downtown St. Louis to Kirkwood, a nearby neighborhood located in western St. Louis County. The ride lasts about 40 minutes, and once you get there, you can grab a bite to eat and explore Kirkwood's quaint downtown area until it's time to catch the train back downtown.

DUFF'S RESTAURANT $–$$
392 North Euclid Avenue
(314) 361-0522
www.dineatduffs.com
Duff's is perfect if you're looking for something a little more upscale, but still casual enough for kids. The Central West End eatery has an eclectic lunch, dinner, and brunch menu that changes seasonally, but there's always an array of sandwiches, soups, pizzas, salads, and entrees, as well as a selection of meatless and "heart-healthy" items for calorie- or cholesterol-conscious diners. The children's menu is available any time the kitchen is open, except during brunch. Then, the Brunch Children's Menu is in effect. Duff's is a popular spot for outdoor dining and weekend brunch. There's free parking available (around the corner) in the McPherson lot and in the Euclid parking lot.

FITZ'S AMERICAN GRILL AND
BOTTLING WORKS $–$$
6605 Delmar Boulevard
(314) 726-9555
www.fitzsrootbeer.com
This root beer microbrewery is an all-around favorite. There's a bottling line on-site, so kids can see the bottles being filled and capped. Fitz's root beer is some of the best you'll ever taste—it's

even won over the taste buds of those who say they don't like root beer. Even the diet version tastes great with no icky aftertaste. Also on tap are cream soda, orange pop, grape pop, ginger ale, and the raspberry/cola–flavored Hip Hop Pop. The menu is just as good, with great burgers (including a great veggie burger), soups, sandwiches, salads, and, of course, root beer floats.

HARD ROCK CAFE $–$$
St. Louis Union Station
(314) 621-7625
www.hardrock.com/locations/cafes
The menu here provides diners with a healthy choice of comfortable favorites, including burgers, sandwiches, salads, and an assortment of barbecued items. A great stained-glass window featuring Chuck Berry lets you know that this link in the Hard Rock chain happens to be in St. Louis, along with a 36-foot-tall replica of Berry's 1959 Gibson ES335 guitar.

LOU BOCCARDI'S $
5424 Magnolia
(314) 647-1151
Lou Boccardi's, in The Hill, is a tiny neighborhood eatery that greets customers with a warm St. Louis–style reception from the family members who run the place. This isn't fancy Italian food, but it's good and it's fresh, and the atmosphere is nothing less than charming. Known for their St. Louis-style pizza, the cozy eatery offers a variety of pasta dishes and salads as well. Closed Sunday.

MAURIZIO'S PIZZA & SPORTS CAFE $
1107 Olive Street
(314) 621-1997
www.maurizios.com
Here you can get excellent fresh, hand-tossed pizzas; pastas; salads; and sub sandwiches. There's also an all-you-can-eat buffet that includes a variety of pizzas, wings, and soda for one reasonable price—just the thing for picky eaters who want different toppings on their pizza. Big-screen TVs will help you keep an eye on all the sports action.

MAX & ERMA'S $-$$
Drury Plaza Hotel, Market and Fourth Streets
(314) 621-5815
www.maxandermas.com

This St. Louis sports–themed restaurant is part of the national chain, but it offers an extensive menu of traditional foods for kids and adults. There's standard kid fare here—chicken fingers, burgers, mac and cheese, corn dogs, grilled cheese, and pasta with marinara sauce—along with a bathtub full of toppings at the build-your-own sundae bar. Kids can even order up their own specialty drinks, such as the Beetle Juice (grape juice and Sprite with gummy bears on the side) or the Volcano Blaster (Coca-Cola and a scoop of ice cream). Parental units can choose from a pretty good selection of eats, ranging from soups, salads, and sandwiches to steaks, pasta, and barbecue.

MIKE DUFFY'S PUB AND GRILL $-$$
124 West Jefferson, Kirkwood
(314) 821-2025
www.mikeduffys.com

Not far from the train station—walking distance, in fact—is this cozy Kirkwood eatery that offers good food at reasonable prices in a casual atmosphere. The menu includes sandwiches, excellent burgers, award-winning chili, soups, salads, appetizers, and other daily specials. On Tuesday nights, kids eat free with the purchase of two adult dinners. There are also a half dozen wrought-iron tables on a small patio for outdoor dining during warm weather. There are two additional locations in the metro area—6662 Clayton Road in Richmond Heights, (314) 644-3700; and 1024 Schnucks Woods Mill Plaza in Chesterfield, (636) 394-8855. Closed Sunday.

OZZIE'S RESTAURANT & SPORTS BAR $-$$
645 Westport Plaza, Maryland Heights
(314) 434-1000
www.ozziesrestaurantandsportsbar.com

Ozzie's is a sports bar and restaurant with good food and loads of sports memorabilia, including the seven Gold Gloves awarded to the Cardinals Hall of Fame shortstop Ozzie Smith. There are 50 regular TVs and five big screens scattered throughout the restaurant, and all are tuned in to a variety of sporting events. Plus, the food is actually very good for a sports bar–type restaurant.

PAM'S CHICAGO STYLE DOGS AND MORE $
6016 Delmar Boulevard
(314) 721-7267
www.pamscsd.com

Don't let the name fool you—they serve a lot more than just Chicago-style hot dogs here. In addition to serving breakfast daily, this tiny eatery in The Loop features "the real deal" for fans of Chicago-style hot dogs. The menu also includes gyros, burgers, salads, sandwiches, tamales, veggie dogs and burgers, breakfast items, and the beloved deep-fried Twinkie. Open daily.

PANERA/ST. LOUIS BREAD COMPANY $
116 North Sixth Street
(314) 588-0423

4651 Maryland Avenue
(314) 367-7636

6630 Delmar Boulevard, University City
(314) 721-7995

6701 Clayton Road, Clayton
(314) 725-9922

1008 Loughborough Avenue I-55, South City
(314) 353-8227
www.panerabread.com

With literally dozens of bakery/cafes throughout the metropolitan area, you're always close to at least one location. The Bread Company—know elsewhere as Panera Bread—is a popular and inexpensive place for breakfast, lunch, or a light dinner. Soups, salads, and sandwiches are the specialties, along with a variety of bagels, croissants, muffins, cookies, lattes, and, of course, breads. The service is fast and the food is good, with the soup selections changing daily. There are a number of vegetarian and low-fat items on the menu, along with the ever-popular PB&J sandwich that "big kids" order almost as often as the little ones. Free Wi-Fi hot spots at all locations.

THE PASTA HOUSE COMPANY $

St. Louis Galleria food court, Brentwood
Boulevard and Clayton Road, Clayton
(314) 863-8882

309 North Euclid
(314) 367-3865

12445 Dorsett Road, Maryland Heights
(314) 878-6676

With 19 locations throughout the metro area, the Pasta House is a popular place with area families. They have a better-than-average menu of pastas with your choice of red sauces or cream-based sauces; appetizers; sandwiches; steaks; veal, chicken, and seafood entrees; as well as salads with their "famous" special salad dressing.

PUJOLS 5 WESTPORT GRILL $$

342 Westport Plaza, Maryland Heights
(314) 439-0505
www.pujols5grill.com

St. Louis Cardinals first baseman Albert Pujols and his wife, Deidre, partnered with a local restaurant group and opened Pujols 5, a high-tech sports bar and restaurant. The food is a cut above the usual sports bar fare, and the menu includes a number of Albert's favorite dishes made from Deidre's own recipes. There are plenty of burgers and appetizers, but the entrees also include grilled chicken, steak, and fish, along with pasta specialties and large salads. In the sports bar area, there are 32 LCD and plasma TVs, and each table is able to control a screen, so everyone can see and hear the game they want.

RACANELLI'S $

6655 Delmar Boulevard
(314) 727-7227

Here you can get really good New York–style pizza by the slice or a whole pie to go. This is more of a pizza stand than a restaurant, but it's great for food on the go. There are a few plastic tables and chairs set up in the common area of this indoor mini mall, which is adjacent to the outdoor common area and market. The restrooms aren't great, but at least they exist.

RIGAZZI'S $–$$

4945 Daggett Avenue
(314) 772-4900
www.rigazzis.com

Rigazzi's on The Hill offers casual Italian dining and has more than 200 items on its extensive menu. Its St. Louis–style pizza (topped with Provel rather than mozzarella cheese) was rated one of the country's best by Bon Appétit magazine. Rigazzi's is known as the "Home of the Frozen Fishbowl," which is an oversize frozen goblet filled with draft beer. (You can, however, order one with soda.) Kids' dinner options include burgers, hot dogs, toasted ravioli, chicken fingers, spaghetti and other pastas, and mini pizza. Small fry's dinners come with fries, applesauce, and a chocolate ice-cream bar. Reservations accepted. Closed Sunday.

SODA FOUNTAIN SQUARE $–$$

1801 Park Avenue
(314) 241-0099
www.sodafountainsquare.net

This Lafayette Square eatery is one of the few family-friendly spots to dine in the hip and trendy neighborhood. Kids of all ages enjoy a visit here, as the retro soda fountain serves up excellent food as well as desserts. Breakfast is served all day (until midnight on Friday and Saturday), along with soups, salads, burgers, sandwiches, and various "home-cooked" plates. Be sure to leave room for dessert, such as old-fashioned ice-cream sodas, milk shakes, floats, splits, and sundaes. Closed Monday.

TED DREWES FROZEN CUSTARD $

6726 Chippewa Street
(314) 481-2652
www.teddrewes.com

A St. Louis tradition since it opened in 1929, Ted Drewes offers the absolute best frozen custard you'll ever put in your mouth. Called "concretes" due to their thickness and the fact that—well, they look like wet concrete—these shakes are so thick that you can turn them upside down and not lose a drop. Create your own concoction

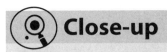 **Close-up**

Corn Mazes and Pumpkin Farms

A unique Midwestern attraction held each fall are corn mazes—mazes made out of cornfields. Some have additional activities, including farmers' markets, hayrides, and live entertainment, and most are open weekends September through Halloween. Most offer a variety of "harvest-time" activities along with pick-your-own-pumpkin options. Hours are subject to change, so it's a good idea to call or log on to the Web sites before you make the drive. All mazes charge an admission fee, with some offering free admission for younger children.

**FORT SPOOKY AT STUCKMEYERS'
FARM** $
249 Schneider Drive
(at Highways 21 and 141), Fenton
(636) 349–1225
www.stuckmeyers.com
Open weekends in October

THE GREAT GODFREY MAZE $
Robert E. Glazebrook Park,
off Illinois Highway 67 at
1401 Stamper Lane,
Godfrey, IL
(618) 466–1483, ext. 1
www.greatgodfreymaze.com
Open September and October,
Friday–Sunday; free admission for kids age
five and under

PIN OAK FARMS **FREE**
Highway E, New Haven
(573) 237–4088
www.pinoakfarms.com
Open weekends in October

RELLEKE'S PUMPKINFEST
Relleke Farms, Sand Prairie Lane,
Granite City, IL
(618) 797–6858
Open daily in October; call for hours

SHRYOCKS CORN MAZE
12 miles east of Columbia, Missouri, on the
north side of Interstate 70,
Millersburg
www.callawayfarms.com
Open early September through early November, Friday–Sunday; free admission for kids
ages three and under

from a list of fixings that includes cookies, candies, fruits, and nuts, or choose from the extensive menu of existing favorites. The sundaes and concretes come in six sizes, but be warned that the concretes are rich and very filling. The "mini"-size concrete is more than enough for most kids and some adults. Plus, everybody always wants to sample what everyone else is having! There's usually a line during warm weather, but it moves incredibly fast, so don't pass up the experience just because there's a crowd. Chances are, you'll be standing in line with local media personalities, elected officials, and people from the neighborhood. Everybody goes to Ted Drewes. Closed during January and February.

TRAINWRECK SALOON **$–$$**
Westport Plaza, Maryland Heights
(314) 434-7222
www.trainwrecksaloon.com
This place looks like a saloon in an old cowboy movie, complete with swinging saloon doors, planked floors, stained glass, and brass tappers, but it offers good food in a family-friendly environment. A large model train circles the bar, and the dining room consists of antique booths and more stained glass. The menu has your choice of ostrich, bison, or "regular" burgers along with ribs, pastas, salads, and desserts. Closed Sunday.

ZIA'S ON THE HILL $-$$
5256 Wilson Avenue
(314) 776-0020
www.zias.com

Another family-owned and -operated restaurant on The Hill, Zia's serves up gourmet Italian specialties in large quantities at moderate prices in a casual, family-friendly atmosphere. Entrees include pastas, veal, chicken, seafood, sandwiches, and salads. Closed Sunday.

WACKY STUFF

BOB KRAMER'S MARIONNETTES $
4143 Laclede Avenue
(314) 531-3313
www.kramersmarionnettes.com

At Bob Kramer's you can discover the world of puppetry through daily demonstrations that show the process of puppet building and five seasonal shows. Lively and entertaining, the shows are fun and humorous for kids and adults alike. Reservations are required. Children under one are admitted free. Shows and demonstrations performed seven days a week.

BUSCH STADIUM $
Clark and Seventh Streets
(314) 345-9565 (tours),
(314) 345-9000 (tickets)
www.stlcardinals.com

Get a bird's-eye view of the home turf (grass, actually) where the National League's St. Louis Cardinals play their home games. The new Busch Stadium, which opened its doors in 2006, is a beautiful red brick venue that features an incredible view of the city skyline. Visit the 2006 World Champs' dugout and the stadium press room, go out onto the warning track, and check out the Redbird Club, Family Pavilion, and one of the party rooms available for rent. Stadium tours are available year-round with the exception of a few major holidays and anytime there's a day game. Tours depart from Gate 5 at 9:30 a.m., 11:00 a.m., 12:30 p.m., and 2:00 p.m. daily.

THE BUTTERFLY HOUSE $
Faust Park, 15193 Olive Boulevard,
Chesterfield
(636) 530-0076
www.butterflyhouse.org

A cultural and educational attraction, at the Butterfly House visitors will see thousands of butterflies in free flight and actually witness the mystery of metamorphosis—from caterpillar to cocoon stage to the larvae's " coming-out party." Children three and under are admitted free.

CHASE PARK PLAZA CINEMAS $
212 North Kingshighway
(314) 367-0101 (recorded movie info)
www.chasepark.com/amenities/cinemas

This five-theater multiplex within the historic Chase Park Plaza Hotel shows the latest Hollywood releases in plush, comfortable surroundings. There's a snack bar that serves all the traditional movie snacks, as well as "adult" beverages for kids 21 and older. Discounted tickets until 6:00 p.m. daily; free valet parking until 5:00 p.m.

ECKERT'S COUNTRY STORE AND FARMS $
951 South Greenmount Road, Belleville, IL
(618) 233-0513

2719 Eckert Orchard Lane, Millstadt, IL
(618) 476-3260

20995 Eckert Orchard Road, Grafton, IL
(618) 786-3445
www.eckerts.com

The Eckert family has turned its three area farms into entertainment centers that feature special children's activities, annual events, festivals, and the Eckert's Country Store and Restaurant. You can get a real farmhand experience as you ride the wagons out to pick your own seasonal fruits and vegetables or take part in the live entertainment. Pig racing is a popular sport around these parts, and Eckert's has it. There are three locations in Illinois, including two farms (in Millstadt and Grafton) and one country store (in Belleville), and all offer various special events and activities throughout the year, such as haunted hayrides, pumpkin bashing, and other events tied to seasonal harvests. Open February through December. Special event admission fees vary.

GALLERIA 6 CINEMAS $
St. Louis Galleria,
I–64/Brentwood Boulevard, Clayton
(314) 725-0808 (recorded movie info)
www.galleria6.stlouiscinemas.com
There are six screens here featuring the top titles from Tinseltown, with a snack bar and mall food court located adjacent to the multiplex. Children under five are not admitted to PG-13 or R rated movies after 5:00 PM. Free parking.

GATEWAY AIR TOURS $$$$
St. Louis Riverfront
(314) 393-2665
www.gatewayarch.com
Take a ride in a helicopter and get a bird's-eye view of St. Louis. The helipad is actually a barge moored on the Mississippi River, right under the Gateway Arch. There are two tours to choose from: The St. Louis Skyline tour lasts about 5 to 6 minutes and flies over the riverfront and downtown St. Louis, and the Explore St. Louis tour, which lasts about 15 minutes, takes visitors around downtown, the riverfront, out to Forest Park, and then to the confluence of the Missouri and Mississippi Rivers in nearby St. Charles. Open Memorial Day through mid-September.

GATEWAY ARCH RIVERBOATS $
St. Louis Riverfront below the Arch
(314) 923-3048, (877) 982-1410
www.gatewayarchriverboats.com
These one-hour narrated sightseeing cruises on the Tom Sawyer or Becky Thatcher riverboats on the mighty Mississippi River offer spectacular skyline views, and they're a great way to cool off on a hot summer day. The paddle wheelers also host special "Blues Cruises," which feature live music, along with dinner cruises and other special event cruises. Three of the five daily cruises include a National Park Service ranger on board, who provides additional information about the river and

its connection to St. Louis. Free admission for kids age three and younger.

MERAMEC CAVERNS $$
I–44, exit 230, Stanton
(800) 676-6105
www.americascave.com
Located one hour west of St. Louis, Meramec Caverns is a fascinating look at the world of caves. Rumored to have served as a hideout for outlaw Jesse James, the cave also has nearby camping, motels, boat rides, and canoe rentals. This is an excellent activity no matter what season you visit, because the cave is always cool in the summer and warm (well, warmer than the air outside) in the winter months. Wear comfortable shoes and be prepared to walk about a mile, total. Tours last about 75 to 80 minutes, and strollers are not allowed. There's a snack bar, gift shop, and restaurant on-site. Boat rides on the Meramec River are also available, or you can rent a canoe or raft and float downriver on your own. Kids can also pan for gold or gemstones at the Meramec Mining Company. There are extra fees for the boat and canoe rentals and the Meramec Mining Company.

MISSOURI BOTANICAL GARDEN $
4344 Shaw Boulevard
(314) 577-9400, (800) 642-8842
www.mobot.org
The Missouri Botanical Garden is an oasis of green and tranquil surroundings that offers something for kids and adults alike. The Climatron Rain Forest, located inside a geodesic-domed conservatory, contains streams, waterfalls, and more than 1,200 species of plants in a natural setting. Visitors to the rain forest will see everything from banana, cacao, and coffee trees to lianas, bromeliads, cycads, passion flowers, and colorful orchids. The Children's Garden offers interactive fun, including climbing in a treehouse, visiting a limestone cave, exploring wetlands, and much more. There is an additional charge to visit this area, but well worth the money. The Kemper Center for Home Gardening has a variety of hands-on activities for kids and adults, including single-day cooking

classes that teach kids and adults how to work together in the kitchen. The garden is also home to the largest traditional Japanese garden in North America, and kids love to feed the koi fish from the lake bridge. (Bring some change for the fish-food machines, because these colorful fish are fun to watch, and they aren't shy about eating in front of strangers.) Also, many special events take place on weeknights during the spring and summer months, including live jazz concert events that encourage families to bring picnics and sit out under the stars. Open daily. Admission is free for children 12 and under.

ST. LOUIS CARRIAGE COMPANY $$
1000 Cerre Street
(314) 621-3334

Carriage rides are a great way to see the city, and it gives kids a chance to check out the sights at a slower pace. Most of the carriage drivers have a dog on board as their "co-pilot," so there's a natural kinship with the little ones. It's also a great way to give tired little feet a break and still keep them occupied. The horse-and-buggy tours start from the front of the Hyatt Regency St. Louis Riverfront Hotel at Fourth and Chestnut Streets, as well as on Laclede's Landing at First and Morgan Streets. Tours are 30 minutes or 60 minutes long.

ST. LOUIS WALK OF FAME   FREE
6500 block of Delmar Boulevard
(314) 727-STAR
www.stlouiswalkoffame.org

More than 100 bronze stars and informative plaques dot the sidewalks of The Loop entertainment district. The stars honor famous St. Louisans who have made their mark in the worlds of entertainment, science, literature, and business and include celebrities such as rock 'n' roll legends Chuck Berry and Tina Turner; hip hop star Nelly; sportscasters Jack Buck and Bob Costas; actors Vincent Price, Marsha Mason, and Cedric the Entertainer; and baseball's Yogi Berra and Bob Gibson. Open daily, 24 hours a day.

UPPER LIMITS ROCK CLIMBING GYM $$
326 South 21st Street
(314) 241-ROCK
www.upperlimits.com

Located next door to Union Station, Upper Limits offers more than 10,000 square feet of sculpted climbing surfaces for beginners and advanced climbers. The gym offers daily rates, gear rental, and instruction. Visitors can try un-roped climbing—or bouldering—which is done close to the ground and doesn't require individual instruction, or learn the top-roping method of climbing. Experienced climbers take a belay test to prove they know what they're doing before participating in activities at the gym, and everyone is required to sign a liability waiver. Kids 14 and under must be accompanied by an adult, and all kids under 18 must have a waiver signed by a parent or guardian to participate. Open daily.

PARKS AND RECREATION

S t. Louis has almost as many intriguing green spaces within its metropolitan borders as it has unique and exciting attractions. Those who enjoy outdoor activities such as running, walking, hiking, and biking can find plenty of places to get in a quick workout, and folks who prefer boating and fishing or tennis and golfing won't have to look too far to find a place to get out and play. In addition to the gloriously scenic, paved, and tree-lined route through the Gateway Arch grounds, there are more than 170 parks throughout the area that offer a great way to commune with Mother Nature. Hikers and bikers can explore a variety of trails—both new and old—on the region's expanding network, including the popular Riverfront Trail along the mighty Mississippi River and Grant's Trail in south St. Louis County. Grant's Trail leads trekkers down an adventurous path to the Grant's Farm wildlife preserve and White Haven, former home of Gen. Ulysses S. Grant. There are also loads of other recreational options, including bowling, canoeing, horseback riding, hunting, skating (in-line and on the ice), and swimming.

PARKS

City Parks

FOREST PARK
Kingshighway, Lindell, Clayton, and
Interstate 64
(314) 289-5300
http://stlouis.missouri.org/citygov/parks/
forestpark
Walkers and runners will find plenty of scenic walkways throughout beautiful Forest Park. Opened in 1876, the park has a 7.5-mile paved pathway that's used by bikers, walkers, joggers, in-line skaters, and the occasional equestrian. There's also a skating rink, handball and tennis courts, stocked lakes for fishing, and a boathouse that rents paddleboats and gondolas for a relaxing way to see Forest Park's tranquil waterways. Four racquetball courts and four handball courts are located north of the Lindell Pavilion and are available on a first-come, first-served basis, and athletic fields for rugby, soccer, volleyball, football, baseball, and softball are open to the public as well. (To purchase permits for groups, call 314-289-5389.) The 1,300-acre park has innumerable picnic spots. Some insist that Art Hill is the best place to pitch a picnic—and get a bird's-eye view of the Grand Basin—while others swear by the shady areas around the World's Fair Pavilion. Forest Park has more than a dozen picnic locations available for rent, including some sites that have shelters.

TOWER GROVE PARK
Kingshighway, Arsenal Street, and
Grand Avenue
(314) 771-2679
http://stlouis.missouri.org/parks/tower-grove/
In 1866 Henry Shaw drew up a proposal for Tower Grove Park and started construction two years later. Today the grand pleasure park that Shaw gave to the citizens of St. Louis is home to softball, soccer, tennis, corkball, and Frisbee games, as well as to the strollers, joggers, and picnickers who revel in the fanciful Victorian pavilions and sculptures that he commissioned. Tower Grove Park, one of only three U.S. parks designated a National Historic Landmark, is almost 300 acres of grassy, tree-lined getaway that offers a variety of recreational options. The park has more than 8,000 types of trees and shrubs that Shaw imported from around the world. Picnickers often head straight for the grassy banks of the lily pond

and its artistic arrangement of stones from the old Lindell Hotel. "The Ruins" are the backdrop to the tranquility of the sailboat pond and its fountain, and there are plenty of large shade trees. Bands perform on the Music Stand, and larger groups hold picnics and family reunions in the numerous Victorian pavilions. Carriage rides through the park are available.

i **Fishing and boating in the heart of the city? Take a paddleboat ride around Post-Dispatch Lake or try your luck at one of the stocked lakes in Forest Park.**

County Parks

CREVE COEUR PARK MARINE AVENUE AND DORSETT ROAD

(314) 615-5454

www.co.st-louis.mo.us/parkscreve

Creve Coeur Park has 1,200 acres of green space and outdoor activities, including fishing, tennis courts, a Frisbee disc-golf course, an archery range, four playground areas, a wildlife area, a sand beach, and a 320-acre lake. While swimming is not allowed in the lake, sailboat captains take to the waterways, along with a competitive powerboat race each summer. The park also has a polo field, 12 picnic sites equipped with barbecue pits and picnic tables, and the Dripping Springs waterfall along the lake's southeast shore. Picnic shelters can be reserved by calling (314) 615-4FUN.

JEFFERSON BARRACKS PARK

533 Grant Road

(314) 544-5714

www.stlouisco.com/parks/j-b.html

Jefferson Barracks Park has more than 400 acres of campgrounds, ball fields, and lush green space. The historic area includes a field archery range, disc-golf course, lighted ball fields, a 2.7-mile paved trail, and the St. Louis County Veterans Memorial Amphitheater. Jefferson Barracks was established in 1826 as the country's first "Infantry School of Practice," and it served as a major military installation until 1946. Named in honor of former president Thomas Jefferson, the post played an important role in westward expansion, as Jefferson Barracks served as a gathering point for troops and supplies bound for service in the Mexican War, Civil War, Spanish-American War, World War I, and World War II. During the summer and fall months, the park plays host to a series of "Blues on the Mississippi" concerts, with local bands performing on Friday evenings. Check the Web site for schedule information.

State Parks

KATY TRAIL STATE PARK

Trailhead located at Riverside and Boonslick Roads, St. Charles

(800) 334-6946

www.mostateparks.com/katytrail

Katy Trail State Park offers something for almost everyone, especially bicyclists, hikers, nature lovers, and history buffs. This park is built on the former corridor of the Missouri-Kansas-Texas (MKT) Railroad—better known as "the Katy"—and when the railroad shut down operation of the St. Charles County to Pettis County route in 1986, the state created a long-distance hiking and bicycling trail that runs almost 200 miles across Missouri. The scenic trail closely follows the route of the Missouri River and travels through dense forests, wetlands, deep valleys, remnant prairies, open pastureland, and gently rolling farm fields. In the spring the trail is brightened with flowering dogwood and redbud, and in the fall the trail comes alive with the rich reds and oranges of sugar maple, sumac, and bittersweet trees. There's plenty of winged wildlife on hand as well, including chickadees, nuthatches, robins, orioles, and woodpeckers, along with red-tailed hawks, turkey vultures, and even bald eagles in the winter months. Because of its location along the Missouri River flyway, the trail hosts migrating birds and waterfowl such as great blue herons, sandpipers, Canada geese, and belted kingfishers.

MERAMEC STATE PARK

Located 3 miles south of Sullivan on Highway 185

(573) 468-6519, (888) MERAMEC (637-2632)

www.mostateparks.com/meramec.htm

The beauty of the Meramec River and its surrounding bluffs, caves, and forests have pleased visitors since the park opened in 1927. This popular 6,896-acre park offers year-round access to camping, picnicking, and trails, as well as seasonal tours of Fisher Cave, one of more than 40 caves in the park. Water enthusiasts can enjoy swimming, fishing, rafting, and canoeing in the Meramec River. Additional facilities include a park store that offers raft and canoe rentals, 210 campsites (including 3 group sites), 20 rental cabins, 22 motel rooms, and a conference center. The visitor center has a mix of educational exhibits, including large aquariums that display the amazing variety of aquatic life found in the river.

PERE MARQUETTE STATE PARK

Route 100, P.O. Box 158, Grafton, IL 62037

(618) 786-3323, ext. 1

http://dnr.state.il.us/lands/Landmgt/PARKS/R4/Peremarq.htm

With plenty of winding roads, hilly terrain, and a plethora of hiking and biking trials, Pere Marquette has no shortage of green space or scenic overlooks. The facility provides plenty of places to camp, fish, bird-watch, and go horseback riding, as well as any number of ways to relax and enjoy the serenity of nature. The upper picnic area offers great scenery, with a view overlooking the majestic Mississippi River, plus occasional visits from the deer, squirrels, and other wildlife who call the park home. A nature-lover's paradise, this 8,000-acre park is famous for the exceptional beauty of its fall colors and for its bald eagles during the winter. Pere Marquette's visitor center offers a three-dimensional map of the park, a 300-gallon aquarium, and a wealth of exhibits about the Illinois River, wildlife habitat, and local history.

ROUTE 66 STATE PARK

Interstate 44, 2 miles south of Eureka

(636) 938-7198

www.mostateparks.com/route66.htm

Route 66 State Park showcases the history and mystique of the historic highway known as "the Mother Road," a roadway that has come to represent American mobility, independence, and the spirit of adventure. Located along the original Route 66 corridor (I–44), the 409-acre park features a variety of recreational activities and historical displays showcasing Route 66. The Bridgehead Inn, a 1935 roadhouse, serves as the park's visitor center and houses a collection of memorabilia. There are also ample opportunities to picnic, exercise, bird-watch, or to just commune with nature, as the park area is home to more than 40 types of birds and a diverse set of trees, plants, and animals. Picnic sites are scattered beneath the shade trees. Level walking, bicycling, and equestrian trails throughout the park are perfect for beginning bike riders. There's also a boat launch, pavilions, and a playground.

PARKS ORGANIZATIONS

MISSOURI STATE PARKS

P.O. Box 176 Jefferson City, MO 65102

(800) 334-6946

www.mostateparks.com

For more than 80 years, the Missouri state park system has preserved and made available the best of the state's natural and cultural resources. Its mission is to preserve and interpret the state's most outstanding natural landscapes and cultural landmarks and to provide outdoor recreational opportunities. State parks and historic sites provide outstanding opportunities to camp, hike, picnic, swim, fish, and relive Missouri history.

ST. LOUIS CITY DEPARTMENT OF PARKS, RECREATION AND FORESTRY

5600 Clayton Road

(314) 289-5300

www.stlouis.missouri.org/citygov/parks

The St. Louis Department of Parks, Recreation

and Forestry maintains the amenities that make the city a good place to live, work, and play. The Parks Division's 105 parks located throughout the city provide pavilions for picnicking, lakes for fishing, ice for skating, and paths for jogging. The Recreation Division offers free access to seven area swimming pools and ten recreation centers; it also runs camps during the summer months and sponsors sports activities throughout the year. You can reserve a picnic pavilion at almost any St. Louis County park. Call (314) 615-4386 for reservations and permits.

ST. LOUIS COUNTY DEPARTMENT OF PARKS AND RECREATION
41 South Central, Clayton
(314) 615-5000
www.stlouisco.com/parks

Each year more than 12 million people visit the 63 parks and nearly 13,000 acres of parkland maintained by St. Louis County Parks and Recreation. There are a number of leisure and recreational facilities for all ages, in addition to "theme parks" where visitors can roam through historic areas and even an animal-farm zoo. Three regional family recreation complexes feature indoor ice-skating rinks, an outdoor Olympic-size pool, and a variety of creative playgrounds.

RECREATION

Bowling

FLAMINGO BOWL
1117 Washington Avenue
(314) 436-6666
www.flamingobowl.net

One of the newest hot spots in downtown St. Louis, Flamingo Bowl is the ultimate bowling alley/nightclub. In addition to lots of hot pink decor, the swanky 12-lane alley features a diverse menu of specialty cocktails and snacks, along with some of the best people-watching in town. Open daily until 3 a.m.

PIN-UP BOWL
6191 Delmar Boulevard
(314) 727-5555
www.pinupbowl.com

The sister "cocktail alley" to downtown's Flamingo Bowl, Pin-Up Bowl is St. Louis's original martini lounge/bowling alley. There are eight bowling lanes, a fantastic digital jukebox, a kitchen, a full bar, and an extensive menu of classic, modern, and signature martinis. A favorite hangout for such local celebs as hip-hop stars Nelly and the St. Lunatics, the "alley-bar" was named to *Condé Nast Traveler*'s inaugural "Hot Nights" list. Open daily until 3 a.m.

TROPICANA LANES
7960 Clayton Road, Clayton
(314) 781-0282
www.tropicanalanes.com

Tropicana Lanes is regularly voted the area's best bowling alley in local publications' readers' polls, and with good reason. This is one big alley—there are 52 lanes—so there's usually not a wait for a lane, even on weekends. The casual, old school attitude and ambience attracts a diverse cross-section of the local population. There are lots of leagues bowling here throughout the week, and there are extended weekend hours to accommodate late-night bowlers.

Canoeing/Rafting

MERAMEC STATE PARK
Located 3 miles south of Sullivan on Highway 185
(573) 468-6519, (888) MERAMEC (637-2632)
www.mostateparks.com/meramec.htm

Water recreation opportunities abound here, and visitors can float down the river in a canoe or raft and enjoy the scenery along the way. Canoe and raft rentals are available in the park's store, and the rental fee includes shuttle transportation, paddles, and life jackets. Weekday floats typically offer substantially more solitude than weekends, as the park is a popular destination for locals looking to "get away from it all."

Cycling

FOREST PARK

Kingshighway, Lindell, Clayton, and I–64

(314) 552-2976

http://stlouis.missouri.org/citygov/parks/
forestpark/

The Forest Park bike path is a 7.5-mile-long, multi-use asphalt trail used for bicycling, in-line skating, jogging, and walking. The path accommodates two-way traffic, and those using the trail are asked to stay to the right of the center stripe to accommodate oncoming traffic. There is also a second "soft path" that is designed for the exclusive use of walkers and joggers.

KATY TRAIL

Trailhead located at Riverside and
Boonslick Roads, St. Charles

(800) 334-6946

www.bikekatytrail.com

The 185-mile Katy Trail, the nation's longest rails-to-trails project, begins in St. Charles, just 30 minutes west of downtown St. Louis. Named for the old Missouri-Kansas-Texas rail-road line and given the nickname "Katy," the flat path is made of crushed limestone gravel and never exceeds a 5 percent grade. Bicycle-rental services are located at trailheads along the 8-foot-wide, wheelchair-accessible trail, which runs nearly 200 miles across the state of Missouri. You can rent bikes at various locations in St. Charles. (For more information see the Day Trips and Weekend Getaways chapter.)

i Rent a bicycle and take your own self-guided tour of the city or the Riverfront Trail. The Gateway Arch Riverfront facility, located below the Gateway Arch on Leonor K. Sullivan Boulevard, offers rentals by the day or by the hour. In addition to standard bikes, it also rents tandems, trailers, and tag-alongs. Helmets are provided. Call (877) 982–1410 for more info or log on to www.gatewayarch.com.

Biking Resources

Are you new to the area and looking for places to ride? Trailnet, a not-for-profit organization, can help. The organization is dedicated to creating and conserving multiuse recreational trails and green-ways and encouraging walking and bicycling for recreation and transportation in the St. Louis bi-state region of Missouri and Illinois. Trailnet hosts a number of events throughout the year, including an Eagle Watch from the Old Chain of Rocks Bridge, "bike-to-work" days, and weekly bicycle rides. For more information contact Trailnet at 3900 Reavis Barracks Road, St. Louis; (314) 416–9930; www.trailnet.org.

Fishing

WASHINGTON STATE PARK

13041 Highway 104, DeSoto

(636) 586-0322

www.mostateparks.com/washington.htm

Surrounded by towering dolomite bluffs, Washington State Park's Big River offers anglers opportunities to catch a wide variety of fish, from catfish and crappie to largemouth and smallmouth bass. The portion of the Big River that extends from the Highway 21 bridge to the Meramec River has been designated by the Missouri Department of Conservation as a Smallmouth Bass Special Management Area, where special regulations regarding length and possession limits apply.

Golf

Is golf your game? Public courses in St. Louis have a tee time just for you. Beautiful courses—many designed by the country's top players and course architects—are located in St. Louis's most scenic settings. With rolling and wooded terrain, bent grass greens, links-style courses, and award-winning designs, the St. Louis area is sure to have a course that suits you. Most of the golf courses listed here offer club and cart rental, driving ranges, and pro assistance.

Golf Courses

ANNBRIAR GOLF COURSE
1524 Birdie Lane, Waterloo, IL
(618) 939-4653, (888) 939-5191
www.annbriar.com

Experience "a little slice of heaven" while playing the majestic Annbriar Golf Course, which features a unique blend of open, links-style terrain on the scenic front nine and wooded rolling terrain on the back nine. The 603-yard 18th hole is a superb finishing hole, with fairway bunkers, a divided fairway, and a deep green with a swale in the middle. Annbriar's precision-placed tee boxes, rolling fairways and lush greens led Golf Digest to rate the facility as one of the country's "Top 500 Places to Play," and its 4.5 star rating ranks it as 7th in the state. Proper course attire is required, and the course allows soft spikes only. Tennis shoes are permitted, or the pro shop personnel will gladly change metal spikes for a fee.

BEAR CREEK GOLF COURSE
158 Bear Creek Drive, Wentzville
(636) 332-5018
www.bearcreekgolf.com

Bear Creek's challenging 18-hole course is considered one of the top public venues in the metro area. Set amid rustic, scenic surroundings in nearby Wentzville, the world-class course was designed by renowned course architect Gary Kern and features a number of challenging holes. The par 4 second and fifth holes are both quite demanding, and the finishing hole is a 440-yard beauty that plays across a lake to a landing area guarded by two deep bunkers and a wooded creekside. Bear Creek offers members and visitors the amenities found at most private country clubs.

FAR OAKS GOLF CLUB
419 Old Collinsville Road, Caseyville, IL
(618) 628-2900
www.faroaksgolfclub.com

Far Oaks Golf Club, is a Goalby-designed course that features a practice facility, 18 holes of championship golf, a Target par 3 course, and an 8,000-square-foot clubhouse complete with a grill and bar, locker rooms and a well stocked pro shop. The course is set among majestic oak trees and has elevation changes usually associated with mountain courses. Far Oaks' PGA professionals offer a variety of instructional programs that range from 30-minute individual lessons to half- and full-day golf schools and clinics. A new dress code has been implemented, banning jeans and cutoffs and requiring shirts with a collar. However, mock short sleeve shirts and turtlenecks are acceptable.

GATEWAY NATIONAL GOLF LINKSERROR! BOOKMARK NOT DEFINED.
18 Golf Drive, Madison, IL
(314) 421-4653, (618) 482-4653,
(800) 482-8856
www.gatewaynational.com

Gateway National Golf Links is an 18-hole, link-style golf course located just 10 minutes from downtown St. Louis. The course, voted the No. 1 course and the best golf value in a St. Louis Post-Dispatch readers' poll, is the only public course in the area that features bent grass fairways. Designed by noted golf course architect Keith Foster, the stunning 5,100- to 7,200-yard championship course combines modern conveniences with a nostalgic feel. Gateway has been voted the No. 1 Public Golf Course in St. Louis, and it is the only facility with bent grass.

KOKOPELLI GOLF CLUB
1401 Champions Drive, Marion, IL
(888) 746-0887, ext. 2
www.kokopelligolf.com

Kokopelli offers 18 challenging holes of golf spread over 160 acres of beautiful terrain. The daily-fee course and facilities were designed by renowned golf architect Steve Smyers and was named one of "America's 100 Best Courses for $100 or Less" by *Travel & Leisure* magazine. Golfweek magazine ranked the facility as the No. 3 course in Illinois. There are five sets of tees, 96 bunkers, rolling fairways, and open greens that provide golfers with a fair—but challenging—day on the links. Play ranges from 5,400 to 7,200 yards and carries a course rating of 71.6 to 75.2. The facility offers a variety of "stay and play" packages that include unlimited golf and practice range access, meals, and hotel accommodations.

NORMAN K. PROBSTEIN COMMUNITY GOLF COURSE AND YOUTH LEARNING CENTER

6141 Lagoon Drive, Forest Park
(314) 367-1337
http://stlouis.missouri.org/citygov/parks/
forestpark/golf.html
At the turn of the 20th century, a number of local businessmen and sportsmen began a campaign for the construction of a municipal golf course. Several sites were suggested, but since the municipality was busy with plans for the coming World's Fair, nothing was done about a golf course for several years. In 1912 Dwight Davis, commissioner of parks and recreation, recommended in his annual report that an 18-hole golf course be developed over the area in Forest Park that was used for part of the World's Fair grounds. Today Forest Park golfers enjoy one of the finest public courses in the country. Each 9-hole course is named for a native Missouri tree—dogwood, redbud, or hawthorne. The Hale Irwin Signature designed facility, with zoysia fairways and a number of water features, is a 27-hole course that includes three 9-hole courses, each of which may be played as a 9-hole course or combined for an 18-hole round. All three courses are Par 35. Audubon Cooperative Sanctuary Program practices have been followed in the design of the course, which helps promote ecologically sound land management and conservation of natural resources. The clubhouse includes Ruthie's Cafe and a golf supply shop. Greens fees are reasonable, and membership packages are available.

QUAIL CREEK CHAMPIONSHIP GOLF COURSE

6022 Wells Road
(314) 487-1988
www.quailcreekgolfclub.com
Quail Creek is a public, 18-hole, par 72 championship course with Bermuda grass fairways and bent grass greens. The facility was designed by Hale Irwin and is located on 150 acres of picturesque hills, creeks, and valleys. Quail Creek's course features three sets of tees and offers a full range of amenities, including a driving range, locker room facilities, private lessons, a fully equipped pro shop, and a full-service restaurant. It is tied for the most difficult public course in the St. Louis area with a slope rating of 141. Golfers with soft spikes or tennis shoes receive a nominal discount, and the facility is open year-round, weather permitting.

SPENCER T. OLIN COMMUNITY GOLF COURSE

4701 College Avenue, Alton, IL
(618) 465-3111
www.spencertolingolf.com
Spencer T. Olin is an Arnold Palmer–designed and managed facility that rated four stars in *Golf Digest's* "Best Places to Play." Located only 30 minutes from downtown St. Louis, the course features zoysia fairways, bent grass greens, and blue rye fescue roughs, with a championship layout playing 6,941 yards from the back tees or 5,049 from the front tees. A championship practice facility features a two-tiered grass tee driving range, practice sand bunker, and putting and chipping greens. The facility hosted the 1996 U.S. Women's Amateur Public Link Championship and the ESPN-televised 1999 U.S Men's Amateur Public Links Championship. Open April through October.

i There are more than 175 parks and green spaces in the city of St. Louis and St. Louis County. There's sure to be one near you!

TAPAWINGO NATIONAL GOLF CLUB

13001 Gary Player Drive, Sunset Hills
(636) 349-3100
www.tapawingogolf.com

Tapawingo's three championship nines, nestled among a scenic environment of rivers, lakes, and hardwood forests, are designed to offer the ultimate golf experience. The course's 27 championship holes were designed by Gary Player, one of only five winners of golf's Grand Slam. Or, as Player himself describes the course: "God designed the first 6 holes. Player Design helped out with the rest." The facility offers three 18-hole course combinations.

Driving Ranges

BARRETT STATION GOLF PRACTICE CENTER

3031 Old Dougherty Ferry Road, Ballwin
(636) 391-6666

Barrett Station is open year-round, so desperate duffers can get their whacks in even when they can't get a tee time. The facility offers lessons from PGA pros, a full-service pro shop that can handle club fitting and repairs, and a driving range with lighted, Bermuda grass tees and pro-turf deshock mats.

TOWER TEE FAMILY GOLF AND RECREATION COMPLEX

6727 Heege Road, Affton
(314) 481-5818
www.towertee.com

Open 365 days a year, Tower Tee is equipped with an 18-hole, par 3 course with mature trees and challenging greens, as well as a 15-target driving range with 30 quickstand Bermuda grass tees, 28 mat hitting stations, and sheltered and heated hitting stations for year-round practice. The facility offers two exceptional Bermuda practice greens with more than 15,000 square feet of putting surface that has been designed to mirror actual playing conditions. There are also seven PGA instructors on staff for individualized instruction. Mini-golf, batting cages, and other kid-friendly activities are available on-site as well. *Golf Range Magazine* ranked Tower Tee as one of the Top 100 golf ranges in America in 2008.

Hiking

CASTLEWOOD STATE PARK

Kiefer Creek Road, off New Ballwin Road
from Highway 100, Ballwin
(636) 227-4433
www.mostateparks.com/castlewood.htm

Between 1915 and 1940, St. Louis residents would take the train each weekend to the Castlewood area for water fun, dancing, and clubhouse partying. Today 1,779-acre Castlewood State Park preserves the history of the former resort. The park stretches for nearly 5 miles, straddling both sides of the Meramec River. Hikers can explore the park on more than 15.5 miles of trails, including the 3-mile Grotpeter Trail that winds through the park's wooded uplands. The River Scene Trail is a 3-mile loop that ascends the tall bluffs along the Meramec River, then descends to the floodplain along the river's edge, and the Chubb Trail is a 7-mile trail that is open to both hikers and equestrians.

ELEPHANT ROCKS

Fort Davidson State Historic Site, Graniteville
(573) 546-3454
www.mostateparks.com/elephantrock.htm

Elephant Rocks, which also has an adjoining campground and 30 picnic sites, is a hike through natural granite formations that look like—you guessed it—elephants. The giant rocks look like a train of circus elephants standing tail-to-trunk. The main path is accessible to almost all ages, and it has views of two quarries, including a red granite one that has provided stone for paving blocks for the St. Louis levee and downtown streets. The main path is very accessible, and the more adventurous can do some climbing. There's also a 1-mile Braille Trail to accommodate hikers with visual disabilities, and it passes a quarry pond that features its own array of animal life.

POWDER VALLEY CONSERVATION NATURE CENTER

11715 Cragwold Road, Kirkwood
(314) 301-1500
www.mdc.mo.gov/areas/cnc/powder

Powder Valley offers 3 miles of paved trails through more than 100 acres of sloping, rocky woods filled with beautiful wildflowers, towering trees, and tangled vines. Located only 20 minutes from downtown St. Louis, the facility offers three trails of differing lengths and topography that can accommodate trailblazers of all skill levels. The Hickory Ridge Trail offers 1-mile and ½-mile loops through cool forested valley, hilltops, a pond, and seasonal creeks that attract a variety of wildlife activity. Tanglevine Trail is a ⅓-mile paved and level trail, dotted with wildflowers and wildlife, while the ⅔-mile-long Broken Ridge Trail takes hikers over steep hills and crisscrosses a creek lined with oak, hickory, and maple trees. The Missouri Department of Conservation also manages Emmenegger Nature Park, more than 100 acres of forested hills overlooking the Meramec River. Hunting and fishing permits can be purchased via the Web site.

ROCKWOODS RESERVATION

2751 Glencoe Road, Glencoe
(636) 458-2236
http://mdc.mo.gov/

In addition to a cave crawl, picnic areas, and education center, Rockwoods Reservation features seven hiking trails among its 1,898 acres of rugged forest, springs, and streams. Each trail offers a different experience and challenge, with distances ranging from 300 yards on the wheelchair-accessible Wildlife Habitat Trail to 3½ miles on the Lime Kiln Loop Trail. The Cobb Cavern Trail is a short jaunt from the parking lot that leads to a huge quarry cave that's especially appealing on a hot day. Some of the trails have steep climbs that could require a breather every hundred feet, while others are paved or partially paved and aren't quite as physically demanding. The scenery includes boulders the size of houses, clear running springs, cathedral stands of white oaks,

beautiful vistas, and the ruins of structures from the property's earlier days as a lumber and quarry resource. The Education Center at Rockwoods offers a detailed topographic map of the area and interpretive brochures for several of the trails.

Hunting

Eastern Missouri offers hunters a selection of several public hunting opportunities. The nearby Emmett and Leah Seat Memorial Conservation Area in Gentry County features 3,164 acres of upland, scattered forests, and grassy pastures. Other options include the Huzzah, Indian Trails, and Brickyard Hills Conservation Areas. For more information call the East-Central Regional Office at (573) 468-3335, or log on to www.mdc.mo.gov/hunt. In addition to offering the means to securing the necessary permits online, the site offers updated information on deer, waterfowl, and turkey hunting; game birds; hunter education courses; youth hunting clinics; and state regulations, seasons, and limits.

Ice-Skating

STEINBERG SKATING RINK

Forest Park
(314) 361-0613
www.steinbergskatingrink.com

One of the nation's largest outdoor skating rinks, the Mark C. Steinberg Memorial Skating Rink has been a popular St. Louis attraction since it opened as an ice rink in 1957. The facility offers ice-skating during the winter and hosts sand volleyball leagues during the warmer months. Skate rentals are available on-site, or visitors can bring their own. Hours of operation vary by season, but the rink's indoor/outdoor Steinberg Cafe snack bar is open year-round.

Soccer

JOE CLARKE SOCCER CAMPS

Washington University in St. Louis
(314) 821-KICK
www.joeclarkesoccercamp.com

Joe Clarke has been a collegiate soccer coach for

more than 25 years, and spent 7 years playing soccer professionally. With a staff comprised of various area high school, college, and professional coaches, the camps offer age-appropriate instruction for all skill levels. Residential and day-long camps take place at Washington University, Parkway Central High School, and Chaminade High School during the summer months. Private team camps and specialized small-group skill-training sessions are also available.

ST. LOUIS SOCCER CAMPS
7542 Lovella Avenue
(314) 647-2385
www.stlsoccercamps.com

St. Louis Soccer Camps is an organization created to increase player knowledge of the game of soccer, facilitate skill development, and enhance the overall desire for advancement to higher levels of achievement. The instructors at the facility are all current or previous coaches or players who participated in soccer at the college level. The weeklong camps are geared to athletes of all skill levels, and mini camps are offered to teams or individuals in order to focus on improving a certain area of the game. The camps also travel to individual team's fields for instructional camps.

ST. LOUIS SOCCER CLUB
One Soccer Park Road, Fenton
(636) 349-3760
www.stlouissoccerclub.com

The Soccer Club is directed by Steve Pecher, former captain of the USA National Team and the St. Louis Steamers. The facility offers a variety of camps for boys and girls of all ages, as well as specialized programs designed to help athletes build strength and endurance, enhance goalkeeping skills, and improve overall game skills.

Swimming

THE AQUATIC CENTER
670 Whitelaw Avenue, Wood River, IL
(618) 251-3110
www.woodriver.org/services/parksand
rec.htm

This $4 million water-recreation complex has something for everyone, including twin four-story waterslides, a 50-meter swimming pool, diving wells with 1- and 3-meter boards, a tot pool, a volleyball court, an observation deck, and concessions. The Aquatic Center has 200 available chaise lounges for those looking to soak up a little sun, and there are at least eight lifeguards on duty at all times. Open Memorial Day through Labor Day.

RAGING RIVERS WATERPARK
100 Palisades Parkway, Grafton, IL
(618) 786-2345
www.ragingrivers.com

Raging Rivers is a popular spot during the hot and steamy St. Louis summers. There are a number of wet and wild attractions to keep the kids cool and occupied, including the Giant Wave Pool, a Swirlpool tunnel flume, the Endless River, Tree House Harbor, and Itty Bitty Surf City for smaller children. Little ones can also play on pint-size waterslides, splash pools, tunnels, and in the Fountain Mountain family interactive area. Open Memorial Day through Labor Day. Inner tube and locker rentals are available for a nominal fee.

Tennis

DWIGHT F. DAVIS MEMORIAL TENNIS CENTER
5620 Grand Drive, Forest Park
(314) 361-0901

The Dwight F. Davis Memorial Tennis Center is named for the donor of the Davis Cup international tennis trophy and the former St. Louis Parks Commissioner who brought active recreation and tennis to Forest Park in 1912. The center, which opened in 1966, offers 19 lighted championship courts and a stadium court. Lessons are available for four-year-olds through adults. The club also hosts the World Team Tennis (WTT) home games of the St. Louis Aces each summer, which bring some of the best professional players to St. Louis over a two-week period.

RICHARD C. HUDLIN TENNIS COURTS
Forest Park
(314) 367-7275
www.forestparkforever.org
Located on the east side of Kingshighway Bou-levard in front of Barnes-Jewish Hospital are the Richard C. Hudlin Tennis Courts, named for an African-American St. Louis tennis coach whose most famous student was Arthur Ashe. These courts are available to the public on a first-come, first-served basis at no charge, and a small public playground is just east of the courts.

TOWER GROVE PARK
Kingshighway, Arsenal Street, and
Grand Boulevard
(314) 776-8722
www.towergrovepark.org
First used in 1911, the three grass tennis courts in Tower Grove Park are the only grass courts remaining in St. Louis. The park, which also fea-tures twelve lighted, hard-surfaced tennis courts, has a well-supplied pro shop and locker facility in the Henry Shaw Memorial Tennis Building, which is located adjacent to the hard-surface courts. Fees for daily use of the courts is usually less than $10 for two people.

YMCAs
YMCA OF GREATER ST. LOUIS
1528 Locust Street
(314) 436-1177
www.ymcastlouis.org
There are 21 YMCA locations throughout the St. Louis area, including two facilities downtown. All offer different activities and amenities with mem-bership, but most offer an extensive schedule of classes and special events, including fitness assessments, swim clubs, and CPR training and certifications. Many also have personal trainers on staff to instruct you how to train safely and effectively. The majority of the family Ys offer child care and special classes for the younger set. Call individual locations for hours of operation, the facility's schedule of events, and the avail-ability of child care.

DOWNTOWN YMCA
1528 Locust
(314) 436-4100
When this 10-story building was built in 1926, it was one of the largest YMCAs in the country. Today the facility features a host of modern ame-nities, including an indoor pool, a full-size gym-nasium, indoor track, Cybex and cardiovascular equipment, free weights, racquetball and hand-ball courts, steam rooms, saunas, whirlpools, and locker rooms. There's also a variety of sports equip-ment available for checkout, including volley-balls, basketballs, racquets, and boxing gloves. The Downtown Y also offers massage therapy, laundry facilities, and even a hair salon. Open daily.

KIRKWOOD FAMILY YMCA
325 North Taylor, Kirkwood
(314) 965-YMCA
The Kirkwood Y is focused on family fun and fitness, and its list of amenities includes two gyms—one full-size and one mini—along with a nursery, indoor track, indoor pool, free weights, cardio machines, Cybex Circuit and Arc Trainers, sauna, locker rooms, family changing area, and equipment checkout that includes weight belts, basketballs, and lap counters for use on the track. Free Child Watch play area for kids 6 weeks to 12 years old.

MARQUETTE YMCA
314 North Broadway
(314) 436-7070
In anticipation of greater needs in the downtown community, the Downtown YMCA opened the Marquette satellite facility in 1987. The state-of-the-art facility, located on the third and fourth floors of the Marquette Building, features a group cycling studio, fitness centers with Cybex equip-ment and cardiovascular machines, free weights, steam rooms, saunas, whirlpools, and locker rooms. Closed Saturday and Sunday.

MID-COUNTY FAMILY YMCA
1900 Urban Drive, Brentwood
(314) 962-9450
Located in nearby Brentwood, this family-focused

location features a 25-meter, L-shaped pool with diving well; a nursery; and a preschool child-care center. There's also a full-size gym, indoor track, strength training and cardiovascular equipment, free weights, a gymnastics center, racquetball courts, a steam room, a sauna, a whirlpool, locker rooms, a family changing area, and sporting equipment checkout available.

SOUTH COUNTY YMCA
12736 Southfork Road, Arnold
(314) 849-YMCA

The South County Y is equipped with two indoor pools—a lap lane pool and a recreational pool—a double-court gym, indoor and outdoor tracks, and a 6,500-square-foot fitness center outfitted with free weights, treadmills, Life Cycles, Precor EFX, Crosstrainers, Stairmasters, Concept II Rowers, and Cybex Circuit machines. Additional activities available to the Y's members and guests include a heavy bag, speed bag, and boxing gloves; racquetball courts; a cycling room; and

a children's center for gymnastics. In addition to the usual lineup of steam rooms, saunas, whirlpool, and locker rooms, there's the Child Watch nursery and the Family Hub, a dedicated space where families can spend time together, play games, use computers, do arts and crafts, and have fun.

WEBSTER GROVES FAMILY YMCA
226 East Lockwood, Webster Groves
(314) 962-YMCA

Webster's facility offers an indoor pool, fitness center with strength training and cardiovascular equipment, free-weight center, aerobics/dance studio, sauna, nursery, locker rooms, and a kids' gym. There's also a family changing area, and basketballs, weight belts, and lap counters available to check out. Both the Webster Groves and Kirkwood locations offer summer day camps, nursery care, and Kids Express for children ages two and a half to eight.

SPECTATOR SPORTS

In St. Louis, sports are much more than tradition—they're an obsession. From the Cardinals, Rams, and Blues to the minor-league baseball and hockey teams to college and high school athletics, almost everyone in this town is into sports at some level.

St. Louis hosted the Olympics as part of the 1904 World's Fair, and since then, the city has laid claim to ten World Series championships, a Super Bowl title, a single-season home run record-holder, and countless other sports highlights. Sports are the lifeblood of St. Louis—the teams, players, and events have a special place in the hearts of the people who live here—so it was no surprise when *The Sporting News* named St. Louis the best sports city in North America.

AUTO RACING

GATEWAY INTERNATIONAL RACEWAY
700 Raceway Boulevard, Madison, IL
(618) 482-2400
www.gatewayraceway.com
Located about 20 minutes from downtown St. Louis, Gateway hosts major-league motor sports events. Gateway features Indy Racing League (IRL), National Hot Rod Association (NHRA) Drag Racing, NASCAR Busch Series, NASCAR Craftsman Truck Series, NASCAR RE/MAX Challenge Series and Infiniti Pro Series, plus weekly drag racing and additional special events. The facility's 1¼-mile oval track and ½-mile drag strip host the NASCAR Busch Series in May, the NASCAR Sears Craftsman NHRA Drag Racing series in June, and the Gateway Indy 250 IRL event each August.

i In 1998 Cardinals' first baseman Mark McGwire hit 70 home runs in one season, smashing the previous record set by Roger Maris. Chicago Cubs' outfielder Sammy Sosa, who was McGwire's closest challenger during the home run race, was on hand when McGwire hit the record-breaking 62nd homer on September 8, 1998. McGwire went on to hit homers 66 through 70 at Busch Stadium as well.

BASEBALL

RIVER CITY RASCALS
Ozzie Smith Sports Complex
900 Ozzie Smith Drive, O'Fallon
(636) 240-BATS, (888) 762-BATS
www.rivercityrascals.com
In June 1999 the River City Rascals joined Frontier League play in a beautiful new ballpark with an old-time feel, T. R. Hughes Ballpark. Located in the Ozzie Smith Sports Complex in St. Charles County, the Rascals' home turf is located about 35 miles west of downtown St. Louis. The stadium has 2,950 permanent seats and a grass berm and picnic area capable of holding an additional 2,200 fans. The Rascals offer a throwback to the old days of baseball, with lots of special events and activities included with the game. Ticket prices are under $10, and there's usually a promotion or giveaway of some sort on any given night.

ST. LOUIS CARDINALS
Busch Stadium, 700 Clark Street
(314) 345-9600
www.stlcardinals.com
Since the team's inception in 1892, the St. Louis Cardinals have made 17 trips to the World Series and had more than 30 players, managers, and executives inducted to the Baseball Hall of Fame in Cooperstown. Legendary players such as

Stan Musial, Bob Gibson, Ozzie Smith, and Mark McGwire have made Cardinals baseball the best game in town for more than a century. McGwire called St. Louis "baseball heaven," and broadcasters and baseball pundits across the country agree, dubbing St. Louis baseball fans the best in the country. Tickets are usually easy to get, whether in advance or at the gate. Scalpers set up shop across the street from the stadium in front of the Hilton hotel and at Mike Shannon's restaurant and you can usually bargain with the sellers and get decent seats for a somewhat reasonable price. Gates open two hours before game time so fans can watch batting practice, and it's an ideal time to try and get autographs from the players. Fans are allowed to walk down into the field box seats behind the dugouts to take photos of the players or get autographs. Management requests that the fans leave the area when the field box ticket holders arrive, so make sure you follow orders from the ushers.

i Looking for some really good seats to a Cardinals game? Check out StubHub .com, the official ticket re-sale site for the Cardinals. Season-ticket holders who can't use their seats for a particular game make their tickets available online for purchase. You can find everything from bleacher seats to field box tickets listed, and the list updates continuously as tickets become available. The sellers set the prices—not the team—so there are great deals and not-so-great-deals. However, it's the best way to score really good seats and authentic tickets.

COLLEGE SPORTS

SAINT LOUIS UNIVERSITY
SLU Athletic Ticket Office
3672 West Pine Boulevard
(314) 977-4SLU
www.slu.edu
A member of the Atlantic 10 Conference, the Saint Louis University men's basketball squad

plays at Chaifetz Arena, their newly opened on-campus venue. The Lady Billikens basketball and volleyball teams play their games at the Bauman-Eberhardt Athletic Center, also located on the midtown campus of SLU. The building, constructed in the 1920s, houses the athletic department offices and SLU's Hall of Fame, which displays trophies and memorabilia from the outstanding accomplishments of individuals and teams throughout Billiken sports history. The SLU baseball and softball teams play at the Billiken Sports Center on the university campus. In nearby Fenton, Missouri, the SLU field hockey teams compete at the Anheuser-Busch Center, a facility located on 32 acres approximately 20 minutes from SLU's midtown campus. Two of the six fields are artificial playing surfaces, which feature state-of-the-art System 90 Astroturf. Robert R. Hermann Stadium offers the men's and women's soccer teams a stellar venue in which to compete. The state-of-the-art field surface is a mixture of blue grasses that covers an area of 155,000 square feet. The Billikens play on a regulation 120-by-75-yard soccer pitch. The addition of permanent seating on the east side of the stadium, along with the expansion of the main grandstand, has increased the facility's seating capacity to 6,050.

i Planning to take MetroLink to Busch Stadium for a game? Downtown and Illinois-side trains are filled to capacity as much as an hour or so before the first pitch, so make plans to get to the station—and the stadium—early.

WASHINGTON UNIVERSITY
1 Brookings Drive
(314) 935-5220
www.bearsports.wustl.edu
A member of the University Athletic Association (UAA), the "Wash U" Bears field highly competitive men's and women's basketball teams, as well as league-leading football, volleyball, baseball, softball, tennis, swimming, track and field, and soccer teams. The university's on-campus athletic

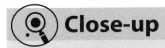 **Close-up**

Batting Practice

Get to Busch Stadium a little early and watch major-league hitters blast baseballs into the bleachers during batting practice. The stadium opens two hours early so ticket holders can witness batting practice by the home and visiting teams. Cardinals players bat first, with the visiting team taking over the batting cage for the last 40 minutes or so. One thing to remember though: As it is with most things in life, batting practice times are subject to change without notice, so you might want to call the stadium to confirm exact times. (314) 345-9600.

BATTING PRACTICE TIMES

12:10 P.M. AND 12:20 P.M. GAMES:
Cardinals batting practice, 9:35–10:50 a.m.
Visiting team batting practice, 10:50–11:30 a.m.

1:15 P.M. GAMES:
Cardinals batting practice, 10:30–11:45 a.m.
Visiting team batting practice, 11:45 a.m.–12:25 p.m.

3:10 P.M. AND 3:15 P.M. GAMES:
Cardinals batting practice, 12:25–1:40 p.m.
Visiting team batting practice, 1:40–2:20 p.m.

6:10 P.M. AND 6:15 P.M. GAMES:
Cardinals batting practice, 3:30–4:45 p.m.
Visiting team batting practice, 4:45–5:25 p.m.

7:10 P.M. GAMES:
Cardinals batting practice, 4:30–5:45 p.m.
Visiting team batting practice: 5:45–6:25 p.m.

facilities include Francis Field, Bushyhead Track, Kelly Field, Mudd Field, the Tao Tennis Courts, Millstone Swimming Pool and Diving Well, Francis Gym, and the Field House.

FOOTBALL

ST. LOUIS RAMS
Edward Jones Dome
701 Convention Plaza
(314) 425-8830
www.stlouisrams.com
The Rams moved from Los Angeles to St. Louis in 1995 and won Super Bowl XXXIV at the conclusion of the 1999 season. The franchise has become an integral part of the city, and the Greatest Show on Turf still takes place whenever the Rams' high-octane offense is clicking on all cylinders. Preseason games start in August, with the regular season continuing through December. Playoff games hopefully take the Rams' season well into January. Single game tickets go on sale in August and usually sell out rather quickly. You can, however, almost always find someone selling tickets outside of the Dome on game day. Depending on how the team is doing dur-

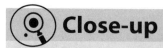 **Close-up**

Amateur Sporting Events

The St. Louis region hosts a number of amateur sporting events each year, including NCAA tournaments and conference championships. (See the Annual Events chapter for special sporting events that take place in the area each year.) And, while it's not an amateur event, St. Louis's Busch Stadium will host the July 2009 Major League Baseball All-Star Game. For more information about St. Louis sports, visit the St. Louis Sports Commission's Web site at www.stlouissports.org. Here are a few of the events scheduled to take place in St. Louis in the near future:

2009 NCAA Women's Basketball Final Four, April 2009, Scottrade Center

2009 NAIA Men's & Women's Outdoor Track & Field National Championships, May 2009, Southern Illinois University–Edwardsville 2010 NCAA Men's Basketball Regional, March 2010, Edward Jones Dome

2010 NCAA Division III Women's Volleyball Championships, November 2010, Washington University Field House

2011 NCAA Men's Ice Hockey West Regional, March 2011, Scottrade Center

2012 NCAA Division I Wrestling Championships, March 2012, Scottrade Center

---

ing that particular season, prices can range from $10 to $150 for a $40 face-value ticket. Prices are highest when the team plays popular rivals like the Pittsburgh Steelers or Green Bay Packers. You are almost guaranteed to find a better ticket deal outside the stadium than you would by going through a ticket agency that scalps tickets, so it's usually a better idea to take your chances on game day. Plus, there are often a lot of good-hearted souls who just want to get their money back on tickets they can't use, and they are less likely to take advantage of you.

i Some of the most successful athletes in the world were raised and trained in St. Louis, including such notables as Olympic track star Jackie Joyner-Kersee, baseball's Yogi Berra and James "Cool Papa" Bell, tennis champ Jimmy Connors, golfer Hale Irwin, and world heavyweight boxing champs Michael and Leon Spinks.

ICE HOCKEY

ST. LOUIS BLUES HOCKEY
Scottrade Center
1401 Clark Avenue
(314) 622-2500
www.stlouisblues.com

A member of the National Hockey League's Western Conference and Central division, the Blues have employed some of the greatest players in history since joining the NHL in 1967. Such old-time hockey heroes as Dickie Moore, Doug Harvey, Glenn Hall, and Jacques Plante helped give the team its start. Later, stars such as Wayne Gretzky, Dale Hawerchuk, and Peter Stastny also would spend time in St. Louis. Legendary architects Lynn Patrick and Emile Francis once ran the Blues, and championship-team builders Cliff Fletcher and Jimmy Devellano had stints on the St. Louis hockey staff. Coaches have included Stanley Cup champions Scotty

Bowman, Al Arbour, and Jacques Demers. The Blues have reached the playoffs 25 times, yet the team still seeks its first Stanley Cup title. The Blues play home games at Scottrade Center in downtown St. Louis, and tickets are usually available for all games at the box office. For tougher tickets—against rivals like Chicago or Detroit—you may have to get to the game a little early and bargain with those selling tickets out front. The regular season runs from October through April, with playoff games (hopefully) taking the season into June. Preseason games usually begin in September.

TENNIS

ST. LOUIS ACES
7730 Carondelet Avenue
(314) 726-2237
www.stlouisaces.com
World-class professional tennis takes place in St. Louis during a two-week period each July. World Team Tennis (WTT) players such as John McEnroe, Andy Roddick, Lindsay Davenport, and Jan-Michael Gambill have competed in the beautiful outdoor setting at the Dwight Davis Tennis Center in Forest Park. Individual match ticket prices range from $30 to $75.

ANNUAL EVENTS

St. Louis will find any excuse to have a party—and to have fireworks. An event just isn't complete without a spectacular pyrotechnics display as part of the grand finale. From First Night festivities on New Year's Eve to every Cardinals home run and victory and the annual holiday tree-lighting ceremony, bombs will be bursting in air on the banks of the mighty Mississippi River.

In addition to a host of house and garden tours in St. Louis's historic areas, there are a number of smaller, eclectic street fairs and block party–style events held throughout the area's many neighborhoods. Some get more media attention and exposure than others, but almost all of them are listed on the St. Louis Convention & Visitors Commission's Web site (www.explore stlouis.com) under the Calendar of Events heading. Since some of the smaller events might skip a year or change locations for whatever reason, it's a good idea to log on to this site or to call ahead to make sure the event is everything you think it will be. Plus, you never know when a new event or festival will pop up in St. Louis. Most of the activities listed are family-friendly and open to all age groups, unless otherwise specified. So, enjoy! After all, a city founded by two guys from New Orleans definitely knows how to let the good times roll.

JANUARY

BASEBALL FORECAST LUNCHEON
Millennium Hotel
200 South Fourth Street
(314) 992-0687
www.stlouissports.org
The Sports Commission hosts its annual Bank of America Baseball Forecast Luncheon in mid-January at the Millennium Hotel in downtown St. Louis. An off-season tradition here in Baseball City, USA, for more than a decade, this event gives fans a forum to hear insight from Cardinals management, media, and other insiders. Each year's luncheon features a theme, based on the participants who will be attending. The event is part of the three-day Cardinals Care Winter Warm-Up, which benefits the philanthropic side of the St. Louis Cardinals organization that's called Cardinals Care. The luncheon is almost always attended by the team manager and a number of top-name current and former Cardinals players.

Members of the sports media are also on hand for the event, which features a three-course lunch and various attendance prizes. The cost is around $30.

CARDINALS CARE WINTER WARM-UP
Millennium Hotel
200 South Fourth Street
(314) 421-3060
www.stlcardinals.com
The St. Louis Cardinals use this event as an opportunity to introduce new players who have been added to the roster during the off-season, as well as showcase favorite players from the past. The event, usually held during the three-day Dr. Martin Luther King Jr. weekend, also raises money for Cardinals Care, which helps kids in the metropolitan area. Team members are on hand to sign autographs and interact with fans—it's a great opportunity to meet Cardinal greats from the past and the present. The cost is around $35.

EAGLE DAYS
Chain of Rocks Bridge
(314) 416-9930
www.trailnet.org
The Missouri Department of Conservation and the Illinois Department of Natural Resources provide visitors the chance to get an "eagle's eye view" of the American bald eagle. Mid-January is typically the most active month for eagles in the area, and state conservation staffers take to the Chain of Rocks bridge with spotting scopes and educational programs. They even bring a live eagle in from the World Bird Sanctuary as part of the educational portions of the free two-day program. It's a great opportunity to see this majestic bird up close and personal, as well as in free flight, fishing for food, and roosting in trees.

MARTIN LUTHER KING JR. DAY
Old Courthouse
11 North Fourth Street
(314) 655-1701
www.nps.gov/jeff
On the date of the federal holiday celebrating Dr. Martin Luther King Jr.'s birthday, a host of St. Louis's African-American leaders gather in the rotunda of the historic Old Courthouse, site of the Dred Scott slavery trials. Activities include speeches and music, as well as the annual Martin Luther King Jr. parade through the streets of downtown. Free.

FEBRUARY

AFRICAN-AMERICAN HERITAGE MONTH
Old Courthouse and Gateway Arch
(314) 655-1701
www.nps.gov/jeff
This month long series of free programs, held at the Old Courthouse and the Gateway Arch's Museum of Westward Expansion, features historical character portrayals, storytellers, concerts, special films, Dred Scott Trial reenactments with visitor participants, Underground Railroad programs, and education programs that salute the contributions of African Americans in St. Louis

and throughout the West. The exhibit "Dred Scott, Slavery, and the Struggle to be Free" is on display on the Courthouse's second-floor rotunda level.

SOULARD MARDI GRAS
Historic Soulard neighborhood, Eighth and Lafayette Streets
(314) 621-8878
www.mardigrasinc.com
The series of Mardi Gras–related events kicks off with the annual Twelfth Night Celebration on January 6 each year, and the party doesn't stop until the last beads have been swept away on Ash Wednesday. In addition to a Cajun cook-off, children's art fair, and a four-day beer fest, Soulard's Mardi Gras includes events such as the Wine Taste and Art Show, Art Taste, a neighborhood house-decorating contest, the Taste of Soulard, Mystic Krewe of Barkus Pet Parade, Wiener Dog Derby, the Grand Parade, and the Fat Tuesday Parade along the streets of downtown. The big parade is held on the Saturday prior to Fat Tuesday each year, and revelers spend the rest of the day celebrating in the streets and bars of Soulard. Various clubs—or "krewes"—host balls throughout the pre-Lenten season, and many are open to the public. Prices vary per activity, although most are free for spectators.

BUILDERS HOME AND GARDEN SHOW
America's Center and the Edward Jones Dome
701 Convention Plaza
(314) 994-7700
www.stlhba.com
The St. Louis Home Builders Association hosts one of the most popular public shows held at the city's convention center each year. The home show includes more than 600 exhibitors featuring building products, an Interior Design Gallery, Kitchen and Bath Showcase, Lawn and Garden Showcase, Pool and Spa Extravaganza, and a number of guest speakers and special seminars on home- and garden-related topics. The cost is $9 for adults, $4 for children ages 6-12.

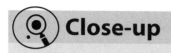 **Close-up**

Mardi Gras

The following is a list of the major festivities that take place during the days of Soulard Mardi Gras each year. The two biggest collections of events are held during the two weekends leading up to Mardi Gras—or Fat Tuesday, which is the Tuesday before Ash Wednesday. There are more events on the "first" Mardi Gras weekend (called "Barkus Weekend"), and many are family-friendly, so feel free to bring the kids. The second weekend (actually, just the Saturday before Fat Tuesday, as well as a repeat performance held at Washington Avenue on Fat Tuesday) is Grand Parade Day, and it is much more suited to an adult crowd due to the party atmosphere and the continuous flow of alcohol. Bars close at 11:00 p.m. in Soulard on Grand Parade Day, and as the local police say, "arrests begin at 11:01 p.m.," so be prepared to mosey out of the area at or before the 11 o'clock "witching hour."

For specific event details and updates, call Mardi Gras, Inc. at (314) 771–5110, or log on to www.mardigrasinc.com.

SCHLAFLY KREWE OF BREWE TENT

On Barkus Weekend, the Schlafly Krewe of Brewe Tent is the place to be for those in search of the three Bs—beer, bands, and beads. Schlafly gives out commemorative Mardi Gras cups and Schlafly beads, but, like the beer, they go fast. But there's music for all three days, so at least you've got that to fall back on. Location is subject to change along with changes throughout the neighborhood, but there are signs to help you find your way around. Free admission.

CHILDREN'S ART FAIR

Who doesn't need their very own crown, scepter, and beads? Your little ones can design their own regal Mardi Gras attire (also known as hat making, creating magic wands, and bead stringing), and there's also Radio Disney personalities, games, and music. The event is held at Concordia Elementary School at Trinity Lutheran Church, at South Eighth and Soulard Streets. The cost is around $5.

WINE TASTE

The Wine Taste offers great wines from Missouri and beyond, live music, tasty snacks, remarkable artwork, and lots of like-minded company. Travel from vineyard to vineyard without leaving the main room of the Mad Art Gallery (2727 South 12th Street), and meet vintners from area wineries and learn about the winemaking business while admiring work by local artists. The cost is $20 to $25.

ART TASTE

Ride the trolleys through the streets of Soulard and check out the eight art studios and galleries that represent the variety of artwork available in the neighborhood. What a great day—mixing eating and drinking with viewing works from local artists. The artists also have their artwork available for purchase at Preservation Hall (1921 South Ninth Street). Free.

TASTE OF SOULARD

The annual Taste of Soulard offers the chance to sample some of the fabulous food you'll find throughout the Soulard neighborhood. More than 25 restaurants serve up special Cajun and

Creole specialties such as jambalaya, red beans and rice, bread pudding with whiskey sauce, and Captain Morgan's Hurricanes. On Saturday, trolleys shuttle diners to all the stops, but it doesn't run on Sunday. The trolley also stops at the Wine Taste and the eight art studios and galleries on the Art Taste. Serious shoppers can hop off at Preservation Hall to purchase artwork and enjoy live music. Tickets can be purchased at any of the participating restaurants, or through Mardi Gras, Inc. at (314) 771–5110. The cost is about $15.

MYSTIC KREWE OF BARKUS PET PARADE

Registration is at the corner of Menard and Allen Streets from 9:00 a.m. to 1:00 p.m., and the parade starts at 1:00 p.m. Each of the first 1,500 canine participants receives a Beggin' Strips goody bag from Purina, and the $5 participant fee is donated to the Open Door Pet Sanctuary. Pets and their owners often come in matching costumes, while others prefer the "natural" look (although clothing is not optional for owners). All owners are responsible for the good behavior of their pets—and vice versa. Check out the stage presentation at the end of the parade to see who is named one of the 13 reigning pet monarchs. The parade starts at Allen and Menard, proceeds south to Russell, and then goes east on Ninth Street and north to Soulard Market Park. Free, but a $5 per-participant donation is encouraged.

NOW THAT'S A WIENER!

The Wiener Dog Derby consists of dachshunds "racing" in one of three categories: Cocktail Wieners, Hot Dogs, or Ball Park Franks. These low-legged creatures tend to wander around more than actually race, as they're usually more interested in inspecting their fellow racers. Bleacher seating lines the course for optimum viewing of the pocket-size pups. Registration is from 10:00 a.m. to 1:00 p.m. and is followed by "Yappy Hour" from 1:00 to 2:00 p.m. (This is when the steely-eyed canines size up their competition and do their pre-race walk-though). Then, at 2:00 p.m., the serious business of racing gets under way at the course in Soulard Market Park. Free for spectators.

IT'S A GRAND OLD PARADE

The annual Soulard Mardi Gras Grand Parade rolls from Busch Stadium and winds up at the foot of the Anheuser-Busch brewery. Each float is decorated to complement the theme for that year, and it traditionally has about 100 units, including marching bands, honor guards, marching krewes, and even Busch Gardens's parade floats fresh from New Orleans's Mardi Gras celebration. There's also a slate of activities and entertainment that takes place before and after the parade in nearby Kiener Plaza, which is located two blocks north of Busch Stadium. Free.

FAT TUESDAY PARADE

On Mardi Gras Day, most of the floats from the Grand Parade held on the Saturday prior make an even grander appearance at this nighttime parade down Market Street. The Fat Tuesday Parade begins at 18th and Market, then proceeds toward the Gateway Arch. The parade disbands near Keiner Plaza, and the party continues into the night. Free.

MARCH

ANNIVERSARY OF THE DRED SCOTT DECISION AT THE OLD COURTHOUSE
11 North Fourth Street
(314) 655-1600
www.nps.gov/jeff

Each year on March 8, the Old Courthouse commemorates the Dred Scott slavery case at the actual location of the trial, which began in 1846. The event features historical re-enactors such as Frederick Douglass, who talks about the impact and significance of the historic decision. Visitors can participate in a reenactment of the trial in the courthouse's restored courtroom and take part in various National Park Service ranger-led programs and other activities throughout the day. Free.

MISSOURI VALLEY CONFERENCE BASKETBALL TOURNAMENT
Scottrade Center
1401 Clark Avenue
(314) 421-0339
www.mvc-sports.com

The Missouri Valley Conference men's basketball championship tourney is played in St. Louis each year in early March, as teams from Bradley University, Creighton, Drake, the University of Evansville, Illinois State, Indiana State, the University of Northern Iowa, Southern Illinois University, Southwest Missouri State, and Wichita State University compete for a spot in the NCAA tournament. All-session tickets are $110; single-session tickets range from $10 to $30.

ST. PATRICK'S DAY PARADE AND RUN
Downtown
(314) 241-7287 for parade info,
(314) 231-2598 for run info
www.irishparade.org

Elaborate floats, marching bands, and giant helium-filled balloons fill the streets of St. Louis for the annual St. Patrick's Day Parade, held the Saturday before March 17. The parade begins at Broadway and Market Street in downtown St. Louis, goes past St. Louis Union Station, and ends

at 23rd Street. A five-mile run, which begins at Ninth and Market Streets and ends in front of St. Louis Union Station, precedes the parade. Runners of all ages and abilities are welcome. Irish festivities take place under the train shed at St. Louis Union Station throughout the day. Free to spectators; $17-$20 to participate in the run.

HERMANN WURSTFEST
Stonehill Winery Pavilion and City Park, Hermann
(800) 932-8687
www.hermannmo.com

The annual Wurstfest is a two-day celebration held in late March that honors Hermann's 160 plus-year history of sausage-making and German culture. Sponsored by the Hermann Area Chamber of Commerce, Wurstfest puts Hermann in the spotlight as the Sausage-Making Capital of Missouri. Visitors are invited to sample and purchase old-world delicacies such as bratwurst, leberwurst, schwartenmagen, and sommer sausage in the pavilion at Stone Hill Winery. The Rhineland Wurstjaegers perform, and there are demonstrations of old-time sausage-making. A panel of celebrity and expert judges evaluates entries in a statewide sausage-making contest. The crowd-pleasing Wiener Dog Derby is held at the city park, where dachshunds compete in the Derby Dash, fashion shows, and the Longest Wiener Dog contest. Many of the area shops and museums feature crafts demonstrations, and local wineries offer tours and wine tastings. The cost is around $5.

APRIL

THE SPIRIT OF ST. LOUIS MARATHON AND FAMILY FITNESS WEEKEND
World's Fair Pavilion in Forest Park, Soldiers Memorial, and America's Center in downtown
(314) 725-9884
www.GoStLouis.org

This three-day event, held in early April, is packed with fitness activities for people of all ability levels. Activities include a 5K run/walk and children's fun run; a marathon, half marathon, and marathon relay; and a health and fitness expo at America's Center. The marathon begins and ends at Soldiers Memorial in downtown St. Louis and takes runners through sections of St. Louis's historic neighborhoods, including Soulard, the Central West End, Forest Park, Clayton, and University City. The 5K run/walk and children's fun run take place in Forest Park. Free for spectators; events are $10 to $260.

GRAND SOUTH GRAND HOUSE AND GARDEN TOUR

South St. Louis neighborhoods
(314) 773-4844
This tour of twelve unique and beautiful residences, held annually in mid-April, showcases the diverse styles of St. Louis city living. The featured homes are located in five of St. Louis's historic neighborhoods: Compton Hill Reservoir Square, Compton Heights, Shaw, Tower Grove East, and Tower Grove Heights. Shuttle buses are available between the homes. The cost is around $14 to $16.

BLUEBERRY HILL DART TOURNAMENT

6504 Delmar Boulevard
(314) 727-0880
www.blueberryhill.com
In late April, Blueberry Hill's Duck Room plays host to the largest and oldest annual pub dart tournament in the United States. This national tournament offers $12,000 in cash prizes for the winners of the men's, women's, and doubles divisions. Free for spectators; around $100 for participants.

ST. LOUIS EARTH DAY FESTIVAL

The Muny Grounds in Forest Park
(314) 962-5838
www.stlouisearthday.org
Exhibits, activities, educational programs, music, and food celebrate Earth Day, April 27, in one of St. Louis's most beloved green spaces. In addition to live music throughout the day, activities and exhibits include the Water Exploration Tent;

a mini-boat regatta; various models of rivers, streams, and dams; a bike rodeo; the chance to create "bike art" from recycled materials; painting an Art Bus; and joining in the annual All Species Parade. The parade, which features everything from bike riders to dog walkers, starts out on The Muny Grounds and winds through the nearby St. Louis Zoo. Free admission.

ST. LOUIS STORYTELLING FESTIVAL

Gateway Arch, Old Courthouse, Missouri Botanical Garden, and more
(314) 516-5948
www.umsl.edu/storytelling
The Storytelling Festival has been spinning yarns for more than 20 years, and it continues to delight people of all ages throughout the metropolitan area. Each year more than 70 regional and featured storytellers gather in St. Louis for this four-day event, held in late April and early May, which features a variety of activities and special events. In addition to special adult storytelling sessions and workshops, there are storytelling programs for the deaf, youth concerts, and a grand finale performance highlighting featured storytellers. Free.

MAY

CENTRAL WEST END HOUSE AND GARDEN TOUR

Central West End neighborhood
(314) 367-2220
www.thecwe.com
This self-guided walking tour features different segments of the CWE neighborhood each year. From the "private places" of Portland Place and Westmoreland Place to the mansions of the Central West End's central corridor, this annual event, which takes place early in the month, is a great way to get an inside look at how the "other half" lives. Most of the houses featured on the tour are where St. Louis's original captains of industry lived—and the houses include everything from ballrooms to soda fountains. The cost is usually around $20.

GREATER ST. LOUIS RENAISSANCE FAIRE
Rotary Park, Wentzville
(636) 928-4141
www.stlrenfaire.com

Held for four weekends from mid-May through early June, the Greater St. Louis Renaissance Faire at Wentzville is a living-history event that seeks to re-create the spirit of 16th-century Renaissance France. The fair invites visitors to immerse themselves in the costumes and mannerisms of the era while perusing the period-inspired offerings of many merchants. Fairgoers can watch the exploits of jousting knights; roam the village shops; enjoy live entertainment, including comedy and music; and interact with colorful villagers, nobles, and assorted peasants. The cost is around $10 and a discount coupon is available on the Web site.

LAUMEIER CONTEMPORARY ART FAIR
Laumeier Sculpture Park
12580 Rott Road
(314) 821-1209
www.laumeier.com

On Mother's Day weekend each year, Laumeier Sculpture Park welcomes more than 150 of the nation's best artists and exhibitors, who sell an impressive array of work in clay, drawing, fiber, glass, jewelry, leather, mixed media, painting, photography, printmaking, sculpture, and wood. There's live music on two stages, and kids love to visit Creation Location, a hands-on activities and entertainment area just for them. In addition to a petting zoo, jugglers, and magicians, Creation Location offers budding artists a chance to create their own sculpture from paper or Mylar, take part in percussion workshops, or watch magicians and balloon artists perform. There are also storytellers, face-painting booths, and stone-carving, wheel-throwing, and guitar-building demonstrations. The cost is around $5.

LEWIS AND CLARK HERITAGE DAYS
Frontier Park, St. Charles
(636) 947-3199
www.historicstcharles.com

In mid-May, history comes alive in St. Charles's Frontier Park, at an event that commemorates the arrival of the famed explorers in 1804. At this authentic reenactment of the Lewis & Clark encampment, visitors can witness the Corps of Discovery making final preparations for their expedition and see full-scale reproductions of a keelboat and two pirogues like the explorers used two centuries ago. Activities include a parade with the Fife and Drum Corps, authentic church services, weapons demonstrations, the ever-popular "skillet throw," and 19th-century crafts. Vendors offer a variety of foods and beverages prepared as they were 200 years ago, and groups portraying military units of the late 18th and early 19th centuries provide tactical demonstrations, including firing cannons and muskets. The largest Fife and Drum Corps muster west of the Mississippi River features a "massed band" of 150 fifers and drummers parading through the park and down Main Street, along with other entertainment such as singers, fiddlers, dulcimer players, games for the kids, and puppet shows. Free.

BATTLE OF FORT SAN CARLOS COMMEMORATION
Jefferson National Expansion Memorial (Gateway Arch)
http://battleoffortsancarlos.org/

This program features music, marching Creole soldiers, costumed re-enactors, and a narrative about activities and feelings on the fateful day of May 26, 1780, when St. Louis defended America's

i St. Louis is home to hundreds of unique special events and activities throughout the year, attracting anywhere from several hundred to several hundred thousand people. For the most complete list of events and activities taking place during your visit, log on to the St. Louis Convention & Visitors Commission's Web site at www.explorestlouis.com, or check out the *St. Louis Post-Dispatch's* online calendar of events at www.stltoday.com.

western frontier against the British in the Revolutionary War. The event is usually held the Saturday before May 26. Free.

GYPSY CARAVAN
(314) 286-4452
www.gypsycaravan-stl.org
Held on Memorial Day for more than 30 years, the Gypsy Caravan is the Midwest's largest daylong flea market, antiques, and crafts fair. Held on the campus of the University of Missouri—St. Louis, the caravan features 500-plus vendors from more than 20 states. Bargain hunters can sort through an incredible selection of antiques, collectibles, knickknacks, and just plain stuff. Some of the offerings include jewelry, furniture, T-shirts, and comic books—just to name a few. Everybody can find something they can't live without. A variety of foods is available for sale on-site, so shoppers won't have to stop shopping for too long. Proceeds from the nominal admission fee ($5) support the Saint Louis Symphony Orchestra. Early birds can get in to see the "good stuff" at 7:00 a.m. for $20.

JUNE

HORSERADISH FESTIVAL
Woodland Park
Pine Lake and Olive Road, Collinsville, IL
(618) 344-0264
www.ci.collinsville.il.us
In early June join in the free fun at the "Horseradish Capital of the World" with a horseradish-eating contest, root-toss competition, live music, food (in addition to horseradish), entertainment, and horseradish-related games. Thanks to the contribution of two-thirds of the U.S. horseradish crop, Collinsville ranks as the world's most concentrated area of horseradish production.

SHAKESPEARE FESTIVAL OF ST. LOUIS
Art Hill in Forest Park
(314) 361-0101
www.shakespearefestivalstlouis.com
See the Bard of Avon's classics under the stars in beautiful Forest Park during the annual fortnight of free performances held in early June. Bring blankets or chairs for lawn seating. Regular performances take place at 8:00 p.m. every night except Tuesday, and the family-friendly Green Show, which features Elizabethan dancers and musicians, educational lectures, and a mini play for children, starts at 7:00 p.m. Thursday night performances are signed for the hearing impaired.

TASTE OF CLAYTON
Shaw Park
Clayton Road and Broadview Drive, Clayton
(314) 290-8474
www.claytonmissouri.com
This family event, held annually in Shaw Park on the first Sunday in June, features Clayton's top restaurants offering samples for a fee. Activities include a family fun area, live music performed throughout the day, and a fireworks extravaganza. The event, sponsored by the Clayton Restaurant Association, draws more than 35,000 people annually. Also featured is a special children's area, "Taste Jr.," an interactive play area where kids can participate in various activities and enjoy special kids' cuisine. Toward the end of the evening, "Taste-too" offers live music, along with an array of desserts, specialty coffees, beer, and wine. The grand finale, a fabulous fireworks display, usually takes place around 9:00 p.m. Admission is free, and the various "tastes" range from $1 to $5.

TASTE OF THE CENTRAL WEST END AND ART FAIR
Central West End, Euclid Avenue corridor
(314) 367-2220
www.thecwe.com
This popular neighborhood event, held in early June, is part street festival, part block party, and features samples from CWE restaurants along with art and music. Local bands provide the music, and local and regional artists show and sell their works. Admission is free, and the various "tastes" range from $1 to $5.

SUSAN G. KOMEN ST. LOUIS RACE FOR THE CURE
200 South Hanley Road, Suite 1070
(314) 721-2900
www.komenstlouis.org
Every year in mid-June, more than 60,000 locals participate in the Komen St. Louis Race for the Cure, which is one of the largest events of its kind in the country. Downtown is overrun with a sea of pink, as men, women, and children spend a Saturday morning walking or running in support of a cure for breast cancer. There is a competitive 5K run, along with a noncompetitive 5K run/walk and a 1-mile Fun Walk, and it is an inspiring way to spend a morning. Registration costs are $20 to $30, and race-day drop-ins are welcome.

CIRCUS FLORA
Grand Center Arts and Entertainment District
(314) 533-1285
www.circusflora.org
Circus Flora was formed in 1985 as a nonprofit theater company specializing in a one-ring European circus. In the intimate red and white "big top," no audience member is more than 40 feet from the ring. For two weeks in mid-June, audiences are treated to wire walkers, jugglers, dancers, galloping horses, and all of the usual trappings of a modern-day circus performance. Circus Flora features original music and a story line that serves as a framework for the acts, bringing the animals, performers, and audience members together in a celebration of life. This show offers kids a chance to feel a part of the action, rather than just being spectators. The cost ranges from $10 to $25.

GREAT RIVERS TOWBOAT FESTIVAL
Mississippi Riverfront on Front Street, Grafton, IL
(618) 786-7000
www.greatriverroad.com/Cities/Grafton/towfest.htm
Learn about life on the Mississippi as you tour a working riverboat and see how river crews live and work aboard the huge barges that cruise America's inland waterways. The festival takes place on the fourth weekend in June each year, and it's a great activity for the whole family. Free.

> **i** During the Fair Saint Louis Fourth of July celebration in downtown, parking is at a premium, so MetroLink is the fastest and most convenient way to get to all of the action.

JULY

FAIR SAINT LOUIS
Jefferson National Expansion Memorial (Gateway Arch)
(314) 434-3434
www.fairstl.org
This annual fair celebrates America's birthday with two days of live concerts, ethnic foods, and nationally known entertainers in downtown St. Louis. The fireworks displays held each evening are a highlight of what has come to be known as "America's biggest birthday party." There's a giant sand sculpture tied to the fair theme each year, along with interactive shows and activities, a Family Fun Village, and other entertainers. Free.

A HISTORIC FOURTH OF JULY CELEBRATION
Old Courthouse
(314) 655-1701
www.nps.gov/jeff
This annual event, held at the historic Old Courthouse, celebrates the Fourth of July with interpreters in period clothing, living-history portrayals, and demonstrations, including appearances by Thomas Jefferson, Abigail Adams, and Frederick Douglass; patriotic music; a tableau vivant (a 3-D "painting" using real people in the scene) and historic vignettes; patriotic speeches; ranger programs; and refreshments of the era. Free.

WORLD'S LARGEST CATSUP BOTTLE SUMMERFEST BIRTHDAY PARTY AND CUSTOM 'N' CLASSIC CAR 'N' TRUCK SHOW BASH

Main Street, Collinsville, IL
(618) 345-5598
www.catsupbottlefestival.com
Celebrate the birthday of Collinsville's world-famous roadside landmark—a giant bottle of catsup—at this family-friendly early-July festival of live music, crafts, food, fun, games, and a car show. Discriminating ketchup lovers can take the "Brooks Catsup Tangy Taste Test" and see if they can tell the difference between catsup and ketchup (even though they're really the same thing). Free.

LIVE ON THE LEVEE

Downtown St. Louis
(314) 434-3434
www.celebratestlouis.org
Live on the Levee is a series of free music concerts that begin in mid-July and continue through early August each summer. Held on Friday and Saturday nights, In addition to live musical performances by artists such as Lyle Lovett, India. Arie, Cheap Trick, Kenny Wayne Shepherd, and Morris Day & The Time, each evening's entertainment is capped off with a stellar fireworks display. Food and beverage vendors are set up on-site.

SOULARD BASTILLE DAY CELEBRATION

Historic Soulard neighborhood
(314) 621-6226
Celebrate St. Louis's French heritage with a series of fun and quirky special events that include food and wine tasting, a street fair, and a bicycle race. Festivities kick off in mid-July with the ceremonial beheading of King Louis and Marie Antoinette and conclude with a bike race through the Soulard neighborhood. In between, there's lots of live music, food, and drinks to be enjoyed by all. Free.

AUGUST

ANNUAL DOWNTOWN RESTAURANT WEEK

Various restaurants
(314) 436-6500
www.downtownrestaurantweek.net
More than two dozen of downtown St. Louis's finest and most popular eateries participate in this annual food frenzy. It's an ideal and economical way to experience dinner at a variety of restaurants. There are no coupons to clip or passes to secure—just visit one of the participating eateries and select from a special 3-course dinner menu for around $25 per person, plus tip and tax. Participants change yearly, so check the Web site to see who's in the mix during your visit.

GREATER ST. LOUIS HISPANIC FESTIVAL

Soldiers Memorial Park
Market and 14th Streets
(314) 837-6100
www.hispanicfestivalstl.com
This free two-day festival is held in early August each year to celebrate St. Louis's ever-increasing Hispanic population. The event tends to move around a bit, but most recently was held at Soldiers Memorial Park in downtown St. Louis. There's plenty of live music, dancing, and other Latin-inspired entertainment, along with Hispanic food booths, arts and crafts, a children's activity area, and information booths. And lots of margaritas.

MISSOURI BLACK EXPO

America's Center
701 Convention Plaza
(314) 361-5772
www.missouriblackexpo.com
Hundreds of local and regional African-American entrepreneurs showcase their businesses during this two-day event, held in the St. Louis Convention Center in early August. In addition to performances by local and national entertainers, Expo activities include a benefit gala, a lecture series, the Annual Festival of Foods Mart, Black

Book Sellers Book Zone, self development and entrepreneurial workshops, a health fair, and free child-care services for those attending the event. Popular events held in conjunction with the Expo include the Budweiser Invitational Amateur Boxing Competition and the Annual Youth Rally, featuring tennis and golf camps for kids. The cost is $8; free for children six and under. Concerts are an additional fee.

FESTIVAL OF THE LITTLE HILLS
Frontier Park and Main Street, St. Charles
(636) 946-7776, (800) 366-2427
www.historicstcharles.com
The Festival of the Little Hills is St. Charles's largest event of the year and draws more than 300,000 visitors during the three-day weekend held in mid-August. Activities include demonstrations by craftspeople and artisans, live music and entertainment, and more than 300 crafts booths with items for sale. There's also a variety of food and beverage booths. Free

MOONLIGHT RAMBLE
Downtown
(314) 644-4660
www.moonlightramble.com
The Moonlight Ramble is the world's largest nighttime bicycle ride, as nearly 13,000 cyclists take to the streets of St. Louis. Registration and other pre-ramble activities get started around 9:00 p.m. and include performances by local bands. The ride, which takes place in late August, begins in downtown St. Louis at the Soldiers Memorial at 12:01 a.m. and ends several hours later in the same location. Recreational bikers as well as more serious-minded cyclists enjoy this event since it's the only time that the streets of St. Louis belong to bike riders first, and automobiles are secondary. Free for spectators; $10 to $25 for participants.

FESTIVAL OF NATIONS
Tower Grove Park
(314) 773-9090
www.intlinst.org/events/festival.asp
The Festival of Nations, a fast-growing celebration that reflects St. Louis's increasingly diverse population, is presented in late August by the International Institute and includes participation from more than 125 area ethnic organizations. Held in beautiful Tower Grove Park, the event features ethnic food booths, handmade items, and nonstop music and dance performances. This family-friendly event includes arts and crafts, a petting zoo, and demonstrations of cultural traditions, including instrument-making and crafts. The Festival of Nations kicks off with a colorful Parade of Nations that features participants dressed in traditional costumes. Free.

SEPTEMBER

JAPANESE FESTIVAL
Missouri Botanical Garden
4344 Shaw Boulevard
(314) 577-9400, (800) 642-8842
www.mobot.org
The Missouri Botanical Garden hosts this festival in honor of Japanese culture each Labor Day weekend. Highlights include tours of the Japanese garden, special art exhibitions, traditional processions, tea ceremonies, kimono demonstrations, traditional music and dancing, a Japanese marketplace, arts and crafts, ikebana, bonsai, martial arts, karaoke, Japanese theatrical performances, cooking demonstrations, food booths, and many more fun family activities, including everybody's favorite, feeding the koi (Japanese carp). Bring plenty of change for the "koi-chow" machines! The cost is $3 to $10.

ST. NICHOLAS GREEK FESTIVAL
St. Nicholas Greek Orthodox Church
4967 Forest Park Boulevard
(314) 361-6924
www.stnicholas.missouri.goarch.org/
GreekFest/
This ethnic food festival and celebration takes place on Labor Day weekend and features authentic food, dance demonstrations, live music, and some of the best baklava you'll ever taste. Imports from Greece are sold in the bazaar, and you can buy desserts to take home as well. Admission is free—and the food is worth every penny.

TOUR DE LAFAYETTE CRITERIUM BICYCLE RACE
Lafayette Square
(314) 772-5724
www.lafayettesquare.org
More than 300 riders participate in this popular bike race, and they represent some of the best cyclists from 20 states. The historic neighborhood of Lafayette Square kicks off Labor Day weekend with a twilight race on Friday night. The mile-long circuit is around Lafayette Park, with participants making about 40 rotations around the park during the race. There are four races, with riders making starts at 6:00, 7:00, 8:00, and 9:00 p.m. Many of the restaurants in Lafayette Square stay open to accommodate racers and spectators, and live music and concessions are available in the mini park. The race is part of the Gateway Cup Series. Free for spectators; $25 for participants.

ST. LOUIS NATIONAL CHARITY HORSE SHOW
National Equestrian Center
880 Freymuth Road, Lake St. Louis
(636) 458-7994
www.stlouishorseshow.com
Riders from 30 states join with horse enthusiasts from around the country at the St. Louis National Charity Horse Show and the $30,000 Grand Prix jumping competition in early September. More than 1,000 riders bring their top mounts to compete in Hunter, Jumper, Saddle Bred, Arabian, and Western events. The event also features a two-day wine-tasting and classic car festival. The cost is $10.

ANNUAL KIRKWOOD GREENTREE FESTIVAL
Kirkwood Park
Geyer Road and Adams Avenue, Kirkwood
(314) 822-5855
www.ci.kirkwood.mo.us
A mid-September weekend of festivities kicks off on a Friday evening with a kids' dog show, canine Frisbee contest, a book fair, and lots of live entertainment. Other events that take place during the weekend include a parade, mini-sailboat regatta, classic car show, and more than 200 booths filled

with different foods and arts and crafts. A Folklife Festival offers a glimpse at what life was like during the 1700s and 1800s, complete with period crafts and music. Free.

HOP IN THE CITY BEER FESTIVAL AT SCHLAFLY TAP ROOM
2100 Locust Street
(314) 241-8101
www.schlafly.com
This local microbrewery hosts an annual beer festival that features live local bands and the chance to sample more than 35 different types of Schlafly beer, as well as products from area wineries. This one-day festival, held in mid-September, takes place under a giant tasting tent on Schlafly's parking lot, and it is a great way for beer lovers to check out a lot of different ales and lagers. European-style foods and regular pub grub are available on-site as well. Free admission; $30-$35 to sample beers.

ST. LOUIS ART FAIR
7818 Forsyth Boulevard, Clayton
(314) 863-0278
www.saintlouisartfair.com
Visual artists from across the nation exhibit an impressive selection of original works of art, including jewelry, paintings, photography, ceramics and pottery, and sculpture and fiber. The three-day event, held in mid-September, features multiple stages of live entertainment, a performing arts village, sand sculptures, and an extensive selection of culinary treats from St. Louis restaurants and eateries. Kids love to visit the Creative Castle, where they can experiment with various art forms and create their own masterpiece to take home. The art fair is one of the most popular local events—a place where participants can socialize as well as shop—and it's a definite must-see. Free.

GREAT FOREST PARK BALLOON RACE
Central Field in Forest Park
(314) 993-2468
www.greatforestparkballoonrace.com
Held the third weekend in September, the Great

Forest Park Balloon Race hosts more than 60 hot-air balloons and draws 200,000-plus spectators each year. The colorful event, one of the most prestigious one-day balloon races in the world, is free for spectators. In 1994 the 10-story-high Energizer Bunny Hot Hare Balloon made its debut at the race and has become a crowd favorite. Festivities begin on the Friday night before the race with the Balloon Glow at the park's World's Fair Pavilion. The nighttime event offers a spectacular view of the balloons fully inflated and "aglow" from their burners. Race-day activities include a performance by the Saint Louis Symphony Orchestra, a parachute team exhibition, and a children's entertainment area. The race officially starts with the launch of the "hare" and "hound" balloons around 4:30 p.m. Free.

FAUST FOLK FESTIVAL
Faust Park
Olive Boulevard and Nooning Tree Drive, Chesterfield
(636) 532-7298
www.st.louisco.com/parks/faust_home.html
For two days in late September, Faust Historical Village comes alive with period re-enactors and artisans demonstrating their crafts, including blacksmithing, metalwork, rail splitting, wheat weaving, making cornhusk dolls, wood carving, silhouette cutting, and others. Live music is featured each day, along with a children's activity area and stagecoach and pony rides. The cost is around $3.

GATEWAY FOOTBALL CLASSIC WEEKEND
1015 Locust Street, Suite 420
(314) 621-1994
www.gatewayclassic.com
The annual Gateway Classic football game is held in late September at the Edward Jones Dome, and the weekend of football festivities includes a college fair, workshops, a fashion show, golf tournament, hospitality receptions, a pep rally and street festival, the Pan-Hellenic Council Greek Village, and live entertainment. Other activities include the Lifetime Achievement Awards Dinner, parties,

a parade, a songfest, and a tailgate party. There's also a wildly entertaining Battle of the Bands half-time show. Tickets range from $12 to $65.

INTERNATIONAL ROUTE 66 MOTHER ROAD FESTIVAL
Downtown Springfield, IL
(800) 545-7300
www.route66fest.com
Celebrate the love of the open road at this nostalgic car show and street festival held in late September. The festival features thousands of classic cars, live music, celebrity appearances, a Route 66 authors' and artists' expo, specialty foods, and performances by stunt drivers and trick motorcycle-riding teams. A highlight of the festival is the world's largest sock hop held at the Prairie Capitol Convention Center, which usually features oldies bands playing hits from the '60s. Free admission; $15 to $50 for sock hop.

MISSOURI CHILI COOK-OFF
Westport Plaza, Maryland Heights
(314) 961-2828
www.westportstl.com
This yearly chili-cooking contest held in late September features more than 100 varieties of chili, and teams compete for "best in show" as well as for a showmanship prize, which participants try to win by using colorful props and costumes to develop a theme for their cooking area. A recent addition to the competition is the homemade salsa division. The grand-prize chili recipe winner goes on to represent St. Louis in the National Chili Cook-Off. Free.

TASTE OF ST. LOUIS
227 South Jefferson
(314) 534-2101
www.tastestl.com
The last weekend in September is traditionally the date for Taste of St. Louis, a three-day event that celebrates food, music, art, and entertainment from the region. Held on the park grounds around the Soldiers Memorial at 14th and Market streets downtown, "Taste" includes national headliners

such as the Neville Brothers, Ozomatli, Live, Son Volt, Shemekia Copeland, and The Roots. Restaurant Row offers visitors a chance to buy "tastes" of specialty dishes from St. Louis restaurants, and the Culinary Stage features a head-to-head battle between area chefs and various culinary demonstrations. The music and art villages offer a variety of live dance and musical performances, as well as art pieces for sale by local artists. Free.

OCTOBER

FALL COLOR CARAVAN
Alton, IL
(618) 465-6676, (800) 258-6645
www.altoncvb.org

Each and every fall, the colors along the National Scenic Byway turn from green to gold, orange, yellow, and red. This free natural spectacle attracts thousands of visitors who enjoy the many festivals, fairs, and roadside stands that pop up each weekend through October. The fall is a great time for a weekend getaway in this part of the country, but it's best to make reservations early—the best hotels and bed-and-breakfasts book up early.

FRIGHT FEST SIX FLAGS ST. LOUIS
Interstate 44 and Allenton—
Six Flags Road, Eureka
(636) 938-4800
www.sixflags.com

Six Flags' annual Halloween extravaganza features "spooktacular" family fun for kids of all ages, including live entertainment, haunted hayrides, storytelling, and, of course, trick-or-treating. A popular activity is "Fearanoia," a nighttime interactive survival game that takes place throughout the 200-acre park. Other attractions include the Mausoleum of Terror and Brutal Planet for those who love a good scare. There are also plenty of non-scary attractions for smaller kids who "spook"

> **i** Beginning in early October, you can check out the beautiful fall foliage along the Great River Road, one of America's Scenic Byways.

easily. The event is held throughout the month of October, on weekends Friday—Sunday. The cost is $37 to $45. Parking additional.

HAUNTED ALTON
Various locations throughout downtown
Alton, IL
(618) 465-6676, (800) 258-6645
www.altoncvb.org

As seen on ABC-TV, Alton is considered to be the most haunted small town in America. The October haunted history tours held throughout the month attract thousands of curious visitors who are hoping to experience something spooky enough to talk about for years. The tours are entertaining, clever, and historic, and they also offer a chance to see beautiful private homes. There are also a number of other activities to enjoy, including an Owl Prowl through Pere Marquette State Park, the McPike Mansion Campout, and the Alton Halloween Parade. Costs vary per activity.

OCTOBERFEST
207 Schiller Street, Hermann
(800) 932-8687
www.hermannmo.com

This traditional German celebration features food, music, oom-pah bands, and dancing, with many area wineries hosting live local bands on weekends throughout the month. In addition to the live entertainment, tours, and wine tastings, the festivities include an arts and crafts sale, studio tours led by wine country artists, German menu items offered by local restaurants, and a biergarten. Weekends only in October. Free.

OKTOBERFEST ECKERT'S COUNTRY STORE AND FARMS
951 Green Mount Road, Belleville, IL
(618) 233-0513

20995 Eckert Orchard Road, Grafton, IL
(618) 786-3445

2719 Eckert Orchard Lane, Millstadt, IL
(618) 476-3260
www.eckerts.com

Activities at this German festival include a ride

on a wagon to the pumpkin patch to search for the "secret" pumpkin, along with country music, pony rides, and more. Eckert's orchards are home to a lot more than just trees in October, as gaggles of ghouls and goblins show up to greet visitors who venture into the orchards after dark. The 20-minute ride isn't too scary, so younger children should be able to enjoy it. If not, they'll just have to amuse themselves with some of the other festivities, including live entertainment and pig racing. Haunted hayrides take place on Friday and Saturday nights at the Millstadt and Grafton farms. The cost is $7.

LOOP IN MOTION ARTS FESTIVAL
The Loop neighborhood/Delmar Boulevard
(314) 725-4466
www.ucityloop.com
The festivals features two days' worth of festivities, starting with the Friday evening gallery/art walk through various exhibits, musical entertainment, and dance performances at more than two dozen locations. See the performance-art piece going on inside the "live window" at Blueberry Hill, along with glass-blowing and ceramic demonstrations at Washington University's Lewis Center. The Loop de Loop Parade takes place on Saturday, followed by live music and dance performances on two stages, children's art activities, a Loop n' Leash Dog Talent Contest, artists' demonstrations, performance art and more. Free.

OKTOBERFEST
Main Street, Frontier Park, St. Charles
(636) 946-7776, (800) 366-2427
www.historicstcharles.com
This two-day, city-wide celebration held in late September or early October pays homage to St. Charles's French and German heritage. Activities include a parade; German bands, foods, and beverage booths; beer gardens; an antique car show Sunday on South Main; German costumes; live music; a children's area; and dozens of craft booths in Frontier Park. Free.

ST. LOUIS WALK OF FAME INDUCTION CEREMONY
Blueberry Hill
6504 Delmar Boulevard
(314) 727-0880
www.stlouiswalkoffame.org
The annual induction ceremony takes place in early October in the heart of The Loop neighborhood on an outdoor stage located at Delmar and Westgate Streets. A local celebrity or TV personality usually emcees the free program, which pays tribute to the newest additions to the Walk of Fame family. Frequently, the honorees make a special effort to attend these ceremonies, and past recipients have included such famous names as Kevin Kline, Marsha Mason, Bob Costas, John Goodman, and Chuck Berry. The brass stars and plaques along the sidewalks of Delmar Boulevard contain summaries of the accomplishments made by famous St. Louisans. There are more than 110 stars and plaques on the Walk of Fame, with additional inductees added each year.

BEST OF MISSOURI MARKET
Missouri Botanical Garden
4344 Shaw Boulevard
(314) 577-9540, (800) 642-8842
www.mobot.org
All things Missouri can be found at more than 100 country stands filled with fruits, vegetables, flowers, plants, herbs, nuts, candies, and baked foods along with handmade arts and crafts. Country and bluegrass musical groups entertain, and the children's activities area features a variety of craft-making opportunities, such as pumpkin or straw hat decorating, bead making, and a chance to get up-close and-personal with a stable full of farm animals. The event is usually held the first weekend of October. The cost is $3 to $10.

HISTORIC SHAW ART FAIR
Shaw neighborhood, 4100–4200 blocks of Flora Place
(314) 771-3101
www.shawartfair.com
More than 125 artists from across the country

display and offer for sale works in a wide variety of media. The fair is set up along the Flora Place Parkway in the historic Shaw neighborhood, which is directly east of the Missouri Botanical Garden. The art fair is juried, and the artists who participate offer some incredibly beautiful and unique pieces. The fair also has children's activities, an eclectic menu of foods available at the food court, and a unique variety of musical performers. The event, which usually takes place the first weekend of October, is held in conjunction with the Missouri Botanical Garden's Best of Missouri Market showcase. The cost is $5; children under 14 are admitted free if accompanied by an adult.

COLUMBUS DAY PARADE AND FESTIVAL
The Hill neighborhood
(314) 837-8830
www.shop-the-Hill.com
The predominately Italian neighborhood known as "The Hill" celebrates the voyage of Columbus to the New World with a parade followed by an Italian festival in Berra Park. The parade begins at Southwest and Kingshighway and winds through the neighborhood, ending at Berra Park at Shaw and Macklind Avenues, where the festival features Italian food and entertainment. Free.

CIVIL WAR LIVING HISTORY WEEKEND AT GRANT'S FARM
10501 Gravois Road
(314) 843-1700
www.grantsfarm.com
This biannual event takes guests back in time, as the 8th Regiment Missouri Infantry performs living-history demonstrations throughout a weekend in mid-October. In addition to setting up camp in the meadow adjacent to Hardscrabble, the former home of Ulysses S. Grant and his family, the re-enactors demonstrate what life was like during the Civil War. Grant's Cabin, nicknamed "Hardscrabble," is open for tours, and an interpreter from the U. S. Grant National Historic Site is on-hand to answer questions. Admission is free, but there is a $10 per car parking fee.

DEUTSCH COUNTRY DAYS – A LIVING HISTORY WEEKEND LUXENHAUS FARM
5437 Highway O, Marthasville
(636) 433-5669
www.deutschcountrydays.org
At this unique and authentic re-creation of early German life in Missouri, held in mid October, costumed artisans present natural dyeing, sad ironing, kloppolei, wood turning, hide tanning, candle dipping, rug braiding, and more. Period music, an antique sorghum press driven by Missouri mules, and a steam powered sawmill add to the festivities. The cost is $5.50 to $15.

GRANT'S FARM HALLOWEEN
Grant's Farm
10501 Gravois Road
(314) 843-1700
www.grantsfarm.com
Grant's Farm Halloween includes activities such as taking a moonlight tram ride through the deer park (bring a flashlight), and participants are encouraged to wear a costume for the costume parade. Visitors can enjoy A variety of shows and activities, including the Mad Science Show—a spectacular science-themed show that will amaze and entertain the small fry, a Creature Feature Show, non-scary classic Halloween characters, and a DJ spinning tunes in the historic courtyard. $20 parking fee per car.

THE HISTORIC HAUNTING AT THORNHILL
Faust Park Historic Village
Olive Boulevard and Nooning Tree Drive, Chesterfield
(636) 532-7298
www.stlouisco.com/parks/faust_home.html
The estate of Frederick Bates provides the setting for this candlelit event. Enjoy storytelling and live animal shows, take a tour of the Bates mansion and family cemetery, and learn all about memorial and burial practices of the early 1800s during this two-day event in late October. Watch a blacksmith and wheat weaver as they demonstrate

and explain the superstitions surrounding their crafts. Children can participate in harvest-time activities and make an old-world jack-o'-lantern. Reservations recommended. The cost is $8.

HALLOWEEN IN THE CENTRAL WEST END
Euclid, McPherson, and Maryland Avenues
(314) 367-2220
www.thecwe.com
The daytime celebration is family-friendly and includes a canine costume parade followed by a kids-only costume parade. After dark the event changes into an adults-only party, with costumed grown-ups getting a chance to strut their stuff during a parade at 9:00 p.m. The assorted bars and restaurants throughout the CWE neighborhood all get into the Halloween spirit as well. Free.

NOVEMBER

ST. LOUIS INTERNATIONAL FILM FESTIVAL (SLIFF)
Tivoli Theatre, Webster University, and Other locations
(314) 367-3378
www.cinemastlouis.org
This annual film festival, held in mid-November, offers 11 days worth of almost non-stop screenings. The festival has grown each year and now showcases works from more than 75 filmmakers, including 260-plus documentaries, shorts and feature films in 136 programs. SLIFF is an open invitational to features, documentaries, and short subjects from all over the world, with special emphasis on American independents, world cinema, and prize-winning short-subjects. SLIFF has received an official designation from the Academy of Motion Picture Arts and Sciences as a sanctioned short-subject qualification event. In addition to the films included in the, New Filmmakers Forum, the festival surveys nearly a dozen additional examples of contemporary American independent cinema. Individual tickets are around $10 each, with discount Festival Punch-Passes available.

MID-AMERICA HOLIDAY PARADE
Downtown
www.christmasinstlouis.org
Held on Thanksgiving morning each year, the Midwest's best holiday parade features marching bands, giant inflated balloon characters the Budweiser Clydesdales, cheerleaders, and lots of colorful floats, carriages, antique cars, dance teams, and even the Cardinals' beloved mascot, Fredbird. Oh—and some guy named Santa Claus. The parade starts around 8:30 a.m. at Broadway and Spruce streets, marches to Market Street, turns west on Market for about 16 blocks, and ends at 20th Street. The entire parade lasts approximately two hours. Free.

ANHEUSER-BUSCH BREWERY CHRISTMAS LIGHTS DISPLAY
Pestalozzi and Broadway
(314) 577-2000
From late November to early January, this display features more than 800,000 red and white lights that adorn almost every tree and building within the historic Anheuser-Busch brewery compound. Visitors can drive along the brewery's main street, which includes the festively lighted Brew House, Clydesdales Stables, the Bevo packaging plant, and other historic buildings. Free.

HOLIDAY FLOWER SHOW
Missouri Botanical Garden
4344 Shaw Boulevard
(314) 577-9400, (800) 642-8842
www.mobot.org
The Missouri Botanical Garden's holiday flower show, held from late November to early January, includes dozens of life-size topiary animals at play in a formal patterned indoor garden. Surrounding a 16-foot moss Christmas tree are hundreds of colorful seasonal plants and flowers, including poinsettias, begonias, gloxinias, anthurium, peperomia, and rosemary. The holiday wreath exhibit is a popular event that features creations by many of the area's top floral designers. The cost is $3 to $10.

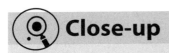 **Close-up**

Annual Events Celebrating Lewis and Clark

In 2004 the St. Louis region celebrated the bicentennial of the Lewis & Clark expedition, and history buffs were treated to a number of exhibits and activities related to the famed explorers' journey. While many of the activities were "one-timers" that were planned specifically for the 200th anniversary, there are still a number of historic sites and annual events that offer insight into the expedition led by Meriwether Lewis and William Clark and the Corps of Discovery.

FEBRUARY

Fête du Bon Vieux Temps
Cahokia Courthouse First and Elm Streets, Cahokia, IL
(618) 332-1782 www.enjoyillinois.com
This colonial Mardi Gras celebration features Lewis & Clark–related tours, activities, and demonstrations at Cahokia historic sites. The fête offers music and dancing reminiscent of the celebrations held by the area's French settlers more than 200 years ago. Lewis and Clark relied on Cahokia as their host community during the winter of 1803–04, and Cahokia residents frequently interacted with expedition members, likely inviting them to participate in Mardi Gras festivities.

MARCH

Louisiana Territory Land Transfer Commemoration
400 South Main Street, St. Charles
(800) 366-2427 www.historicstcharles.com
This annual ceremony includes a reenactment of the announcement of the Louisiana Territory land transfer from France and Spain to the United States.

MAY

Annual Lewis & Clark Departure Day
Lewis and Clark State Historic Site 1 Lewis and Clark Trail, Hartford, IL
(800) 224-2970 www.lewisandclarkillinois.org
The highlight of the Departure Ceremony is a re-creation of the departing Corps' keelboat and pirogues from the confluence of the Missouri and Mississippi Rivers. There are also plenty of frontier crafts, skills demonstrations, and colonial-cuisine cooking lessons.

Lewis and Clark Heritage Days
Frontier Park, St. Charles
(636) 947-3199 www.historicstcharles.com

This annual event commemorates the arrival in St. Charles of Lewis and Clark and the Corps of Discovery. For more information, see the full write-up on page 154.

DECEMBER

Annual Event of the Arrival at Camp River
Dubois 1 Lewis and Clark Trail, Hartford, IL
(618) 251-5811 www.lewisandclarkillinois.org
The celebration of the arrival of the Lewis & Clark expedition features reenactors arriving at the mouth of the River Dubois to establish their 1803–4 winter encampment, as well as demonstrations of period skills, crafts, and military operations.

VICTORIAN CHRISTMAS
Old Courthouse
11 North Fourth Street
(314) 655-1600
www.nps.gov/jeff

This month-long event, which celebrates the holiday season as it was in the Victorian era, kicks off at the end of November with the lighting of a 25-foot Christmas tree with musical accompaniment by the Compton Heights Concert Band. The celebration continues daily with noontime concerts in the Old Courthouse Rotunda throughout December, museum galleries depicting holiday celebrations at different times in St. Louis's history, and daily holiday tours and education programs. Free.

WAY OF LIGHTS CHRISTMAS DISPLAY
National Shrine of Our Lady of the Snows
442 DeMazenod Drive, Belleville, IL
(618) 397-6700
www.snows.org

From 5:00 to 10 p.m. each night from late November to early January, the shrine is aglow with more than one million white lights along a mile-and-a-half stretch that winds through the grounds. Visitors can drive through a collection of electro-art sculptures and life-size figures depicting the Christmas story, then stop off at the visitor center for a look at the Christmas tree display. The Christmas Village features plenty of things to see and do, including storytelling, coloring, and face painting, along with activities at the Children's Theatre, caroling, and a live animal display. Free admission, but donations are appreciated.

WILD LIGHTS
The St. Louis Children's Zoo in Forest Park
(314) 781-0900
www.stlzoo.org

From late November through December, you can stroll through the St. Louis Zoo's enchanting holiday wonderland and enjoy thousands of colorful lights, animated displays, seasonal music, and storytelling, and you can meet Blitzen and Miracle, two live reindeer who live at the zoo year-round. The "Winter Wizard" uses audience members to help tell his stories, and the Kids' Corner offers hands-on craft-making activities for the younger set. The zoo's Lakeside Cafe remains open throughout the event for dinner, snacks, and hot cups of cocoa and coffee. The cost is $4.

DECEMBER

CHANUKAH: FESTIVAL OF LIGHTS CELEBRATION
Missouri Botanical Garden
4344 Shaw Boulevard
(314) 577-9400, (800) 642-8842
www.mobot.org

Chanukah is a traditional Jewish holiday celebration that includes festive music and a menorah-lighting ceremony. The daylong event includes stories of Chanukah told by puppets, storytellers, and musicians. An Israeli shuk (market) with an array of Chanukah merchandise, Chanukah cookie decorating, and children's craft workshops round out the festivities. The cost is $3 to $8.

CHRISTMAS IN HERMANN
207 Schiller Street, Hermann
(800) 932-8687
www.hermannmo.com

At Kristkindl Markt, reminiscent of Christmas markets in Germany, booths brim with all manner of treasures, from delicate glass ornaments to local wines and sausages. Old-fashioned carolers serenade shoppers, and when it's time for a break, the schnellimbuss (food stand) serves up steaming bowls of soup, homemade cookies, and mugs of mulled cider. The market features items such as weavings, jewelry, Polish pottery, handmade soaps, homemade sausages, baskets, European glass ornaments, German Christmas items, and more. Free.

Also enjoy the Candlelight House Tours in the Hermann historic district, which afford visitors a rare glimpse inside some of Hermann's most beautiful historic homes, all decked out for the holidays. The cost is $10. Lastly, you can also celebrate the season in Hermann at

Weihnachtsfest, at the Deutschheim State Historic Site (109 West Second Street; 573-486-2200; www .mostateparks.com/deutschheim.htm). This Christmas open house, held annually in early December in conjunction with the Kristkindl Markt, features craft demonstrations, 19th-century Christmas trees, and toy collections from yesteryear. German cookies are served, and admission is free.

LAFAYETTE SQUARE HOLIDAY PARLOUR TOUR AND TASTE OF LAFAYETTE SQUARE
Lafayette Square neighborhood
(314) 772-5724
www.lafayettesquare.org
During this one-day event in mid-December, visitors can take a self-guided walking tour of 12 homes and experience the elegance and gentility of St. Louis in the late 1800s with a glimpse of the Victorian "painted ladies" all decked out in their holiday finery. Lafayette Square has become one of the "hot spots" in town, thanks to a bumper crop of new restaurants and bars and revitalized loft and apartment living spaces. Activities during the holiday house tour include a Victorian teahouse, historic carriage rides, carolers, live music, and an art and antiques fair. The cost is usually $12 to $15.

KWANZAA: FESTIVAL OF THE FIRST FRUITS
Missouri Botanical Garden
4344 Shaw Boulevard
(314) 577-9400, (800) 642-8842
www.mobot.org
Kwanzaa, named for the Swahili term that means "first fruits," celebrates the richness of African-American culture and is centered around the feast table of the harvest. A Kwanzaa ceremony highlights a day of storytelling, craft and jewelry workshops, and authentic African drumming and musical performances. The festival is held in late December. The cost is $3–$8.

FIRST NIGHT ST. LOUIS
Grand Center Arts and Entertainment District
(314) 289-8121
www.firstnightstl.org
Celebrate the New Year at First Night St. Louis, a visual- and performing-arts festival held in the Grand Center Arts and Entertainment District on New Year's Eve. Events take place on the main stage at the intersection adjacent to the Fox Theatre, inside Grand Center's concert halls, theaters, buildings, and churches, as well as outside at its streets and parks. The alcohol-free evening kicks off at 6:00 p.m. with an opening ceremony that lights the streetscapes and buildings, creating "lighted works of art," and ends with a grand fireworks display at midnight. Featured entertainment includes musicians, storytellers, dancers, actors, puppeteers, and visual and media artists. Indoor events take place in the College Church, Continental Life Building, Woolworth Building, Sheldon Concert Hall, the Dance Tent, Third Baptist Church, and the Grandel Theater. The cost is around $10.

THE ARTS

It's no surprise that a city responsible for launching so many talented actors, musicians, and writers over the years would have a lively, contemporary music, dance, and theater scene. In addition to a long list of musical artists, playwright Tennessee Williams spent his formative years in St. Louis, as well as poets T. S. Eliot and Maya Angelou. Actors from Hollywood's golden age, such as Betty Grable, Vincent Price, Virginia Mayo, and Buddy Ebsen, as well as current favorites such as John Goodman and Kevin Kline, all have called St. Louis home. (These artists, and many others from the worlds of sports, music, science, education, and technology, are honored with brass stars and plaques on the St. Louis Walk of Fame. See the Attractions chapter for more information.) With all this history and glitter, it's easy to see why St. Louis is such a culture-rich city.

One focal point of the St. Louis arts scene is the Grand Center Arts and Entertainment District, located just minutes west of downtown, which is home to a variety of the city's most popular arts organizations, including the renowned Saint Louis Symphony Orchestra (SLSO). SLSO plays within the friendly confines of Powell Symphony Hall. Other Grand Center neighbors include the tremendously entertaining St. Louis Black Repertory Company, which stages performances at the Grandel Theatre, and the acoustically perfect Sheldon Concert Hall, home to various jazz, folk, and chamber music performances throughout the year.

Live-theater options continue to expand in St. Louis, and one of the newest events has quickly become an annual tradition. The St. Louis Shakespeare Festival debuted in June 2001, and it continues to present free, professional-caliber Shakespearean theater, and does it among the lush greenery of Forest Park. There are a multitude of small, independent theater groups ranging from "small-town" municipalities' productions of Oklahoma! to the more avant-garde groups who tackle serious social issues and offer a more controversial night at the theater. There's also the annual St. Louis International Film Festival, which presents an aggressive series of films and related events during its 10-day run.

Other live-theater options include the Repertory Theatre of St. Louis and Opera Theatre of St. Louis, both at suburban Webster University. Opera Theatre, which makes a special effort to attract younger audiences, prefers a fresh and "American" style, with the performances done in English and featuring outstanding young artists alongside members of the Saint Louis Symphony Orchestra.

In addition to Webster University, St. Louis's numerous colleges and universities contribute to the local arts scene as well. Washington University and Saint Louis University both offer excellent galleries and exhibits, along with a growing number of neighborhood galleries in places like Washington Avenue, Maplewood, Clayton, and the Central West End.

Local arts groups include the Regional Arts Commission (RAC) and their cadre of "Arts Commandos," the Missouri Arts Commission, and the St. Louis Arts & Education Council.

Even with all of this, St. Louis's local arts scene continues to expand, with the opening of the Contemporary Art Museum St. Louis and the building designed by architect Tadao Ando that houses the Pulitzer Foundation for the Arts.

In addition to free general admission, most Forest Park attractions also offer free times for admission to their special exhibits and programs. Check with individual attractions for specific dates and times.

ARTS ORGANIZATIONS, DANCE, GALLERIES, MUSEUMS, MUSIC, AND THEATER.

Arts Organizations

ART ST. LOUIS
917 Locust Street, third floor
(314) 241-4810
www.artstlouis.org
Art St. Louis is a not-for-profit visual arts co-op gallery, organization, and advocate that exhibits work by established and emerging artists from the St. Louis region. It produces a quarterly art magazine, presents exhibits year-round in the gallery and at off-site locations, and has a slide registry and art leasing and purchasing programs. The gallery is free and open to the public. Expanding beyond gallery walls, Art St. Louis curates year-round, bimonthly exhibits of works by Art St. Louis member artists at a variety of off-site locations, including Arts in Transit/Bi-State Development Agency, Fleishman-Hillard, Louderman Lofts, St. Louis Development Corporation, St. Louis Regional Commerce and Growth Association, and the World Trade Center–St. Louis.

CENTER OF CREATIVE ARTS
524 Trinity Avenue
(314) 725-6555
www.cocastl.org
The mission of the Center of Creative Arts (COCA) is to provide an integrated forum to foster the appreciation of the arts in the greater St. Louis community by producing and presenting performances, exhibitions, and educational programs. COCA is a Missouri not-for-profit corporation founded in 1986 and housed in the former B'nai Amoona Synagogue, which is listed on the National Register of Historic Places. COCA is respected region-

ally and nationally for its vibrant, high-quality arts programs, and its education department is designed to address a need in the community for visual- and performing-arts activities for children and their families. More than 6,000 people enroll in the educational programming annually, making it the largest arts-education institution in the bi-state area. The programs are taught by professional artists/instructors. The Family Theatre Series presents innovative, family-oriented entertainment by nationally and internationally known performing artists, and past performances have run the gamut from the juggling and wisecracking Flaming Idiots to the crazy costumes and dance moves of the Frogz dance troupe.

GRAND CENTER
634 North Grand Boulevard, Suite 10-A
(314) 533-1884
www.grandcenter.org
Grand Center is home to more than two dozen arts groups and offers the broadest range of exceptional arts and entertainment in the St. Louis region. Dance St. Louis, the Black Repertory Company, Portfolio Art Gallery, and the Pulitzer Foundation for the Arts are just a few of the numerous artistic outlets that call Grand Center home.

THE PULITZER FOUNDATION FOR THE ARTS
3716 Washington Boulevard
(314) 754-1850
www.pulitzerarts.org
The Pulitzer Foundation for the Arts seeks to foster a deeper understanding and appreciation of the relationship between contemporary art and architecture. Through its works of art, library, and collaborative programs with other cultural and educational institutions, the foundation serves artists, architects, scholars, students, and members of the general public. The building, designed by Pritzker Prize–winning architect Tadao Ando, provides a tranquil place for contemplation, enjoyment, and study. Works by George Braque, Alberto Giacometti, Juan Gris, Henri Matisse, Pablo Picasso, Mark Rothko, and Richard Serra are among those on permanent display.

ST. LOUIS ARTISTS' GUILD
Two Oak Knoll Park, Clayton
(314) 727-9599
www.stlouisartistsguild.org

St. Louis's oldest and largest visual arts center, the St. Louis Artists' Guild is housed in a restored 1920s mansion located in Oak Knoll Park in Clayton. Since 1886 the guild has been the regional center for artists and art lovers, and its mission remains "to encourage excellence and appreciation in the visual arts" by providing programs, classes, and exhibitions. The guild also holds national, regional, and local competitions; hosts national exhibitions; and participates in collaborative and exchange exhibitions with other art organizations. Closed Monday.

ST. LOUIS REGIONAL ARTS COMMISSION
6128 Delmar Boulevard
(314) 863-5811
www.art-stl.com

The St. Louis Regional Arts Commission (RAC) promotes, encourages, and fosters arts and cultural institutions throughout the St. Louis region by creating an environment that nurtures local artists. In addition to serving as a clearinghouse for local arts organizations and volunteers, RAC funds numerous popular music festivals and events throughout the region, including Taste St. Louis and performances with the Saint Louis Symphony Orchestra. (See the Annual Events chapter for more information.)

SOUTH CITY OPEN STUDIO AND GALLERY (SCOSAG)
Tower Grove Park
4255 Arsenal Street
(314) 865-0060
www.scosag.org

Located in a renovated gatehouse in Tower Grove Park, the studio welcomes drop-in visitors as well as students in the ongoing classes offered in drawing, painting, clay, bookbinding, and more. Kids are encouraged to explore art at their own pace and can choose from a variety of hands-on art activities. Young artists ages 5

to 17 can explore everything from drawing and painting to ceramics and bookmaking. Call for reservations and class schedules.

Dance
DANCE ST. LOUIS
634 North Grand Boulevard, Suite 1102
(314) 534-6622
www.dancestlouis.org

Dance St. Louis stages performances at the Fox Theatre, Blanche Touhill Performing Arts Center, and the Edison Theatre on the campus of Washington University. The organization brings some of the greatest dancers and dance companies in the world to St. Louis audiences each year.

Galleries
ATRIUM GALLERY
4728 McPherson Avenue
(314) 367-1076
www.atriumgallery.net

The Atrium Gallery serves the St. Louis–area private sector and corporate markets with quality contemporary works by regional, national, and international artists. The facility specializes in large-scale original works such as paintings, sculpture, drawings, and photography and includes works from artists such as Bruce Beasley, Robert Forbes, Ellen Glasgow, Carl Goldhagen, Kirk Pedersen, Doug Salveson, Jane Schneider, Janet Sorokin, and William Yonker. Educational programs include the Art Buffet, a luncheon lecture series, and the Sunday Salon, where artists' talks take place during the opening weekends of each exhibit. Closed Tuesday.

BARUCCI GALLERY
8101 Maryland Avenue, Clayton
(314) 727-2020
www.baruccigallery.com

The Barucci Gallery offers contemporary works by regional and national artists that specialize in sculpture, painting, and art glass. A four-time recipient of the Top 100 Retailer of Craft award from *Niche* magazine, the lively space features a variety of serigraphs, ceramics, watercolors, acrylics, jewelry, and hand-blown glass art pieces. There's also an on-site frame shop. Closed Sunday.

BELAS ARTES MULTICULTURAL CENTER & ART GALLERY
1854 Russell Boulevard
(314) 772-ARTS
www.belas-artes.net
Belas Artes is a combination gallery and multicultural center in one charming space. The gallery features a variety of works by international artists and celebrates myriad ethnicities and cultures. There are four "themed" rooms—African-Latino, Middle Eastern, European–North American, and ZenAsian—and the center hosts a number of activities and special events, including art fairs, music and dance classes, and themed evenings that feature ethnic foods combined with music, movies, and art exhibitions.

COMPONERE GALLERY OF ART AND FASHION
6509 Delmar Boulevard
(314) 721-1181
www.componere.com
In French, componere means to gather together, as in small mosaics of an artistic whole. This gallery features artwork with a contemporary urban look along with a sense of humor and has special monthly exhibits of regional works. One hundred fifty regional artists are represented with original works and limited-edition Iris prints. St. Louis city and rural scenes are represented in watercolor, oil, photography, collographs, and monotypes. Componere is locally known for its large inventory of affordable jewelry, creative blown glass, lovely functional and raku ceramics, as well as clay sculptures and carved wood.

CRAFT ALLIANCE
6640 Delmar Boulevard
(314) 725-1177, ext. 22
www.craftalliance.org
Established in 1964, Craft Alliance is a nonprofit visual-arts center dedicated to excellence in arts education and reaching a diverse public through instruction and exhibition of fine art in the craft media. The gallery features functional and sculptural contemporary art in clay, metal, wood, fiber, and glass by regional and national artists. A second location is now open at 501 North Grand Boulevard (314) 534-7528 in the Grand Center Arts & Entertainment District. Both locations are closed on Monday.

JCC ART GALLERY
2 Millstone Campus Drive
(314) 432-5700, ext. 3194
www.jccstl.org
The JCC Art Gallery features ongoing exhibitions, as well as work for sale such as Judaic graphics by Mordechai Rosenstein, ceramics by Herb Gralnick, glass objects, small sculpture, photography, and hand-painted silk scarves and ties.

KODNER GALLERY
7501 Forsyth Boulevard, Clayton
(314) 863-9366
www.kodnergallery.com
This gallery features fine 18th-, 19th-, and 20th-century paintings, watercolors, drawings, and sculpture by European and American masters, Impressionists, regionalists, and artists of the Old West, including artists such as Thomas H. Benton, Antoine Blanchard, Bernard Buffet, Edouard Cortes, Frederick C. Frieseke, Joan Miró, Pablo Picasso, Frederic Remington, and many more. Closed Sunday.

MAD ART GALLERY
2727 South 12th Street
(314) 771-8230
www.madart.com
Housed in a 1930s deco-style neighborhood police station, this Soulard gallery hosts a number of contemporary and unique art exhibits. In addition to supporting local up and-coming artists, Mad Art is the site of various and sundry fun and funky special events, including the annual Art Prom, independent film screenings, performance art, and just about anything else you can imagine.

During the ever-popular Soulard Mardi Gras festivities, Mad Art hosts a wine tasting and gallery show that usually includes live music and prime people-watching opportunities.

MARIANIST GALLERIES
1256 Maryhurst Drive, Kirkwood
(314) 965-0877
www.melsmart.com

This gallery, located right next to Vianney High School in Kirkwood, features studio and exhibition space for three artists. Works displayed here include acrylics on canvas; handmade paper; painted metal; stone, brass, and copper sculpture; fresco; stained glass; watercolors; paper cutouts; and ceramics. Closed Sunday.

PHILIP SLEIN GALLERY
1319 Washington Avenue
(314) 621-4634
www.philipsleingallery.com

Located in the burgeoning downtown Loft District, the Philip Slein Gallery is a cozy space but features an impressive array of contemporary artists from across the country. The month-long exhibitions feature artists such as Gary Panter, Brandon Anschultz, Phyllis Galembo, Michael Noland, and Art Chantry. Open Tuesday through Saturday.

R. DUANE REED GALLERY
7513 Forsyth Boulevard, Clayton
(314) 862-2333
www.rduanereedgallery.com

This Clayton gallery features an extensive selection of nationally recognized artists specializing in contemporary paintings, works on paper, sculpture, ceramics, glass, and fiber. The facility is known as the exclusive St. Louis location for artists such as Ken Anderson, Jane Barrow, Aaron Karp, Nancy Rice, and Philip Slein, as well as contemporary glass by Dale Chihuly, Pohlman-Knowles, Marvin Lipofsky, and others. Reed also features ceramics by Rudy Autio, Bennett Bean, Chris Federighi, and Patricia Degener, along with fiber artists such as John Garrett, Mary Giles, and John Sauer. Closed Sunday and Monday.

THE SHELDON ART GALLERIES
3648 Washington Boulevard
(314) 533-9900
www.sheldonconcerthall.org

The Sheldon Art Galleries is a nonprofit facility that houses five galleries permanently devoted to photography, architectural history, art collections about the history of jazz, and children's art. Each gallery sticks with its overall theme, and past exhibits have included everything from Linda McCartney's rock-star photos to the history of the automobile's role in suburbia. The Bellwether Gallery features St. Louis artists, and the History of Jazz Galleries always spotlights jazz musicians or events. The Gallery of Photography often showcases antique advertisements and newspaper photos that depict the area's history, while the Bernoudy Gallery of Architecture and the Gallery of Children's Art feature obvious objects for their themes.

i Prefer a little culture served up with your trim? Then head over to The Loop's D-Zine Hair & Art Studio (6679 Delmar Boulevard; 314–727–0708), a combination art gallery and beauty salon. The high-end, full-service salon features exhibitions by local artists and is open daily. Walk-ins are welcome.

STEIN GALLERY
21 North Meramec Avenue, Clayton
(314) 726-6616
www.steingallery.com

The Stein Gallery specializes in 19th- and 20th-century art, featuring works in all media. The extensive collection of prints, drawings, paintings, sculpture, and photography includes the work of internationally known artists such as Balthus, Henri Matisse, Marc Chagall, Pablo Picasso, Georges Rouault, Pierre Auguste Renoir, and Henri Toulouse-Lautrec. Stein's contemporary works include pieces by names such as Jim Dine, Helen Frankenthaler, Roy Lichtenstein, Richard Serra, Ernest Trova, and Andy Warhol, and fine-art photography by Annie Leibovitz, Arnold

Newman, and William Eggleston is also featured. Closed Sunday.

WHITE FLAG PROJECTS
4568 Manchester Road
(314) 531-3442
www.whiteflagprojects.org
This alternative, nonprofit gallery—voted best gallery in the 2008 Riverfront Times poll, presents exhibitions by contemporary visual artists from St. Louis and around the world. In addition, the 2,000-square-foot gallery hosts special events that include interactive and performance art and "exhibitions-as-parties" like the New Year's Eve show. Located in the up-and-coming neighborhood known as The Grove, White Flag Projects offers six regular exhibitions and four short-term projects each year. Call for hours.

Museums

CONTEMPORARY ART MUSEUM ST. LOUIS
3750 Washington Boulevard
(314) 535-4660
www.contemporarystl.org
The Contemporary Art Museum St. Louis is a leading institution for contemporary art in an innovative environment. "The Contemporary" is a non-collecting museum that presents art and ideas through changing exhibitions, community partnerships, educational programs, lectures, and discussions. There is an on-site cafe (Tempt) and museum store (Muse) as well. Closed on Monday, but Thursday is free for all ages. The museum is located in Grand Center just east of Grand Avenue and the Fox Theatre.

HISTORIC SAMUEL CUPPLES HOUSE
Saint Louis University Mall
(314) 977-3575; (314) 977-3570 (recording)
www.slu.edu/the_arts/cupples
The Cupples House is an opulent Richardsonian Romanesque 42-room mansion on the National Register of Historic Places that features fine and decorative arts and a 1,000-piece antique glass collection. Located on the campus of Saint Louis University next to the Pius XII Library, the venue

features revolving exhibitions and highlights from the university's permanent collection. Closed Sunday and Monday.

LAUMEIER SCULPTURE PARK
12580 Rott Road (at Geyer Road)
(314) 821-1209
www.laumeier.org
Laumeier Sculpture Park is a 98-acre park designed to enrich people's lives and encourage creative thinking through the presentation of interpretive exhibitions, educational programs, contemporary art, and art experiences in a park setting. The outdoor collection of more than 80 sculptures is available to the public year-round, and many works represent current or unique approaches to art in a natural environment. The goal of Laumeier is to expand public awareness of sculpture and highlight the achievements of 20th- and 21st-century artists. Check out the free iPod tour for an informative stroll through the beautiful facility. Closed Monday.

MILDRED LANE KEMPER ART MUSEUM– WASHINGTON UNIVERSITY
Forsyth and Skinker Boulevards
(314) 935-4523
www.kemperartmuseum.wustl.edu
Founded in 1881, this is the oldest art museum west of the Mississippi River and is considered one of the finest university museums in the country. Now well into its second century, the Mildred Lane Kemper Art Museum continues to realize the university's role of cultural leader by acquiring and exhibiting contemporary and historical art for both academic and public education. In the mid 1980s the museum embarked on an acquisition program to fill important historical gaps, such as Thomas Cole's *Aqueducts Near Rome* (1832), contemporary art since the 1970s, and pieces from such artists as Shusaku Arakawa, John Baldessari, Josef Beuys, Jenny Holzer, Barbara Kruger, Annette Lemieux, and Tim Rollins. The permanent collection also includes works by Pablo Picasso, George Caleb Bingham, and other major 19th- through 21st-century artists. Closed Tuesday and university holidays.

MUSEUM OF CONTEMPORARY RELIGIOUS ART (MOCRA)

3700 West Pine Pedestrian Mall
(314) 977-7170
http://mocra.slu.edu

Located on the campus of Saint Louis University, MOCRA is the world's first interfaith museum dedicated to the ongoing dialogue between contemporary artists and the various faith traditions. Its unique space and blend of group and solo exhibitions, along with a strong permanent collection, have garnered MOCRA significant national attention. Admission is free, but a donation is suggested. Closed Monday.

SAINT LOUIS ART MUSEUM (SLAM)

Forest Park
1 Fine Arts Drive
(314) 721-0072
www.slam.org

SLAM is one of the leading comprehensive art museums in the country, and its permanent collection ranges from ancient to contemporary, including works by a number of world-renowned artists. The American art collection includes scenes from the Western frontier by George Caleb Bingham and Charles Wimar, paintings by American Impressionists such as John Henry Twachtman and Frederick Carl Frieseke, works by Abstract Expressionists such as Mark Rothko, and the pop imagery of Roy Lichtenstein and Andy Warhol. The ancient art collection includes Assyrian, Coptic, Egyptian, Greek, Iranian, Islamic, Near Eastern, Persian, Roman, and Syrian works, as well as the mummy Amen-Nestawy-Nakht. The facility has works from virtually every culture and time period, with a highly-regarded collection of Oceanic and pre-Columbian art, as well as ancient Chinese bronzes, European and American art of the late 19th and 20th centuries, with a particular strength in 20th-century German paintings. SLAM offers numerous special exhibitions as well as a research library, special events, and educational programming.

SAINT LOUIS UNIVERSITY MUSEUM OF ART (SLUMA)

3663 Lindell Boulevard
(314) 977-3399
http://sluma.slu.edu

SLUMA is housed in a four-story, historic French Revival mansion on the Saint Louis University campus. The museum exhibits items relevant to the Jesuit philosophy and ideals by local, national, and internationally acclaimed artists, including Joachim Probst, Miguel Martinez, Thomas Huck, Edward Boccia, and Renato Laffranchi, as well as the work of Saint Louis University artists. Additional displays include the Marion Cartier Collection and the John and Ann MacLennan Gallery of Asian Art. A museum shop, tours, and volunteer opportunities are available. Open Wednesday through Sunday, except for national holidays. Free admission.

Music

COMMUNITY MUSIC SCHOOL OF WEBSTER UNIVERSITY

470 East Lockwood, Webster Groves
(314) 968-5939
www.webster.edu/cms/

The Community Music School of Webster University is a private school for the arts that offers educational programs and performance opportunities in music. Classes are available for all ages and skill levels, and the instructors are professional teachers who also happen to be performing musicians. Individual and group classes are offered at the school, which is accredited by the National Association of Schools of Music and a certified member of the National Guild of Community Schools for the Arts.

OPERA THEATRE OF ST. LOUIS

Loretto-Hilton Center at Webster University
Big Bend and Edgar Roads, Webster Groves
(314) 961-0644 (box office),
(314) 961-0171 (office)
www.experienceopera.org

Not every Midwestern city can claim to have

one of the country's most acclaimed opera companies. To see why opera has made such an impact in the St. Louis area, plan a visit in May or June, when there are rotating productions of classic and contemporary opera sung in English. The Repertory Theatre of St. Louis, which also performs at the Loretto-Hilton Center, offers a thrilling live theater experience with a season of cutting-edge drama, contemporary comedy, and classics on the main stage and in the studio theater. The season runs from September through April each year.

SAINT LOUIS SYMPHONY ORCHESTRA
718 North Grand Boulevard
(314) 533-2500 (general info), (314) 534-1700 (box office)
www.slso.org

The Saint Louis Symphony Orchestra is a world-renowned ensemble that performs a broad musical repertoire and offers a number of live performances geared to younger audiences. There are Kinder Konzerts, performances that incorporate instruction and music for kids in kindergarten to grade three; Young People's Concerts, which are targeted at children in grades four through six; and a Young Adults Concert Series, a program for older students that is part of the symphony's community partnership program. Featuring performances by world-renowned musicians such as Yo-Yo Ma, Itzhak Perlman, and Wynton Marsalis, the critically acclaimed orchestra has received six Grammy Awards and more than 50 Grammy nominations.

Theater

BLANCHE M. TOUHILL PERFORMING ARTS CENTER
University of Missouri–St. Louis
One University Boulevard
(314) 516-4949
www.touhill.org

Located on the campus of the University of Missouri–St. Louis (USMSL), "The Touhill" hosts an amazing variety of performances, ranging

from lecture series and operas to comics and contemporary concerts. There are two separate theaters housed within the facility, the 300-seat Desmond and Mary Lee Theater and the 1,600-seat Anheuser-Busch Hall. Both spaces have an intimate feel and state-of-the-art audiovisual components. Past performances include comic Bob Newhart, Kathy Griffin, Marilyn McCoo & Billy Davis Jr., the Explosions: Percussion Festival, and the Great Russian Nutcracker.

EDISON THEATRE WASHINGTON UNIVERSITY
6445 Forsyth Boulevard
(314) 935-5000
www.edisontheatre.wustl.edu

The highest quality national and international artists in music, dance, and theater perform innovative new works or contemporary interpretations of classical works at the Edison Theatre throughout the year. The annual OVATIONS series brings such diverse performances as West African dance, Shakespearean plays, "Sweet Honey in the Rock," Luna Negra Dance Theater, and Trey McIntyre Project.

THE FOX THEATRE
527 North Grand Boulevard
(314) 534-1678
www.fabulousfox.com

The Fox originally opened as a vaudeville palace in 1929 and later became a monument to the movies, hosting film premieres and other live entertainment for more than seven decades. Today the Fox presents Broadway shows, family shows, and concerts and is as popular for its daytime tours of the facility as it is for its shows.

MUNICIPAL OPERA ASSOCIATION (THE MUNY)
Forest Park
(314) 361-1900
www.muny.com

One of the oldest and largest outdoor theaters in the country, the Muny, located in Forest Park, hosts a number of popular musicals each summer. There are also year-round performances by the Muny Kids and Teens performing troupes, both of which serve as community outreach programs of the Muny Opera. The season runs from mid-June through mid-August nightly.

REPERTORY THEATRE OF ST. LOUIS
Loretto-Hilton Center at Webster University
Big Bend and Edgar Roads, Webster Groves
(314) 968-4925
www.repstl.org

Each season the Rep offers a wide variety of plays on two stages. Both the Mainstage Productions and Studio Theater shows feature some of the best local actors and occasional guest stars. Productions range from beloved favorites such as *My Fair Lady* and *Twelfth Night* to Edward Albee's *The Goat, or Who Is Sylvia?* Both companies-within-a-company provide lively—and sometimes controversial—theatrical experiences. There are nightly shows Tuesday through Sunday.

> **i** There are a limited number of free "lawn seats" available for every performance at the Muny. Grab a blanket and get there early to make sure you get a spot.

ST. LOUIS BLACK REPERTORY COMPANY
Grandel Theatre in Grand Center
3610 Grandel Square
(314) 534-3810
www.theblackrep.org

The Black Rep offers contemporary works by African-American playwrights and musical presentations throughout its season, which runs from January through June. Each season features a central theme, but every performance is a truly unique night at the theater. From lively musicals to thought-provoking satire, the Black Rep offers one of the best theatrical experiences in the region. It was voted Best Theater Company in the 2008 *Riverfront Times* readers' poll. Show times vary with each production, so call for more information.

DAY TRIPS AND WEEKEND GETAWAYS

As if there wasn't already enough to do in St. Louis! But, if you've got a bit of a road warrior in you, your need to hit the open road is understandable. Luckily, St. Louis is situated in the middle of some pretty interesting country, so you're only a couple of hours from a diverse collection of entertaining things to see and do. From exploring rock formations and the prehistoric past to wandering through the heart of America's history, there's something around here for just about everyone. History buffs can trace the path of explorers Lewis and Clark from St. Charles, Missouri, or walk in the footsteps of honest Abe Lincoln in Springfield, Illinois. Wine aficionados can sample their way through Missouri's wine country as hikers and bikers set off along the beautiful Katy Trail. Those who just can't get enough time behind the wheel will enjoy the natural beauty along the Great River Road as well as the nostalgic photo opportunities along historic Route 66. From the most quaint bed-and-breakfast inns to the kitschiest greasy-spoon diner, chances are that you can find whatever it is you're looking for somewhere within an approximate 120-mile radius of St. Louis. And all of the suggested destinations are close enough that you can make it back to St. Louis for the evening, and just far enough away to feel like you "got away from it all."

MISSOURI WINE COUNTRY

Augusta and Hermann, Missouri

America's first wine district was created in the hills of Missouri, just west of St. Louis. Take Interstate 70 west to Highway 19 south into Hermann, about 70 miles, and you'll be in the heart of the state's wine country. In the mid 1800s German immigrants from the Rhine River Valley planted vineyards and constructed wine cellars in and around the small towns of Augusta and Hermann. Augusta, which was first settled in 1836 on the bluffs overlooking the river, soon became the epicenter of German cultural traditions. Today there are more than two dozen wineries in Missouri, and many have tasting bars and picnic areas that are great places to spend an afternoon. During September and October many of the wineries have special events and live entertainment on weekends, and if you time your visit right, you can enjoy some spectacular fall foliage as well. Admission is free to all of the wineries, except during special events (such as during Labor Day weekend and Octoberfest).

Montelle Winery (Highway 94, 1 1/2 miles east of Augusta; 636-228-4464; www.montelle.com), perched high atop Osage Ridge, offers glorious views of the Missouri River, the village of Augusta, and the surrounding wine-growing region. Both the Augusta Winery (corner of Jackson and High Streets, Augusta; 888-MOR-WINE; www.augustawinery.com) and the Mount Pleasant Winery (5634 High Street, Augusta; 800-467-WINE; www.mountpleasant.com), which offer stunning views of rolling hills and lush green flatland that connect the hill country to the Missouri River, are relaxing places to spend an afternoon, sitting outside on the patio and enjoying the view—and the vino. Mount Pleasant also offers indoor seating for those who prefer to sit and sip in climate-controlled confines. The Augusta Grocery has all sorts of snacks that go well with wine, including platters of assorted cheeses, fruits, crackers, and deli meats, while the Mount Pleasant Grill offers salads, sandwiches, veggie wraps, and the house specialty: flatbread baked with sun-dried tomatoes and Fontina cheese and served with a basil pesto dipping sauce.

Both the grocery and the grill are located on-site of the Mount Pleasant Winery. Louis P. Balducci Vineyards (3½ miles west of Augusta, 6601 Highway 94 South; 636-482-VINO; www.balducci vineyards.com) is Augusta's newest "winey" kid on the block. The Balduccis produce nearly a dozen various vinos and serve a limited kitchen menu (Friday through Sunday only), but there are beautiful vistas and special events throughout the year. Blumenhof Winery (on Highway 94, 7 miles west of Augusta; 800-419-2245; www .blumenhof.com) is located in Dutzow, Missouri's oldest German settlement, which was founded in 1832. The winery's German heritage is evident in its architecture and in the warm, friendly ambience. Farther west in Hermann, Missouri, the Stone Hill Winery (1110 Stone Hill Highway; 800-909-WINE; www.stonehillwinery.com) offers tours, wine tastings, live music, and special events such as the occasional "grape stomping." For more information visit www.missouriwine.org.

> ℹ️ On weekends in October, many area wineries offer round-trip bus service from several St. Louis locations.

This quaint small town was founded in 1799 by followers of Daniel Boone. In the fall of 1833, a dozen Catholic families from Hanover, Germany, settled in Washington, and the German influence is still evident today. Washington put itself on the map in 1850 when it built a steamboat landing on the bank of the Missouri River. In 1855 John B. Busch, brother of Adolphus Busch of Anheuser-Busch fame, started a brewery in Washington that bottled the original Busch beer. Today, the brewery building still stands and houses several modern-day captains of industry. Other locally manufactured products include the zither (a musical instrument similar to the dulcimer) and corncob pipes. In fact, Washington has the only factory in the world that still manufactures corncob pipes.

Downtown Washington's historic shopping district has a unique collection of small galleries, specialty shops, antiques stores, and restaurants. Elijah McLean's (600 West Front Street; 636-239-9463, www.elijahmcleans.com) is a full-service restaurant located in a mansion that once was a private residence. The restaurant sits atop a hill overlooking the Missouri River and offers an elegant yet casual atmosphere. The very reasonably priced Sunday brunch offers a wide variety of options, including peel-and-eat shrimp, fresh fruit, pancakes or eggs Benedict made to order, beef Stroganoff, baked fish, fried chicken, cold salads, cooked veggies, and a dessert table filled with pastries, muffins, and cakes. The Basket Case Deli/Creamery Hill Cafe (323A West Fifth Street; 636-239-7127) offers sandwiches, homemade soups, salads, fresh seafood, steaks, and pastas, and the Gourmet Cafe and Moonlight Restaurant (1381 High Street, No. 111; 636-390-9131) serves up specialty sandwiches, vegetarian dishes, salads, and entrees with a Southwestern flair.

In addition to the wineries, other nearby attractions include Purina Farms (200 Checkerboard Drive, Gray Summit; 636-451-2223, www .purina.com), a hands-on educational center that features interactive exhibits, wagon rides, a petting arena, farm-animal barn, pet shows and demonstrations, and other special events. It's located about 30 minutes from downtown Washington. And, about 10 minutes from Purina Farms is the Shaw Nature Reserve (Highway 100 and Interstate 44, exit 253, Gray Summit; 636-451-3512, www.mobot.org/MOBOT/naturereserve/). This division of the Missouri Botanical Garden has an educational visitor center, five-acre wildflower garden, and 13 miles of nature trails. The Bascom Manor House, a two-story, modified Italianate Victorian home built in 1879, is also located on-site and available for tours.

There are several very different bed-and-breakfast options to choose from, including the Central Hotel (1017 Maupin Avenue, New Haven; 573-237-8540; www.centralhotelnh.com), a vintage 1879 hotel that has been restored to its original charm. There are five guest rooms, and each includes a private bath and all of the modern amenities. The Heritage Valley Bed 'N' Breakfast (1668 Four Mile Road, Washington; 636-239-7479;

www.heritagevalleybnb.com) is a hand-hewn log cabin that features a fully-equipped kitchen and bathroom, along with the always-important central heating and air-conditioning. There are two loft-style bedrooms available, and the cabin can accommodate up to seven guests. The Cottages of Hunter's Hollow Bed and Breakfast Inn (200 Powell Avenue, Labadie; 636-451-0303, www.huntershollowbandb.com) offers a country retreat that will make you think you've journeyed "across the pond." The Compleat Angler is decorated with fishing gear such as hand-tied flies and English rods, while the Fox and Hounds cabin offers the ambience of an English hunting lodge. Visit the Washington, Missouri, Web site at www.washmo.org for additional information and updates, or call them toll-free at (888) 7WASHMO.

St. Charles, Missouri

Another town to the west of St. Louis on I–70 is St. Charles, a river city with its own unique historical perspective. The city was founded in 1769 by French-Canadian fur trader Louis Blanchette and named Les Petites Cotes, or the Little Hills. During the great westward expansion, thousands of pioneers passed through here, replenishing supplies one last time before departing into the new territory. St. Charles is the location of the Lewis and Clark Rendezvous, Missouri's First State Capitol, the origin of the Boone's Lick Trail, and home to Daniel Boone. For more details on St. Charles, check out the Web site www.historic stcharles.com.

The First Missouri State Capitol and State Historic Site (200-216 South Main Street; 636-940-3322, www.mostateparks.com/firstcapitol .htm), on St. Charles's historic Main Street, has been completely restored and furnished with period pieces from the 1820s. The 10-block-long, 200-year-old street was Missouri's first and largest historic district. A trolley travels among the street's more than 125 one-of-a-kind stores, where you can shop for framed art, antiques, old and reproduction signs, Victorian accessories, lamps, collectible figures and plates (at the largest store of

its kind in Missouri), stained glass, quilts, pottery, floral arrangements, and decorating accents from every period. Frenchtown, a historic St. Charles neighborhood, is a haven for antiques lovers with more than 20 unique stores, including the United States' largest selection of vintage architectural products, hardware, plumbing, molding, ceilings, intricate gingerbread, lighting accessories, weathervanes, and cupolas.

When you get hungry, you can stop at Lewis and Clark's American Restaurant and Public House (217 South Main Street; 636-947-3334, www.lewisandclarksrestaurant.com), which offers traditional American fare served in a 100-year-old, three-story renovated building with a patio overlooking Main Street and the river. Miss Aimee B's (837 First Capitol Drive; 636-946-4202, www .saucemagazine.com/missaimeeb/) features indoor and outdoor dining for breakfast, lunch, or dessert in a historic house built in 1865. Other options include Bella Garden Cafe (524 South Main Street; 636-724-6006), which has its own "Bella Wraps" and lighter fare, including deli sandwiches, and the St. Charles Vintage House Restaurant and Wine Garden (1219 South Main Street; 636-946-7155, www.stcharlesvin tagehouse.com). The restaurant serves American cuisine, and the beautiful wine garden plays host to a number of weddings and special events.

For more history, check out the Lewis & Clark Boat House and Nature Center (1050 Riverside Drive; 636-947-3199, www.lewisandclark center.org), a "hands-on" museum that traces the adventure of Lewis and Clark into the wilderness of the West. Displays feature Indian tribes, the men of the expedition with their equipment and artifacts, and a walk-through forest.

Feeling a little adventurous yourself? Katy Trail State Park offers a unique opportunity for people of all ages and interests. Whether you are a bicyclist, hiker, nature lover, or history buff, the trail offers opportunities for recreation, a place to enjoy nature, and an avenue to discover the past. The trailhead located at Riverside and Boonslick Roads in St. Charles is at mile marker 39.5. Katy Trail State Park (www.mostateparks.com/katytrail/

index.html) is built on the former corridor of the Missouri-Kansas-Texas Railroad, which is better known as "the Katy." When the railroad ceased operation of the route from St. Charles County to Sedalia, Missouri, in 1986, it was turned into an extraordinary long-distance hiking and bicycling trail that would eventually run almost 200 miles across the state. The section of trail between St. Charles and Boonville has been designated an official segment of the Lewis and Clark National Historic Trail, and the entire trail is part of the American Discovery Trail. The trail also has been designated as a Millennium Legacy Trail. Bike rentals are available in and around St. Charles, including at Katy Bike Rental (2998 Highway 94 South, Defiance; 636-987-2673, www.katytrailbikerental .com). Also, the Bass Pro Shops Sportsman's Warehouse (1365 South Fifth Street, St. Charles; 636-688-2500, www.basspro.com) has all of the hunting, fishing, and camping apparel and merchandise you could possibly ever need.

Defiance, Missouri, approximately 20 miles away from St. Charles, features the Historic Daniel Boone Home and Boonesfield Village (1868 Highway F, Defiance; 314-798-2005 www.linden wood.edu/boone/), which includes the four-story home built by Boone and his sons in 1810, where Boone lived until his death in 1820. The house has seven fireplaces, a ballroom, and a variety of everyday items such as a collection of flintlock long rifles, Mrs. Boone's butter churn and sewing basket, Daniel's writing desk, and the family dishes. There's also a Missouri frontier village that includes a one-room schoolhouse; church; general store; gristmill; pottery; printer's, carpenter's, and dressmaker's shops; and other homes.

If you're yearning for more modern, nighttime action, the Ameristar Casino (St. Charles riverfront; 636-949-7777, www.ameristar casinos.com) has more than 3,000 slots and video poker machines, 95 table games, and live poker. The casino frequently hosts nationally known entertainers in the Bottleneck Blues Bar and the Casino Cabaret lounge. Dining options include Pearl's Oyster Bar, 47 Port Street Grill, Falcon Diner, and the Landmark Buffet. Other nighttime entertainment options include concerts by top-name rock, country, pop, and R&B bands at the nearby Verizon Wireless Amphitheater (14141 Riverport Drive; 314-298-9944, www .livenation.com), which many locals still refer to as "Riverport Amphitheater." The St. Charles County Family Arena (2002 Arena Parkway; 636-896-4200, www.familyarena.com) hosts concerts year-round. Baseball fans can enjoy minor-league baseball at its most entertaining level with a visit to see the Rascals. The River City Rascals (900 Ozzie Smith Drive, O'Fallon; 636-240-BATS, www .rivercityrascals.com), a professional minor-league baseball team, plays in nearby O'Fallon from June to August.

Need a place to rest your weary head? In Frenchtown, the five-room Bittersweet Inn (1101 North Third Street, St. Charles, 636-724-7778, www.bittersweetinn.com) is a beautifully decorated home built in 1864. It has been elegantly restored and features a beautiful garden, front veranda, and spacious guest rooms. Also located in the historic Frenchtown neighborhood, the Alexander-Wentker House, also known as the Victorian Memories Bed-and-Breakfast (709 Fourth Street; 636-940-8111; www.victorianmemories .com), is a retreat just TWO blocks from the popular antiques district.

Caves and Rivers

About an hour west of St. Louis on I–44 is Stanton, Missouri, home of Meramec Caverns (I–44, exit 230; 800-676-6105; www.americascave .com), which continues to be a big draw for kids and families. Billed as "Mother Nature's Museum," the caverns offer an up-close and personal look at mineral and rock formations that are truly breathtaking. Tucked under the foothills of the Ozark Mountains, the cave was mined by French colonial miners and Civil War garrisons who used the cave's natural minerals to manufacture gunpowder. Another selling point that adds to the cave's mystique is the story that outlaw Jesse James and his gang used the cave as a place to stash their loot and horses during the 1870s. There's also an underground river and the "Stage Curtain," which is said to be the largest single cave formation in the world. Other activities available around these parts include boat rides, canoe rentals, camping, and panning for gold.

Missouri's scenic Onondaga Cave (I–44, exit 214 at Leasburg; 573-245-6600; www .mostateparks.com/onondaga.htm) is open for tours as well, along with the nearby Cathedral and Fisher Caves. The latter two are geared toward the more adventurous, as tours are done the old-fashioned way—with handheld lanterns. Float trips are a popular activity here, with the Meramec River and Huzzah and Courtois creeks beckoning locals and visitors alike during the hot summer months.

Another popular spot for spelunkers and divers is the Bonne Terre Mine (39 Allen Street, Bonne Terre; 888-843-3483; www.2dive.com), the world's largest man-made caverns and lake. The spot was mined for more than 100 years. Walking, boat, and scuba tours of the mine, which was filmed by noted oceanographer Jacques Cousteau, are available.

Hannibal, Missouri

Legendary author Samuel Clemens, better known as Mark Twain, called the tiny town of Hannibal home. Located about two hours north of St. Louis on U.S. Highway 61, Hannibal plays host to events straight out of the pages of Twain's books, such as fence-painting and frog-jumping contests. The town is home to the Mark Twain Boyhood Home & Museum (120 North Main Street; 573-221-9010, www.marktwainmuseum.org). Tours are also available of the Becky Thatcher House, the John M. Clemens Justice of the Peace Office, and Grant's Drug Store. The Twain Museum features interactive exhibits that examine some of the author's major works, including The Adventures of Tom Sawyer, The Adventures of Huckleberry Finn, and Roughing It. The exhibits include a stagecoach, a steamboat replica, and 15 Norman Rockwell illustrations that were commissioned for special editions of Tom Sawyer and Huck Finn in the 1930s. Hannibal as History is an exhibit that looks at the town's architecture from its earliest

days through buildings completed in the early 1900s and includes everything from residences and schools to public buildings and factories. The most recent addition to the museum is a biographical exhibit of Mark Twain. This section allows visitors to investigate Twain's family, his publishing career, his dabbles in politics, and similar topics. For more Twain fun, the Mark Twain Cave complex (one mile south of downtown on Highway 79; 573-221-1656; www.marktwain cave.com) offers a variety of activities, including one-hour tours of the cave that showed up in Twain's books about Tom and Huck. The complex includes a campground, a visitor center, and the Rock Shop, where you can pan for gemstones.

Bed-and-breakfast accommodations in downtown Hannibal include Lula Belle's Restaurant, Lula Belle's Bed and Breakfast (111 Bird Street; 573-221-6662, www.lulabelles.com) Main Street Bed and Breakfast and The Painted Lady Bed and Breakfast. All four are run by the folks at Lula Belles. In addition to Lula Belle's, you can grab a bite to eat at The Abby Rose Tea & Lunch Room (110 North Main Street, 573-221-1226, www.abbyrose.com) or the family-friendly fun zone Sawyer's Creek (11011 Highway 79, 573-221-8000, www.sawyerscreek.com). For information on these or other Hannibal attractions, call the Hannibal Convention and Visitors Bureau at (573) 221-2477, or log on to www.hanmo.com.

SOUTHERN ILLINOIS WINE COUNTRY

Great River Road

The Great River Road (www.greatriverroad.com), from nearby Alton, Illinois, to Kampsville, is one of America's National Scenic Byways. From St. Louis take I–70 west to Highway 367/U.S. Highway 67 North. If you get tired of the beautiful scenery afforded you by the mighty Mississippi River, you can take a break and enjoy the soaring limestone bluffs on the other side. These bluffs were first noted by 17th-century explorers Marquette and Joliet. Just north of the tiny town of Alton, you'll see an image of a piasa bird painted on the bluffs.

The fierce, serpent-like bird of Native American legend gives the area its name, Piasa Country.

Alton (www.visitalton.com) was founded in 1818, and it soon became one of the largest communities in the state. In the 1830s Illinois was a free state, while just across the Mississippi River, Missouri was a slave state. Alton resident Rev. Elijah Lovejoy became a vocal opponent of slavery and published the Alton Observer, an abolitionist newspaper. The Underground Railroad, a secret route used by slaves to escape into free territory, went directly through Alton, and in 1858 the final Lincoln-Douglas debate was held in the city.

In Alton and nearby Grafton, there are a number of quaint restaurants, cafes, antiques shops, and bed-and-breakfast inns. Some of Alton's most popular restaurants include Tony's (312 Piasa Street; 618-462-8234), Cane Bottom/My Just Desserts (31 East Broadway; 618-462-5881, www.myjustdesserts.org), and The Big Muddy Pub (204 State Street; 618-463-1095, www.bigmuddypub.com). For overnight accommodations, Alton's Beall Mansion (407 East 12th Street; 618-474-9100, www.beallmansion.com) and Jackson House (1821 Seminary Street; 618-462-1426, www.jacksonbb.com) are two of the region's most popular bed-and-breakfasts. Alton is also home to the Alton Belle Casino (219 Piasa; 800-711-GAME, www.argosycasinos.com), and nearby Hartford, Illinois, is the location of the Lewis and Clark State Historic Site (Illinois Highway 3 at New Poag Road; 618-251-5811, www.campdubois.com), which is the site of the famed explorers' Camp DuBois. Nearby Elsah's Maple Leaf Cottage Inn (12 Selma Street, 618-374-1684) and Green Tree Inn Bed and Breakfast (15 Mill Street; 618-374-2821, www.greentreeinn.com) bed-and-breakfasts offer relaxing alternatives to the standard hotel experience. For more information about the Great River Road or Piasa Country, call the Greater Alton/Twin Rivers Convention and Visitors Bureau at (800) ALTON-IL, or log on to www.visitalton.com.

Abraham Lincoln's Springfield, Illinois

Just two hours northeast of St. Louis on Interstate 55 is the Illinois state capital, Springfield. Here you can tour the Lincoln Home (426 South Seventh Street; 217-492-4241, ext. 221, www.nps.gov/liho/), where the Lincolns lived from 1844 to 1861, and the Abraham Lincoln Presidential Library and Museum (212 North Sixth Street; 800-610-2094; www.alplm.com). This facility has the world's largest collection of documentary material related to the life of Lincoln, America's 16th president. The museum features state-of-the-art exhibits, interactive displays, and multimedia programs. Lincoln's pre presidential years and his years in the White House are featured prominently, but one of the most entertaining areas is Mrs. Lincoln's Attic. Here, kids can try on clothes from the era, play with period toys, and, yes, play with Lincoln Logs. The Old State Capitol (1 Old Capitol Plaza, 217-785-7960, www.Illinoishistory.gov) is where Lincoln debated Stephen Douglas on the slavery issue.

You can visit the Lincoln Tomb at Oak Ridge Cemetery, where Lincoln; his wife, Mary; and sons Tad, Eddie, and Willie are buried. You can also walk through the restored living-history village of New Salem, where Lincoln lived before beginning his political career. Visit the Illinois State Museum (502 South Spring Street, 217-782-7386, www.museum.state.il.us/) for a look at the history of the state through permanent and changing exhibits, interactive elements, and audiovisual effects.

Or, if you prefer, you can follow the signs to go "off-roading" on the historic two-lane highway of Route 66. There are several Route 66–related icons in and around Springfield, and one that is definitely worth checking out is Shea's Gas Station Museum (2075 Peoria Road, Springfield; 217-522-0475). Shea's is a favorite photo stop for Route 66 travelers from around the world—for both its charming and eclectic collection of gas station memorabilia and for its "celebrity" owner, Bill Shea. Bill is always happy to share stories about his collection and his years on the Mother Road. It's free to tour the museum—Bill only asks that all visitors leave their signature in his guest book. The photographs are worth the visit themselves. Closed Sunday and Monday. Another popular spot along the route is the Cozy Drive In (2935 South Sixth Street, Springfield; 217-525-1992). The original owner of this traditional diner, Ed Waldmire, invented the Cozy Dog, or as it's more commonly known, the corn dog. The Waldmire family still serves up Cozy Dogs, french fries, and stories of the Mother Road with travelers from around the world from Monday through Saturday. They also have managed to accumulate an eclectic assortment of memorabilia since opening in 1949.

Some other fun stops along the Mother Road include the Route 66 Twin Drive-In Theatre (700 Recreation Drive, Springfield; 217-698-0066, www.route66-drivein.com), one of the state's few remaining drive-ins. The facility opens at dusk, with double features nightly from Memorial Day to Labor Day. Or, check out the Route 66 Dream Car Museum (Old Route 66, Williamsville; 217-566-3799), a collection of vintage autos from the collection of two private citizens. The venue, which features sock hops and car cruises throughout the year, is open seasonally, so call first.

Built in 1871, the Rippon-Kinsella House (1317 North Third Street, 217-241-3367, www .ripponkinsella.com) is an antiques-filled Victorian B&B located minutes from downtown Springfield. The Henry Mischler House Bed and Breakfast (802 East Edwards, 800-525-2660, www.mischler house.com) is a Queen Anne Victorian house built in 1897. Relax in front of the cozy fireplace or enjoy the private garden and water fountains during the warmer months. For more information about Springfield, Illinois, call (800) 678-8767 or log on to www.visit-springfield.com.

RELOCATION

The St. Louis area is a great place to live, work, and raise a family, and it offers affordable living, good educational resources, and a variety of cultural and sports-related activities. To say that St. Louis is a city of neighborhoods is to quote a local cliché—but it's true. From its ethnically inspired neighborhoods, where the earliest immigrants banded together to re-create their lives in familiar surroundings, to today's artists' enclaves and suburban attempts at bohemia, there's a place for almost every personality in the greater St. Louis region. Luckily for its inhabitants, St. Louis—the region and the city—is home to a diverse assortment of neighborhoods that are rich in history, architecture, and character.

The city consists of a number of distinct neighborhoods, including a resurgent downtown that is a popular place for young professionals and older empty-nesters looking to enjoy city living in the Midwest. A mile or so to the south, Soulard, which is one of the city's oldest neighborhoods, is reminiscent of the residential enclaves in New Orleans's French Quarter, complete with brick mansard-style buildings, neighborhood groceries and pubs, and a historic centerpiece known as the Soulard Farmers Market. In Lafayette Square, Victorian homes line the 30-acre Lafayette Park, and the neighborhood has retained much of the charm of the late 1800s. A few miles to the west, along the city's western boundary, is the Central West End (CWE). The CWE and its magnificent estates make it one of St. Louis's grandest neighborhoods, and the stately mansions and regal "private places" are neighbors with a host of diverse shops, restaurants, and pubs. Renovated single- and multifamily housing is located along the Skinker-DeBalivere area that borders Forest Park, while The Hill neighborhood is home to dozens of Italian restaurants, bakeries, and groceries alongside quaint brick homes and shotgun-style houses. In the St. Louis Hills neighborhood, just southwest of The Hill, you'll find stately two-story homes surrounding Francis Park and charming brick bungalows that look like gingerbread houses. The southwestern edge of the city is where many city employees call home. Due to a residency law that requires all city employees live within the city limits, this area of town is home to many city government employees. In Richmond Heights and Maplewood, young families and artists are revamping the neighborhood's stately homes and businesses that have been around since the early 1900s. Clayton and Ladue are two of St. Louis's toniest suburbs, while Webster Groves and Kirkwood bring their own brand of small-town charm to the metropolitan region. For those who really want to "get away from it all" at the end of the workday, there's Chesterfield, Wildwood, Town & Country and points west—West County, that is, and the suburban melting pot that occupies the far edge of St. Louis County.

DOWNTOWN

St. Louis's downtown has undergone a tremendous resurgence. More people are moving back downtown to take advantage of the influx of new housing options, including an incredible number of spacious and charming lofts, condominiums, and new apartments. Twice a year, in the spring and fall, the Downtown St. Louis Partnership (www.downtownstlouis.org) produces a free downtown housing tour that shows prospective residents all of the new and exciting living spaces cropping up throughout the area. Downtown is becoming an open door to St. Louis's arts and

The Regional Commerce and Growth Association (RCGA) (314–231–5555; www.stlrcga.org) offers a variety of relocation publications, including the Welcome Book, the Greater St. Louis Apartment Guide, and Selecting the Right School for Your Child.

entertainment resources, with a wide variety of museums, galleries, nightclubs, restaurants, and event venues all located within the two square miles known as downtown. The 21st-century St. Louis region has crowned downtown as its centerpiece, and Washington Avenue, which was once known as the nation's premier garment district, is now a regional destination known for restaurants, nightlife, and the hundreds of new living spaces that have been carved out of the city's historic buildings. As of 2006, downtown St. Louis is home to 10,000 residents living in more than 7,000 lofts, condos, apartments, town houses, and single-family homes. Downtown St. Louis has become one of the most sought-after neighborhoods in the area, and the types of rental/ownership options continue to change at an incredible pace. From studio apartments (around $500/month) to $1 million penthouses, the Loft District has choices for every budget and lifestyle. Live/work spaces are enjoying increased popularity as well, with many residents opting to just "commute" to another part of their building to put in their 40 hours a week. By the end of 2008 approximately 11,000 residents called downtown home, thanks to, an influx of additional housing options and amenities, such as restaurants, shops, grocery stores, pharmacies and other neighborhood necessities. Strong resident/tenant organizations are at the forefront of the improvements to downtown, and each group hosts a number of special events and cocktail hours designed to help residents get to know one another and keep up with what's new in the neighborhood.

Soulard/Benton Park

One anchor of the Soulard neighborhood is the stately red brick monstrosity known as the Anheuser-Busch InBev Brewery. Soulard, St. Louis's oldest neighborhood, is chock-full of red brick single-family homes, apartments, and town houses that are in varying degrees of rehab. In addition to a sprinkling of restaurants and galleries, Soulard is home to some of St. Louis's best blues music clubs. The lively neighborhood was named for Antoine Soulard, a Frenchman who surveyed colonial St. Louis for the King of Spain and originally owned this tract of land just minutes south of the Gateway Arch. A collection of 19th-century homes constructed of St. Louis's signature red brick hug the sidewalks and hide restaurants' elaborate courtyards in the back, where outdoor dining is offered from spring through fall. The historic churches of Soulard, many built by St. Louis's immigrant communities, welcome visitors throughout the year. The Soulard neighborhood marks its French heritage with a Bastille Day celebration each July and an 11-day Mardi Gras fête each year. The Soulard Farmers Market serves as the neighborhood's centerpiece, where locals and visitors alike swarm to buy fresh produce, flowers, baked goods, and exotic spices.

Next door, the Benton Park neighborhood is enjoying a rehab-resurgence as well. Benton Park began to build up soon after the Civil War and, by 1875, had become a semi-urbanized district. Benton Park is known by many for its proximity to the Cherokee Street Business District, which borders the southern edge of the neighborhood. Traditionally a working-class neighborhood, it has seen many changes in recent years, thanks to a boom of revitalization. One of the neighborhood's greatest assets has been the quality of 19th-century housing stock, with three-quarters of the houses in Benton Park consisting of one- to two-family units. In recent years, the area north of the park has changed dramatically, as many young professionals have moved to the area, paying prime market rates for the single-family homes and doing extensive rehab on the properties. This blue-collar neighborhood built by German immigrants has transformed into a more demographically diverse area during recent years, and it has begun to attract larger numbers of middle-class home owners, immigrants of various nationalities, and a large population of artists. In addition to refurbished houses, there has been construction of about a dozen new "historic-like" buildings. The new homes are mainly of frame construction but have brick façades to blend in with the surroundings. The neighborhoods are defined by Gravois, Cherokee and Potomac, Jefferson, and Interstate 55. The distance to downtown is less than 1 mile, and the airport is approximately 14 miles away. The predominant price range of housing varies greatly, mostly dependent upon the level of renovations needed and/or completed, and the assigned school district is the St. Louis Public Schools and St. Louis Magnet Schools.

Lafayette Square

Lafayette Square is among St. Louis's most picturesque neighborhoods, and it too has seen a rebirth due to home owners who are willing to invest in a unique fixer-upper. Named after a Revolutionary War hero who visited St. Louis in 1825, Lafayette Square surrounds beautiful Lafayette Park, a 30-acre oasis of greenery within the urban landscape. Stately 1870s and 1880s Victorian homes, or "painted ladies," frame the square, and the grand dames have been called the finest and largest collection of Victorian-era architecture in the country. The area has won the title of one of the "Prettiest Painted Places" in America, and its annual house and garden tour and yearly holiday parlor tours are always well attended. Developers have begun converting many of the historic area's long-neglected manufacturing facilities and warehouses into unique and stylish lofts and apartments. As more residents flock to the area, the burgeoning neighborhood continues to attract even more restaurants, specialty shops, and galleries. The neighborhood has seen its own new construction boom, as developers have seized upon the renewed interest in the area to build new lofts and condos.

Convenient to downtown (2 miles) and Lambert–St. Louis International Airport (14 miles), the predominant price range varies greatly, depending on the level of rehab needed. Lafayette Square residents attend St. Louis Public Schools or area magnet schools. For information on the Lafayette Square neighborhood, call (314) 772-5724 or log on to www.lafayettesquare.org.

WEST OF DOWNTOWN

Central West End

Perched on the edge of Forest Park, St. Louis's Central West End (CWE) is full of tree-lined private streets marked by large, stately homes and charming sidewalk cafes, art galleries, antiques shops, bookstores, and boutiques. The 1904 World's Fair led to great development in the CWE, as mansions went up quickly all around Forest Park. The neighborhood was once the site of St. Louis's most notorious entertainment district, Gaslight Square. Gaslight Square, a bohemian mecca of clubs, antiques shops, art galleries, and fine restaurants, reached its zenith in the late 1960s and attracted worldwide attention. Today the CWE includes most of the city's private streets and luxury apartment buildings, along with some of the finest commercial and religious architecture. While there is not any one prevalent style or dominant building type, the overall detail and quality of construction reflects the strong sense of prosperity that built the district. Private places, or gated streets, include Portland Place and Westmoreland Place on the west side of Kingshighway, and Hortense Place and Lenox Place on the east side of Kingshighway. The CWE is one of the city's largest neighborhoods, ranking second in population, and it is just 3 miles from downtown and 10 miles from the airport. Both are accessible by MetroLink, the bi-state area's light-rail system. The predominant price range for housing can be anywhere from $175,000 to $2.5 million, and area students are assigned to St. Louis Public Schools or magnet schools.

The Hill

Between the 1880s and 1920s, Italian immigrants laid claim to The Hill, and the residents have maintained the colorful traditions in this lively neighborhood. Even the fireplugs, which set a colorful boundary for the neighborhood, are painted green, white, and red in tribute to the flag of Italy. Baseball's Yogi Berra and Joe Garagiola grew up on these streets, where neighbors still know each other by name and an evening out can still include a game of bocce (Italian lawn bowling). Row upon row of tiny, neatly kept houses with equally tiny yards squeeze close to the street, and neighborhood restaurants, shops, and taverns dot many corners. Elegant gourmet restaurants and mom-and-pop trattorias stand next to tiny Italian grocery stores crammed full of imported and homemade delicacies. Some of the traditional Italian community icons have faded over the years in the neighborhood. The Hill was one of the city's purest ethnic neighborhoods and its most stable, tightly woven community. Although it is not as ethnically pure as it once was, the Italian population is still just less than 70 percent of the residents. This well-maintained neighborhood consists of traditional brick bungalows, interspersed with shotgun houses, apartments, and larger single-family homes. St. Ambrose Place, located south of Hereford Street and Bischoff Avenue, is a modern subdivision of single-family, two-story homes built in the late 1980s in response to the neighborhood's housing shortage. The Hill has a very strong retail business community, including many of St. Louis's favorite restaurants and import stores, and educational options include St. Ambrose Parish School, Shaw Community School, Visual and Performing Arts Magnet School, and O'Fallon Technical High School. The Hill is convenient to Interstate 44 and Interstate 40, and it's an approximate 3-mile trek to downtown and about 10 miles to the airport.

Richmond Heights/Maplewood

Richmond Heights and Maplewood are suburban areas located along the border of the city of St. Louis. Richmond Heights is actually sandwiched between St. Louis and the city of Clayton, which serves as the center of the county's government offices and services. Legend has it that before the Civil War, a young lieutenant named Robert E. Lee, who was stationed in St. Louis with the Army Corps of Engineers, came upon land that today is known as Richmond Heights. He was struck by its beauty and remarked how much it reminded him of Richmond in his home state of Virginia. "Heights" was added later because the land is at one of the highest elevations in St. Louis County. Richmond Heights is nestled south of Clayton and offers beautifully maintained older homes on tree-lined streets. It consists primarily of single-family homes, including upscale housing in Lake Forest and Hampton Park, as well as charming middle-income homes. Homes in the area range substantially in size and architectural style, and most are between 30 and 50 years old. There are a number of modest homes that are well suited for the first-time home buyer as well as a variety of larger homes located near Tilles Park.

Richmond Heights also benefits from its close proximity to the up-and-coming city to its south called Maplewood. Once known as one of the shopping Meccas of St. Louis County, Maplewood's downtown business district bustled with commercial activity throughout the 1940s, '50s, and '60s. During the late 1960s and throughout the '70s, Maplewood suffered the same fate as most older, inner-ring suburbs, as many people moved to newer communities in west St. Louis County. Today Maplewood has experienced an influx of new blood as many young couples have taken advantage of the good home buys. Similarly, there's been renewed interest in the city's main drag, Manchester Road, due to the area's low retail rental rates and property values, and it now bustles with an eclectic mix of retail, restaurants, coffeehouses, specialty shops, jewelers, office-supply stores, and nightspots.

The Schlafly microbrewery opened its second location in Maplewood, and the Bottleworks restaurant and beer garden has been a welcome addition to what has become a rejuvenated neighborhood. Richmond Heights and Maplewood are both located about 10 miles from downtown St. Louis and 12 miles from the airport. The predominant price range for housing is anywhere from $150,000 to $750,000, and the public schools in the area include Brentwood, Maplewood–Richmond Heights, Clayton, and Ladue.

University City/The Loop

University City is a mix of neighborhoods offering an outstanding variety of new and existing housing, including multiple-family apartments, condominiums, and single-family housing, along with the bustling entertainment district known as The Loop. U City, as it is often called, is a city of parks, with the most park acreage per mile. Located at the western edge of the Central West End and anchored at its southern border by Washington University, U City is a vibrant, diverse community with good theater, an excellent public library, and a lively restaurant and retail district. Just a block from The Loop are two arts organizations, the Center of Contemporary Arts and the Saint Louis Symphony Community Music School, which both promote the visual and performing arts with education for the community and performances. Downtown is only 8 miles away, and the airport is about 7 miles down Interstate 170. The average price for a home in U City is around $250,000, and students are assigned to University City's public schools.

Clayton

Clayton, the seat of St. Louis County government, is best known for its commerce by day and its restaurants by night. Dozens of fine restaurants, elegant hotels, and fine-art galleries have found a home in the heart of the Central Business District of Clayton. The housing here ranges from homes built for the captains of industry in the 1920s and '30s to new luxury condominiums in neighborhoods with coffee shops, restaurants, antiques stores, and vest-pocket parks that invite friendly encounters with neighbors of all ages. Architec-

tural styles range from traditional-looking homes to mansions that resemble English country manor houses, along with a few examples of Spanish architecture thrown in for good measure. At the eastern edge of Clayton, the architecture dates from the close of the 1904 World's Fair. A main artery, Wydown Boulevard, is one of the most beautiful boulevards in the area, with lanes for bicyclists and a median that is usually full of walkers, runners, and spectacular flowering trees. Restaurants and shops line the commercial area and Central Business District, and Shaw Park offers recreational activities such as swimming and tennis. Clayton is about 8 miles from downtown St. Louis and 12 miles from the airport. Homes range from $150,000 to $1 million-plus, with an average home price of just under $600,000, and students attend the distinguished Clayton schools.

Ladue

Ladue is one of the area's oldest and most affluent neighborhoods, and it contains some of the finest estates, million-dollar homes, and the highest-priced residential subdivisions in the area. The styles of houses in this area range from traditional architecture to modern luxury homes, and most are situated on elegant, beautifully landscaped lots of one to three acres. Ladue offers a pastoral, country atmosphere with convenient access to St. Louis and Clayton's business districts, as well as a variety of exclusive shops—including the upscale Plaza Frontenac shopping mall—restaurants, antiques stores, and country clubs. Several old and distinguished landmark restaurants are located in the Ladue area, and tradition is a recurring theme. Downtown St. Louis is 10 miles to the east, and the airport is only about 8 miles to the north. The average home price is around $1.2 million, but residents get the added benefit of Ladue public schools.

Wydown-Skinker/DeMun Area

The Wydown-Skinker neighborhood is located in the far west end of the city of St. Louis, by the city limits on the west, Forsyth Boulevard on the north, Forest Park/Skinker Boulevard on the east, and Clayton Road on the south. The neighborhood was part of the grounds of the 1904 World's Fair, and it remains one of the most upscale and expensive neighborhoods in the city. Large homes, many built in the 1920s, grace tree-lined private streets, and there are a number of high-rise and two- and four-family apartment buildings, along with condominiums and newly constructed lofts. The neighborhood is adjacent to the DeMun Avenue business district, which features an assortment of shops, restaurants, and other businesses. This area is an extremely stable (and expensive) neighborhood, most of the properties here are maintained to high standards, and it offers easy access to Interstate 64/U.S. Highway 40. Downtown is merely 4 miles away, and the airport is an approximate 11 mile drive. Home prices for this area average about $350,000.

SOUTH/SOUTHWEST

Whereas St. Louis is made up of disparate neighborhoods and personalities, St. Louis County is made up of disparate communities. More than 90 different municipalities make up St. Louis County, and each one has a character and personality all its own. For more information about the numerous cities and towns in the county, call (314) 615-5000 or log on to www.co.st-louis.mo.us.

Kirkwood

Kirkwood, the first planned suburb west of the Mississippi, has an authentic small-town flavor. Home to beautiful old houses with broad, open lawns framed by mature trees and sidewalks lining the streets, Kirkwood is often called "Queen of the Suburbs." Its train depot in the city's business district was built in 1893 so that early residents could become the first suburbanites to commute from Kirkwood to office buildings in downtown St. Louis. Kirkwood has settled into its role as a desirable bedroom community conveniently located an easy drive from downtown, but it has retained its strong historic traditions along with

its quiet lifestyle. Kirkwood's homes and businesses have reflected many diverse architectural styles throughout the town's history, including Victorian, Italian Villa, Italianate, Gothic Revival, Greek Revival, and Tudor Revival. The city has more than 300 acres of parkland, including the centrally located Kirkwood Park, which is home to an aquatic center, ice rink, outdoor amphitheater, ball fields, tennis courts, picnic sites, and playground areas. Homes sell for an average price of $330,000, and both downtown and the airport are about 15 miles away. Kirkwood residents attend schools in the Kirkwood district.

Webster Groves

A suburban municipality, Webster Groves originated as five separate communities—Webster, Old Orchard, Webster Park, Tuxedo Park, and Selma—along adjacent railroad lines. These communities merged in 1896 in order to implement public services and develop a unified city government. Since then Webster Groves' tree-lined streets and abundance of beautiful single-family homes have continued to attract new residents. Nestled among clusters of elm, oak, and maple trees are many spectacular homes, boasting large wraparound porches, second and third stories, gingerbread trim, and abundant, verdant lawns. Webster has received the "Tree City USA" award for more than 20 years and is often compared to the historic areas of New England. Contemporary housing options are also available, with many "newer" neighborhoods built during the 20th century. From custom homes and condo complexes to townhomes and apartment complexes, there is a variety of housing options in Webster. The geographic and economic diversity of the area is evident in the variety of neighborhoods that make up the city, along with the cooperation of the members of the community. Home prices average around $253,000. Downtown St. Louis is about 14 miles to the east, and the airport is about 16 miles from the heart of town.

Chesterfield

You'll find a mixture of the old and the new in Chesterfield and its neighboring communities. From country estates and custom-built homes to the new construction of tract housing and apartments, Chesterfield is one of St. Louis's most popular and fastest-growing areas. A number of businesses have moved to the Chesterfield area in order to take advantage of its prime office space and nearby corporate airfield. There are still many heavily wooded areas with winding lanes and magnificent views of wildlife, however, and the Missouri River can be seen from various points of the area. There are also innumerable parks, lakes, and picnic areas for the outdoorsy types, as well as excellent indoor recreational facilities for almost every sport. The Chesterfield Mall offers first-class shopping options, and many of the area's most popular restaurants have opened locations in or around this West County suburb. Chesterfield is 24 miles from downtown St. Louis and 20 miles from Lambert–St. Louis International airport. Housing prices range from $125,000 to $650,000, and the area is served by the Parkway and Rockwood school districts.

St. Louis Hills/Southampton

St. Louis Hills is located in the southwest area of St. Louis, with boundaries of Hampton Avenue to the east, Gravois to the south, Chippewa Street to the north, and the River Des Peres to the west. St. Louis Hills still holds the distinction of being the last large subdivision created in the city—as well as the home to the original Ted Drewes Frozen Custard stand on historic Route 66 (Chippewa Street).

Many residences, built in the 1930s and '40s, reflect a unique charm and individuality. St. Louis Hills is full of tree-lined residential streets, churches, and schools, as well as developing businesses and plenty of open green spaces. Low crime incidences reflect the commitment of neighbors working with city police to provide a safe environment in which to live, work, and play.

i The cost of living in St. Louis is very reasonable. The average price for a typical 2,200-square-foot home with a two-car garage is about $150,000.

St. Louis Hills and the Southampton neighborhood, which is located on the east side of Hampton Avenue, are located close to major highways (I–44 and I–55), and alternate routes make for an easy commute from home to most points in the metropolitan area. Southampton is best known for its numerous blocks of owner-occupied single-family homes and the affordability of its housing stock. Many of the homes in Southampton are similar in style and design to the homes next door in St. Louis Hills, but they're priced significantly lower. Housing prices in St. Louis Hills and Southampton range from $130,000 to $300,000-plus, depending on what side of Hampton you choose. Downtown is about 12 miles away, and the airport is approximately 13 miles away.

REAL ESTATE

The city of St. Louis is home to more than 80 distinct and charming neighborhoods, including The Hill, Dogtown, Lafayette Square, the Central West End, Soulard, The Ville, and Washington Avenue's loft district. Each offers a unique way of life for its residents, and each is a colorful addition to the metropolitan quilt that is St. Louis. St. Louis County also offers myriad tiny towns and charming municipalities to call home, each with its own personality. From the traditional suburban outpost to small-town charm, there are plenty of options for area residents.

Real Estate Agencies

COLDWELL BANKER GUNDAKER RELOCATION OFFICE
2458 Old Dorsett Road, Suite 100, Maryland Heights
(314) 298-5006
www.cbgundaker.com

Coldwell Banker Gundaker, with more than 25 offices in the St. Louis region, serves 200-plus communities in the city of St. Louis and St. Louis County; St. Charles, Jefferson, Franklin, Warren, and Lincoln Counties; and most of east-central Missouri. When Coldwell Banker and Gundaker Realtors merged in 2001, the result was a real estate company with an annual sales volume exceeding $6 billion. Coldwell Banker Gundaker has more than 2,500 sales associates, and offers a relocation team to help newcomers find the right community or neighborhood. The team also provides insight into local schools, transportation, amenities, and more, as well as helping customers find temporary accommodations if needed; and assisting those who are part of a temporary assignment or company relocation program to plan and execute a move to St. Louis.

DIELMANN SOTHEBY'S INTERNATIONAL REALTY

8301 Maryland Avenue, Suite 100
(314) 725-0009
www.dielmannsothebysrealty.com

Led by veteran local Realtor Andy Dielmann, Dielmann Sotheby's International Realty offers comprehensive real estate services to sellers at every price point, but the company is best known for its dealings with luxury homes and high-end condominiums. Dielmann Sotheby's is an affiliate of Sotheby's International Realty, and the St. Louis area office has more than 100 real estate agents and can accommodate clients who speak Afrikaans, English, French, German, Hindi, Russian, or Spanish.

EDWARD L. BAKEWELL, INC.

7716 Forsyth Boulevard, Clayton
(314) 721-5555, (800) 341-4791

4140 Manchester Avenue, St. Louis
(314) 571-7979
www.bakewellinc.com

Edward L. Bakewell specializes in homes located in the Central West End, Clayton, Ladue, University City, Webster Groves, and Chesterfield. One of St. Louis's oldest, family-owned, full-service real estate firms, it has been in business since 1910. Fifty percent of Bakewell's 50-plus, full-time sales associates have been actively engaged in real estate for at least 10 years, and most have spent their careers with Edward L. Bakewell.

GLADYS MANION, INC.

8227 Maryland Avenue, Clayton
(314) 721-4755
www.gladysmanion.com

This company was founded in 1936 by the late Gladys Manion and is currently run by her grandson, Stafford H. Manion. During its history, Gladys Manion, Inc. has grown dramatically in sales and knowledge of the market but maintains itself as a moderate-size agency. This agency focuses on higher-end housing, representing exclusive real estate properties such as Bellerive Country Club Grounds, Muirfield, Twin Creek, and Twin Farms. Manion also represents a number of unique condo developments in Clayton, such as Kingsbury Place, Kingsbury Terrace, Kingsbury Court, Old Town Village, North Central Place, Taylor Park Condominiums, and "The Residence." The agency is the residential agent for major St. Louis corporations, including Nestle Purina, A. G. Edwards, Anheuser-Busch, Jefferson Smurfit, Enterprise Rent-A-Car, and Monsanto, as well as for the St. Louis Rams, St. Louis Cardinals, and St. Louis Blues.

JANET MCAFEE, INC.

9889 Clayton Road
(314) 997-4800
www.janetmcafee.com

Since 1975 Janet McAfee, Inc. has been helping St. Louisans buy and sell homes in some of St. Louis's finest residential neighborhoods. McAfee's 100-plus sales agents know St. Louis's high-end residential communities well, and the firm is focused on the central corridor of the city of St. Louis and St. Louis County, including Clayton, Ladue, Richmond Heights, University City, and west St. Louis County properties. Corporate relocation is an important facet of the business, and the company is the Realtor of choice for many of the area's larger corporations. McAfee is the exclusive St. Louis representative of Who's Who in Luxury Real Estate and RELO, the largest network of leading independent residential real estate firms in the country.

LAURA MCCARTHY REAL ESTATE
124 North Gay Avenue, Clayton
(314) 725-5100
2730 North Ballas Road, Town and Country
(314) 569-1177
www.lauramccarthy.com
Laura McCarthy is an exclusively residential, primarily suburban St. Louis real estate company that specializes in the area's established, upscale neighborhoods. The company was founded in 1944 and is still considered a respected name in St. Louis real estate. There are two offices in the St. Louis area with a staff of more than 100 agents who deal with properties in University City, Clayton, Ladue, Frontenac, Olivette, Creve Coeur, Brentwood, Warson Woods, Glendale, Kirkwood, Webster Groves, Des Peres, and Town and Country. McCarthy agents are knowledgeable about the area's array of private schools, medical facilities, and housing featuring various kinds of architecture, as well as the communities that offer exceptional youth soccer, baseball, and basketball programs.

RE/MAX PROPERTIES WEST
16100 Swingley Ridge Road, Chesterfield
(636) 532-5900, (800) 949-0490
www.remax-propertieswest-chesterfield-mo.com
This West County RE/MAX office specializes in residential and commercial properties in Chesterfield, Ladue, Ballwin, Wildwood, Creve Couer, Clayton and St. Charles, and features more than 90 agents.

RE/MAX RESULTS
6407 Hampton Avenue
(314) 352-7770
www.remax.com
More than 15 sales associates work out of this independently owned and operated RE/MAX office, specializing in properties available throughout the Richmond Heights, Webster Groves, Kirkwood, University City, and city of St Louis areas. Both this office and the aforementioned RE/MAX Properties West office are part of the RE/MAX real estate network, which started in Denver in 1973. Today this global franchise spreads across 43 countries on six continents and includes nearly 80,000 sales associates in more than 4,400 offices worldwide.

Apartments and Rental Housing
If you're looking to rent for a while before settling into a more permanent residence, St. Louis has plenty of new and not-so-new apartments and houses, as well as duplexes, carriage houses, and garage apartments to suit almost every taste. The Central West End has a number of renovated carriage houses and former servants quarters that can be rented, and a number of spacious one- and two-bedroom flats can be found in South City and the Southampton neighborhoods. Downtown has dozens of rental properties available, ranging from studio apartments to luxury lofts, and the outer regions of St. Louis County are equipped with large apartment complexes that can accommodate most price ranges. University City has numerous apartments throughout the area, but they get snapped up quickly right before school starts in the fall, and any vacancies are usually filled when the students return from the holiday break.

For a good look at what's available and where to find it, check out the classified ads in the Friday through Sunday editions of the *St. Louis Post-Dispatch* or the weekly *Riverfront Times*, or go to the Post Dispatch's Web site, www.stltoday.com, for daily updates to the online classifieds.

There's a free publication called Apartment Guide that lists most of the area's apartment complexes, and it is distributed via street-corner boxes alongside those for the *Post-Dispatch, Riverfront Times, Employment Weekly,* and the *St. Louis American.*

Metropolis St. Louis, a grassroots organization of young St. Louisans dedicated to making St. Louis a more vital place to live, has a Web site that features a number of housing options. In addition to listings of individual apartments (instead of complexes), the site includes extended-stay options and area houses for sale throughout the city. Log on to www.mstl.org and click on the "Relocating" link for details. Or, visit the universal find-whatever-you're-looking-for Web site, www.craigslist.com and click on St. Louis and housing.

DRIVER'S LICENSES AND VEHICLE REGISTRATION

If you have a valid driver's license issued by another state or one that expired less than 184 days ago, you will only have to take the written, vision, and road-sign tests, not the driving test. A valid out-of-state license, one additional proof of identification, and proof of a Social Security number are required. After passing the tests, new residents can proceed to a Department of Revenue driver's license office. For the location nearest you, check the blue pages of the phone book. For the easiest one-stop shopping, however, visit the State of Missouri's motor vehicle office located at 4626 South Kingshighway (314) 752-5100. You can take the tests and get a new driver's license and new license plates all at one place. Missouri driver's licenses are $10 (good for three years) and $20 (good for six years).

Within 30 days of moving into the state, you'll need to register your vehicle at one of the Missouri Department of Revenue contract offices (see sidebar on page 194). In addition to passing a safety and vehicle emissions inspection, applicants must provide proof of auto insurance, a title or other proof of ownership, and a statement of non-assessment from the county tax assessor. Missourians pay personal property taxes on their cars, so you'll need proof that you are not delinquent for last year's taxes before your vehicle can be registered. Safety inspections are available at most local full-service gas stations throughout the area, and the Gateway Clean Air Program (888) 748-1AIR; www.gatewayclean air.com) performs emissions inspections. For a complete licensing checklist, or to get additional information, call the Missouri Department of Motor Vehicles at (573) 751-4450, or log on to http://dor.mo.gov/.

Illinois residents have up to 90 days to get their new driver's license, but the state adheres to the same 30-day rule for vehicle registration. For more information call the Illinois office of the Secretary of State at (800) 252-8980 or log on to www.cyberdriveillinois.com.

VOTER REGISTRATION

You can register to vote in Missouri by completing a Missouri Voter Registration Application and taking it to the St. Louis City Election Board (300 North Tucker Boulevard; 314-622-4336, www.stlelections.com) in downtown St. Louis. You can also take the application to a deputy registrar in your community or a voter registration agency (DMV, Health and Social Services, Community and Regional Affairs, or recruitment offices of the armed forces of the United States), or it can be mailed to the elections office in your jurisdiction. The St. Louis County Election Board (12 Sunnen Drive, Maplewood; 314-615-1800, www.co.st-louis.mo.us/ELECTIONS/) has more than 600 registration sites, including most city halls, libraries and schools. The deadline for registering to vote in an election is the fourth Wednesday prior to the election.

CHAMBERS OF COMMERCE

The St. Louis Regional Chamber and Growth Association (RCGA) (1 Metropolitan Square, Suite 1300; 314-231-5555; www.stlrcga.org) is an all-encompassing chamber of commerce and economic development organization for the greater

St. Louis region. RCGA services the city of St. Louis and St. Louis County, as well as the Missouri counties of St. Charles, Lincoln, Warren, Franklin, and Jefferson. On the Illinois side of the river, RCGA's territory includes the counties of St. Clair, Jersey, Madison, Clinton, and Monroe. The organization's 4,000-strong membership base makes up nearly 40 percent of the bi-state's regional workforce. Businesses of all sizes, including nonprofits, government agencies, labor organizations, and a variety of other area institutions, make up RCGA's membership, and the organization markets the region nationally and internationally to attract targeted industries to the area and help spur economic development.

Department of Revenue Motor Vehicle and Driver's License Contract Offices

St. Louis City:

4628 South Kingshighway; (314) 752-3177

1330 Aubert Avenue, Room 102B; (314) 454-1071

AAA St. Louis License Office 3917 Lindell Boulevard; (314) 531-0700

St. Louis City Hall License Office 1200 Market Street, Room 106; (314) 622-4231

St. Louis County locations:

9503 Gravois Road, Affton; (314) 631-1311

1711 Clarkson Road, Chesterfield; (636) 530-9500

32 North Central Avenue, Clayton; (314) 863-5331

3238 Laclede Station Road, Maplewood; (314) 645-1044

LIBRARIES

The centerpiece of the St. Louis Public Library (SLPL) system is the Central Library branch (1301 Olive Street; 314-241-2288). The main library and the collection of branch locations offer books, magazines, audio and video cassettes, CDs, CD-ROMs, DVDs, and many other kinds of materials. Library cards are free to city of St. Louis, St. Louis County, and St. Charles County residents and property owners, as well as to those attending school or working in the city. This also includes those who live in and/or pay taxes in the following library districts: Brentwood, Kirkwood, Maplewood, Richmond Heights, Rock Hill, University City, and Webster Groves. You can apply for a library card in person at any SLPL location, and current identification is required at the time of registration and renewal. Library cards are valid for one year and may be used at all SLPL locations. For minors 17 and younger, guardians may approve borrowing privileges.

The SLPL's Film Library, located at the Central branch, offers a wide variety of films in two primary collections: Rotating and Public Performance. The Rotating Collection contains thousands of popular titles from every era and genre, including the same titles available in the big-name video stores. The Public Performance Collection offers an array of documentaries, educational films, and other media that are invaluable to educators, lecturers, and home-schoolers, including current titles, fiction and nonfiction books on tape and CD, and a collection of film-related books.

There are 17 branch locations within the SLPL system, including Baden, Barr, Buder, Cabanne, Carondelet, Carpenter, Central, Central Express, Charing Cross, Divoll, Film Library, Julia Davis, Kingshighway, Schlafly, Machacek, Marketplace, and Walnut Park. For more information call (314) 241-2288 or log on to www.slpl.lib.mo.us.

TOURISM BUREAUS

GREATER SAINT CHARLES CONVENTION AND VISITORS BUREAU

230 South Main Street, St. Charles
(800) 366-2427
www.historicstcharles.com

MISSOURI DEPARTMENT OF TOURISM

P.O. Box 1055
Jefferson City, MO 65102
(573) 751-4133, (800) 579-2100
www.visitmo.com

ST. LOUIS CONVENTION & VISITORS COMMISSION

701 Convention Plaza, Suite 300
(314) 421-1023, (800) 916-0040
www.explorestlouis.com

Visitor information centers are located in the Main and East terminals of Lambert–St. Louis International Airport, at Kiener Plaza St. Louis Union Station downtown, in Forest Park, and at Seventh Street and Washington Avenue inside the America's Center convention complex.

THE TOURISM BUREAU OF SOUTHWESTERN ILLINOIS

10950 Lincoln Trail
Fairview Heights, IL
(618) 397-1488, (800) 442-1488
www.thetourismbureau.org

HEALTH CARE AND WELLNESS

The St. Louis area is home to more than 50 hospitals, and its health-care facilities are among the best in the nation. Both Washington and Saint Louis universities have medical schools—which makes St. Louis one of only a few cities in the country that has two major medical schools. Two outstanding pediatric hospitals, St. Louis Children's and Cardinal Glennon Children's, take care of the region's tiniest patients.

Many patients from outside the metropolitan area as well as from other countries look to St. Louis for medical care, making St. Louis's facilities competitive with the likes of such prestigious medical institutions as the Mayo Clinic and the Sloan-Kettering Institute. In 2000 BJC International Health Services (IHS) was formed to help attract international patients to St. Louis and assist them through the health care process, and the medical schools of Washington and Saint Louis universities have also helped to promote St. Louis as a major health center.

HEALTH DEPARTMENTS

CITY OF ST. LOUIS DEPARTMENT OF HEALTH
634 North Grand Boulevard
(314) 612-5100
www.stlouis.missouri.org/citygov/health
The city health department provides a number of health- and safety-related services for St. Louis residents, including implementation of mosquito spraying (an absolute necessity in St. Louis) and school immunizations to AIDS/HIV testing and information on lead poisoning. The city health department also oversees the local restaurant industry to make sure that eating and drinking establishments maintain healthy cooking and dining environments, enforces laws and regulations that protect public health and ensure safety, and evaluates the effectiveness, accessibility, and quality of personal and community health services.

ST. LOUIS COUNTY DEPARTMENT OF HEALTH
111 South Meramac Avenue, Clayton
(314) 615-0600
www.co.st-louis.mo.us/doh
The St. Louis County Department of Health offers comprehensive health care, including prevention and primary care, at public health centers, nursing facilities, and mental-health centers throughout St. Louis County. This health department also provides information on communicable disease control, sexually transmitted diseases, and biological terrorism.

URGENT-CARE/WALK-IN HEALTH CENTERS

Urgent-care facilities are designed to provide faster treatment for minor injuries and illnesses at much lower costs than are usually incurred in hospital emergency rooms. These clinics specialize in treating minor medical problems such as the flu, pulled muscles, minor cuts, sprained ankles, and sore throats. The following clinics are open daily.

AFTER-HOURS PEDIATRIC URGENT CARE CENTER
1751 Clarkson Road, Chesterfield
(636) 519-9559
www.afterhoursstl.com

Highway K & Laura Hill
O'Fallon, MO
(636) 379-9633

ST. LOUIS CONNECTCARE–SMILEY URGENT CARE CENTER
5535 Delmar Boulevard
(314) 879-6300
www.stlconnectcare.org

ST. LUKE'S URGENT CARE
233 Clarkson Road, Ellisville
(636) 256-8644

5551 Winghaven Boulevard, O'Fallon
(636) 695-2500
www.stlukes-stl.com

HOSPITALS

BARNES-JEWISH HOSPITAL
1 Barnes-Jewish Hospital Plaza at
South Kingshighway
(314) 747-3000
www.barnesjewish.org
Barnes-Jewish—often just called "Barnes"—is the largest hospital in Missouri, a result of the 1996 merger between Barnes Hospital and the Jewish Hospital of St. Louis. As the flagship hospital of BJC Health Care, Barnes-Jewish has an excellent reputation in patient care, medical education, research, and community service, and it is the primary adult teaching hospital of the Washington University School of Medicine. The facility has a 1,700-member medical staff that includes full-time faculty of Washington University and a number of private physicians. The medical staff is supported by a staff of more than 900 residents, interns, and fellows, as well as professional nurses, technicians, and service and support personnel. The hospital's collective of facilities and services includes the Center for Advanced Medicine and the Alvin J. Siteman Cancer Center. The Siteman Center is the only NCI-designated cancer center in the region, and the Charles F. Knight Trauma and Emergency Center is the only American College of Surgeons–verified Level I trauma center in St. Louis. The Rehabilitation Institute of St. Louis, a joint venture of BJC Health Care, Health-South, and the Washington University School of Medicine, is the only free-standing

rehabilitation hospital within a 120-mile radius of St. Louis, and this 80-bed facility offers inpatient and outpatient rehabilitation services as well as rehab-related research and acute inpatient medical therapy services.

i In 2008, Barnes-Jewish Hospital ranked 12th in the nation on the Best Hospitals Honor Roll according to *U.S. News & World Report.*

BARNES-JEWISH WEST COUNTY HOSPITAL
12634 Olive Boulevard
(314) 996-8410
www.barnesjewishwestcounty.org
Barnes-Jewish West County Hospital is a 113-bed facility in west St. Louis County that offers a full range of health care services and medical and surgical specialties. Barnes-Jewish West is noted for excellence in orthopedics and sports medicine, cosmetic surgery, urology, dermatology, general medicine, and diagnostic services. The radiology department is equipped with the latest technology and specialized equipment, such as high-speed MRI and spiral CT capable of 3D imaging, and it also offers complete noninvasive cardiac and diagnostic procedures.

CARDINAL GLENNON CHILDREN'S HOSPITAL
1465 South Grand Boulevard
(314) 577-5600
www.cardinalglennon.com
Cardinal Glennon Children's Hospital, a member of SSM Health Care, serves more than 200,000 children every year, from the tiniest newborns to adolescents. All of the hospital's physicians and nurses are specifically trained for pediatric medicine, and Glennon is a teaching hospital affiliated with Saint Louis University Schools of Medicine and Nursing. The hospital's Dan Dierdorf Emergency and Trauma Center is a 24-hour, Level 1 emergency center that is specially designed to treat children, and the hospital's Acute Care Center handles children whose conditions do

not require the critical care services of an emergency room, but who are faced with such classic childhood conditions as fever, vomiting, diarrhea, colds, or infections. The Bob Costas Cancer Center is a 16-bed inpatient facility that includes a four-bed bone marrow/stem cell transplant unit, Pediatric Research Institute research facilities, and the St. Louis Cord Blood Bank, which provides stem-cell bone-marrow transplants. The sophisticated resources available in Glennon's Pediatric Intensive Care Unit are ready for patients with diverse medical needs: transplant surgery patients, young victims of serious traumatic injuries, and children who need extra corporeal membrane oxygenation (ECMO). There's also a Pediatric Rehabilitation Institute that is the only facility of its kind in the St. Louis region, and a state-of-the-art Surgery Center and Neonatal Intensive Care Unit.

Emergency Phone Numbers at a Glance

Animal Control: (314) 353-5838

Life Crisis Services, Inc.
suicide prevention hotline:
(314) 647-HELP

Hazardous Materials hotline:
(314) 444-5555

Missing Persons: (314) 444-5555

St. Louis Poison Control Center:
(314) 772-5200 or
(800) 222-1222

CHRISTIAN HOSPITAL NORTHEAST DIVISION
11133 Dunn Road
(314) 653-5000
www.christianhospital.org
Christian Hospital, a member of the BJC Health Care network, is a 493-bed acute-care facility located in north St. Louis County. It offers a full range of health care services and an array of medical and surgical specialties. Noted for its cardiology services, the nonprofit hospital's medical staff comprises more than 600 physicians and more than 2,500 health care professionals. It's also known for outstanding cancer care, psychiatric care, diabetes treatment, and substance-abuse programs.

DEPAUL HEALTH CENTER
12303 DePaul Drive, Bridgeton
(314) 344-6000
www.ssmdepaul.com
SSM DePaul Health Center is a full-service Catholic hospital in northwest St. Louis County. The 450-bed facility specializes in emergency services and treats such ailments as chest pain, acute illness, and trauma in its Level II trauma center,

and it also has mental-health services, substance-abuse programs, and a Senior Specialty Center for older patients with special needs. DePaul's Heart Institute features the latest in prevention, diagnosis, and treatment of heart problems, and the hospital's state-of-the-art facilities enable its surgeons to perform procedures such as laparoscopic gallbladder surgery; laser and microsurgery of the eye, ear, nose, and throat; and maxillofacial surgery.

MISSOURI BAPTIST MEDICAL CENTER
3015 North Ballas Road
(314) 996-5000
www.missouribaptist.org
Missouri Baptist is a 489-bed acute-care hospital located in west St. Louis County that offers a variety of medical and surgical services. The facility specializes in women's health, heart services, cancer services, and orthopedics, and the hospital's Cardiac and Vascular Center offers a comprehensive list of services focused on prevention, diagnosis, intervention, and rehabilitation, along with a range of wellness programs and activities. Missouri Baptist is an affiliate of BJC Health Care.

SAINT LOUIS UNIVERSITY HOSPITAL
1635 Vista Avenue
(314) 268-5800
www.sluhospital.com
Saint Louis University Hospital (SLU), part of the Tenet St. Louis network, is a 356-bed academic teaching hospital for Saint Louis University's health-sciences professional clinical programs, including the university's school of medicine. The facility offers treatment for a variety of diseases and disorders and features specialty treatment for bone, joint, and brain diseases; cancer; and cardiovascular and digestive diseases and disorders. In addition to its trauma and emergency medicine facilities, the hospital includes the Endovascular Treatment Center and the Adult Congenital Heart Disease Specialty Clinic. SLU also utilizes the Cyber Knife Stereotactic Radiosurgery System in its arsenal of treatments of tumors and lesions in what were previously considered "inoperable" areas of the brain, lung, neck, and spine.

ST. LOUIS CHILDREN'S HOSPITAL
1 Children's Place at South Kingshighway
(314) 454-6000
www.stlouischildrens.org
St. Louis Children's Hospital has been providing specialized care for children for more than a century and offers a full range of medical services, including pediatric cardiology and cardiothoracic surgery, pediatric organ transplants, cancer care, neurology, and neurosurgery. The hospital is affiliated with the Washington University School of Medicine, which is ranked as one of the top five medical schools in the country. St. Louis Children's is a member of BJC Health Care, the first fully integrated health care system in the country to join an academic medical center with suburban-, rural-, and metropolitan-based health care facilities. Children's also has stellar specialty facilities, including a comprehensive cerebral palsy center, the Cleft Palate and Craniofacial Deformities Institute, and the most active pediatric lung transplant program in the world. Other specialties include the cochlear implant program, pediatric eye care, epilepsy and seizure disorders, and pediatric plastic surgery. In 2007 *Child* magazine named the facility as one of the "10 Best Pediatric Hospitals" in the nation, and US News & World Report rated it one of the nation's best in the 2008 edition of "America's Best Children's Hospitals."

ST. MARY'S HEALTH CENTER
6420 Clayton Road, Richmond Heights
(314) 768-8000
www.stmarys-stlouis.com
SSM St. Mary's Health Center is a 600-bed facility with more than 800 physicians on staff, representing all medical specialties. The hospital is a major tertiary hospital affiliated with Saint Louis University Medical School and offers services that include comprehensive obstetrics and cardiology services, including high-risk obstetrics and open-heart surgery, total joint replacement, and advanced breast cancer detection approaches, including the stereotactic needle core biopsy, an outpatient procedure that allows physicians to extract tiny tissue samples without surgery. St. Mary's Emergency Department is a state-of-the-art facility that provides special facilities for OB/GYN patients, a decontamination room to treat chemical exposures, and an area specifically designed to quickly identify and treat heart problems.

PHYSICIAN REFERRAL SERVICES
The following is a list of referral services for area physicians. All participating doctors are affiliated with specific hospital systems within the metropolitan area, and many are affiliated with area teaching hospitals, including Washington and St. Louis Universities.

BJC Health Care System (314) 362-WELL
SLU Care (314) 977-4440
SSM Health Care (314) SSM-DOCS
St. Louis Children's Hospital Answer Line
    (314) 454-KIDS
Washington University Physicians
    (314) TOP-DOCS

i If you have a medical emergency during your stay in the St. Louis area, St. Mary's Health Center (6420 Clayton Road) in nearby Richmond Heights offers more immediate attention than many of the larger hospitals' emergency rooms.

MENTAL-HEALTH RESOURCES

MENTAL HEALTH AMERICA OF EASTERN MISSOURI.
1905 South Grand Boulevard
(314) 773-1399
www.mhaem.org
The Mental Health America of Eastern Missouri is a not-for-profit, nongovernmental, charitable corporation that deals with the entire spectrum of mental health and mental illness. The organization is affiliated with Mental Health America, the oldest and largest volunteer movement in the country devoted to mental health and mental illness. MHAEM serves citizens in St. Louis City and St. Louis County, as well as residents of St. Charles, Lincoln, Warren, Franklin, and Jefferson counties

MISSOURI DEPARTMENT OF MENTAL HEALTH
5400 Arsenal Street
(314) 877-0370
www.dmh.missouri.gov
This organization combats the stigma associated with mental illness, developmental disabilities, and substance addiction and provides services to the community such as suicide prevention, counseling, and comprehensive psychiatric services for children and adults throughout the state.

PROVIDENT COUNSELING ADMINISTRATIVE OFFICE (FOR INFORMATION AND FIRST APPOINTMENTS)
2650 Olive Street
(314) 533-8200, (800) 782-1008
www.providentc.org
Provident, with locations in St. Louis City, West County, South County, Jefferson County, and Belleville, Illinois, offers counseling for addiction, domestic abuse, life crisis, and victims of sexual, physical, and emotional abuse. Their community services involvement includes youth-focused programs, skills development, and assistance with child custody and supervised visitation agreements.

i Traveling with Fido or Mr. Boots? In the event of a medical emergency that involves the beloved family pet, head for the Animal Emergency Clinic at 9937 Big Bend Boulevard (314) 822–7600, which is open 24 hours a day, 7 days a week.

HOSPICE CARE

BJC HOSPICE
9890 Clayton Road
(314) 872-5050
www.bjchospice.org
BJC offers a holistic and multidisciplinary approach to patients who have a physician-determined six-month prognosis. Treatment and care are provided by a skilled team of health care professionals sensitive to the emotional and spiritual needs of both adult and pediatric patients. The facility has locations in Illinois (618) 463-7100, Sullivan, Missouri (573) 468-3630 and Parkland, Missouri (573) 760-8550.

SSM HOSPICE
10143 Paget Drive
(314) 989-2700
www.ssmhomecare.com
SSM Hospice, part of the SSM Health Care system, provides home care services throughout the bi-state region as well as hospice care at its Paget Drive location. SSM serves clients in the city of St. Louis and St. Louis County, as well as St. Charles, Jefferson, Franklin, Warren, Lincoln, and eastern Montgomery counties.

VISITING NURSE ASSOCIATION HOSPICE CARE (VNA)

9450 Manchester Road, Webster Groves
(314) 918-7171
www.vnastl.com

VNA services numerous hospitals and private nursing facilities throughout the greater St. Louis area and also provides in-home care. The VNA team includes nurses, social workers, home health aides, and members of the clergy, and it even offers follow-up care to help families deal with grief.

ALTERNATIVE MEDICINE

For those who prefer alternative or holistic health practices to the standard offerings of Western medicine, there are a number of practitioners who feel they can poke, crack, stick, and massage you to a healthier and more harmonious sense of well-being. While these techniques tend to be less invasive and produce fewer side effects than those associated with traditional medicine, there has been less research and independent verification of the benefits of holistic approaches as well.

BRENTWOOD CENTER OF HEALTH

2558 South Brentwood Boulevard
(314) 961-8940
www.bcoh.org

This multispecialty health clinic, which focuses on women's health, offers customers a more holistic approach to healing via acupuncture, physical therapy, massages, yoga, Chinese herbs, tai chi, infant massages and support for the treatment of lymphedema. The therapists at the center also offer alternative medicine treatments for fertility issues, menstrual cycle regulation, pain, and other maladies. Closed Sunday.

CHESTERFIELD HEALTH CENTER

1851 Schoettler Road, Chesterfield
(636) 227-0903
www.logan.edu

Operated by the Logan College of Chiropractic, Chesterfield Health Center offers a full range of ser-

vices. In addition to consultations, physical exams, X-rays, and lab work, spinal adjustments, rehab programs, physical therapy, and a variety of "take-home" treatments are offered. Closed Sunday.

WEBSTER GROVES HEALTH CENTER

8071 Watson Road
(314) 961-2451
www.logan.edu

Operated by the Logan College of Chiropractic, this clinic offers the same services as Chesterfield Health Center (see listing). Closed Sunday.

WELLNESS COMMUNITY OF GREATER ST. LOUIS

1058 Old Des Peres Road, Des Peres
(314) 238-2000
www.wellnesscommunitystl.org

The Wellness Community (TWC) is a national nonprofit organization that provides support and education to people who have been diagnosed with cancer. St. Louis's chapter is one of 23 TWC organizations located throughout the United States. Through participation in professionally led support groups, educational workshops, and mind/body classes utilizing the Patient Active Concept, people affected by cancer can learn vital skills that enable them to regain control, reduce isolation, and restore hope regardless of the stage of their disease.

SUPPORT ORGANIZATIONS

ALZHEIMER'S ASSOCIATION, ST. LOUIS CHAPTER HELPLINE

9374 Olive Boulevard
(314) 432-3422
www.alzstl.org

This association offers support, education, and services for those suffering from Alzheimer's. Caregivers can get legal, financial, and medical assistance, as well as resources for adult day care and hospice services. The toll-free phone number is staffed 24 hours a day.

ST. LOUIS EFFORT FOR AIDS (EFA)
1027 South Vandeventer, Suite 700
(314) 645-6451
www.stlefa.org
The St. Louis EFA provides education about prevention of HIV and offers support and services to individuals living with HIV and AIDS. Besides mental-health services and numerous support groups throughout the area, the organization offers educational programs, assistance with workplace reentry, and information on treatment options.

ST. LOUIS PEREGRINE SOCIETY (SLPS)
2343 Hampton Avenue
(314) 781-6775
www.peregrinesoc.org
This society has been helping cancer patients and their families since 1949. Serving both the city of St. Louis and St. Louis County, SLPS funds recreational programs for children with cancer; offers nutritional supplements for adult patients; provides prescription and transportation assistance, equipment, and medical supplies; and assists with the purchase of prosthetic devices.

SUSAN G. KOMEN BREAST CANCER FOUNDATION–ST. LOUIS AFFILIATE
9288 Dielman Industrial Drive
(314) 569-3900
www.komenstlouis.org
The St. Louis affiliate of the Susan G. Komen Breast Cancer Foundation does an excellent job raising awareness about breast cancer and signs up more than 60,000 people each year to participate in the annual Komen Race for the Cure, held in June. St. Louis has one of the highest attended events in the country, with more than 64,000 participants in 2006. During October, National Breast Cancer Awareness Month, the local affiliate produces a number of additional fund-raising activities and events. The organization also provides information on group meeting dates for breast cancer survivors, educates breast health volunteers, and hosts an annual survivor event in May. There's also a strong speakers bureau in place and a support group for children and grandchildren of breast cancer patients.

EDUCATION AND CHILD CARE

S t. Louis was the site of the country's first public kindergarten in 1873, and it has long been a leader in education. Many of the current institutions were "firsts," including the first educational facility, medical school, and advanced degree program offered west of the Mississippi River. Today the region includes more than 100 school districts and 300 private schools. The post-secondary educational scene is rife with well-respected colleges, universities, technical schools, and community colleges, which attract students from around the world. With all of this cultural diversity and educational opportunities, it's odd that St. Louis remains a region that is absolutely fascinated by its high schools. Newcomers and visitors are often greeted with the question, "So—where did you go to high school?" by unwitting locals who don't know that the out-of-towners are, well, from out of town. Many attribute the question to nosy locals trying to figure out what economic situation you were born into, while others see it as a way of trying to figure out if you have mutual friends or acquaintances. Whatever the reason, it's always a good opening line or a way to break the ice with a stranger in a business or social setting. St. Louisans remain loyal to their beloved alma maters as well, with Friday night often set aside as high school football nights in many current and former high school households.

PUBLIC SCHOOLS

City of St. Louis

ST. LOUIS PUBLIC SCHOOLS
801 North 11th Street
(314) 231-3720
www.slps.org

Like so many major cities, St. Louis's public school system has had its share of problems. In 2003 the school system was declared a provisionally accredited district, and it remained at that status as of 2008. In October 2006 the Missouri Department of Elementary and Secondary Education released summary data of Missouri school districts' Annual Performance Reports (APR) for the 2005–6 school year. The APR of St. Louis Public Schools (SLPS) shows that the district earned only 39 of 66 performance points needed for full accreditation, so the district remains provisionally accredited.

There are about 28,000 students in the SLPS system, from preschool through grade 12. SLPS has a total of 84 schools, which includes 52 elementary schools, 17 middle schools, 14 high schools, and 4 special schools. Of the 84 the district offers 27 magnet schools, including 14 elementary, 8 middle, and 5 high schools. Magnet school programs include Montessori, basic instruction, individually guided education, military academies, visual/performing arts, international studies, math, science and technology, multimedia electronic graphic arts, and the gifted academies.

The racial mix for SLPS is 81 percent African American, 14 percent Caucasian, and 5 percent Asian, Hispanic, or Indian. More than 80 percent of the students in the SLPS system are eligible for free and reduced lunches.

Teachers in the SLPS system average 12 years of experience each, with more than 44 percent of the administrators, teachers, and support staff holding advanced degrees. The average student-teacher ratio is 18 to 1, and more than 87 percent of the teaching staff have acquired life, professional, and continuing professional certificates. SLPS also provides special education and early-childhood special education programs, coordinates Parents as Teachers and Gifted Education programs, and offers advanced placement and technical offerings such as agricultural science, business education, health occupations, computers, marketing, family and consumer science, and trade/industrial education.

Students are assigned to city schools based on the parents' address. For each address in the city, there is an assigned elementary, middle, and high school, and usually the assigned school is the closest one to each address. Parents may enroll students who are new to the school district at the Recruitment and Counseling Center at 801 North 11th Street, and they need to bring proof of address as well as the child's birth certificate and immunization record. Preschool students (three and four years old), kindergarteners (five years old), and first-graders (six years old) must be age-eligible before August 1.

Assignment to one of the district's magnet schools is based on the results of a lottery process, which allows each child an equal chance to be accepted in accordance with the priority guidelines established by the district. Parents can list up to three schools that they would accept as a magnet school selection. Each magnet school features a different educational focus or theme. For example, Kennard Classical Junior Academy (CJA), the only full-time, gifted public elementary school in the area, features a curriculum that is designed to challenge students' analytical and critical thinking skills. Primary-school students at Marshall Multimedia Electronic Graphic Arts (MEGA) magnet school, however, work with the hottest computer technology to learn three-dimensional drawing, special effects, and virtual-reality skills that are useful for careers in graphic design and software and Web site development.

Students also have the opportunity to attend a magnet cluster, which is three schools—one elementary, one middle, and one high school—that offer a continuous, interdisciplinary instructional program emphasizing high academic achievement. The International Studies Magnet Cluster focus is world languages, cultures, and global awareness, which allows students to develop skills in problem solving, critical thinking, technology, and language proficiency.

Besides the St. Louis–born population, the magnet cluster consists of students and teachers from such countries as Bosnia, China, Ethiopia, Herzegovina, India, Italy, Laos, Morocco, Poland, Romania, Russia, Somalia, Spain, and Vietnam. One of the program's key components is that all students must study a world language throughout their school career. Students at Soldan High School are introduced to the school's theme through Introduction to International Studies, a required course for Soldan freshmen. At the high school level, students can even take classes that earn college credit at the University of Missouri–St. Louis. In addition to Soldan, the ISC course of study is taught at Dewey Elementary and Bunche Middle Schools.

i The St. Louis Regional Chamber & Growth Association (RCGA) offers two publications to help relocated families find child-care and educational facilities throughout the bi-state region: A Parent's Guide to Choosing Child Care and Selecting the Right School for Your Child. Call the RCGA at (314) 231–5555 or log on to www.stlrcga.org for a complete list of materials available

St. Louis County

There are almost as many school districts in St. Louis County as there are municipalities—your neighborhood school is truly that. The vast collection of county schools is broken down into districts for Affton, Kirkwood, Ritenour, Bayless, Ladue, Riverview Gardens, Brentwood, Lindbergh, Rockwood, Clayton, Maplewood–Richmond Heights, Special School District, Ferguson-Florissant, Mehlville, University City, Hancock Place, Normandy, Valley Park, Hazelwood, Parkway, Webster Groves, Jennings, Pattonville, and Wellston. The Clayton, Kirkwood, and Ladue school districts are renowned for offering students a quality education from elementary through high school. Clayton and Ladue Horton Watkins high schools, located in the upscale suburbs of Clayton and Ladue, respectively, are well respected academically and athletically. For specific information about the various county school districts, call or log on to the individual municipality's Web site.

CLAYTON SCHOOL DISTRICT
#2 Mark Twain Circle, Clayton
(314) 854-6000
www.clayton.k12.mo.us
The Clayton School District encompasses three elementary schools, one middle school, and one high school. The district strives to maintain its student to teacher ratio of 12:1, and Clayton schools are considered one of the nation's premier school systems and are regularly ranked among the county's best in terms of Missouri Assessment Program (MAP) and Adequate Yearly Progress (AYP) results. Nearly half of its teachers—46 percent—have more than 16 years of teaching experience, and student demographics are 70 percent Caucasian, 22 percent African American, and 8 percent Asian, Hispanic, or Native American. Clayton's The Family Center offers a variety of parent-child and parent education programs, support groups, and a Special Services Program that features development screening, early childhood special education, and individual and family counseling.

i Immunizations required to enter school in Missouri include diphtheria, tetanus, pertussis, polio, measles, rubella, mumps, and hepatitis B. For details call the Missouri Department of Health at (800) 699–2313.

KIRKWOOD SCHOOL DISTRICT R-7
11289 Manchester Road, Kirkwood
(314) 213-6100
www.kirkwood.k12.mo.us
The Kirkwood district continuously produces students who consistently score above state and national standardized tests through personalized learning, smaller classes, and gifted and special-education programs. There are five elementary schools, two middle schools, and one high school in the district, which has been accredited with

distinction by the Missouri Department of Education. In 1992 Kirkwood High School (KHS) became a member of the Coalition of Essential Schools, a national educational communication network founded in 1984. KHS's membership in this coalition stresses a more focused, community-based effort in the school district's continuing efforts to improve the high school's educational opportunities. The student teacher ratio is 17:1, and the demographic make-up is 75 percent Caucasian, 18 percent African American, and 7 percent Asian, Hispanic and Indian.

LADUE SCHOOLS
1201 South Warson Road
(314) 993-6447
www.ladue.k12.mo.us
The Ladue Schools system includes four elementary schools, one middle school, and one high school. The tiny district was recognized by the state of Missouri for Distinction in Performance each year from 2001 to 2006. Ladue High offers an impressive educational environment for students in grades 9 through 12. The annual enrollment averages 1,200, and the student-teacher ratio is 13 to 1. Demographically, the high school breaks down as 72 percent Caucasian, 17 percent African American, 9 percent Asian, 2 percent Hispanic, and 1 percent other. The average per-pupil expenditure is a little more than $12,300.

PRIVATE SCHOOLS

Catholic Parochial

CATHOLIC EDUCATION OFFICE
20 Archbishop May Drive
(314) 792-7302
www.archstl.org/education
The Archdiocese of St. Louis operates the oldest and largest school system in the state, which is also the seventh-largest archdiocesan school system in the country. The percentage of families who choose Catholic schools for their children here is among the highest in the country, with about 50,000 students enrolled in the various elementary and high schools. All of the

archdiocese's 121 elementary schools are currently accredited by the Missouri Chapter of the National Federation of Non-Public School State Accrediting Associations, and its high schools are accredited by a recognized state, regional, or national accrediting association. These include the North Central Association of Schools and Colleges (NCA), National Federation of Non-Public School State Accrediting Associations–Missouri Chapter, Independent Schools Association of the Central States (ISACS), or University of Missouri Committee on Accrediting Non-Public Schools.

The archdiocese has 29 Catholic high schools that provide academic programs in secular subjects, as well as formal courses in the authentic teachings and practices of the Catholic Church, which offer the opportunity for Christian witness and service, liturgical celebrations, and personal guidance for growth in faith. The diversity provided by the schools afford a Catholic secondary education to students with a broad range of abilities, talents, and interests. The high schools are owned and operated by the archdiocese, and the administration of these coed and single-sex schools falls under the jurisdiction of the Superintendent and the Board of Catholic Education. Area archdiocesan high schools include Bishop DuBourg, Cardinal Ritter College Prep, John F. Kennedy, Rosati-Kain, St. Mary's, St. Pius X, and Trinity Catholic High School. Regional high schools, operated and supported by the archdiocese and the parishes in their region, include Duchesne in St. Charles, St. Dominic in O' Fallon, and St. Francis Borgia Regional High School in Washington. Parish high schools are a collaborative effort of the parish and the archdiocese and include St. John the Baptist College Prep in south St. Louis, St. Vincent in Perryville, and Valle Catholic High School in Ste. Genevieve. All three of these schools are coeducational.

Private Catholic high schools in the city of St. Louis and St. Louis County are sponsored and operated by specific religious communities that are financed through tuition, local funding, subsidies from the religious communities,

and endowments. These schools operate under authorization of the Archbishop, and the religious education program of these schools is under the jurisdiction of the Superintendent. All of the private Catholic schools are single-sex, with one exception, Gateway Academy. The private Catholic high schools for boys are Chaminade College Prep, Christian Brothers College High School, DeSmet Jesuit, Saint Louis University High, St. John Vianney, and St. Louis Priory School. The girls' private Catholic schools are Cor Jesu Academy, Incarnate Word Academy, Nerinx Hall, Notre Dame, St. Elizabeth Academy, St. Joseph's Academy, Ursuline Academy, Villa Duchesne School, and Visitation Academy.

CHRISTIAN BROTHERS COLLEGE HIGH SCHOOL
12433 North Outer Forty, Chesterfield
(314) 336-2000
www.cbchs.org

Christian Brothers College (CBC) is a Lasallian community founded by followers of St. John Baptist de La Salle in 1849. CBC's St. Louis campus was the first college of the Christian Brothers in the Americas, and it remains one of the most prestigious Catholic high schools in the region. A perennial powerhouse in academics and athletics, the all-male CBC has produced many of St. Louis's most celebrated athletes and corporate tycoons. CBC accepts applications for students entering ninth grade, and applications are due by December of the preceding year. Admission is based on the applicant's grades, scores on standardized tests, behavior reports from teachers and principals, and the ever-important "past association with CBC," including those who have relatives who are alumni of the school. Typically, CBC receives many more applicants than it can accept, so the admissions process is very competitive. The 240,000-square-foot campus includes an academic wing with 52 classrooms, a 3,000-seat athletic stadium, a 400-seat performing-arts center, a 500-seat dining hall, and an 1,800-seat gym.

NERINX HALL HIGH SCHOOL
530 East Lockwood, Webster Groves
(314) 968-1505
www.nerinxhs.org

Nerinx was founded by the Sisters of Loretto in 1924 as an independent, private Catholic school, and it remains one of the area's top college-preparatory high schools for women. It is always a major player in athletics, academics, and community services, so getting into the school is quite an accomplishment. Applications to the school, as well as the other Catholic schools in the area, are handled through the Archdiocese of St. Louis. Nerinx's student body represents all factions of the metropolitan area, and almost 95 percent of the 600 students are Roman Catholic. The school admits about 150 freshmen each year, and applications are submitted during early December of the previous year. Selection to the school is based on the student's grade-school report cards, standardized testing, and interviews held on campus. Nerinx's beautiful, tree-lined campus is located adjacent to Webster University in Webster Groves, a St. Louis suburb.

ROSATI-KAIN
4389 Lindell Boulevard
(314) 533-8513
www.rosati-kain.org

Rosati-Kain, a Catholic college-prep school for young women, is located in the Central West End neighborhood. Rosati-Kain was established from two separate educational institutions named for the first two Archbishops of St. Louis—Joseph Rosati and John Joseph Kain—that were merged to form one school in 1911. Today's student body is made up of girls from throughout metropolitan St. Louis. The school is accredited by the North Central Association and the Missouri Department of Education, and all of the courses offered are college preparatory. Athletics are a big part of the culture at Rosati-Kain, and the school has competitive teams in tennis, track, volleyball, softball, basketball, soccer, and swimming. The school application procedures are the same as those used by other area Catholic schools that are affiliated with the Archdiocese of St. Louis.

SAINT LOUIS UNIVERSITY HIGH SCHOOL
4970 Oakland Avenue
(314) 531-0330
www.sluh.org

Saint Louis University High School (SLUH), an all-boy Catholic, Jesuit educational institution, was founded in 1818 as St. Louis Academy. The school grew rapidly and eventually included a college, which was granted a charter as Saint Louis University in 1832. Located next door to the Saint Louis Science Center, SLUH remains one of the largest private schools in Missouri. The 1,000 students are drawn from more than 121 area elementary and middle schools, and SLUH's student body is comprised of young men from diverse geographic and economic backgrounds. Saint Louis University High is a major player in the local sports and scholastic scenes and boasts a number of prominent St. Louisans among its alumni. The school accepts applications for students entering the ninth grade, and applications for admission after the ninth grade, such as transfer students, are considered only on a space-available basis. Admission is based on the applicant's grades, scores on standardized tests, and an interview with the applicant and his parent or guardian. Like most of the more popular Catholic schools, the admissions process is extremely competitive.

INDEPENDENT SCHOOLS

INDEPENDENT SCHOOLS OF ST. LOUIS
101 North Warson Road
(314) 567-9229
www.independentschools.org

The Independent Schools of St. Louis, a nonprofit professional association established in 1972, includes 46 independently governed elementary and secondary schools throughout the St. Louis region. Each school undergoes a rigorous examination process every seven years to procure and maintain accreditation, and most member schools belong to the Independent Schools of the Central States (ISACS) and the National Association of Independent Schools (NAIS). Schools that are members of Independent Schools of St.

Louis provide a complete range of educational opportunities for students from kindergarten through grade 12 and include those that focus on traditional models of excellence in education as well as special-needs schools that specialize in areas that include learning differences or emotional and behavioral problems.

PRIVATE ELEMENTARY SCHOOLS

CLAYTON ACADEMY & PRESCHOOL
7501 Maryland Avenue, Clayton
(314) 727-0833
www.claytonacademy.org
Clayton Academy is a focused, coeducational, elementary- and middle-school facility that provides customized teaching in small groups. The facility mandates that the maximum class size be limited to ten students and places great importance on providing a creative atmosphere. Clayton Academy began in 1980 as a toddler/infant-care center and preschool and opened its private elementary school in 1991. The school adheres to the theory that every child learns differently, and educators tailor the programs to meet the specific needs of each child. All of the academy's teachers are accredited and hold master's degrees in education, and the facility is equipped with classrooms that are designed to engage and maintain children's attention.

COMMUNITY SCHOOL
900 North Lay Road
(314) 991-0005
www.communityschool.com
Founded in 1914, the Community School is an educational facility for children age three through the sixth grade. Located in the St. Louis suburb of Ladue, the campus is situated on a 16-acre wooded site that includes birds and forest creatures, native trees, and wildflowers, which provides an excellent backdrop for studying science and ecology. The curriculum at the Community School emphasizes fundamental skills augmented by classes in computers, art, woodworking, music, band, drama, physical education,

and French. The school is committed to diversity and multicultural awareness. The student-teacher ratio is 7 to 1, which allows the faculty to give individualized attention to each child.

NEW CITY SCHOOL
5209 Waterman Avenue
(314) 361-6411
www.newcityschool.org
New City is an elementary school that believes children possess numerous talents, and it is the role of the educator to identify and nurture those talents. The school, which features full-time specialist teachers in art, pre-primary movement, performing arts, physical education, library, science, and Spanish, is the most racially and socio-economically diverse of all of the St. Louis Confederation schools. New City's faculty has been utilizing the theory of Multiple Intelligences since the school's founding in 1988, and it has received nationwide attention for its efforts. The school is a member of the National Association of Independent Schools and offers programs for children age three through the sixth grade. Yearly enrollment is about 400 students, and admission is based on an in-person visit that allows teachers to observe the child in work and play situations, along with formal and informal assessment of the child's skill development.

PRIVATE SECONDARY SCHOOLS

CHAMINADE COLLEGE PREPARATORY SCHOOL
425 South Lindbergh Boulevard
(314) 993-4400
www.chaminade-stl.com
Chaminade College Preparatory School (CCPS) is an independent Catholic school for young men in grades 6 through 12 and provides a wide range of athletic, cultural, social, and religious activities as part of its total education program. Academically, Chaminade offers a rigorous curriculum that requires students to take classes that include religious studies, classical/modern languages, social studies, fine arts, practical arts, and numerous

sciences. As in all area high schools, athletics are tremendously popular here, and Chaminade regularly produces championship teams at the middle school, junior varsity, and varsity levels. In addition to the usual lineup of sports teams, CCPS offers hockey, water polo, golf, wrestling, and volleyball, and its athletic facilities are superior to those found in many professional, minor-league sports organizations. In addition to studying and playing sports, the students perform a total of 30,000 service hours per year. Students in grades 6 through 11 must work from 20 to 50 total hours per school year, while seniors are required to complete a 50-hour service project. The projects are coordinated through the school's Campus Ministry and religious-studies classes.

CROSSROADS COLLEGE PREPARATORY SCHOOL
500 DeBaliviere Avenue
(314) 367-8085
www.crossroads-school.org
Since 1974 Crossroads School has offered a coeducational, college-preparatory curriculum for students in grades 7 through 12. The school is known for its rich history of cultural diversity, and it approaches learning through intellectual, personal, and social growth in an atmosphere that is academically challenging but encourages respect for individual differences. The small school has an annual enrollment of about 200 students and strives to maintain close student/teacher relationships. Crossroads emphasizes exploration and self-expression in the classroom and features a curriculum that is sequential and interdisciplinary, often taking students beyond the classroom by utilizing the arts and educational opportunities available throughout the area.

JOHN BURROUGHS SCHOOL
755 South Price Road, Ladue
(314) 993-4040
www.jburroughs.org
John Burroughs is a coeducational, college-preparatory school that offers a liberal-arts education for students in grades 7 through 12. Founded in 1923, the school strives to balance academics,

the arts, and athletics with community service and environmental awareness. The 40-acre campus includes seven student-use buildings, and the school has as an outdoor facility located in the Missouri Ozarks that is used for education and community building. Burroughs offers small classes to enhance the students' ability to learn, and the school stresses ethics, diversity, student government, outdoor education, and other activities to supplement its curriculum. There's an on-site academic support program that is available to assist students with writing, math, and study skills. Admission is based on school records, recommendations, an entrance examination, and an interview, and the applicant's personal qualities are a major consideration.

MARY INSTITUTE AND ST. LOUIS COUNTRY DAY SCHOOL (MICDS)
101 North Warson Road
(314) 995-7367
www.micds.org
MICDS, a coed facility, is the result of a 1992 merger of two separate institutions: Mary Institute and Country Day School. Today MICDS offers a liberal-arts nonsectarian education for its 1,200 students from junior kindergarten through grade 12. The elementary school uses a developmentally interactive and interdisciplinary educational model that features a homeroom teacher who works with children in the core academic areas, and specialists in computers, science, studio art, drama, music, woodworking, Spanish, and physical education. Grades five through eight receive a unique blend of single-sex education—in mathematics, science, language arts, phys ed, and history—and coeducational learning in fine arts and foreign languages. High school students receive a challenging selection of academic choices, including Advanced Placement classes. The average class size is 16 students, and the pupil to teacher ratio is 8:1. There is a variety of activities, athletics, and opportunities to participate in the school's arts programs, as well as a strong emphasis placed on community service at all grade levels. MICDS is another of the area's heavy hitters when it comes to local athletics,

producing competitive teams in lacrosse, crew, field hockey, water polo, and ice hockey, in addition to the major sports like football, baseball, and basketball.

THOMAS JEFFERSON SCHOOL
4100 South Lindbergh Boulevard
(314) 843-4151
www.tjs.org
Founded in 1946, "TJ" offers a rigorous, core classical curriculum to an international array of boarding and day students in grades 7 to 12. The average class size is 14, and the overall student to teacher ratio is 7:1. Seven faculty members live on the grounds, and the scenic 20-acre campus features seven cottage-style dorms, two academic buildings, a gym, an athletic field, and tennis courts. In addition to stressing college preparatory work, the school has a variety of arts and activities offerings, and places high importance on the students' role in the community and personal responsibility.

UNIVERSITIES

FONTBONNE UNIVERSITY
6800 Wydown Boulevard, Clayton
(314) 862-3456
www.fontbonne.edu
Fontbonne University, a four-year, coeducational liberal-arts institution, is a small school that caters to approximately 3,000 students, many of whom are working professionals. The school offers 34 majors, 25 minors, and 16 master's degree programs that span a variety of disciplines, including a major in deaf education, communication disorders, dietetics, and business. Fontbonne, founded by the Sisters of St. Joseph of Carondelet in 1923, is accredited by the Higher Learning Commission and is a member of the North Central Association of Colleges and Schools.

LINDENWOOD UNIVERSITY
209 South Kingshighway, St. Charles
(636) 949-4949
www.lindenwood.edu
Lindenwood University is a four-year liberal-arts

college situated on a historic 500-acre campus in St. Charles. Lindenwood offers more than 120 undergraduate and graduate degree programs that include everything from art history and computer science to fashion design and pre-law. The school has an annual enrollment of nearly 15,000 students and features on-campus housing in traditional residence halls, apartment-style housing, married and single-parent, and nontraditional student housing options. The university, which is regularly named one of America's best Christian colleges, is accredited by accredited by the Higher Learning Commission of the North Central Association of Colleges and Schools.

MARYVILLE UNIVERSITY
13550 Conway Road
(800) 627-9855
www.maryville.edu
Maryville University was founded in 1872 by the Religious of the Sacred Heart, but it has evolved into an independent, coeducational university that offers 50 undergraduate programs, ranging from accounting to e-marketing to music therapy. Master's degrees offered at the school include education, nursing, rehabilitation counseling, business and health administration, and occupational and physical therapy. The university's 3,500 students, about half of which are undergraduates, includes more than 1,000 "Weekend College" students and a few hundred graduate students. Maryville has two coed residence halls and student apartments on campus that can accommodate 600 students. Classes here are kept small—traditionally averaging about a dozen students each—and the on-campus Academic Success Center and Advising Center offer individualized academic consultation and career exploration.

SAINT LOUIS UNIVERSITY
221 North Grand Boulevard
(800) SLU-FOR-U
www.slu.edu
Saint Louis University (SLU), founded in 1818, was the first institution of higher learning west of the Mississippi. The university was the first to have a graduate school in the "new" western region and

the first to begin schools of philosophy, divinity, medicine, law, and business. It was also the first Catholic university in the nation to have any of these constituent schools and specialized faculties. Today SLU educates 12,700-plus students and offers more than 85 undergraduate and 50 graduate programs in arts and sciences, business, engineering and aviation, nursing, public service, social service, and allied health professions. The school is known as a hotbed of collegiate soccer talent, with numerous pro players coming out of the Billikens' program. In fact, soccer is such a tradition at SLU that the school doesn't even have a football team. SLU is a NCAA Division I school and a member of the Atlantic 10 Conference. The school opened a new $80 million on-campus arena in 2008. Chaifetz Arena, the new home of the Billikens' basketball teams, also hosts a variety of live events such as concerts, graduation ceremonies, and other performances.

The SLU School of Medicine—one of the 12 schools that SLU comprises—was established in 1836. The Frost Campus at Grand and Lindell Boulevards in midtown St. Louis has been the site of the central administration since 1888. The university's College of Arts and Sciences, Graduate School, School of Law, College of Philosophy and Letters, John Cook School of Business, School of Social Service, and School for Professional Studies are all located on the Frost Campus, along with the Parks College of Engineering and Aviation. Parks College was founded in 1928 as the first federally approved air college and has been a part of SLU since 1946. The Health Sciences Center, located about a mile from the main campus, is home to the university's schools of medicine, nursing, allied health professions, and public health.

UNIVERSITY OF MISSOURI–ST. LOUIS
8001 Natural Bridge Road
(314) 516-5000
www.umsl.edu
UMSL, pronounced UM-zul by locals, is the largest university in the St. Louis area and the third largest in Missouri. Part of the University of Missouri system, the St. Louis location offers more than 50 undergraduate degree programs, seven pre-

professional programs, 34 master's-level degrees, and 15 doctoral programs. The commuter school has a full range of extracurricular activities and events, including nearly 200 clubs, organizations, and NCAA Division II sports teams. The campus, located in northwestern St. Louis County, is easily accessible by public transportation, including its very own MetroLink stop. The school's culturally diverse student population includes representatives of 47 states and more than 100 countries. UMSL works in cooperation with more than 400 St. Louis–area companies and organizations to offer internships, cooperative education, and work-study programs. The school offers a variety of scholarships, loans, grants, and work-study opportunities to make college an affordable option for more St. Louisans.

WASHINGTON UNIVERSITY
1 Brookings Drive
(314) 935-5000
www.wustl.edu
Washington University, founded in 1853, is counted among the world's leaders in teaching and research, drawing students and faculty from throughout the United States and more than 110 countries. "Wash U," as it's most commonly called, has an undergraduate enrollment of more than 6,000 full time undergraduates, as well as graduate and professional students, with a student-to-faculty ratio of 7 to 1.

In addition to 90 programs and 1,500 courses contributing to bachelor's, master's, and doctoral degrees, the school offers a broad spectrum of traditional and interdisciplinary fields and additional opportunities for minor concentrations and individualized programs. Wash U's 169-acre Hilltop Campus features stunning Collegiate Gothic architecture, including a number of buildings on the National Register of Historic Places. The 59-acre Medical Campus, located near the main campus in St. Louis's Central West End neighborhood, includes the Washington University School of Medicine and the associated hospitals and institutes that make up the Washington University Medical Center. According to the 2008 edition of U.S. News & World Report's "America's

Best Colleges" guide, 19 of Washington University's schools, academic areas, and departments are ranked in the top 10 of U.S. News & World Report's rankings of graduate and professional programs. Wash U also offers exemplary programs in such disciplines as art, architecture, business, law, engineering, and social work.

The university is a member of the National Collegiate Athletic Association (NCAA) Division III and has been a member of the University Athletic Association (UAA) since the late 1980s. Athletically speaking, the Lady Bears are perennial champions in both basketball and volleyball. The Wash U women's basketball team won the Division III national championship four years in a row and the volleyball team was national champion seven times between 1989 and 1996 and again in 2003. Women's sports at Wash U also include softball, tennis, and soccer. The football team has won three Missouri Valley Conference titles, three UAA titles, and has produced 44 All-Americans. Wash U's additional men's athletics include soccer, swimming and diving, tennis, and track and field.

WEBSTER UNIVERSITY
470 East Lockwood, Webster Groves
(314) 968-6991
www.webster.edu
Webster is a private, independent, nondenominational, comprehensive institution with national and international campus centers. Since its beginnings in 1812, the university has expanded its outreach tremendously and now offers programs to students at 68 sites throughout the United States. In addition to the beautiful, tree-lined "headquarters" in nearby Webster Groves, the university has more than 100 campuses in the U.S. and around the world. Webster instituted its first European campus in Geneva, Switzerland, in 1978, and the university's flexible, American-style higher education has attracted students of many nationalities. Today there are additional European campuses, in London; Vienna, Austria; and the Netherlands, along with campuses in Bermuda, Shanghai, and Thailand. Webster University has expanded the breadth of its educational offerings

to include bachelor's and master's degree programs for the School of Business and Technology, College of Fine Arts, School of Education, Barnes College of Nursing and Health Sciences, and the College of Arts and Sciences. There are 13 undergraduate degrees offered, along with nine graduate degrees. The 47-acre St. Louis campus has an enrollment of more than 5,000 students and offers a range of classes for traditional students, adult learners, corporate and military personnel, and international students. Webster's annual film series is a popular cultural attraction for students and non-students throughout the region.

OTHER HIGHER EDUCATION

LOGAN COLLEGE OF CHIROPRACTIC
1851 Schoettler Road, Chesterfield
(636) 227-2100
www.logan.edu
Established in 1935, Logan College is accredited by the Council on Chiropractic Education and the North Central Association of Colleges and Schools. The facility features a state-of-the-art educational/learning environment within a 112-acre wooded, hilltop campus. The academic programs at Logan College are offered year-round, and the classes are set up on trimesters of 16 weeks each. Degree programs available to students include the Accelerated Science Program (ASP), bachelor of science in human biology, and the doctor of chiropractic degree program. In addition to completing class work, student interns from the college get hands-on experience by working with patients at Logan College Health Centers and at six off-campus health centers.

There are 12 colleges and universities, eight professional schools, and seven community colleges in the St. Louis metropolitan area.

ST. LOUIS COLLEGE OF PHARMACY
4588 Parkview Place
(314) 367-8700
www.stlcop.edu

St. Louis College of Pharmacy (StLCoP) is a private, independent, nonsectarian college located in the Central West End's medical community. Founded in 1864, the school is the oldest college of pharmacy west of the Mississippi River. Unlike other pharmacy schools, StLCoP doesn't have a pre-pharmacy program—students are automatically admitted into the six-year Doctor of Pharmacy program beginning in year three, as long as they've successfully met the progression requirements. And, due to its location in such a sports-crazed town, the college offers NAIA Division II men's and women's basketball, cross-country, cheerleading squad and dance team, and an extensive intramural sports program. The college's doctor of pharmacy and baccalaureate in pharmacy programs are accredited by the American Council on Pharmaceutical Education and the Higher Learning Commission, North Central Association of Colleges and Schools.

ST. LOUIS COMMUNITY COLLEGE
300 South Broadway
(314) 539-5000
www.stlcc.cc.mo.us
St. Louis Community College (STLCC) is the largest community college system in Missouri and one of the largest in the United States. The school, which offers 11 college transfer options and more than 90 career programs, has an enrollment of more than 32,500. STLCC has four main campuses—Florissant Valley, Forest Park, Meramec, and Wildwood—and offers programs that are designed to fill the needs and special interests of each campus's surrounding area. All three offer freshman- and sophomore-level college transfer, career and developmental programs, and non-credit continuing education courses that include on-site career training, recreational subjects, and even instructional television. There are three additional education centers located throughout the region: the South County Education and University Center (4115 Meramec Bottom Road), Downtown Education Center (300 South Broadway), and the William J. Harrison Education Center (4666 Natural Bridge Road).

CHILD CARE

In addition to multiple locations of national child-care facilities such as KinderCare, La Petite Academy, Montessori, and Children's World Learning Centers, there are more than 1,800 public and private child-care centers throughout the bi-state area. Many churches and social-service organizations offer preschool and child-care facilities, as well as many of the region's public school districts.

Referral Agencies
CHILD DAY CARE DEVELOPMENT CENTER
4236 Lindell Boulevard, Suite 300
(314) 531-1412, (800) 467-CDCA
www.childcarestl.org
The Child Day Care Association (CDCA) is the central planning, training, and coordinating not-for-profit agency for quality child care in the greater St. Louis area. CDCA provides licensing, regulatory information, and listings of more than 60 affiliated child-care programs and providers in St. Louis, St. Charles, and Illinois.

ILLINOIS NETWORK OF CHILD CARE RESOURCE AND REFERRAL AGENCIES (INCCRRA)
CHASI–Child Care Resource and Referral Program
2133 Johnson Road, Suite 100A, Granite City, IL
(800) 467-9200
www.chasiccrr.org
The southern region of INCCRRA, which includes Madison, Bond, St. Clair, Clinton, Washington, Monroe, and Randolph counties, is served by the Children's Home and Aid Society of Illinois (CHASI) program. CHASI is an informational resource for families, child-care providers, employers, and communities in southwestern Illinois that includes child-care options, referrals, licensing, and child-care issues. The INCCRRA is an organization of regional Child Care Resource & Referral (CCR&R) agencies serving communities throughout the state of Illinois.

Child-Care Providers

CHILDGARDEN CHILD DEVELOPMENT CENTER
4150 Laclede Avenue
(314) 531-8148
www.childgardencdc.com
Childgarden provides comprehensive early-childhood development services and early intervention services to children with special needs. The facility, which opened in 2001, is a joint venture between the Easter Seals Society of Missouri and St. Louis Arc, an organization that offers services and support to people with developmental disabilities and their families.

DOWNTOWN CHILDREN'S CENTER
607 North 22nd Street
(314) 621-1131
www.downtownchildcare.com
The Downtown Children's Center (DCC) is a nonprofit, nationally accredited child-care program that offers programs for infant/toddler care, kindergarten, preschool, and summer camps. In 2008, the center moved into a new state-of-the-art facility just west of downtown's central core. Enrichment programs include computer classes, dance/gymnastics, kinder concerts, Spanish, and weekly visits to the library and assorted field trips. DCC is a nonsectarian day-care center that represents an alliance of businesses, child-care professionals, and working parents that provides quality care near the city's central business district. Children are admitted without regard to race, religion, or national origin, and scholarships are awarded to students based on financial need. In 2006 the enrollment of kids ages 6 weeks to 12 years old topped out at around 100.

ℹ Preschool and Child-Care Facilities Christian Academy of Greater St. Louis Preschool, 11050 North Warson Woods Road; (314) 429–7070; www.cagsl.com. Kids Play, Chesterfield Crossing Center, Chesterfield, (636) 532–4600; Lafayette Center, Manchester, (636) 227–1800; Deer Creek Crossing Center, O'Fallon, (636) 379–9494; www.kidsplayfun.com.

THE GODDARD SCHOOL
1633 Kehrs Mill Road, Chesterfield
(636) 519-0808
1157 Smizer Mill Road, Fenton
(636) 343-7007
6040 Telegraph Road, Oakville
(314) 293-1200
www.goddardschool.com
Goddard is an early-childhood development center that offers full- and part-time programs for infants and toddlers, preschool, and after-school care. There are also a number of summer programs available. The school offers age-appropriate activities that help children learn a variety of subjects, including language art, manners, personal safety, and art history.

THE WESTPORT SCHOOL
1915 Ross Avenue, Maryland Heights
(314) 878-5339
www.thewestportschool.com
The Westport School features teachers with degrees in early-childhood education and offers full- and half-day programs. In addition to infant and toddler care, the facility has programs for preschoolers ages three to five, kindergarten "readiness," and summer day-camp options for school-age kids.

WORSHIP

I n spite of what appears to be an overwhelmingly Catholic population, St. Louis is home to a broad cross-section of religious beliefs. There are a variety of places of worship for all denominations—and the nondenominational—as well as facilities celebrating the Hindu, Islamic, Quaker, and Buddhist religions. There are also Chinese, Korean, and Spanish churches throughout the region, and a Church of Scientology in nearby University City.

The Catholic Church was first in the territory and remains the largest. The French government mandated it—somewhat—with its Code Noire. The Code, decreed in 1724, allowed only Catholics to cross the Mississippi River, although after the Spanish took control of the region, it wasn't stringently enforced. So, when Pierre Laclede and Auguste Chouteau arrived 40 years later, Roman Catholicism was the de facto "official" religion of the region.

Organized religion of any type was somewhat of a rarity during the early decades of St. Louis. It is said that visitors were surprised at the festive social lives of St. Louis's citizens, as well as the scarcity of churches. These reports compelled Bishop William Duborg to relocate the Diocese of Florida and Louisiana to the city in 1818, and he ordered plans to begin building a church immediately. Bishop Duborg himself held the first mass in the new edifice on Christmas day, 1819.

Running both the Florida and Louisiana territories was a big job, so the bishop divided them and formed the Diocese of St. Louis in 1826. Joseph Rosati was named as the first bishop in 1827, and he soon realized that the burgeoning river town was fast outgrowing its only church. In 1831 Rosati blessed the cornerstone of a new cathedral located at Walnut and Second Streets, and the new cathedral opened in 1834. Now known as the "Old Cathedral," it became a basilica in 1961 by decree of Pope John XXIII in recognition of its significance in spreading Catholicism into the American West. In 1914 a new cathedral, located on Lindell Boulevard in the Central West End, replaced the original cathedral basilica, and the building is still referred to as the "New Cathedral" by the local citizenry. The stunningly beautiful structure has the world's largest collection of hand-tiled mosaics, and it is a popular tourist

site for Catholics and non-Catholics alike. In 1999 Pope John Paul II visited St. Louis and held mass at the basilica, which is located across the street from the Archdiocese of St. Louis.

The Catholic Church provided needed social services as well, constructing a hospital facility in 1845. In 1933 Saint Louis University's Fermin Desloge Hospital made an additional contribution to the region's health care needs. The church also created the Guardian Angel Settlement Association in 1911, which ran its Guardian Angel Day Nursery. In post-World War II St. Louis, Cardinal Archbishop Joseph Ritter was an early leader in improving race relations in the city, overseeing the desegregation of both the Archdiocese school system and Saint Louis University in the 1940s.

Despite the Code Noire of the 18th century, a modest Jewish community existed in St. Louis in the early 1800s, and by 1837 there were enough Jews in the area to hold services. Louis Bomeisler, a German from Philadelphia, is thought to have conducted the first service for Rosh Hashanah in that year, and he set about ordering a Torah, prayer books, and Taleisim for the group. In 1841, 12 men met at the Oracle Coffee House located at Second and Locust Streets to write the constitution for Achdut Yisrael, the United Hebrew Congregation, and they were soon joined by two more congregations. B'Nai Brith and Amoona El sprouted quickly, and they eventually merged into B'Nai El. B'Nai El erected its own building in 1855, when Jewish philanthropist Judah Touro of Providence, Rhode Island, donated $5,000 to build the new facility at Sixth and Cerre Streets. Dubbed the "coffee mill" for its eight sides and turret, B'Nai El was the first synagogue west of the Mississippi River, but United Hebrew soon followed suit, dedicating its new building later that year. By 1860 the Jewish population had increased to approximately 5,000 people.

i **Pope John Paul II's visit in 1999 drew 110,000 people to the Dome at America's Center and the adjacent convention center. It was the largest indoor gathering in U.S. history.**

By 1900 all the local Jewish congregations were part of the new American brand of Judaism. The first group in St. Louis met in 1863, forming Shaare Emeth (Gates of Truth) in 1866. Three years later the congregation built a synagogue at 17th and Pine Streets, and it soon became one of the leading Reformed congregations west of the Mississippi. Both United Hebrew and B'Nai El changed to Reformed as well, and there was growing concern about this "Americanized" brand of Judaism. In 1924 local Orthodox Jews organized Vaad Hoeir as a union of all local Orthodox Jewish congregations.

Like the Catholics, the Jewish community was a social force in St. Louis. Charitable assistance started in 1871, with help for refugees from the Chicago fire. As Russian Jews immigrated to America, members of the local Jewish community found themselves facing constant needs to help recent arrivals. In addition to providing food, clothing, and shelter, Jewish relief agencies offered a home for the aged and infirmed, as well as English classes to help immigrants assimilate into their new environment. In 1902 Jewish Hospital opened at Delmar and Union Boulevards, and it moved to its current Central West End location in 1927. In the late 1990s Jewish Hospital

i **The Saturday edition of the St. Louis Post-Dispatch includes several pages of special events and activities taking place that weekend at area houses of worship. There's also a lengthy listing of active churches, synagogues, and fellowship halls throughout the bi-state region and the times of their individual services.**

merged with Barnes Hospital to form Barnes-Jewish Hospital, which is now considered one of the most respected hospitals in the country.

In 1817 missionary John Mason Peck arrived in St. Louis and established the First Baptist Church, comprised of a mostly African-American congregation. In 1825 Peck ordained former slave John Berry Meachum, and within two years Meachum was the pastor at First Baptist Church, where he soon began running schools for black children as well. The Baptists were active abolitionists, as their demographics prove—of the 46 Baptist churches on the Missouri Association roster, the two largest black churches had more than 1,400 members, while the 13 largest white churches had a little more than 1,000 parishioners.

Other Protestant denominations arrived in town at about the same time. In 1817 the Presbyterians showed up and built their first church building less than seven years later. The Episcopalians followed in 1819, founding Christ Church at Second and Walnut Streets (now known as Christ Church Cathedral), and in 1821 the Methodists arrived. For the most part, these denominational churches were formed by Americans moving to the region from other parts of the country, such as New England and the southeastern seaboard.

During the late 1830s the first Lutherans came from Saxony in order to practice their more conservative Lutheranism. Within 10 years they created Trinity Lutheran Church and the Lutheran Church-Missouri Synod, and they also moved the Concordia Seminary here.

By the 1840s African-American congregations in St. Louis began to blossom. Second African Baptist (now Central Baptist) started in

1846 with a special emphasis on training young clergy and laymen for local and international mission work. The other large black denomination in St. Louis was the African Methodist Episcopal (AME) Church. The AME movement began when Richard Allen led a group of black parishioners out of a Philadelphia church in 1787 to form their own worship service. Started in 1840, St. Paul's AME was the first black Methodist church west of the Mississippi, and St. Peter's, an outgrowth of St. Paul's, followed seven years later. St. Paul's constructed its first building in 1866 and finished its new edifice in 1872, making it the first church west of the Mississippi built by and for African Americans. St. James AME, by contrast, worked after 1885 to establish an African-American presence in The Ville.

As with the Catholic and Jewish congregations, black churches have a history of social consciousness. During the post-war civil rights movement, Ministers and Laymen for Equal Educational Opportunity staged marches on the St. Louis Public School Board in the late 1950s over the de facto segregation in public educa-

tion. Antioch Baptist Church was among the first churches to house Head Start and day-care programs, and St. James AME initiated James House in 1970 on the old Poro College site as the first church-developed housing project in St. Louis. Unlike most other Protestant branches, black churches have a legacy of leadership in relating faith and action.

The Church of Jesus Christ of Latter Day Saints facility located in southwest St. Louis was the first church building erected by Mormons in the area. Before occupying their new home, the Mormons in St. Louis had a rather uncertain existence dating from 1831. During the period of their great westward migration to Utah in the mid-19th century, many Mormons stayed in St. Louis, numbering as many as 4,000 in 1850. The modern revival of the Mormons in St. Louis occurred in 1896 when they began holding meetings in a small storefront. However modest their beginnings might have been, today's Mormon population enjoys worshipping together in the beautiful temple in west St. Louis County that was finished in the mid-1990s.

RETIREMENT

Just because you retire in St. Louis doesn't mean you have to slow down. Seniors remain a vital part of the local community, and their presence can be seen and felt in a variety of ways. From volunteering with local arts organizations to working one-on-one with inner-city kids who need a hand with their schoolwork, St. Louis seniors don't have to worry about having too much time on their hands. There are also a number of local organizations that can help senior citizens with everything from hot meals and computer classes to finding just the right dancing partner.

According to the St. Louis Department of Human Services, residents over the age of 65 represent 14 percent of the city's population, which is more than one in every seven people. It should be noted that these figures represent the city "proper," which is merely a portion of the metropolitan area's 2.6 million residents. However, the services and facilities available to today's seniors reflect the large role that older Americans play in the St. Louis community.

SENIOR SERVICES

COUNTY OLDER RESIDENT PROGRAMS (CORP)
121 South Meramec Avenue, Clayton
(314) 615-4516, (314) 615-4425 (TTY)
www.co.st-louis.mo.us/dhs/CORP.html
CORP, a division of the St. Louis County government, provides quality service to county residents age 60 and older and targets the primary needs of older adults through a variety of programs and services. In addition to assistance with transportation needs, tax preparation, and home care and repair, CORP provides area seniors with home visits/telephone reassurance, legal assistance, computer classes, and volunteer opportunities. The list of programs also includes several projects that highlight active aging. Broadway Fantasies is a song-and-dance revue highlighting the musical talents of some of the area's older adults. Seniors can also participate in a number of "lower-profile" activities, such as computer clubs, bowling leagues, and various special-interest clubs.

THE MID-EAST AREA AGENCY ON AGING (MEAAA)
14535 Manchester Road, Manchester
(636) 207-0847
www.mid-eastaaa.org
The MEAAA is a comprehensive resource for older adults, including information on transportation, long-term care facilities, senior centers, programs, and services. The nonprofit agency has been around since 1973 and is one of ten area agencies on aging in the state. MEAAA programs and services are available for anyone age 60 and older who lives in St. Louis, Franklin, Jefferson, or St. Charles Counties in Missouri.

ST. LOUIS AREA AGENCY ON AGING (SLAAA)
634 North Grand Boulevard, 7th Floor
(314) 612-5944
http://stlouis.missouri.org/government/hslaaa.html
SLAAA provides a comprehensive and coordinated system of community-based services for older adults in the city of St. Louis. The agency's objectives are to secure and maintain maximum independence and dignity in a home environment, and to encourage economic, social, and personal independence for older persons by

providing opportunities for employment, socialization, and volunteer activities in the community. The primary services available within the city are broken into four categories: community services, in-home services, alternative living, and financial assistance. These services are funded through SLAAA or other community-based organizations and range from support groups, health care services, and legal assistance to case management/care coordination and in-home services to help seniors live independently.

RETIREMENT COMMUNITIES

There are a number of retirement communities located throughout the greater St. Louis metropolitan area, and the services offered range from independent, on-the-go living to centers equipped with full-care nursing facilities. Depending on medical needs and lifestyle preferences, there are a variety of choices of retirement communities that will work within almost any budget. Here is a list of popular communities in St. Louis that have numerous locations and offer a menu of amenities and medical care facilities. For a complete listing of retirement communities in the region, check with the senior-services agencies listed at the beginning of this chapter. They can also let you know about new facilities and extended services available to seniors in the area.

BETHESDA BARCLAY HOUSE
230 South Brentwood Boulevard, Clayton
(314) 725-1000

BETHESDA DILWORTH
9645 Big Bend Boulevard,
Webster Groves/Kirkwood
(314) 968-5460

BETHESDA GARDENS
420 South Kirkwood Road, Kirkwood
(314) 965-8100

BETHESDA MEADOW
322 Old State Road, Ellisville
(636) 227-3431

BETHESDA ORCHARD
21 North Old Orchard Avenue, Webster Groves
(314) 963-2100

BETHESDA SOUTHGATE
5943 Telegraph Road
(314) 846-2000

BETHESDA TERRACE
2535 Oakmont Terrace Drive
(314) 846-6400

THE OAKS AT BETHESDA
Big Bend Road just west of Berry Road
(314) 965-8100
www.bethesdahealth.org
Bethesda Health Group, one of St. Louis's premier senior-living and skilled nursing care residences, has eight facilities in the St. Louis area. The properties offer a continuum of care, from independent living or supportive care to full care and special care. The company's senior-living communities offer a comfortable and secure environment where residents can come and go as they please, prepare meals in their apartment, or "eat out" in one of the beautiful dining rooms. Bethesda's supportive care is designed for residents who need assistance with daily activities such as bathing, dressing, or monitoring of medications, and the full nursing care residences provide residents with more personal attention and extensive nursing care. Bethesda also has three different facilities that can accommodate residents suffering from Alzheimer's and varying levels of dementia.

THE BRENTMOOR AND THE BRENTMOOR COURT
8600 Delmar Boulevard
(314) 995-3811

Brentmoor Place
1001–21 North McKnight Road
(314) 994-3011
www.brentmoor.com
The Brentmoor retirement communities feature

spacious independent and assisted-living apartments with fully equipped kitchens, health and fitness centers, and weekly housekeeping service. Residents can also take advantage of a full social calendar, scheduled van transportation, controlled building access, a complimentary happy hour, and meals in the Carriage Club Restaurant.

FRIENDSHIP VILLAGE OF SOUTH COUNTY
12503 Village Circle Drive, Sunset Hills
(314) 842-6840
www.friendshipvillagesouth.com
This retirement community overlooks the Meramec Valley and features apartments and cottage units with satellite cable TV, housekeeping services, laundry, personal garden areas, transportation, a salon, and a nursing facility. The South County life-care community also has a therapeutic swimming pool and hot tub, ballroom, billiard room, and activities such as woodworking and creative and cultural arts.

FRIENDSHIP VILLAGE OF WEST COUNTY
15201 Olive Boulevard, Chesterfield
(636) 733-0153
www.friendshipvillagewest.com
The West County location of the Friendship Village communities features 34 landscaped acres of apartment homes that offer 24-hour security, satellite TV, maid service, a computer lab, exercise programs, and recreational activities. The location also features an on-site bank, convenience store, library, beauty shop, and a 120-bed skilled nursing facility for residents who need more specialized care.

THE GATESWORTH
1 McKnight Place
(314) 993-0111
www.thegatesworth.com
A high-end retirement community, the Gatesworth is designed for independent seniors. Residents can enjoy a relaxed lifestyle with fine dining and an activity level that fits their preferences. The award-winning, locally owned community offers a full range of care with services

such as weekly housekeeping, 24-hour security/emergency response, nursing assistance, and a full-time resident services director and staff. Amenities include chauffeured transportation, fine dining and special events, an on-site bank, fitness and arts centers, rooms for cards and billiards, a library, a convenience store, a business and computer center, beauty and barber shops, a restaurant/lounge, and a full-service day spa.

> **i** The St. Louis Fire Department's "R.U.O.K." daily telephone reassurance program is a free service available to senior citizens and disabled individuals who are living on their own. If there is no answer after three attempts, emergency crews are dispatched to your home. For more information call the St. Louis Fire Department at (314) 533–3406.

VOLUNTEER OPPORTUNITIES

Whatever your interests are, there's probably an organization in the area that could use a little help. From animal shelters to arts organizations, St. Louis has just the place for eager volunteers to put in a good day's work.

There are a number of festivals and sporting events held throughout the year that operate on "volunteer power." Events such as the St. Louis Art Fair, Taste of St. Louis, Live on the Levee, Soulard Mardi Gras, and Fair Saint Louis are always looking for a few extra helping hands. For more information on these and other popular festivals, see the Annual Events chapter.

CENTER OF CREATIVE ARTS
524 Trinity Avenue
(314) 725-1834, ext. 105
www.cocastl.org
The Center of Creative Arts (COCA) provides an integrated forum to foster the appreciation of the arts in the greater St. Louis community through live performances, exhibitions, and educational programs. Volunteers work in the theater, gallery, and front office and provide support for

COCA staffers in the education and membership departments. Front-of-house opportunities include greeters, ushers, ticket takers, merchandise sales, and even driving performers around, along with working backstage with wardrobe or in technical production. Volunteers also help with set-up and staffing for special events and fundraising activities held at the center.

THE FOX THEATRE
527 North Grand Boulevard
(314) 534-1678
www.fabulousfox.com
The lavishly decorated "Fabulous Fox" Theatre presents various live entertainment options, including Broadway shows, music and comedy concerts, family shows, and more. Volunteers work as ushers for anything and everything that takes place at the theater, including concerts, shows, and various family-entertainment events.

MISSOURI BOTANICAL GARDEN
4344 Shaw Boulevard
(314) 577-5187
www.mobot.org
The Missouri Botanical Garden (MBG) is home to more than 30 gardens, a world-famous botanical research center, and an active education division that offers visitors a chance to discover and share knowledge about plants and their environment. Volunteers can work with specialists in the garden's 13 divisions, including horticulture, research, Web site design, conservation and restoration, and the library. The education division utilizes volunteer instructors, interpreters, and garden docents, and the information and membership services desks put volunteers to work answering questions from visitors and signing up new members. There are additional volunteer opportunities at MBG's other attractions, including the Shaw Nature Reserve, Butterfly House, and Earthways Center.

MISSOURI HISTORY MUSEUM
Forest Park Lindell and Skinker Boulevards
(314) 454-3187
www.mohistory.org

The Missouri History Museum helps make the history of the region accessible to residents, students, and visitors by offering a variety of permanent exhibits, temporary touring exhibitions, and related special events. Volunteer staffers greet visitors, conduct specialized tours as exhibit "interpreters," help with the cleaning and preservation of artifacts, staff the gift shops and information desk, assist with research, help with recruitment, and occasionally work with curators to install exhibitions.

REGIONAL ARTS COMMISSION
6128 Delmar Boulevard
(314) 863-5811
www.art-stl.com
The Regional Arts Commission (RAC) promotes, encourages, and fosters the arts and cultural institutions throughout the St. Louis region by nurturing local artists. RAC calls its volunteers "Arts Commandos," who sign on for a four-month tour of duty that will take them to any one of 150 different nonprofit arts organizations. Commandos assist with projects and fund-raising activities, including everything from stuffing envelopes, tending bar, or taking tickets to painting workspace, scrubbing floors, and moving scenery. Commandos are from all walks of life—professionals, community volunteers, retirees—and participants have the opportunity to experience the arts with a hands-on, approach to serving the community.

SAINT LOUIS ART MUSEUM
Forest Park
1 Fine Arts Drive
(314) 655-5287
www.slam.org
Saint Louis Art Museum (SLAM) volunteers can work as tour guides; meet and greet visitors at the visitor services desk; staff the gift shop; assist with research in the museum library, resource center, and curatorial departments; assist with exhibit preservation and repair; provide administrative support; staff special events; and undergo training to become a museum docent.

SAINT LOUIS SCIENCE CENTER
5050 Oakland Avenue
(314) 289-4412
www.slsc.org

Saint Louis Science Center (SLSC) volunteers help the community understand past, present, and future developments in science and technology in an educational and fun environment. Volunteers help visitors explore and experience the multitude of hands-on exhibits and activities, work as greeters, sign up new members, perform administrative tasks, staff special events, repair and clean exhibit items, and assist with electronic security monitoring.

ST. LOUIS BLACK REPERTORY COMPANY
Grandel Theatre
3610 Grandel Square
(314) 534-3807
www.theblackrep.org

The Black Rep produces a slate of theater, dance, and other creative presentations that heightens the social and cultural awareness of its audiences. Volunteers work as ushers for performances and special events, as well as work concessions and check-in tables, provide administrative support, and assist with the production of the annual Woodie Awards show.

ST. LOUIS CONVENTION & VISITORS COMMISSION
701 Convention Plaza, Suite 300
(314) 421-1023
www.explorestlouis.com

The St. Louis Convention and Visitors Commission (CVC) is the sales and marketing organization that promotes St. Louis as a convention and leisure-travel destination to regional, national, and international visitors. Volunteers provide information about the area attractions, restaurants, and arts and culture institutions to out-of-towners who stop by area visitor information centers. Two additional options include: the Gateway Greeters, a group of friendly faces who make sure visitors receive a warm welcome and friendly assistance at the airport; and the Convention Volunteer Team, whose members help convention delegates explore St. Louis and navigate around the America's Center convention complex.

SAINT LOUIS ZOO
Forest Park
(314) 781-0900, ext. 261
www.stlzoo.org

This world-class zoo, which serves as an educational and recreational resource for the community, has more than 11,000 animals as well as a survival center for endangered species. Volunteers act as tour guides; teach classes at the zoo and in local schools; chair planning committees; staff fund-raising events and private parties; help the zoo's horticulturist with planting, watering, and weeding; work the information booth; assist gift shop staffers; and work with members of the Wildside Walkers fitness program.

Phone Numbers at a Glance:

American Association of Retired Persons (AARP): (888) OUR-AARP

Catholic Center: (314) 533-1887

Illinois Department on Aging, Senior Help Line: (800) 252-8966

Lutheran Senior Services: (888) LSS-LIVING

Meals on Wheels St. Louis: (314) 268-1523

Missouri Department of Health and Senior Services: (573) 751-6400

Missouri Elder Abuse Hotline: (800) 392-6210

St. Louis Area Agency on Aging: (314) 612-5918

St. Louis County Older Resident Programs: (314) 615-4516

MEDIA

The St. Louis media scene is similar to those in most major American cities in the 21st century. It includes one daily newspaper and a variety of weekly papers that serve diverse audiences throughout the area. The *St. Louis Post-Dispatch* is the only daily in town, and the weekly *St. Louis American* garners a high African-American readership. St. Louis's weekly alternative newspaper, the *Riverfront Times,* plays devil's advocate/pot stirrer when it comes to local issues, and the publication is an authority on the local and national music scene. For whatever reason—probably St. Louis's ongoing inferiority complex regarding Chicago—the *Chicago Tribune* is available daily from paper machines on street corners throughout downtown.

Television newscasts and radio formats mimic those in most metropolitan areas as well, with most network affiliates offering standard local newscasts in addition to network programming. The local TV stations include four network affiliates, NBC, CBS, ABC, and FOX, along with KPLR, a local station affiliated with the CW network, and KETC, the PBS station in town.

In 2008, the FOX affiliate (KTVI, Channel 2) and KPLR (Channel 11) merged news operations, allowing the stations to stagger news, programming and community affairs programs. The mega-station produces nine hours of news every day. Weekday mornings, Fox 2 News is on the air from 5:00 to 9:00 a.m., and again from 11:00 a.m. to noon. On Saturday and Sunday, the morning news runs from 9:00 to 10:00 a.m. The station offers an hour-long 5:00 p.m. newscast seven days a week, as well as a half-hour newscast at 6:00 p.m. weeknights. Channel 2 returns at 9:00 p.m. nightly with another hour of news, followed by a more in-depth take on the day's top stories with "FOX 2 News Edge" at 10:00 p.m. Channel 11 (KPLR) broadcasts and hour-long newscast on weeknights.

KSDK (NBC) and KMOV (CBS) are virtually tied at the top of the ratings heap, trading out "No. 1 newscast in St. Louis" honors regularly.

The FOX, CBS, and NBC affiliates go head-to-head at 5:00 p.m. and 6:00 p.m., while the CBS and NBC affiliates battle weekdays at noon, 5:00, 6:00, and 10:00 p.m. Local FOX, NBC, and CBS all have locally based morning news shows, and KDNL sticks with ABC's "Good Morning America" for the duration. WRBU, My 46, offers shows such as "Tyler Perry's House of Payne," "The Insider," "My Wife and Kids," and "George Lopez." KPLR remains the local CW affiliate, home to popular shows like "America's Next Top Model," "Gossip Girl," and "Smallville."

In the world of St. Louis radio, there are three major conglomerates that control most of the stations in town: Emmis Broadcasting, Clear Channel, and Infinity Broadcasting. KMOX-AM remains the king of news/talk, while upstarts news/talk KTRS-AM and KFNS-AM offer a host of sports/talk shows as well. KTRS broadcasts Cardinals games and KMOX handles Blues hockey and the University of Missouri's football and men's basketball games. The Rams' official radio station is on the FM side of the dial at 103.3 KLOU.

For local cable television, locally based Charter Communications is the cable provider. Charter, headquartered in Town and Country, recently bought out the other area cable providers, leaving the bi-state region with a somewhat confusing cable TV system, and it also provides broadband Internet access. Fortunately, there is an abundance of satellite TV dish providers in the area for those who feel they need more "control" over their channel-surfing options.

NEWSPAPERS

Daily

BELLEVILLE NEWS DEMOCRAT

120 South Illinois Street, Belleville, IL
(314) 241-4098
www.bnd.com

Founded in 1858, the *Belleville News Democrat* (BND) was a family-owned newspaper from 1891 to 1972, when it was purchased by Capital Cities/ABC, Inc. In 1997 the paper was acquired by Knight Ridder. The paper serves the second-largest metropolitan area in Illinois, a bustling, fast-growing, and diverse region located just across the Mississippi River from St. Louis. Readership is estimated to be 150,000 daily and 185,000 on Sunday, with a circulation of 53,387 daily, and 65,760 on Sunday. The paper serves eight Illinois counties, with delivery primarily to St. Clair and southern Madison Counties. The *News Democrat*'s main office houses editorial, advertising, and administration staff, and its focus is on local, regional, and national stories, along with Illinois state politics, sports, and features. The Web site features news, columns, and information for and about the southern Illinois and St. Louis metro areas. Subscriptions are $18 per month, and daily copies are 50 cents (weekdays) and $1.25 (Sunday) each.

ST. LOUIS POST-DISPATCH

900 North Tucker Boulevard
(314) 340-8000
www.stltoday.com

Most often referred to simply as "the Post," the *St. Louis Post-Dispatch* is the only daily in town. It also publishes the *Suburban Journals* twice a week, with stories of special interest devoted to different sections of the metro area. Considered too liberal by conservatives and too conservative by liberals, the *Post*, part of Lee Enterprises, occupies a precarious position within the community. Staff members of the *Post-Dispatch* produce a reasonably accurate report of regional, national, and international news. Sections of the paper include the Main News, or the "front section," which is news of the nation, the world, and high-profile regional stories. Main News is responsible for national and international coverage and oversees the *Post-Dispatch*'s Washington Bureau. Metro News includes local and regional coverage, including the St. Louis region as well as Missouri and Illinois. The department has offices in the city of St. Louis, St. Louis County, St. Charles County, Jefferson County, and Jefferson City in Missouri, and in Madison and St. Clair Counties and the city of Springfield in Illinois. Metro News bureaus include the St. Charles, Jefferson County, North and South St. Louis County, Clayton, and Jefferson City bureaus in Missouri, and in Belleville, Edwardsville, Springfield, and the Illinois State House in Illinois. The Features section includes stories found in the Everyday, Arts & Entertainment (A&E), Get Out, Let's Eat, Travel, StyleWest, and Lifestyle sections. The Features department's work includes everything from the comics and movies to television and recipes, as well as the fine arts and fashion—plus everything in between. The Business section covers local, national, and international business news, as well as news that affects the pocketbooks of the region. *Post-Dispatch* sports staff members cover professional, collegiate, prep, and amateur sports competitions, highlighting the activities of all local pro and semipro teams. The online news department provides stories for the paper's Internet site, www.stltoday.com, which is updated as events occur throughout the day. The Web site receives news updates from the *Post-Dispatch* reporters, the Associated Press, and other wire services to keep online visitors up-to-date with the latest information of interest to the St. Louis area. They also monitor online discussions of sports and news topics in their various blogs and reader forums. The daily circulation rate is more

i The first daily newspaper in the country was the *St. Louis Herald,* which began publication in 1834. Today's *St. Louis Post-Dispatch* was founded by Joseph Pulitzer, father of the prestigious Pulitzer Prize, in 1878.

than 278,000, and approximately 407,000 on Sunday. Daily subscriptions are about $3 a week, and the newsstand price is 50 cents (weekdays) and $1.25 (Sunday).

THE TELEGRAPH
111 East Broadway, Alton, IL
(618) 463-2500
www.thetelegraph.com
Local news has been the heart and soul of this newspaper since it first began publishing in 1836. *The Telegraph* works diligently to bring the readers of Madison, Jersey, Calhoun, Macoupin, and Greene counties local news and information, leaving the national news to the larger dailies in the area. Readership for *The Telegraph* is approximately 60,000 per day, and the newspaper's Web site provides updated news and information, as well as community-events listings. Subscriptions for daily home delivery are around $180 per year.

i Didn't grab a paper this morning? Log on to the St. *Louis Post-Dispatch's* Web site (www.stltoday.com) for an online version of the newspaper, as well as breaking and updated news throughout the day.

RIVERFRONT TIMES
6358 Delmar Boulevard, Suite 200
(314) 615-6666
www.riverfronttimes.com
The staff of this free weekly alternative newspaper likes to keep the pot stirred on local issues. Most often referred to simply as "the RFT," the paper usually assumes the role of devil's advocate on issues affecting the region. Most of its news coverage is focused on issues that are important to St. Louis's young adults, and readers look to the paper for its investigative reporting, news and commentary on local politics, and the most comprehensive arts and entertainment coverage in the St. Louis area. Indeed, the publication is usually taken very seriously for its extensive coverage of the local and national music scene. Founded in 1977 as St. Louis's alternative newsweekly, the

RFT has cultivated a weekly circulation of about 100,000. But, due to the "pass-along" nature of the paper, its weekly reach is estimated to be closer to 250,000 readers. Copies of the RFT begin appearing in news racks throughout the area by late afternoon each Wednesday.

i Pick up a free copy of the *Riverfront Times* for a comprehensive listing of entertainment options throughout the week. It's published on Wednesday.

ST. LOUIS AMERICAN
4242 Lindell Boulevard
(314) 533-8000
www.stlamerican.com
The *St. Louis American* is Missouri's largest, most widely read weekly newspaper targeted to African Americans. The *American*, which comes out on Thursday, publishes more than 70,000 copies, is free, and is distributed to more than 845 locations throughout the city of St. Louis, St. Louis County, St. Charles County, and portions of Illinois. The *American* reaches 40 to 45 percent of black households in the metropolitan area. Founded in 1928, the paper is rapidly gaining regional and national acclaim. Coverage includes stories from an African-American perspective, including religion news, entertainment, sports, and profiles of successful local African Americans in business, health care, and public service. Updated daily, the paper's Web site offers up-to-date information on local and national news, along with sports, weather, entertainment, and a local business directory. Subscriptions are available for $40 per year.

ST. LOUIS BUSINESS JOURNAL
1 Metropolitan Square, Suite 2170
(314) 421-6200
http://stlouis.bizjournals.com/stlouis/
The *St. Louis Business Journal* (SLBJ) concentrates on local business news and information, along with sales-prospecting resources and a variety of financial information. The papers are sold at

convenience stores, hotel newsstands, bookstores, and in newspaper boxes throughout the downtown area. The Web site version of the paper is updated throughout the day with late-breaking business news and features the week's top stories and popular items from the print version, which reaches more than 160,000 readers per week. A yearlong subscription costs $74, and the newsstand copy cost is $2.

ST. LOUIS JEWISH LIGHT
12 Millstone Campus
(314) 432-3353
www.stljewishlight.com

The *St. Louis Jewish Light,* a weekly community newspaper, was established in 1947. The publication is part of the Jewish Federation of St. Louis and is distributed to approximately 14,500 households. Special issues include Wedding Planner, Bar/Bat Mitzvah Planner, Health and Fitness, Senior Living, Dining Guide, holiday issues, an issue celebrating Israel's anniversary, and the annual Guide to Jewish Life in St. Louis.

SUBURBAN JOURNALS
900 North Tucker Boulevard
(314) 340-8000
www.yourjournal.com

Even though the various *Suburban Journals* are owned by the same company that owns the *Post-Dispatch,* the regionalized newspapers see themselves as a separate—but equal—news source for readers throughout the area. The Post-Dispatch won't run any feature story that was first covered by one of the *Journals,* and vice versa. The *Journals* have separate staffs and run many of the same headline stories, but usually include stories of interest to their particular neighborhood or area of the county. In addition to obituaries, birth, anniversary, wedding, and engagement announcements, each *Journal* runs an extensive number of community calendars, providing a place for groups to publicize their fund-raising events. There are 25 editions (and 9 editorial locations) for the family of *Suburban Journals,* with each one focusing on local news and feature stories.

The *Journals* run stories about community government, school boards, neighborhood associations, community organizations, and the myriad chambers of commerce, along with coverage of news from local police and fire departments. The news focuses on local people, including community leaders, teachers, and small-business owners. The pro teams are largely ignored, but there is exhaustive coverage of high school, junior high, middle school, and elementary school athletes. In 2009, the *Suburban Journals* began charging a $20 annual subscription fee for the papers, which previously were free and landed on your doorstep each week whether you asked for it or not. Circulation numbers for the freebies were estimated at 500,000 per week.

WEST END WORD
625 North Euclid, Suite 330
(314) 367-6612
www.westendword.com.

This small, neighborhood newspaper is distributed throughout the Central West End (CWE) neighborhood, midtown and downtown St. Louis, as well as to neighboring University City, Clayton, Brentwood, and Richmond Heights. The free paper, which consists mainly of local feature stories and CWE-specific classified advertisements, can be picked up at Schnucks and Straub's grocery stores in the Central West End, as well as at select retail stores, restaurants, apartment buildings, condominiums, and office buildings. *West End Word's* weekly circulation is approximately 25,000, which includes 3,000 door-to-door deliveries to homes in the CWE.

MAGAZINES

ALIVE MAGAZINE
3115 South Grand, Suite 400, East St. Louis, IL
(314) 446-4056
www.alivemag.com

ALIVE offers readers the latest info on beauty, fashion, entertainment, and what's happening on the region's social scene. The slickly produced monthly is free and available at more than 1,000 locations throughout the bi-state area, including health clubs, salons, restaurants, shops and night-spots. *ALIVE* also puts on a variety of cocktail party–type events that draw large crowds of the city's young hipsters, and they seem to have their finger on the pulse of what's hot and trendy in St. Louis. The circulation of this popular monthly is 50,000.

SAUCE MAGAZINE
1820 Chouteau Avenue
(314) 772-8004
www.saucemagazine.com
This entertaining and informative tabloid-style magazine offers insight into what's happening at local restaurants and markets as well as the latest trends being used by St. Louis chefs. The free monthly is available at area eateries and food stores, and the Web site features a handy listing of restaurants that can be searched by cuisine, location, and special attributes like "kid-friendly," "outdoor dining," "business lunch," etc. *Sauce* also highlights cocktail trends, live music and enter-tainment listings in the region, and has a good overall feel for "the scene."

ST. LOUIS COMMERCE
1 Metropolitan Square, Suite 1300
(314) 444-1104
www.stlcommercemagazine.com
St. Louis Commerce magazine is published each month by the St. Louis Regional Chamber and Growth Association (RCGA), a membership-driven organization that works to attract and grow business in the St. Louis metropolitan area. The slick, glossy magazine includes stories on local businesses and regional corporations that are enjoying success in the St. Louis area. Regular features include shorter pieces on national and local trends, the RCGA calendar, profiles of local businesspeople, details about new construction and/or development in the area, and Newsmak-ers, which highlights activities and accomplish-ments by local individuals and organizations. A yearly subscription (12 issues) is $60, and the estimated circulation is 4,000 to 5,000.

ST. LOUIS MAGAZINE
1600 South Brentwood Boulevard, Suite 550, Brentwood
(314) 918-3000
www.stlmag.com
St. Louis Magazine is a shiny, slick publication that concentrates its editorial pages on the city's movers and shakers and the hot spots that attract them. The colorful feature stories highlight various restaurants, clubs, and shops in the metro area and provide some insight into city issues, local personalities, and what's happening in the local arts, sports, and political arenas. There's also a nod to the city's ever-intriguing social scene, and pieces that detail the current fashion and food trends, both nationally and locally. A one-year subscription costs about $20, and the circulation is around 50,000.

TELEVISION

St. Louis is the 21st largest broadcast market in the country, with an estimated viewing audience of 1.1 million television households. The local dial's lineup includes four network affiliates—NBC, CBS, ABC, and FOX—as well as two popular local/independent stations and a local religious station, KNLC Channel 24. Many St. Louisans opt for cable or satellite programming as well, and cable TV subscribers only have one choice for a provider: Charter Communications. Headquar-tered in nearby Town and Country, Charter is a Wired World Company owned and operated by Microsoft cofounder Paul Allen.

RADIO

Like other major cities in the United States, St. Louis has argued over which station was "first" on the air. Documentation exists that shows WEW, owned by Saint Louis University, actually originated the first "broadcasts," which came in the form of Morse Code transmissions of weather information in 1913. By 1921 the station was regularly broadcasting weather information via "radiophone" that is, using voice.

Today three major radio conglomerates control most of the stations in town: Emmis Broadcasting, Clear Channel Worldwide, and Infinity Broadcasting. All three are represented in the St. Louis market, with each company controlling a stable of local stations. One exception to the corporate culture of radio is KDHX-FM 88.1, a community station that offers a diverse lineup of programming, ranging from blues, reggae, and indie rock shows to programs on environmental, political, and gay and lesbian issues. Another station, once called the "Mighty MOX," is KMOX-AM, a famed news/talk radio station with tremendous "reach" throughout the region.

KMOX remains the king of news/talk and Blues hockey game broadcasts in spite of the fact that they lost the broadcasting rights to Cardinals baseball games to rival KTRS. KTRS-AM 550 raided KMOX's overflowing talent pool when it first hit the airwaves in 1997, and brings an alternative news/talk/sports option to the region. KFNS-AM/FM, or, as it is often called, "K-Fans," challenges both stations with its sports/talk format, and all three stations offer a variety of baseball, football, and hockey players' and coaches' shows. KLOU-FM 103.3, an "oldies/super hits" music station, also broadcasts the St. Louis Rams games and several football-related shows during the season.

As in most cities, the formats and personalities on local radio stations are subject to change without notice, and you often feel like you need a scorecard to keep up with who's in, who's out, and who's going where on the local airwaves.

St. Louis Television Stations

Station	Network	Channel	Web site
KTVI	FOX	2	www.fox2ktvi.com
KMOV	CBS	4	www.kmov.com
KSDK	NBC	5	www.ksdk.com
KETC	PBS	9	www.ketc.org
KPLR	CW	11	www.cw11tv.com
KNLC	IND	24	www.knlc.tv/
KDNL	ABC	30	www.abcstlouis.com
WRBU	MNT	46	www.my46stl.com

St. Louis Radio Stations

AM Stations

Call Letters	Frequency	Format	Nickname
KTRS	550	News/Talk	The Big 550
KFNS	590	Sports	The Fan
KJSL	630	Christian	
KSTL	690	Gospel	
KWRE	730	Country	
WEW	770	Variety	
KFUO	850	Christian	
WGNU	920	Christian	
KXEN	1010	Christian	
WRYT	1080	Religious	
KMOX	1120	News/Talk	The Voice of St. Louis
WSDZ	1260	Disney	
KSIV	1320	Religious	
KSLG	1380	FOX Sports	
WIL	1430	Country	
KIRL	1460	Gospel/Jazz	
WESL	1490	Urban Contemporary	
KATZ	1600	Gospel	

FM Stations

Call Letters	Frequency	Format	Nickname
KDHX	88.1	Community Radio	
WSIE	88.7	Public Radio	
KWMU	90.7	NPR	
KSIV	91.5	Christian	
WIL	92.3	Country	
KSD	93.7	Country	The Bull
KSHE	94.7	Rock	K-She
WFUN	95.5	R&B	Foxy 95
KIHT	96.3	Rock	K-Hits
KFTK	97.1	Talk	
KYKY	98.1	Adult Contemporary	Y-98
KFUO	99.1	Classical	
KATZ	100.3	Hip-hop	The Beat
KFNS	100.7	Sports	The Fan
WXOS	101.1	ESPN, Sports/Talk	
KEZK	102.5	Soft Rock	
KLOU	103.3	Greatest Hits	
WHHL	104.1	Hip-hop, R&B	Hot 104.1
KMJM	104.9	R&B	Majic 104.9
KPNT	105.7	Alternative	The Point
WARH	106.5	'70s, '80s, '90s	The Arch
KSLZ	107.7	Top 40	Z-107.7

INDEX

ABOUT THE AUTHOR

Dawne Massey is a freelance writer who, after visiting St. Louis frequently to satisfy her obsession with professional baseball, moved to the Gateway City in 1994 to work for the St. Louis Convention & Visitors Commission. A native of Memphis, Tennessee, she graduated from Memphis State University (Go Tigers!) with a bachelor's degree in journalism and worked for WHBQ-TV before joining the Memphis Convention and Visitors Bureau. There, she became an inadvertent expert on "all things Elvis" as well as a fervent activist regarding the supremacy of STAX versus Motown. After relocating "up-river" in St. Louis, she discovered a vibrant roots music scene and like-minded people who believe that Cardinals baseball, Rams football, and authentic Italian food are three good reasons to get out of bed every morning. She lives in a work-in-progress 1940s bungalow in St. Louis's Southampton neighborhood with a high-maintenance, work-in-progress cat named Creole. Just one cat—she is not a crazy cat lady.